Multivariate Statistics for Personnel Classification

Multivariate Statistics for Personnel Classification

Phillip J. Rulon
Graduate School of Education, Harvard University

David V. Tiedeman
Graduate School of Education, Harvard University

Maurice M. Tatsuoka
University of Illinois

Charles R. Langmuir
University of Utah on assignment to Haile Selassie I University

John Wiley & Sons, Inc.   New York · London · Sydney

Preface

Our interest in the psychological profile in personnel work spans two decades. The pursuit of this interest led to the understanding of the problem of personnel classification in terms of probability theory presented in this book.

The book starts from first principles and proceeds by easy stages so that those without background in mathematics or statistics can understand personnel classification in terms of probability theory. Many illustrations are included. Principles of geometry and matrix algebra are introduced at appropriate places and the book thus resembles a programmed text. Those who comprehend needed principles should advance as rapidly as possible.

The exposition attempts to teach through induction. The book therefore begins in terms of one test, then considers two tests, and proceeds to add tests until any number of variables, in fact, T of them, has been discussed. In each sequence of variables, scores for one person are first considered. Then scores for two persons are considered. We augment the sequence of persons until the statistical issues of the individuals who belong to one group have been discussed. Then two groups, three groups, and so on to G groups are considered in sequence. This programmed type of organization offers an opportunity to bypass explanatory text as soon as a concept is mastered.

If a series of objects can be only one of G kinds and if the designation of each object is not known but the location and dispersion of the density distribution of the objects are known for each group, the objects can be most accurately reidentified by use of the topological procedures developed in Chapter 6. This is a logical fact. It is also a fact, as Cronbach and Gleser (1957, p. 104) note, that topologies of this nature ignore information the tests may offer about the success a person is likely to enjoy in the group to which he is assigned. Should topology therefore underlie the theory of personnel classification? We develop the argument in this book that topology should be accorded this role.

v

However, the theory of personnel classification has grown from the theory of personnel selection. In personnel selection, acceptable persons are picked from those who apply. The basis of acceptance is taken to be the likelihood of reaching a designated standard of performance in the groups which are to be formed through classification of personnel selected. The extension of selection logic to personnel classification assumes that the tests do not themselves offer information about the predisposition of an applicant for one type of work or another. The tests are therefore permitted to guide the decision of a personnel adviser only in terms of the likelihoods of performance at the desired level in the several jobs under consideration. We note in Chapters 1, 9, and 11 that this selection procedure leads to some indefensible consequences. These consequences have not been considered in relation to decision theory in personnel work as it has been advocated by Cronbach and Gleser (1957). We consider both aspects of the problem in Chapter 10 where we present an index which combines the information from discriminant and regression analysis.

The answer to personal decision does not lie in theories of personnel decisions advanced by Cronbach and Gleser or us. People decide where they will apply for work. This aspect of the problem is not considered here by us or by Cronbach and Gleser. However, Tiedeman and Field (in press) deal with the logic of personal decision of this nature. Their argument requires the understanding developed in this book. Perhaps the needed separation of theories of personal and personnel decision will come sooner if we have widespread consideration of personnel classification through regression procedures (Cronbach and Gleser, 1957), personnel classification through topology (this book), and personal decision (Tiedeman and Field, in press). That is the purpose of this book.

Although the subject of the book may be considered advanced because it deals with personnel classification in terms of any number of tests and groups, two aspects of advanced statistics are omitted for simplicity. Our treatment does not consider whether the sample dispersion should be estimated using one less than the number of cases in a group or not. (The reader is advised that this book consistently uses the number of cases in the group as the divisor of the sample sums of squares and cross products in estimating the dispersion in a group.) In addition, except for the single test of dimensionality included in Chapter 8, the book largely omits discussion of sampling error. There is only a single significance test presented in the book as a result. However, the reader is referred to Rao (1952) for general discussion of sampling error in relation to the study of personnel topologies. Particular attention should be given to Section 7d (pp. 258–271) of Rao's text. The section offers a fairly exact test of significance of the differences among groups. Such a test logically encompasses the entire subject of this book. If the average test scores of groups vary significantly, personnel classification becomes possible with such tests. If groups do not differ in that systematic fashion, personnel classification with such tests is meaningless.

We are each indebted to our employer for time devoted to the preparation of this book. We are also indebted to the Educational Research Corporation and the Human Resources Research Center, U.S. Air Force, for special resources. In addition, Tiedeman acknowledges the further contribution of resources by the Center for Advanced Study in the Behavioral Sciences and the National Institute of Mental Health. The first revision of the initial draft was accomplished while he was a Fellow of those institutions during 1963–64.

P. J. Rulon
D. V. Tiedeman
M. M. Tatsuoka
C. R. Langmuir

Contents

ix

Multivariate Statistics for
Personnel Classification

Personnel Classification and the Job Psychograph

Chapter 1

Personnel Work and the Psychological Profile

Personnel Classification in Personnel Work

In Industry. Several different kinds of personnel decisions take place during a single day in the operation of a large industrial plant. Applicants for advertised positions are considered. The personnel adviser decides whether an applicant is qualified for the job he is seeking. If the company does consider him qualified, he may be assigned immediately to that job. On the other hand, the company may assign him to a totally different job because of his qualifications for more demanding and/or rewarding work. The applicant unqualified for the job he was seeking may still be considered by the company because there may be other available jobs for which the applicant is qualified.

The responsibility which is centered in the personnel office of a large concern to assign work to employees is not limited to the allocation of work to newly hired employees. There is usually daily activity in a large firm which requires reassignment of work functions to those who have been employed for some time. Most of this work reassignment occurs in the unit in which the employee is presently assigned, and is managed by the one in charge of the productivity of a group of men. Whenever the reassignment of work functions takes the form of job reclassification, however, the personnel office of the plant is usually responsible for performing the transition. Job reclassifications can originate in a number of different ways. For instance, an employee may become dissatisfied with his work on one job and request transfer. He may do so with or without knowing specifically what other opportunity is available, and with or without knowing definitely about another opening and its requirements. The company may also initiate the problem of job reclassification, of course. This may stem from eliminating one kind of job and creating other

3

kinds. It may also arise from the realization that an employee is not performing satisfactorily in one job but may in another.

It may be advantageous to the company in the process of classifying and/or reclassifying employees to set fixed deadlines for this activity. This policy has the effect of allowing the company to consider the requests of a group of people considered simultaneously rather than one at a time. Regardless of whether classification is undertaken daily, weekly, monthly, or even sporadically, it has specific characteristics which distinguish it from selection, which may also be a function of the personnel office. It is the purpose of this book to distinguish classification from selection. But first let us continue to explore the magnitude of the function of personnel classification.

In the Employment Service. Each state maintains a public employment service. Such a service is usually responsible for placing applicants who seek the assistance of the service and for the administration of unemployment insurance, if necessary. Those who seek the help of a public employment service are ordinarily required to take the General Aptitude Test Battery (United States Department of Labor, 1962). The personnel officer responsible for advising applicants seeking placement is frequently known as an employment counselor. The employment counselor records the work history of the applicant and uses this and the results of the General Aptitude Test Battery to determine the jobs for which the applicant is eligible. The applicant is then helped to secure an available job.

The United States Employment Service has made numerous studies of the General Aptitude Test Battery. These studies have given rise to the designation of aptitude patterns and minimum scores on the necessary patterns for many jobs throughout the country. This procedure, which is used to suggest the possible application of abilities, does not necessarily result in the use of these aptitudes, as we will show. But we are now considering the type of personnel work in which classification is an important function.

In School and College. The teacher continuously assesses the progress of his students and classifies each of them in relation to what he considers it possible for the student to do in the future in view of what he knows the student can do now. This is an aspect of the classification problem, however, that we will not consider further. The aspect of classification which is relevant in this study concerns assigning students to specific curricula in high school or to majors in college.

As the student approaches the ninth grade, he is required to elect a pattern of courses. These courses influence the choice of work opportunities for which the student is qualifying himself. For instance, the opportunities available to the student who decides to prepare himself for entrance into college will be different from those available to the student who does not. The school counselor is usually given the responsibility for supervising the election of courses that students are required to take during the eighth grade and afterward. The counselor knows the stated wishes, educational history, and test scores of each pupil, and the qualifications which the school requires for each curriculum. The counselor is likely to use aptitude scores in his supervision of these elections because the curricula available usually are defined in terms of aptitude, to some degree.

A similar limitation on future opportunities is necessary, for some students elect to continue their education in college. Toward the end of the freshman year, most colleges require the election of a major. A major is a pattern of courses defined by certain members of the faculty. Since this election is again a limitation on work opportunities available upon completion of the major, counselors usually supervise the student's choice of a major and help him to consider his aptitudes and those required by various jobs. The information needed for such supervision is different from that required for the selection of students. We shall begin to delineate this as we consider the final context in which personnel classification is a significant aspect of personnel work.

In an Armed Service. Personnel officers, who are likely to be known as career counselors in the armed services, classify drafted and volunteer personnel during the period of basic training which is provided for all enlisted personnel. The Air Force is an example.

All airmen are given the Airman Classification Battery during the first week of basic training. During the third week of training each airman has a guidance conference with a career counselor. On the basis of the airman's education, experience, abilities, preferences, and the current Air Force manpower requirements, he is recommended for assignments in from three to five career fields. A career field is a grouping of related Air Force specialties involving basically similar knowledge and skills. A relatively small number of airmen with prior service or readily adaptable skills may be placed in some specialized assignment by the counselors.

Career guidance requires judgment that an airman will perform effectively in the recommended career field. This judgment is based partially on aptitude indices. Aptitude indices are scores on the several factors measured by the Airman Classification Battery. In nearly every instance the indices correlate positively with grades earned later by the airman when he goes to an Air Force technical school (Gragg and Gordon, 1950). It has been customary to use the known relation between the indices and school achievement to predict the success an airman is likely to exhibit in the various career fields for which he is considered. These estimates have a great influence on his guidance and eventual assignment.

Predictions of relative success can be obtained only from studies of Air Force experience with groups of airmen. Valid data for each study satisfy four conditions: (1) each group is a representative sample of a population of which the incoming airmen are also members; (2) the test information is obtained before the airman's entry in the Air Force specialty; (3) the airmen studied are members of the Air Force specialty; and (4) data are available which furnish a criterion that indicates which airmen were relatively successful in the Air Force specialty and which were less successful. When data satisfying these four conditions are available, a regression equation can be obtained to predict the success an airman can be expected to attain in the specialty. When Air Force experience has been tabulated for several different specialties, an incoming airman's probable success can be predicted for each one. However, these various predictions give no indication of the career field that the airman might select if given the opportunity to choose his assignment. Such information simply does not enter into the calculations. This will now be developed more fully.

Group Membership, Not Success in a Group, Is the Primary Datum in Classification

To clarify the previous discussion, suppose that the specialty designations of the several groups used to compute the prediction equations were mislaid. From the test scores of each airman we could still compute a prediction of his success in each specialty. But this estimate would provide little information useful for reassigning him to the group of which he was actually a member.

Tiedeman and Sternberg (1952) studied the relation between standardized sophomore grade averages and freshman verbal reasoning scores of two groups of high school pupils, one group enrolled in college preparatory and the other in the business curriculum. Their scatter diagrams are shown in Fig. 1.1. Suppose that the curriculum designations of these 207 pupils were not known. What are the problems involved in trying to ascertain the correct group for each pupil? The statistical picture is represented in Fig. 1.2, which shows the scatter diagram for all 207 pupils and the two regression lines, which are the same as those in Fig. 1.1. The regression line for predicting a pupil's grade average in the business curriculum is seen to have nearly the same slope and to be placed above the line for predicting grade average in the college preparatory curriculum.

A counselor who is given both regression equations and the verbal reasoning scores of these 207 pupils might try to divide the individuals into the two curriculum groups by computing for each pupil first, his predicted success in the college preparatory curriculum and next, his predicted success in the business curriculum. If he uses the regression equation

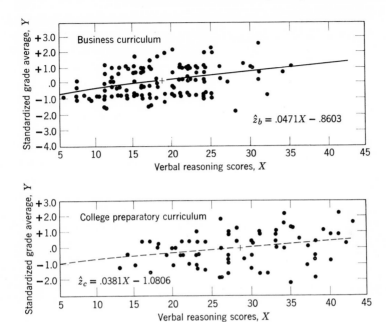

Fig. 1.1

derived from the data on college preparatory pupils and predicts the success of all pupils in the college preparatory curriculum, he will obtain a distribution as shown in Fig. 1.3a. Clearly some of these pupils have a much higher predicted grade average in the college preparatory curriculum than others do. This is also true, of course, of predicted grades in the business curriculum. Making use of the regression equation derived from the data on business curriculum pupils and predicting the business curriculum success of all 207 pupils results in the distribution in Fig. 1.3b.

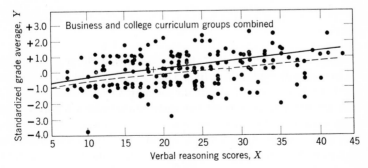

Fig. 1.2.

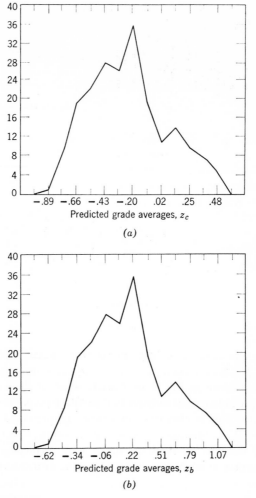

Fig. 1.3 *Predicted grade averages (all pupils). (a) refers to the college preparatory;
(b) refers to the business.*

The distributions shown in both figures are strikingly similar, differing
only in the scale along the base line. This is bound to happen when only
one predictor, in this instance, verbal reasoning score, is used. When more
than one predictor is used, these two distributions will still appear similar
and differ mostly in the scale along the base line. There is nothing about
either of these distributions, and nothing in a comparison between them,
that indicates the curriculum of any pupil at that time.

Accordingly, the information which the regression equations seem to provide the counselor is misleading as to curriculum choice. Suppose the counselor considers the poor performer whose predicted grade average for the college preparatory curriculum is $-.89$ (see Fig. 1.3a) and for the business curriculum, $-.62$ (see Fig. 1.3b). The difference between predictions would seem to indicate that this individual should enter the business curriculum, where the prediction for him is not as bad as it is for him in the college preparatory curriculum. This argument may be sound for this poorly performing individual; consider, however, the five students at the other end of the distribution for whom the predicted grade average in the college preparatory curriculum (Fig. 1.3a) was .48 and in the business curriculum, 1.07 (Fig. 1.3b). Apparently these five individuals should also be advised to elect the business curriculum. In fact, examination of the predictions pupil by pupil for the entire group in this guidance situation indicates that all of the pupils would be assigned to the business curriculum if the decision were based upon predicted success as measured by standardized grade average.

Substantially more information is available concerning curriculum choice if the individual identities of the groups are maintained, as in Fig. 1.4. As seen in Fig. 1.4a, it is clear that the students in the college preparatory curriculum have higher predicted grade averages in that curriculum than in the business curriculum. Figure 1.4b shows that when success is predicted in the business curriculum, the college preparatory group still has higher predicted success than the business curriculum group does.

If it were entirely sound to advise a student to consider a certain curriculum on the basis of his relatively higher predicted success in that curriculum than in others, we should expect to find the two groups trading places between Figs. 1.4a and b. Figure 1.4a should appear just as it does: those students actually in the college preparatory curriculum have higher predicted grade averages in that curriculum than do the students in the other curriculum. When success is predicted in the business curriculum, we should find the reverse. We should find that the students actually in the business curriculum have higher predicted grades in that curriculum than do the students in the other curriculum. However, as shown in Fig. 1.4b, this is not true. Those who are predicted to perform outstandingly in the business curriculum tend to enter the college curriculum and not the business curriculum.

When one is screening a group of applicants for a particular job, it is appropriate to assume that all the applicants have chosen to enter the job. The best selection will be achieved by choosing those applicants who are estimated to perform best. However, when alternative job assignments are available, it is not appropriate to assume that applicants will prefer the

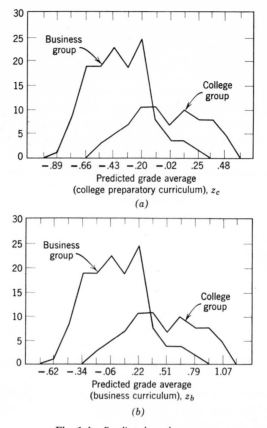

Fig. 1.4 *Predicted grade averages.*

job in which they are predicted to be most successful. We must remember that a person may decline a job because he is likely to be too *successful* (that is, he is "too good for that job") as well as because he may be *unsuccessful* at it.

There is an exact correspondence between the three frequency polygons in Figs. 1.4 and 1.5. The distributions of verbal scores for each curriculum given in Fig. 1.5 differ from the predicted grade average only in the scale. The transformations of verbal reasoning scores to predicted standardized grade averages in either the college preparatory or business curricula had no effect on the overlap of the groups. The *verbal reasoning scores alone give exactly the same information concerning curriculum choice as do the predicted standardized grade averages in either curriculum.* This is always true if there is only one predictor. We show in subsequent chapters that the inference of group membership from predicted scores when more than

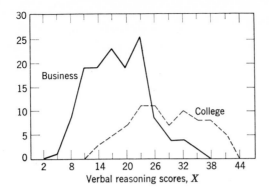

Fig. 1.5 *Frequency polygon of two curriculum groups.*

one predictor is available is likely to be less reliable than the inference from the test scores themselves.

At Waltham High School, pupils who do well in verbal reasoning in the ninth grade are likely to be in the college preparatory curriculum in the tenth grade, whereas pupils who obtain lower scores are usually in the business curriculum. This is not surprising. Preparation for college work undoubtedly requires greater verbal facility than is required in preparing for stenographic and clerical work. If those pupils with high verbal reasoning facility were guided away from college preparatory work simply because they could do still better in high school commercial subjects, the talents of the best students would be diverted from their most useful development. Ability would be wasted by oversupplying the lower level and undersupplying the higher level.

That there is a tendency for persons to choose jobs consistent with their levels of ability is illustrated in Stewart's (1947) tabulation of Army General Classification Test (AGCT) scores according to the civilian occupation from which the army personnel came. Stewart's summary of AGCT data on occupations for which 50 or more cases were available is reproduced in Fig. 1.6.

Accountants (Group 1) clearly have higher scores than do general bookkeepers (Group 16). Considering intelligence, the AGCT scores predict that accountants would be more successful bookkeepers than the actual bookkeepers. However, the fact remains that the persons with higher AGCT scores tended to be accountants, not bookkeepers. Putting it another way, the more intelligent bookkeepers gravitate toward accounting. There is, of course, overlap of the distributions, but the central difference is substantial. Only 25% of the bookkeepers exceed the median score of accountants. Recommending that accountants become bookkeepers because they will be better bookkeepers than the present ones robs society of its supply of accountants. Bookkeeping can be performed by somewhat less intelligent people; accounting probably cannot.

Very often, education and jobs are organized to accommodate people at various levels of various abilities. Studies suggest that people are aware of these levels, and that this awareness influences their choices of education and occupation. Individual choices can be predicted to some extent from knowledge about the persons before they enter their jobs. A typical example is seen in Fig. 1.7, which shows data from the Differential Aptitude Test.

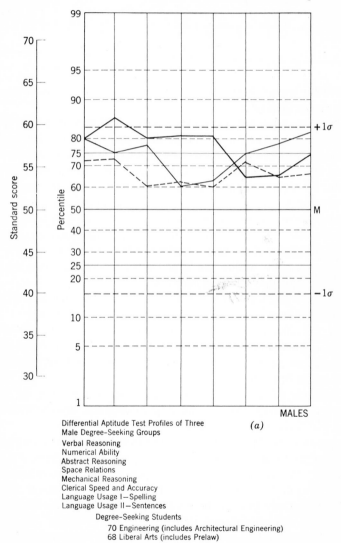

Differential Aptitude Test Profiles of Three
Male Degree-Seeking Groups

    (a)   MALES

Verbal Reasoning
Numerical Ability
Abstract Reasoning
Space Relations
Mechanical Reasoning
Clerical Speed and Accuracy
Language Usage I—Spelling
Language Usage II—Sentences

Degree-Seeking Students

70 Engineering (includes Architectural Engineering)
68 Liberal Arts (includes Prelaw)

Fig. 1.7 *Reproduced from* Occupations, *Vol. XXX, No. 8, pp. 588–9, 1952.*

The test scores were obtained while the boys were still students in high school. The career classification for the boys was determined two or three years later. Thus the classification represents the careers that the boys were pursuing at the time of the followup. Figure 1.7*a* indicates distinct differentiation in level of ability between those students who chose to seek a college degree and those who went to work (Fig. 1.7*b*). There is also differentiation among the three types of degree-seeking students and between the two categories of employed males. The levels of boys' aptitudes are related to

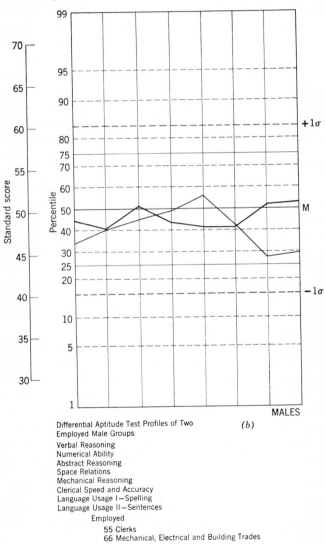

Differential Aptitude Test Profiles of Two   *(b)*
Employed Male Groups

Verbal Reasoning
Numerical Ability
Abstract Reasoning
Space Relations
Mechanical Reasoning
Clerical Speed and Accuracy
Language Usage I—Spelling
Language Usage II—Sentences

Employed

55 Clerks
66 Mechanical, Electrical and Building Trades

the jobs they enter. *The level of their career choices could have been predicted while the boys were still in high school.*

The boys who chose to continue their education in engineering obtained higher scores in all eight areas of the Differential Aptitude Test while in high school than did those who chose jobs in the mechanical, electrical, and building trades. Engineers being trained can surely learn building trade tasks, and they would be expected to perform the tasks better than the men presently in these jobs. This expectation does not mean, however, that the men seeking engineering degrees should actually be in the building trades. Engineering study requires more ability than men in the trades exhibit. Within a hierarchy of jobs requiring similar aptitudes, advising a man to take the job in which he will perform best *wastes manpower*; it oversupplies the low level and fails to supply the higher levels.

Many jobs require various degrees of diverse abilities. It is the responsibility of a personnel head in a plant to know the ability requirements for each job, to estimate the capabilities of each employee he advises, and to assign him to a job so that each job will have qualified employees.

Personnel Classification and the Psychological Profile

To illustrate the advising and assignment procedure in practice, and to apply the preceding discussion to personnel problems in a large plant, we introduce a hypothetical example involving two abilities, mechanical and clerical, and two jobs, mechanic and clerk. To make the illustration as simple as possible, let us assume that the scores on the tests have been standardized for the population of employees and that the two abilities are not correlated. The bivariate distribution of mechanical and clerical ability can then be represented by the scatter diagram given in Fig. 1.8. The scatter diagram represents the mechanical and clerical abilities of all employees available for assignment to career fields.

A mechanic's job requires better-than-average mechanical ability, so let us assume that the ideal assignment of an employee is one who is $1\frac{1}{2}$ standard deviations above the mean in mechanical ability. Although clerical ability is unquestionably useful in maintaining engines, we shall regard mechanical ability as more important. We therefore assume, to simplify the illustration, that clerical ability 1.0 standard deviation (SD) *below* the mean is adequate and represents, in combination with appropriate mechanical ability, the ideal employee. The job of clerk, on the other hand, requires more clerical ability and less mechanical ability. We will assume, for the example, that the numerical statements are clerical ability, $+1.5$, and mechanical ability, -1.5 SD. These hypothetical ideal values as well as the relative numbers of employees whose scores meet the specifications are indicated by crosses on Fig. 1.8.

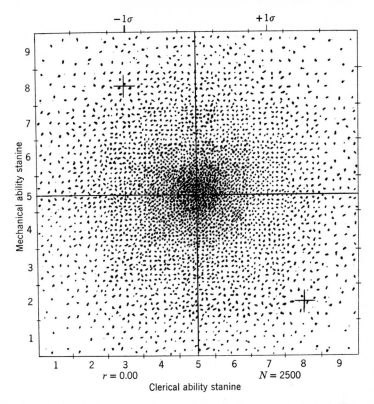

Fig. 1.8   *Hypothetical scatter diagram of mechanical and clerical ability stanine scores.*

The frequency with which employees are found with the exact combination of abilities specified for each job is obviously small and very much smaller than the number required. Consequently, it is necessary that employees whose scores place them in the vicinity of the ideal points be assigned to these jobs.

The assumed ideal specifications do not necessarily represent minimum requirements. The company may be well satisfied with a mechanic whose mechanical ability is less than +1.5 but whose clerical ability is greater than −1.0 SD. Within a maintenance gang some variation can be efficiently utilized by permitting the better clerks and poorer mechanics to do more than the usual share of difficult paperwork, and vice versa.

It is sometimes suggested that the problem is solved by assigning to the job of mechanic only employees whose mechanical ability is higher than +1.5 SD. The suggestion might be a practical working rule if the job of mechanic were the only job that the personnel officer had to fill. Some other jobs also require mechanical ability, and a few may require even greater ability. The rule actually would prove wasteful. It satisfies one need by neglecting others. It robs higher-level mechanical jobs of the talents they require.

The best solution is to choose a suitable central point to aim for, and decide upon the desirable amount of variation around the central point, both decisions being conditioned by the actual distribution of abilities in the supply of available men.

Let us apply these ideas to the hypothetical example. The scatter diagram in Fig. 1.8 describes the actual supply of employees. From this population a large number of men are to be identified as mechanics. We begin by identifying those individuals whose scores meet the specifications exactly, that is, -1.0 SD in clerical ability and $+1.5$ SD in mechanical ability. These men are labeled mechanics. Since we have not found a sufficient number, we relax the specifications to include score points in the vicinity of the specified values. A question arises immediately concerning the limits of the acceptable "neighborhood," that is, how large a deviation is permissible. It is quite clear from the known facts about the distribution of the available supply of men that a large group can be found only by accepting quite large deviations from the central specification point.

We might also ask about the form of this specific region. In this situation we notice that it is easier to find score points near the center of the population, and we know that mechanical ability greater than specified may compensate for clerical ability less than specified. If we follow these principles we find that the region containing the score points which we consider acceptable for mechanics increases and takes on a characteristic form. This can be seen in a scatter diagram of the individuals finally included in the group. Figure 1.9 is an example. The central point of the distribution is -1.0 on the clerical scale and $+1.5$ on the mechanical, in accordance with specifications. The standard deviation is 0.60, somewhat less than the standard deviation in the population of employees. The correlation within the group is $r = -0.25$. Two of the isofrequency, or contour, ellipses characterizing the ideal bivariate distribution are superimposed on Fig. 1.9 as a simplified indication of the location and form of the region of score points which describe the individuals. The density, which is greater in the center, is such that one-half the individual score points lies inside the small ellipse and one-half outside. And 90% lie inside the large ellipse.

Similar considerations for the job of clerk lead us to conclude that the score points of clerks will be distributed in a differently located, but quite similar, bivariate distribution. The two groups, mechanics and clerks, are represented by contour ellipses in Fig. 1.10.

In a hypothetical example it is easy to imagine a point specifying the

The Geometry of the Psychological Profile

Chapter 2

The One-Variate Case

A Preview

An obvious aspect of the profile problem is the manner of representing test scores for interpretation or, more precisely, interpretative decisions. Although questions of validity are implicit in any decision problem, the explicit subject of our analysis is the manner of representing valid data, the means of extracting the maximum information, and the method of presenting the information in the most useful form. The answers to the questions which arise in the statistical simplification or reduction of the data, that is, the solutions to the profile problem, flow naturally from the elementary characteristics of the data themselves. The solutions, in fact, are dictated by the logical concepts underlying the idea of frequency distributions of data; they are: the concept of the mean, central tendency or centroid as a description of a group; the concept of variation among the members of a group; and the concept of covariation within a group.

The development begins with the simplest possible instance—one score of one man. The case is generalized by adding men so that the group contains two, three, four, and finally any number N of men. The initial problems of representing the data of one test and distinguishing among the members of one group are thus developed from the beginning. A second group is then introduced and the problem of comparison between groups is examined in the simplest instance. A third group is added, and finally the case is generalized to any number G of groups.

The same procedure is followed with variates. A second test is introduced and the logical elements of the bivariate case are developed first for one group, then for two groups, and finally for G groups. It is easy to see that the same procedure can be applied to extend the number of variates. We shall find that the logical solution that solves the simple instances is also the solution to the profile problem in the general case where N persons are each measured with T tests and are known to be sorted into G groups.

Analyses of the simple cases of concrete examples get the most attention.

The logical concepts are developed in detail, in a familiar statistical setting, and with complete computations of the example.

The Indoor–Outdoor Score of the Activity Preference Inventory

In the following example, we shall consider World Airlines, a company employing over 50,000 persons and operating scheduled flights. This company naturally needs many men who can be assigned a particular set of functions. The mechanics on the line who service the equipment of World Airlines form one of the groups which we shall consider. A second group are the agents who deal with the passengers of the airline. A third are the men in operations who coordinate airline activities.

The personnel officer of World Airlines has developed an Activity Preference Inventory for the use of the airline. The first section of this inventory contains 30 pairs of activities, each pair naming an indoor activity and an outdoor activity. One item is

_____ Billiards : Golf _____

The applicant for a job in World Airlines checks the activity he prefers. The score is the number of *outdoor* activities marked.

Joe Armand, Tom Baslik, and Bill Flint

Joe Armand checked the Activity Preference Inventory when he applied for a job in World Airlines. Joe was hired and asked to return in several days for assignment to a job. His score is indicated in a roster available in the personnel office of World Airlines. It may be recorded on an answer sheet, or a list, or on a record, such as the personnel folder which World Airlines maintains for each of its employees. We shall refer to the written record of names and scores as a roster, whether the roster be in the form of a separate card for each employee or a listing of names and scores:

Apprentice	Social Security Number	Number of Outdoor Activity Preferences
Armand, Joe	123-45-6789	22

Our first question is: What does a personnel officer know about Joe? The officer can say that Joe preferred the outdoor activity named in 22 of the 30 pairs, preferred the indoor activity in 8 of 30 pairs, and that Joe prefers 14 more outdoor than indoor activities. These statements exhaust the information conveyed by the roster.

The personnel officer may also indicate this information graphically by constructing a vertical line marked with convenient intervals to indicate the possible score values. Joe's score may be indicated as a point on this line, as in Fig. 2.1a. This construction is called a profile stalk. Joe's position on the profile stalk may also be indicated by placing an × to

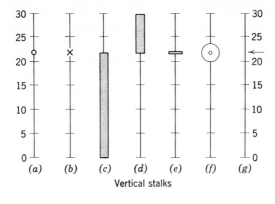

Vertical stalks

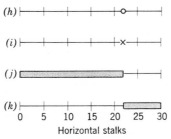

Horizontal stalks

Fig. 2.1

indicate the point. It may also be shown by constructing a wide black bar from 0 to 22, or by dropping a wide black bar from 30. These devices are illustrated in Fig. 2.1. Obviously the same graphic representation could be constructed on a horizontal scale. *All of these representations are called profiles.* All have a common basic idea. No matter what graphic device is used, the number 22 which summarizes Joe's marking of the test is thought of as a point on a line or a location on a scale. Although we shall find that this precise geometric concept encounters difficulties in its graphic application to test score profiles, the concept is indispensable.

The profile representation adds no information to that given in the roster. It provides only a visual model of the numerical score. Further interpretative information *is* added by introducing preference scores of other employees.

Suppose Tom Baslik's score is included in the roster. The roster now reads:

Apprentice	Social Security Number	Number of Outdoor Activity Preferences
Armand, Joe	123-45-6789	22
Baslik, Tom	987-65-4321	18

The personnel officer can now make the simplest comparison, one man with another. We note specifically that the two scores are represented by two locations or points on a line, and that the difference between the scores is represented by a distance along the line. Joe Armand prefers more outdoor activities; Tom Baslik prefers fewer; the men are separated by a distance of 22 minus 18, or 4 outdoor preferences. We note also that the difference and the distance are the same if we score the test by counting indoor preferences. The same facts are represented by writing the numbers in a column.

$$22$$

$$18$$

When writing the scores this way we assume an unwritten column heading, Outdoor activity score. We *understand* further that the unwritten heading of the first row is "Armand, Joe," whereas that for the second row is "Baslik, Tom." Double lines may be used to enclose the column of numbers.

$$\left\| \begin{matrix} 22 \\ 18 \end{matrix} \right\|$$

This is a matrix. If the column of numbers were enclosed in square brackets or large parentheses, the arrangement would also be called a matrix.

$$\begin{bmatrix} 22 \\ 18 \end{bmatrix} \qquad \begin{pmatrix} 22 \\ 18 \end{pmatrix}$$

A matrix of scores such as

$$\left\| \begin{matrix} 22 \\ 18 \end{matrix} \right\|$$

is simply an unlabeled reproduction of a roster. The matrix *implies* the existence of column and row headings.

The facts recorded in the matrix may be indicated on the profile stalk by some symbol to mark the two points. In Fig. 2.2 both locations can be observed and the distance between the men is equally obvious. It is to be noted, however, that the simplest extension, namely two scores, has restricted the graphic methods; the device of Fig. 2.1c and d cannot be used.

Thus roster, matrix, and profile convey identical information, that is, Joe Armand scores 22, Tom Baslik 18, and Joe Armand preferred the outdoor activity in four more pairs of indoor–outdoor activities than did Tom Baslik. Consideration of Tom Baslik's score increased the under-

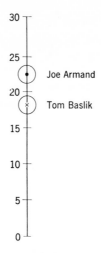

Fig. 2.2 *Two employees on an outdoor profile stalk.*

standing of Joe Armand's score, and vice versa. Each score became a reference point for comparison with the other.

A third employee, Bill Flint, may appear on the personnel officer's roster.

Apprentice	Social Security Number	Number of Outdoor Activity Preferences
Armand, Joe	123-45-6789	22
Baslik, Tom	987-65-4321	18
Flint, Bill	432-19-8765	20

The third score may be inserted in the matrix of scores, and Bill's

$$\begin{Vmatrix} 22 \\ 18 \\ 20 \end{Vmatrix}$$

score may be located by a symbol on the profile stalks, as in Fig. 2.3. Roster, matrix, and profile representations give the same information. The outdoor activity preferences of Joe Armand are now known to exceed the outdoor activity preferences of two, rather than one, employee. Although this represents an increase in the amount of information available, the utility of the information has not been greatly increased. It is obvious that the example must be enlarged by the addition of more employees' scores.

Before turning to the problems of score representation in a larger group, we remark that the profile representation of the preference information

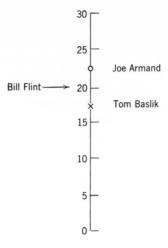

Fig. 2.3

for Joe, Tom, and Bill is different from roster and matrix representations in two respects. The marking of points on a single profile stalk is the simplest form of representation of numbers on a Cartesian axis. This representation discloses at first glance the rank of the outdoor activity preferences of Joe, Tom, and Bill; roster and matrix representations do not. Roster and matrix representations show the sequence, which is customarily alphabetic by name, in which the activity preference scores are recorded; profile and Cartesian representations do not. Thus there is a difference between matrix and Cartesian forms of representation. For purposes of score interpretation, we usually consider that the numerical sequence in which the scores for several employees are written is unimportant but that the numerical rank of the score is important. For this reason, we might conclude that profile representation is superior to matrix representation. However, we must remember that profiles and Cartesian representations can always be constructed from rosters and matrices but that rosters and matrices cannot always be reconstructed from profiles.

The Problem of One Group

World Airlines is a large company which must recruit men if it is to maintain its work force at full strength. Furthermore, many of its jobs require the acquisition of special information, and are sufficiently complex and important to require a period of supervised practice before an employee is accorded the full status of doing more independent work. World Airlines therefore maintains an apprentice system for six months for inducting its skilled employees into its operations. The jobs we shall consider in this example require a high school education, and induction is subject to service as an apprentice for a period of six months.

World Airlines recruits apprentices from high school. In the spring of each year, applicants for apprentice training in major cities are called together and given the Activities Preference Inventory and other tests. These scores are used to pick those applicants who will be hired and inducted as apprentices. Joe Armand, Tom Baslik, and Bill Flint are three of a group of 135 applicants tested in New York City who survived this preliminary screening and are now employed by World Airlines, although they still are to receive assignment to a type of apprentice training.

The pool of apprentices which includes Joe, Tom, and Bill consists of 135 men. The Activity Preference Inventory scores appear in a roster, as in Table 2.1. The roster can be represented as a matrix:

$$\begin{Vmatrix} 21 \\ 21 \\ 27 \\ \vdots \\ 21 \end{Vmatrix}$$

The matrix will contain 135 scores. When we do not need to know the numerical value of each one of the scores, we can simplify and save space by using a shorthand form. The form creates an impression of the matrix without reproducing it entirely. The first two or three scores and the last score are usually reproduced and the other scores which belong in the matrix are indicated by dots.

Whether one thinks of the outdoor activity preferences of Joe's group as a roster or a matrix, one point becomes clear immediately. Neither roster nor matrix provides a visual impression of the location of the group's scores or the differences that characterize the men. Consequently, we turn next to a profile representation of the roster.

The inadequacies of an attempt to indicate a roster of 135 scores on a profile stalk by graphic symbols such as dots, $\times$'s, or asterisks lead to two basic decisions. First, we abandon the identification of the score points by name, and second, we adopt the notion of frequency at a point. These decisions lead us directly to the concept of a graphic frequency distribution plotted on a Cartesian axis. In effect, we abandon the profile representation as not useful for many scores in a group and substitute the more general Cartesian representation, using one axis to indicate the score values, as in the profile stalk, and a second axis to show the frequency with which each score occurs in the roster. The results are shown in Fig. 2.4.

Table 2.1 *Roster of Scores*

Apprentice Number*	Number of Outdoor Activity Preferences	Apprentice Number*	Number of Outdoor Activity Preferences	Apprentice Number*	Number of Outdoor Activity Preferences
1	21	46	15	91	20
2	21	47	14	92	13
3	27	48	13	93	20
4	16	49	13	94	11
5	14	50	20	95	16
6	20	51	19	96	22
7	19	52	19	97	21
8	9	53	17	98	18
9	23	54	11	99	27
10	14	55	14	100	24
11	22	56	18	101	16
12	20	57	17	102	13
13	20	58	10	103	20
14	18	59	17	104	20
15	25	60	11	105	12
16	17	61	23	106	18
17	10	62	21	107	20
18	17	63	19	108	6
19	15	64	11	109	20
20	21	65	18	110	17
21	18	66	22	111	20
22	20	67	17	112	13
23	22	68	11	113	20
24	29	69	13	114	22
25	15	70	11	115	19
26	21	71	23	116	19
27	20	72	21	117	16
28	21	73	20	118	15
29	21	74	17	119	14
30	20	75	13	120	18
31	25	76	13	121	18
32	14	77	11	122	23
33	20	78	16	123	13
34	16	79	17	124	19
35	11	80	13	125	15
36	16	81	16	126	15
37	16	82	26	127	14
38	20	83	24	128	13
39	13	84	17	129	19
40	22	85	16	130	17
41	10	86	14	131	24
42	24	87	13	132	18
43	20	88	16	133	14
44	19	89	16	134	12
45	20	90	11	135	21

* Since the name of the apprentice and his social security number are not essential to the example, a serial identifying number is used.

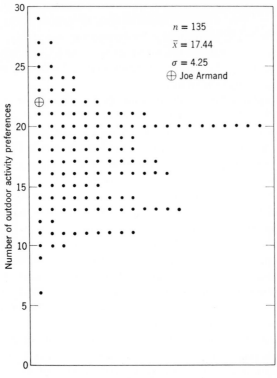

Fig. 2.4

At this point, several ideas must be considered. When we give up the identification of the scores by name we eliminate the possibility of constructing the matrix from the frequency distribution. This distribution, however, can always be reproduced from the matrix. When we attempt to indicate scores as points on a line, the repetition of particular values leads us to think of concentration or density of points along the line. We cannot graphically represent the density by superimposing dots on a line, but we can use the idea of density in thinking about the group, and we can show it graphically by using Cartesian representation. We also recall that the purpose of turning to profile representation of the matrix was to obtain a visual summary of the information contained in the details of the matrix. The results in Fig. 2.4 reveal the essential features.

The number of dots indicates the size of the group. The center of the group is visually located near a score of 18. The size of the differences among the members of the group is indicated by the scattering of individuals, and the variation is shown by the graphic shape of the representation. The visual impressions of these four fundamental characteristics of every frequency distribution and, of course, every test score matrix, may be made more precise by computing the familiar statistics: N, the number of scores; $\bar{X}$, the mean score; V or σ^2, the variance; and noting that the shape of the pictorial representation looks very much like a sample from a normal distribution.

The computations for the distribution in Fig. 2.4 are $n = 135$, $\bar{X} = 17.44$, $\sigma^2 = 17.92$. The standard deviation σ is 4.25.

We now have 134 profiles with which we can compare the profile of Joe Armand. The possible comparisons are readily seen in Fig. 2.4 where Joe's profile is marked by the $\oplus$ at a score of 22. Figure 2.4 shows that only 14 of Joe's group had more outdoor preferences than Joe did. If we consider Joe's score to be a midscore in the group of six scores at 22, in accordance with customary statistical practice, we can say that 87% of the group have lower scores. Thus it would seem that Joe has rather outstanding outdoor preferences. Is this good or bad?

Up to this point we have confined our consideration of the score to the number of *outdoor* activities preferred. This scoring system is arbitrary. Had we counted the number of *indoor* activities preferred, Joe's score, instead of being higher than the scores of 87% of his group, would have been lower than the scores of 87%. Joe's position would have been "bad" instead of "good," if the usual interpretation of percentiles is invoked. With this example in mind we ask the reader to suspend the natural inclination to evaluate the score, and to think of scores in a more general way as locations in a frequency distribution.

The example provides no data to guide a value judgment or a prediction of behavior. The personnel officer does not know how the number of outdoor preferences correlates with any of the criteria with which he is concerned. He does not know whether a greater number of *outdoor* preferences or a greater number of *indoor* preferences is a positively oriented predictive indicator of some later performance. It is possible, however, to locate the score in relation to the center or average of the group. The mean score indicates the number of outdoor activities a typical member of the group prefers. It is a good approximation of the number of outdoor preferences of a large fraction of Joe's group. Since the mean locates the center of a group and is a good estimate of a large proportion of the most typical members, it is frequently thought of as the best single score value that can be used to describe the location of the group as a whole.

As soon as we have accepted this concept of a single location to characterize the group, we notice its limitations. An outstanding fact about people is that they are different. The statistical use of the mean is sometimes criticized because it *seems* to imply that the members of the group are all the same. Using the Cartesian idea that a score is represented by a point on a line and the difference between scores is a distance along the line will solve the problem. The difference between an individual's score and the mean score is a numerical statement of his atypicalness. The difference measures how far he is from the typical point. We shall call such a difference a deviation from the mean, or sometimes a deviation score, or even more simply, a deviation.

Even though the deviation score is a direct measure of atypicalness, we encounter a difficulty in interpreting particular values because we have no familiar comparison measures. We know that if a deviation is zero, the man is typical, but we expect most of the men in a group to be more or less different. We do not know how large a deviation has to be before we should think of a man as really atypical. We obtain the necessary interpretive information by looking at the distribution of the group. Before examining the details of the group distribution, we discern that it would be advantageous to find a way of translating deviation scores into some easily interpretable statement about atypicalness. We would like to obtain a type of interpretation that would have the same meaning for every distribution we might consider.

The graphic representation of the group scores in Fig. 2.4 is reproduced as a conventional frequency distribution in Table 2.2. Inspection of either the figure or the table shows that a score of 30 is atypical in Joe's group; in fact, it is so atypical that even the man who marked the largest number of outdoor activities is more like the average member. We note two facts about the man who did mark the largest number ($X = 29$). First, he *is* a member of the group, and, second, he is atypical. He is so atypical that the scores of the 134 other men are closer to the mean. We ascertain this fact by computing the deviation of the largest and smallest scores:

$$29 - 17.44 = 11.56 \quad \text{and} \quad 6 - 17.44 = -11.44$$

The man who chose the smallest number of outdoor activities is also atypical. His score is almost as far from the mean as the highest score is. His score is lower than all the other 134 scores and it is farther from the mean than 133 of them.

We are approaching the concept of the percentile equivalent of a score. An outdoor preference score of 29 is so high that more than 99% of the group's scores are lower, and a score of 6 is so low that more than 99% of the scores are higher. If similar computations were made for each score value, we would have a table of percentile equivalents. The percentile concept, however, does not quite meet our need. We are concerned with a

Table 2.2 *Frequency Distribution of the Group*

Number of Outdoor Activity Preferences	Frequency
29	1
28	–
27	2
26	1
25	2
24	4
23	4
22	6
21	10
20	20
19	9
18	9
17	11
16	12
15	6
14	9
13	13
12	2
11	9
10	3
9	1
8	–
7	–
6	1
	$n = 135$

statement of typicalness or atypicalness. We are not concerned with notions of superiority-inferiority. The percentile statement includes the notion of rank order—a score is interpreted as being higher or lower than the typical score—and is too easily translated to mean better or worse than the average. Our concept of atypicalness rests on the notion of distance from the typical without regard to direction. Our concept requires that we avoid the kind of value judgments associated with percentiles.

An example will reveal the slight modification of the percentile idea that our concept of atypical deviation requires. By counting the frequencies in Table 2.2 we can determine the number of scores higher than any particular value we choose. Thus we find that 14 scores are higher than $X = 22.5$. (In accord with conventional statistical practice, we regard the score value 23 as the midpoint of the interval from $X = 22.5$ to $X = 23.5$.) From the fraction 14/135, we find that 10% of the group's scores are more divergent in the plus direction than is $X = 22.5$. By similar counting we find that 14, or 10%, are more divergent in the opposite direction than $X = 11.5$. With respect to atypicalness, these two points on the score scale are equivalent. We express the degree of atypicalness for direct interpretation as the percent of the whole group who are even less typical, that is, 20%. We have thus disposed of the problem of the direction of divergence: a score at the ninetieth percentile is regarded as just as unusual as a score at the tenth percentile. Altogether, 20% are more unusual.

A numerical statement expressing this interpretation of distance from the centroid of a group will be called a centour score or centour equivalent. Thus if an apprentice's score is said to be equivalent to a centour of 30, the statement means that 30% of the group were farther away from the middle of the group and 70% were nearer. A centour of 95 means "close to the center"; a centour of 5 means "far from the center."

Although the centour score idea is simple, there are some statistical problems that have been avoided in the initial explanation. The reader may have noticed that our argument rests on two propositions that seem to be inconsistent in the data. First, we have said that equal absolute distances from the centroid represent equivalent atypicalness, and second, we have introduced the idea that deviations which occur with equal frequency are equivalent. In the example, we found that the score point $X = 22.5$ was exceeded by 14 members of the group and that another 14 men scored lower than $X = 11.5$. The absolute values of the distances from the centroid are $|22.5 - 17.44| = 5.06$ and $|11.5 - 17.44| = 5.94$. When the distance is computed, the score points are seen to be unequally divergent. The discrepancy arises in the example because of the chance irregularities in the frequency distribution. The problem of the inconsistency disappears in any general instance where the data may be appropriately described by a normal distribution. The use of the normal distribution in the calculation of centour equivalents is illustrated in detail when we consider the case of two groups.

Before returning to the problems of profile representation, it should be noted that the centour equivalent is a two-tailed concept. A score which is either plus 1.0 SD or minus 1.0 SD is equivalent to a centour of $16 + 16 = 32$. The areas in both tails of the normal distribution are added to determine the total fraction which is more divergent. The centour scores in Table 2.3 were computed for the normal distribution which most closely approximates the group distribution in Fig. 2.4.

Table 2.3 *Centour Equivalents for the Group (Assuming a Normal Distribution)*

Mean = 17.44	$\sigma = 4.25$
Number of Outdoor Activity Preferences	Centour Equivalent
29	01
28	01
27	02
26	04
25	07
24	12
23	19
22	28
21	40
20	55
19	71
18	89
17	92
16	74
15	57
14	42
13	30
12	20
11	13
10	08
9	05
8	03
7	01
6	01

Percentiles and Profile Representation

In the preceding section we explored the problem of using profile representation in representing scores for a group. This led us into the concepts of frequency distributions and the centour score. We return now to the problem of profile representation of a single score, and inquire into the application of the percentile concept to the individual profile.

Table 2.4 records the percentile equivalents of the group scores tabulated in the diagram of Fig. 2.4 and the frequencies of Table 2.2.

Early in this chapter we constructed a profile representation of Joe Armand's outdoor score. Obviously, it is possible to perform the same kind of construction using the percentile scores instead of the original raw

Table 2.4 *Percentile and Standard Score Equivalents of Scores in the Group (Computed from Table 2.2)*

Raw Score	Standard Score	Percentile
29	+2.72	99+
28	2.49	99
27	2.25	98
26	2.02	97
25	1.78	96
24	1.55	94
23	1.31	91
22	1.07	87
21	0.84	81
20	0.60	70
19	0.37	60
18	0.13	53
17	−0.10	46
16	−0.34	37
15	−0.57	30
14	−0.81	25
13	−1.05	17
12	−1.28	11
11	−1.52	7
10	−1.75	3
9	−1.99	1
8	−2.22	1
7	−2.46	1
6	−2.69	1−

scores. Such constructions for the three apprentices of our example are shown individually in Fig. 2.5. The three men are marked on the same profile stalk in Fig. 2.6, and the two kinds of profile scales, raw score and percentile rank, are shown together for comparison.

The purpose of the profile construction is to provide a visual impression of a score and a readily determined interpretation of it. The visual impressions provided by the raw score and percentile scale profile are quite different. This observation brings us to the following.

Profile Problem 1A. Should profiles be constructed on a percentile score scale or a raw score scale? In resolving this problem, we recall that our interpretation of the number of outdoor activity preferences expressed by Joe, Tom, and Bill did *not* depend on the *visual impression* obtained from

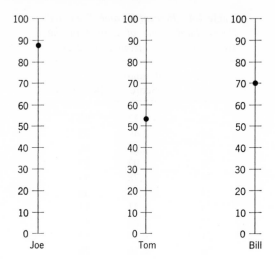

Fig. 2.5 *Profiles on percentile scales.*

representation of their scores. It depended on the order and relative frequency with which scores like those of Joe, Tom, and Bill actually occurred in the group. The interpretation of a profile is not affected by the graphic method chosen. It depends solely on the frequency distribution tabulated from the score matrix.

Figure 2.7 represents the relation between the percentile and raw score

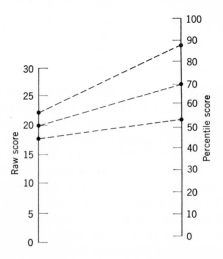

Fig. 2.6 *Comparison of raw score and percentile scales.*

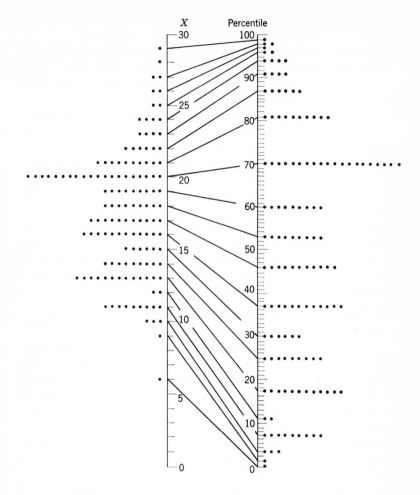

Fig. 2.7 *Correspondence between raw scores and percentiles.*

scales and the frequency distributions obtained on each scale. It shows that raw scores and percentile ranks have identical rank order, and none of the personnel head's earlier impressions concerning the relative standing of Joe, Tom, and Bill is contradicted by either type of representation.

Figure 2.7 also reveals that the frequency with which different scores are represented is not changed by expressing the scores as percentiles. The same fraction of the group exceeds a given percentile rank as exceeds the raw score corresponding to that percentile rank.

When interpretations are based on the order and relative frequency of different scores, it makes no difference whether profiles are represented by a raw score or a percentile rank scale.

In computing centour scores, we used the convenient symmetry and well-known distribution of areas under the normal curve. Because the original data in the matrix are very similar to the ideal curve, the centours computed by use of the normal distribution were very nearly the same as would be computed from the actual fractions of the sample. Consequently, centour scores computed on the basis of the mean and standard deviation of percentile ranks would lead to erroneous statements about the typicalness or atypicalness of the percentile ranks of the outdoor activity preferences of Joe, Tom, and Bill.

Conversion of profiles to a percentile representation does not alter the order or relative frequency interpretations of profiles, but the use of percentiles is inconsistent with the use of the normal distribution in the computation of centour scores. Raw score representation is consistent with all three qualities desired, whereas percentile rank representation is consistent with only two of three qualities. We conclude that raw score representation, at least for the data of this example, is superior.

Standard Scores and Profile Representation

In our previous consideration of a score expressed as a deviation from the mean we mentioned the problem of determining how large a deviation has to be in order to be regarded as atypical. The discussion which followed led to the concept of the centour. We now return to the problem of finding a unit of measurement or comparison for the deviation score, and its use in profile representation. The unit of measurement used for illustration is the standard deviation of the distribution.

A standard score designated by the symbol z is equal to the deviation score divided by the standard deviation. The equation is

$$z = \frac{X - \bar{X}}{\sigma}$$

where X is the raw score as in the original matrix, $\bar{X}$ is the mean score, and σ is the standard deviation. The standard score thus describes the size of a deviation score $(X - \bar{X})$ as a certain number of standard deviations; it describes the location of the score X as a certain number of standard deviations from the mean. A score of 40 in a group with the mean equal to 50 and the standard deviation equal to 5 is two standard deviations below the mean. The standard score is minus 2.0.

$$z = \frac{40 - 50}{5} = -2.0$$

Similarly computed, a score $X = 54$ is equivalent to $z = +.80$.

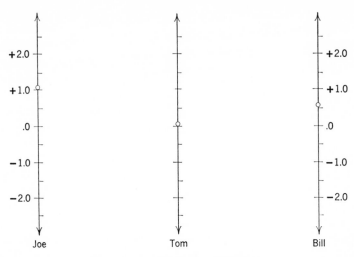

Fig. 2.8 *Standard score profile stalks.*

Standard scores computed for the group example are recorded in Table 2.4. These standard scores could be used as the basis for constructing profiles of the three apprentices. These profiles are shown in Figs. 2.8, 2.9, and 2.10. The one-to-one correspondence of the raw to standard scores is obvious. We have changed the numerical value of the centroid by shifting

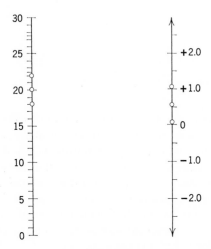

Fig. 2.9 *Comparison of three passenger agents on raw score and standard score profile stalks.*

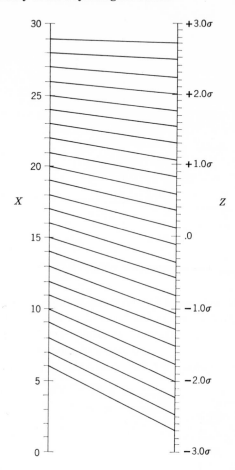

Fig. 2.10 *Correspondence between raw scores and standard scores (from Table* 2.4).

the mean from 17.44 in the X scores to zero in the z scores. This change is commonly called a translation of the origin. And we have changed the numerical value of the standard deviation from 4.25 in the X distribution to 1.0 in the z distribution. This change is called a transformation of the scale. Neither the translation nor the transformation has changed the basic character of the frequency distribution. The change has only standardized the origin and unit of measurement for the interpretation of scores.

The personnel adviser presented with profiles constructed with standard scores knows that Joe is 1.07 SD above the mean; Tom, .13 SD above the mean; and Bill, .06 SD above the mean. All three apprentices maintain the same relative position as was given by the number of their *outdoor* preferences. In fact, the standard scores indicate that Bill's location on the scale is halfway between that of Joe and Tom, exactly as the raw score indicated. Except for orienting interpretation to the mean and standard deviation of the group, the standard score transformation adds no new information. The transformation to standard scores has no influence on the *rank* a score holds in a given distribution, or the relative value of differences among individuals. Consequently, if we obtain centour scores for direct interpretation, it makes no difference whether we use the number of outdoor activities preferred, translated scores such as deviations from the mean, or transformations such as standard scores. Centour scores have a further advantage in that it makes no difference whether we think in terms of the number of *outdoor* activity preferences or the number of *indoor* activity preferences.

This example solves the following.

Profile Problem 1B. Should profiles be presented on a standard score scale or on a raw score scale? Since standard scores and raw scores stand in a linear relationship with each other, the order of the scores, the relative frequency with which the scores occur, and the shape of the distribution of scores are identical on both scales. When centour scores provide the framework for interpretation, identical values will result from calculations using either raw scores or standard scores.

Matrix Representation

Previously, a matrix was identified as a form for representing the scores in a roster. We shall use the now familiar example of the standard score transformation to develop equal familiarity with the matrix notation. In the single-group, single-variable case, matrix notation provides no advantage over ordinary scalar algebra in dealing with the equation $z = (X - \bar{X})/\sigma$. For multivariate examples, however, we shall find that the complications of ordinary algebraic notation are much simplified by matrix methods. In explaining matrix representation we shall also make explicit the geometric relationships which are implicit in the transformation of raw scores to standard scores. We begin with the simplest situation that illustrates matrix rules, namely, a roster of two scores.

The matrix of two scores (Joe Armand and Tom Baslik) is

$$\left\Vert \begin{matrix} 22 \\ 18 \end{matrix} \right\Vert$$

A score will be designated X_p where the subscript p stands for the pth person and may be any one of $p = 1, 2, 3, \ldots, n$, so that $X_1 = 22$ and

$X_2 = 18$. The matrix may be denoted by the symbol X and a matrix equation may be written

$$X = \begin{Vmatrix} X_1 \\ X_2 \end{Vmatrix}$$

The single matrix equation then represents two scalar equations, specifically:

$$\begin{array}{c} X_1 = 22 \\ X_2 = 18 \end{array} \quad \text{or} \quad X = \begin{Vmatrix} X_1 \\ X_2 \end{Vmatrix} = \begin{Vmatrix} 22 \\ 18 \end{Vmatrix}$$

If the elements (scores) in the column matrix X are written in the same order in a row, the resulting row matrix is named the *transpose* of X and is written X'.

$$X' = \| X_1 \quad X_2 \| = \| 22 \quad 18 \|$$

One matrix may be added to or subtracted from another matrix provided they have the same size and shape, that is, the same number of row elements and column elements. The result of addition or subtraction is a matrix. The elements in the new matrix are obtained by addition or subtraction of the elements *in the same position* in the original matrices. Thus X can be subtracted from X as follows:

$$X - X = \begin{Vmatrix} 22 \\ 18 \end{Vmatrix} - \begin{Vmatrix} 22 \\ 18 \end{Vmatrix} = \begin{Vmatrix} 0 \\ 0 \end{Vmatrix}$$

X' can be subtracted from X':

$$X' - X' = \| 22 \quad 18 \| - \| 22 \quad 18 \| = \| 0 \quad 0 \|$$

But X' cannot be subtracted from X because X has one column of two rows and X' has one row of two columns.

Multiplication may be performed on a matrix. To multiply a matrix by a scalar quantity, that is, a constant number, multiply every element of the matrix by the scalar:

$$3X = 3 \begin{Vmatrix} 22 \\ 18 \end{Vmatrix} = \begin{Vmatrix} 66 \\ 54 \end{Vmatrix}$$

and

$$3X' = 3\| 22 \quad 18 \| = \| 66 \quad 54 \|$$

It is obvious that the product of a matrix and a scalar quantity may be written in any order; it makes no difference whether we write 3 times X or X times 3.

Two matrices may be multiplied under certain conditions by using a rule of procedure. The result of the multiplication is a matrix. Thus the product of a matrix A and a matrix B is a matrix C, and such a matrix product is written

$$C = AB$$

Before proceeding with the rule for calculating a matrix product it will be advantageous to extend the idea of a matrix to include more than one column and more than one row.

A matrix in general is a rectangular array of elements arranged in r rows and t columns. We may think of a matrix A which consists of 2 rows and 3 columns, as composed of elements a_{11}, a_{12}, a_{13}, in the first row and a_{21}, a_{22}, a_{23} in the second row:

$$A = \begin{Vmatrix} a_{11} & a_{12} & a_{13} \\ a_{21} & a_{22} & a_{23} \end{Vmatrix}$$

The numerical subscripts identify the row and column position occupied by the element. It is convenient to use the alphabetic subscripts i, j to identify the general element. The symbol a_{ij} then denotes the element which lies in the ith row and the jth column. Numerical values of the elements in the 2×3 matrix A might be

$$A = \begin{Vmatrix} 2 & 7 & 5 \\ 4 & 3 & 6 \end{Vmatrix}$$

where $a_{11} = 2$, $a_{12} = 7$, etc. Similarly a 3×2 matrix B may be written

$$B = \begin{Vmatrix} b_{11} & b_{12} \\ b_{21} & b_{22} \\ b_{31} & b_{32} \end{Vmatrix}$$

Numerical values of the (b_{ij}) might be

$$B = \begin{Vmatrix} 2 & 4 \\ 7 & 3 \\ 5 & 6 \end{Vmatrix}$$

For the particular numerical values illustrated, the matrix B is the transpose of A and A is the transpose of B. These are written

$$A = B' \qquad \text{and} \qquad B = A'$$

The product AB is a matrix C which contains elements c_{ij}:

$$AB = C = \begin{Vmatrix} c_{11} & c_{12} \\ c_{21} & c_{22} \end{Vmatrix}$$

The procedure for computing the c_{ij} is to multiply the pairs of elements in the ith row of A and jth column of B and add the products. The unavoidable ambiguity of expressing this algebraic rule in nonalgebraic language is clarified in the example. The matrix equation $AB = C$ written as complete matrices is, in general,

$$A \quad \cdot \quad B \quad = \quad C$$

$$\begin{Vmatrix} a_{11} & a_{12} & a_{13} \\ a_{21} & a_{22} & a_{23} \end{Vmatrix} \cdot \begin{Vmatrix} b_{11} & b_{12} \\ b_{21} & b_{22} \\ b_{31} & b_{32} \end{Vmatrix} = \begin{Vmatrix} c_{11} & c_{12} \\ c_{21} & c_{22} \end{Vmatrix}$$

and in the particular numerical example is

$$A \quad \cdot \quad B \quad = \quad C$$

$$\begin{Vmatrix} 2 & 7 & 5 \\ 4 & 3 & 6 \end{Vmatrix} \cdot \begin{Vmatrix} 2 & 4 \\ 7 & 3 \\ 5 & 6 \end{Vmatrix} = \begin{Vmatrix} c_{11} & c_{12} \\ c_{21} & c_{22} \end{Vmatrix}$$

The element c_{11} lies in the top left corner of the matrix C in row 1, column 1 ($i = 1$ and $j = 1$). Pairing the elements "row by column," multiplying, and adding, we obtain

$$c_{11} = a_{11}b_{11} + a_{12}b_{21} + a_{13}b_{31}$$

which, in numerical values, is

$$c_{11} = 2(2) + 7(7) + 5(5) = 78$$

In the illustration the numbers in parentheses are the column elements of B. The element c_{12} which lies in the first row and second column of C is obtained in the same way from the first row in A and the second column in B:

$$c_{12} = 2(4) + 7(3) + 5(6) = 59$$

The complete matrix C is

$$C = \begin{Vmatrix} 78 & 59 \\ 59 & 61 \end{Vmatrix}$$

The explanation of the fact that C is a 2×2 matrix should be clear from this example of matrix multiplication. The process associates each row of A with each column of B in turn, Since there are two rows in A and two columns in B there will be two rows in C and two columns in C. In general, in the matrix product $C = AB$, the order (size) of C is determined by the number of rows in A and the number of columns in B.

Before we use these methods in dealing with the score matrix X, we note an important fact about matrix multiplication: two matrices may be multiplied only if the number of elements in the rows of the first matrix is equal to the number of elements in the columns of the second matrix. We have computed a product AB, but we cannot compute a product BA because the number of columns in the first matrix of the product is not equal to the number of rows in the second matrix.

We return now to the 2 by 1 matrix of scores X and find the product $X'X$:

$$X'X = \|22 \quad 18\| \cdot \left\|\begin{matrix} 22 \\ 18 \end{matrix}\right\|$$

We note that this matrix product will be a one by one (1×1) matrix, that is, a single element. The numerical result is

$$X'X = 22(22) + 18(18) = 484 + 324 = 808$$

The result is the square of the first score plus the square of the second score, or the sum of the squares of the scores in the matrix. In the notation of scalar algebra, the matrix product $X'X$ would be written $\sum X_p^2$.

The mean of these two scores is 20. If this value is subtracted from each of the scores, the differences $x = (X - \bar{X})$ are deviation scores. The deviation scores are:

$$x_1 = X_1 - \bar{X} = X_1 - 20 = 22 - 20 = +2$$
$$x_2 = X_2 - \bar{X} = X_2 - 20 = 18 - 20 = -2$$

If the mean is plotted on a Cartesian axis:

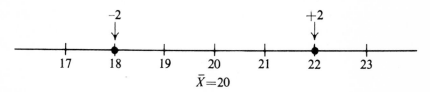

the deviations $+2$ and -2 show the distance of the two scores from the mean in the same way that the raw scores 22 and 18 are located with reference to zero on the profile stalk. This *change of origin* may be shown graphically on a scale where the number zero is assigned to represent the mean:

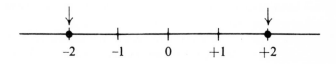

In many statistical computations, notably the variance

$$\sigma^2 = \Sigma(X - M)^2/N$$

the deviation scores are the numbers of principal interest. The matrix

$$x = \left\| \begin{matrix} +2 \\ -2 \end{matrix} \right\|$$

is the matrix of the deviation scores and represents the two points $+2$ and -2, just as the matrix

$$X = \left\| \begin{matrix} 22 \\ 18 \end{matrix} \right\|$$

represents the two raw score profile points. We have seen that the matrix product $X'X$ is the sum of the squares of the raw scores. By the same rule, the matrix product $x'x$ is the *sum of the squares of the deviation scores*

$$x'x = \| +2 \quad -2\| \ \left\| \begin{matrix} +2 \\ -2 \end{matrix} \right\|$$

$$= (+2)(+2) + (-2)(-2) = 8$$

When we divide $x'x$ by the number of scores, we obtain the variance σ^2. For the numbers $X = 22$ and $X = 18$, the variance is $8/2 = 4$, and the standard deviation is the square root of the variance, or 2.

Transforming the raw scores to deviation scores may be represented as a matrix subtraction. We first define the matrix $\bar{X}$ to have the same shape and size as the matrix X, and to contain as elements the mean in place of each X, thus

$$\bar{X} = \left\| \begin{matrix} 20 \\ 20 \end{matrix} \right\|$$

Then the matrix $x = X - \bar{X}$ is

$$x = X - \bar{X} = \left\| \begin{matrix} 22 \\ 18 \end{matrix} \right\| - \left\| \begin{matrix} 20 \\ 20 \end{matrix} \right\| = \left\| \begin{matrix} +2 \\ -2 \end{matrix} \right\|$$

The subtraction of the $\bar{X}$ matrix from the X matrix is equivalent to shifting the origin of measurement from the original zero of the raw score axis to the mean of the scores on that axis.

In analysis of variance the basic numbers in the calculations are sums of squares which are denoted by the matrix product $X'X$, or sums of squared deviations from the mean $x'x$. The scalar equations $\sum X^2 = \sum x^2 + n\bar{X}^2$ and $\sum x^2 = \sum X^2 - n\bar{X}^2$ are easily expressed in the matrix idiom because $\bar{X}'\bar{X} = n\bar{X}^2$. In the numerical illustration,

$$\bar{X}'\bar{X} = \|20 \quad 20\| \cdot \left\|\begin{matrix} 20 \\ 20 \end{matrix}\right\| = 2(20)^2$$

Thus the matrix equation

$$x'x = X'X - \bar{X}'\bar{X}$$

is the matrix formula for the sum of the squares of the deviation scores if X is a column of scores.

This rule holds for any number of scores. However, before we take up the case of three scores, let us use the trivial case in which we know the number of outdoor activity preferences of Joe Armand only. In this instance the score is a 1 by 1 matrix

$$X = \|22\|$$

and, writing as a row everything that was written as a column,

$$X' = \|22\|$$
$$X'X = 22(22) = 484$$

The mean of this distribution of one score is 22. Therefore:

$$\bar{X} = \|22\| \quad \text{and} \quad \bar{X}' = \|22\|$$
$$\bar{X}'\bar{X} = 22(22) = 484$$

Finally:

$$x'x = X'X - \bar{X}'\bar{X} = 484 - 484 = 0$$

We continue by extending the illustration to the case $n = 3$. The 3 by 1 matrix for Joe Armand, Tom Baslik, and Bill Flint is

$$X = \left\|\begin{matrix} 22 \\ 18 \\ 20 \end{matrix}\right\|$$

The mean of these three scores is $\bar{X} = 20$. The $\bar{X}$ matrix is now 3 by 1:

$$\bar{X} = \left\|\begin{matrix} 20 \\ 20 \\ 20 \end{matrix}\right\|$$

The matrix of deviation scores is

$$x = \left\|\begin{matrix} 22 \\ 18 \\ 20 \end{matrix}\right\| - \left\|\begin{matrix} 20 \\ 20 \\ 20 \end{matrix}\right\| = \left\|\begin{matrix} +2 \\ -2 \\ 0 \end{matrix}\right\|$$

The *translation* of axis, accomplished by subtracting the matrix $\bar{X}$ from the matrix X, is indicated in a graphic representation of the locations of the three scores:

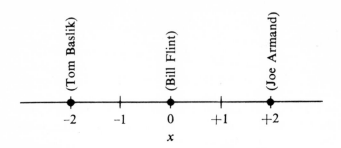

The translation retains the original information concerning Joe Armand, Tom Baslik, and Bill Flint. The three apprentices are in exactly the same relation as in the profile representation of their outdoor activity preferences. Joe Armand still prefers two more outdoor activities than Bill Flint and four more than Tom Baslik.

The transpose of x is

$$x' = \|+2 \quad -2 \quad 0\|$$

and the matrix $x'x$ is

$$x'x = \|+2 \quad -2 \quad 0\| \cdot \left\|\begin{matrix} +2 \\ -2 \\ 0 \end{matrix}\right\| = (4 + 4 + 0) = 8$$

The result is the sum of the squares of the deviation scores.

The matrix product $X'X$ is

$$X'X = \|22 \quad 18 \quad 20\| \cdot \left\|\begin{matrix} 22 \\ 18 \\ 20 \end{matrix}\right\| = (484 + 324 + 400) = 1208$$

And the product $\bar{X}'\bar{X}$ is

$$\bar{X}'\bar{X} = \|20 \quad 20 \quad 20\| \cdot \left\|\begin{matrix} 20 \\ 20 \\ 20 \end{matrix}\right\| = (400 + 400 + 400) = 1200$$

The difference between the matrix product $X'X$ and the matrix product $\bar{X}'\bar{X}$ is

$$X'X - \bar{X}'\bar{X} = (1208) - (1200) = 8 = x'x$$

The variance is 8 divided by 3, or approximately 2.67. The standard scores $z = (X - \bar{X})/\sigma$ for the group of three men can be written in a matrix. Each standard score is a deviation score multiplied by the same scalar quantity $1/\sigma$. The matrix of standard scores Z contains elements z_{ij}, each being a standard score.

$$Z = \frac{1}{\sigma} \begin{Vmatrix} +2 \\ -2 \\ 0 \end{Vmatrix}$$

The three scores in the Z matrix can be graphically represented on a standard score scale:

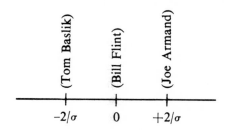

The *transformation* effected by multiplying $(X - \bar{X})$ by a constant *alters the size and meaning of the scale units.* A return to the scale units can be accomplished by multiplying each of the scores in Z by σ:

$$x = \begin{Vmatrix} +2 \\ -2 \\ 0 \end{Vmatrix} = \sigma \begin{Vmatrix} \dfrac{+2}{\sigma} \\ \dfrac{-2}{\sigma} \\ \dfrac{0}{\sigma} \end{Vmatrix}$$

These principles hold for any size sample. For the apprentices, the roster of the 135 men is represented by the matrix X (135 rows):

$$X = \begin{Vmatrix} 21 \\ 21 \\ 27 \\ \vdots \\ 21 \end{Vmatrix}$$

The transpose of X contains 135 columns:

$$X' = \begin{Vmatrix} 21 & 21 & 27 & \dots & 21 \end{Vmatrix}$$

and the product $X'X$ is

$$X'X = \|21 \quad 21 \quad 27 \quad \cdots \quad 21\| \begin{Vmatrix} 21 \\ 21 \\ 27 \\ \vdots \\ 21 \end{Vmatrix}$$

$$= 21(21) + 21(21) + 27(27) + \cdots + 21(21) = 43,480$$

The mean of the 135 scores is 17.44. The matrix $\bar{X}$ is

$$\bar{X} = \begin{Vmatrix} 17.44 \\ 17.44 \\ \vdots \\ 17.44 \end{Vmatrix} \qquad \text{(135 rows)}$$

and the transpose of $\bar{X}$ is

$$\bar{X}' = \|17.44 \quad 17.44 \quad \cdots \quad 17.44\| \qquad \text{(135 columns)}$$

Thus:

$$\bar{X}'\bar{X} = \|17.44 \quad 17.44 \quad \cdots \quad 17.44\| \begin{Vmatrix} 17.44 \\ 17.44 \\ \vdots \\ 17.44 \end{Vmatrix}$$

$$= 17.44(17.44) + 17.44(17.44) + \cdots + 17.44(17.44) \qquad \text{(135 terms)}$$
$$= 135(17.44)^2 = 41,060.7360$$

The sum of squared deviations is

$$X'X - \bar{X}'\bar{X} = 43,480 - 41,050.7360 = 2419.2640 = x'x$$

The variance is obtained by dividing $(X'X - \bar{X}'\bar{X})$ by $n = 135$. The variance is 17.92; the standard deviation is 4.25.

The matrix of standard scores for the group is then given by the matrix equation:

$$Z = \frac{1}{4.25}(X - \bar{X})$$

Thus we see that matrix and Cartesian representations are closely associated. The visual impression of first moving the origin from a raw score of zero to the mean of the set of scores (*axis translation*) and then converting the deviation units to standard deviation units (*axis transformation*) is written algebraically in the equation

$$Z = \frac{1}{\sigma}(X - \bar{X})$$

Passenger Agents and Mechanics

Comparison with Two Groups of Employees

When outdoor activity preference data are available for only the group of apprentices of which Joe Armand is a member, the personnel head can interpret Joe's score in the following ways.

1. About 87% of the group preferred fewer *outdoor* activities.
2. About 13% of the group preferred fewer *indoor* activities.
3. About 28% of the group have outdoor activity preferences more deviant from the group mean.
4. The number of Joe's outdoor preferences is 1.07 SD *above* the mean of the group.
5. The number of Joe's indoor preferences is 1.07 SD *below* the mean of the group.

These five statements exhaust the information that the single group data provide for advising an employee about the selection of a job in World Airlines. None of the information is particularly helpful for personnel classification.

We will assume that before Joe Armand receives advice about a choice of type of apprentice training for which he is eligible, Activity Preference Inventory scores are obtained for many apprentices. After a waiting period long enough to permit the most recently tested apprentices to complete their training and adjust to their duty assignments, three facts were ascertained for each apprentice:

1. The apprentice's present job in World Airlines.
2. Whether the apprentice now performs his duties satisfactorily.
3. Whether the apprentice is now satisfied with his duty assignment.

With this information about each apprentice, the entire group can be divided according to job assignments. Within each job subdivision we can identify a group of men who are satisfactory workers and who are also satisfied with their assignment. For our example we use a group of 85 satisfactory and satisfied passenger agents (or agents, for short) and a group of 93 satisfactory and satisfied mechanics. We assume that Activity Preference scores were obtained for each man before his training and assignment. The scores are initially recorded in rosters, as in Tables 2.5

Table 2.5   *Roster of Scores. Number of Outdoor Activity Preferences Expressed by Satisfactory and Satisfied Passenger Agents*

Apprentice Number	Score	Apprentice Number	Score	Apprentice Number	Score
1	10	30	10	58	12
2	14	31	3	59	16
3	19	32	6	60	15
4	14	33	11	61	7
5	14	34	13	62	6
6	20	35	11	63	9
7	6	36	8	64	9
8	13	37	5	65	20
9	18	38	11	66	5
10	16	39	14	67	14
11	17	40	22	68	8
12	10	41	16	69	14
13	17	42	12	70	15
14	10	43	12	71	15
15	10	44	15	72	14
16	18	45	11	73	15
17	6	46	11	74	11
18	10	47	15	75	10
19	15	48	15	76	7
20	8	49	15	77	11
21	6	50	17	78	14
22	10	51	12	79	18
23	1	52	7	80	14
24	14	53	14	81	17
25	13	54	22	82	13
26	21	55	22	'83	9
27	12	56	18	84	13
28	12	57	16	85	16
29	5				

and 2.6. The rosters may be represented as matrices X_1 and X_2 where the subscripts 1 and 2 identify the two groups:

$$X_1 = \begin{Vmatrix} 10 \\ 14 \\ 19 \\ \vdots \\ 16 \end{Vmatrix} \quad \text{and} \quad X_2 = \begin{Vmatrix} 20 \\ 21 \\ 15 \\ \vdots \\ 19 \end{Vmatrix}$$

We proceed directly to the problem of profile representation of the data.

Table 2.6 *Roster of Scores. Number of Outdoor Activity Preferences Expressed by Satisfactory and Satisfied Mechanics*

Apprentice Number	Score	Apprentice Number	Score	Apprentice Number	Score
1	20	32	20	63	23
2	21	33	19	64	22
3	15	34	17	65	13
4	15	35	20	66	25
5	11	36	21	67	23
6	24	37	17	68	17
7	18	38	11	69	21
8	14	39	14	70	15
9	13	40	18	71	19
10	17	41	13	72	22
11	16	42	22	73	17
12	15	43	25	74	21
13	24	44	19	75	24
14	14	45	20	76	21
15	14	46	21	77	15
16	18	47	17	78	24
17	14	48	18	79	19
18	12	49	21	80	23
19	16	50	17	81	21
20	18	51	17	82	20
21	19	52	17	83	18
22	13	53	16	84	23
23	28	54	22	85	17
24	17	55	19	86	17
25	24	56	16	87	17
26	19	57	18	88	17
27	22	58	21	89	19
28	22	59	15	90	17
29	21	60	19	91	25
30	18	61	14	92	16
31	23	62	15	93	19

Profile Representation

We have the outdoor preference scores of the group of apprentices of whom Joe, Tom, and Bill are examples. We find that the scores of these men—that is, the undifferentiated sample of apprentices in an arbitrarily assigned grouping—have no value in the evaluation or classification of the men; an apprentice's score does not assist a personnel head in deciding upon the wisdom or appropriateness of a variety of possible assignments for the apprentice. The example provides scores for the individual members of two groups. We are seeking methods of examining the data for interpretive value in the advising and assignment situation. It is important to notice that our fundamental purpose requires that the groups be selected or differentiated in a meaningful way.

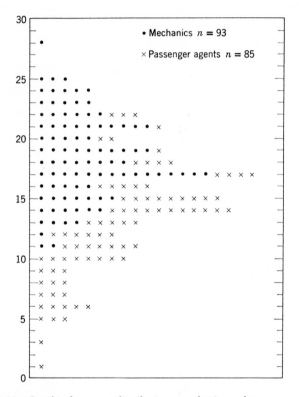

Fig. 2.11 *Graphic frequency distribution—mechanics and passenger agents.*

Three decisions regarding procedure develop from the results of our previous investigation of the profile problem. First, we show the collection of individual profiles by means of the frequency distribution for visual inspection. Second, we use a raw score scale; and third, we retain the identity of our two job groups.

Various ways of representing these data graphically are shown in Figs. 2.11 to 2.13. In Fig. 2.11 the two groups are plotted on a single scale, and the two kinds of specialties are differentiated by the symbols used to represent frequencies—×'s indicate agents and •'s indicate mechanics. Figure 2.12 presents the same data in a somewhat more meaningful fashion by separating the groups of ×'s and dots, so that the shape of the separate group score distributions can be seen. In this form of graphic representation the important facts about group overlap become clearer. Figure 2.13 plots the same scores on opposite sides of the profile stalk, the

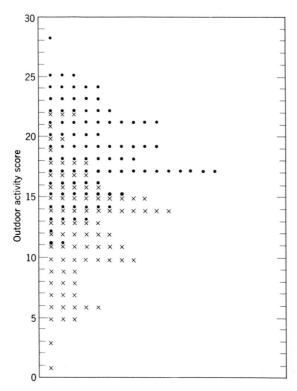

Fig. 2.12 *Graphic distribution of two groups—mechanics and passenger agents.*

agents on the left, the mechanics on the right. Exactly the same data are also represented in the two frequency distributions in Table 2.7.

If Figs. 2.11 and 2.12 are confusing, we can examine the representation in Fig. 2.13 or, alternatively, the frequency distributions in Table 2.7. We conclude certainly that the groups are quite different. We also observe that many of the individual members of either group are very similar to those of the other group. On the other hand, a considerable number of the individuals in either group are not at all like any members of the other group.

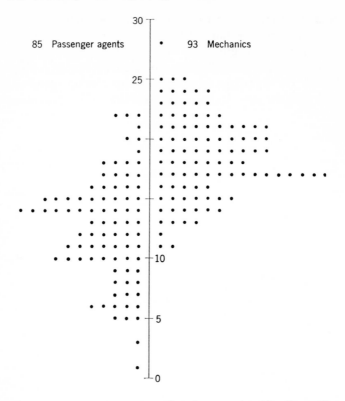

Fig. 2.13 *Comparison of two groups plotted on opposite sides of a profile stalk.*

If we have the score of an individual who is not a member of either group—he may be, for example, an incoming apprentice—we can ask the question: Which group does it appear he should belong to? Joe Armand, for example, obtained a score of 22. When compared with agents' scores, his score is extreme. A very small proportion of agents obtained scores as high as 22. When compared with mechanics, Joe Armand does not seem so divergent. Seventeen of the mechanic group obtained higher scores. Such comparisons in terms of absolute frequencies could be continued endlessly, and could be observed for each individual score.

The mean of the agents' frequency distribution is 12.59. We compute Joe Armand's deviation from the agent group and find $(22 - 12.59) = +9.41$. The mean of the mechanic distribution is 18.54. We compute Joe Armand's deviation from the mean of this group as $(22 - 18.54) = +3.46$. We observe that Joe deviates more from the agents' centroid than he deviates from the mechanics' centroid. We can continue such calculations

Table 2.7 *Frequency Distributions of Outdoor Preference Scores—Two Groups*

Score	Passenger Agents	Mechanics
30		
29		
28		1
27		
26		
25		3
24		5
23		5
22	3	6
21	1	10
20	2	5
19	1	10
18	4	8
17	4	15
16	5	5
15	9	7
14	11	6
13	5	4
12	6	1
11	7	2
10	8	
9	3	
8	3	
7	3	
6	5	
5	3	
4		
3	1	
2		
1	1	
0		

and comparisons of deviations from score points endlessly, and we can perform them for each individual.

All the problems we encountered with the group scores in our analysis of the single group are present here in each group separately. The groups are of different size, and statements concerning absolute frequencies are not comparable since they depend upon the number of individuals in the group. Statements of comparison between absolute deviations are pointless because the two groups differ in the variation among the members. Although we may have many doubts concerning the best way to represent the score and to discuss the individual scores, Fig. 2.13 clearly shows that the number of preferences for outdoor activities indicated by an apprentice is related to the job in World Airlines to which he is assigned and in which he is satisfied and performing satisfactorily.

Percentile Representation

Following the procedure developed in the one-group example, we may represent an individual's score as a profile using a percentile scale. With basic data available from two different groups, we require two percentile statements for each individual score. Thus, Joe Armand's score of 22 is equivalent to the 98th percentile in the agent group and the 82nd percentile in the group of mechanics. With respect to outdoor activity preferences, Joe Armand excels a larger percentage of apprentices who became agents than apprentices who became mechanics. There seems to be no simple way of expressing the meaning of the difference, nor does any intuitive evaluation of the difference appear helpful.

Our observations are equally confusing if we consider the indoor activity preferences as the appropriate scoring rule. The number of indoor activity preferences of Joe Armand exceeded the indoor activity preferences of 2% of the agent group and 18% of the mechanic group. With respect to indoor activity preferences, Joe Armand excels a larger percentage of the mechanic group than of the agent group. Joe's outdoor activity preferences exceed those of more of the agent group, whereas his indoor activity preferences exceed those of more of the mechanic group. All the confusions inherent in the single-group evaluation of the percentile representation of profiles are here doubled by the necessity of considering two groups for each apprentice. The idea of rank order and superiority-inferiority which is customarily associated with percentile scales does not assist in the basic problem of expressing similarity-divergence measures.

Figure 2.13 shows that high-scoring apprentices are more likely to be discovered in a group of mechanics and that low-scoring apprentices are more likely to be found in a group of agents, but that some high-scoring men turn out to be agents and some low-scoring men turn out to be mechanics. The important fact is that both types of men, the high-scoring agents and the low-scoring mechanics, are satisfied apprentices performing satisfactorily in their assignments. This points directly to the centour concept as the solution to the interpretation of profiles.

Standard Score Representation

The profile of an individual score may be represented on a standard score scale. We have a choice of procedure: we may standardize on agents or on mechanics, or on the combined group of 178 men. The problem of this choice leads to the following.

Profile Problem 2. On which group should the raw scores be standardized? If we merge the groups, we increase the number of cases, but in the merger we lose the meaningful classification of individuals which is the objective of our analysis.

Since the means and standard deviations of the two distributions are not identical, the standard score scale derived from each group separately will be different. This is apparent in Table 2.8, which shows the standard score equivalents computed for each group.

Table 2.8   *Standard Scores for Two Groups*

Number of Outdoor Activities	Standard Score Equivalent	
	Passenger Agents	Mechanics
29	3.67	2.96
28	3.45	2.67
27	3.22	2.39
26	3.00	2.10
25	2.77	1:82
24	2.55	1.54
23	2.33	1.26
22	2.10	0.98
21	1.88	0.69
20	1.66	0.41
19	1.43	0.13
18	1.21	−0.15
17	0.99	−0.43
16	0.76	−0.72
15	0.54	−1.00
14	0.32	−1.28
13	0.09	−1.56
12	−0.13	−1.84
11	−0.36	−2.13
10	−0.58	−2.41
9	−0.80	−2.69
8	−1.03	−2.97
7	−1.25	−3.25
6	−1.47	−3.54
5	−1.70	−3.81
4	−1.92	−4.10
3	−2.14	−4.38
2	−2.37	−4.66
1	−2.59	−4.95

The transformation $z = (X - \bar{X})/\sigma$ simply moves the origin of the raw score scale and changes the unit of the scale. Standard scores do not alter the *form* of the distribution. Consequently, if raw scores for employees in *both* jobs are converted to standard scores on the basis of the mean and standard deviation of the passenger agents, the appearance of Fig. 2.13 would not be altered. Only the numerical symbol designating each scale point would be changed. The same invariant characteristic of the frequency distribution would appear if Fig. 2.13 had been plotted in terms of standard scores for the mechanics. The labels on the scale would be different, but the contrast of agents and mechanics would not be altered.

Centour scores for the mechanics would be identical whether computed in terms of the agent standard scores or in terms of raw scores. The same invariance is true for centour scores of the agents based on mechanic standard scores. In fact, the centour is invariant for any linear transformation of raw scores. Nothing is achieved by converting raw scores of both specialties to the standard scores of one of the groups before centour scores are computed. The visual impression of the frequency distributions and the calculation of the centour scores of individuals are unaltered by the addition of groups.

The answer to Profile Problem 2 is: If a statement concerning the probability of membership in a job is desired, the statement is achieved directly from the raw score data of each group. Nothing is gained by any linear transformation of raw scores before determination of the probability estimate. This latter statement is true not only of a transformation to the standard scores of either group alone, but also of the transformations to the standard scores of any other group, including a combination of groups. Thus Profile Problems 1 and 2 are really not problems as long as the interpretation of individual scores rests on the centour equivalents or a similar statement of relative frequency.

Centour Computation

Certain fundamental statistical ideas influence our choice of methods for computing centour equivalents. The idea of a statistical population, homogeneous in some respect, lies at the foundation of our logical derivation of the centour concept. In the example, one such population consists of passenger agents, another consists of mechanics. Each population is homogeneous in that every employee who is a member of the population is a satisfied and satisfactory member of a single class identified by the job. The ideal centours interpret the distance of a score point from the centroids of the populations in terms of the relative frequency with which even greater divergence occurs among all the scores in the populations.

Although we think of the populations as existing and wish to interpret our score for a single employee in relation to the population characteristics, we do not have the scores of the population for inspection or computation. We conceive of the population as being represented by a frequency distribution, whose characteristics are described by four statistical statements: (1) the size of the population N; (2) the true mean score in the population M; (3) the variance of the population σ^2, or the standard deviation σ; and (4) a statistical description of the appearance of the distribution. Although we do not know the numerical values of the statistics, we can incorporate the concept of their existence in our thinking and in algebraic analysis. Our logical argument for the choice among methods of computing centours will stem from the idea of an unknown basic population of scores.

We do have some information about the populations. In the illustration we have 93 scores of mechanics. We think of these 93 scores as representative of the population of all satisfactory and satisfied mechanics. Their scores comprise a sample of a statistical population. Long experience with observation of samples lends convincing support to two propositions: first, a second sample will be different; it will be characterized by a different mean, a different variance, and different frequencies at the score values; it may contain a different number of individuals. Second, if many samples are compared, most of the differences will be small. This leads us to regard the true value of a statistic for the population as the value we expect to find in any one sample. We think of the sample statistic as an *estimate* of the unknown true value in the population. We also observe that, as the size of the samples increases, the differences between samples become smaller. Similar experience with repeated samples indicates that the appearance of a sample frequency distribution stabilizes when the size of the sample is increased. The irregularities and unevenness of the frequencies located at adjacent score points are smoothed out, and the appearance of successive samples seems to approach the same basic form. These observations from experience, and the statistical theory formulated to give precise interpretation of experiments with samples, suggest the following illustration.

The outdoor activity scores of the 93 mechanics represent a sample. Since this sample is hypothetical and was constructed to be an illustration, it is possible to define precisely the statistical population from which it is taken. The 93 scores were, in fact, drawn by a mechanical random sampling process from a hypothetical population in which the mean, or expected value in a sample, is 19.0. The standard deviation in the population is 3.72. The exact form of the population distribution is binomial; it is so nearly the same as a normal distribution that for all practical purposes it may be regarded as a normal distribution. From these statistics of the population we can compute the true centour equivalents of any score.

The computation of true centour scores—that is, centour equivalents in the population distribution—proceeds directly from the statistics. It is not necessary to count frequencies in a tabulated distribution. First, the standard score in the population distribution is computed for each raw score value. We designate this standard score z_t. A score $X = 28$ deviates from the population mean $+9$ units on the raw score scale. The standard score z_t is computed by dividing the deviation by the standard deviation of the population $z_t = +9/3.72 = +2.419$. The value of z_t is computed for each score. The result of these computations is presented in the third column of Table 2.9. Each of these standard scores may be used to determine from a table of the areas of a normal distribution the proportion which exceeds the value of z_t. This table indicates that the area in the tail

Table 2.9 *Centours Calculated for a Hypothetical Normal Population — Mechanics*

	$M = 19.0$		$\sigma = 3.72$	
Raw Score X	Deviation from Mean $(X - M)$	Standard Score z_t	Percent Exceeding z_t	Centour Equivalent
28	+9	+2.419	0.8%	01.6
27	+8	+2.150	1.6	03.2
26	+7	+1.882	3.0	06.0
25	+6	+1.613	5.3	10.6
24	+5	+1.344	8.9	17.8
23	+4	+1.075	14.1	28.2
22	+3	+0.807	21.0	42.0
21	+2	+0.538	29.5	59.0
20	+1	+0.269	39.4 ↑	78.8
			50%	
19	0	0.000	50%	100.0
18	−1	−0.269	39.4	78.8
17	−2	−0.538	29.5	59.0
16	−3	−0.807	21.0	42.0
15	−4	−1.075	14.1	28.2
14	−5	−1.344	8.9	17.8
13	−6	−1.613	5.3	10.6
12	−7	−1.882	3.0	06.0
11	−8	−2.150	1.6	03.2
10	−9	−2.419	0.8%	01.6

in the portion of the curve beyond $+2.419$ SD is 0.0078, or $\frac{8}{10}$ of 1%. The values obtained from the normal distribution table for each value of X are entered in the fourth column of Table 2.9.

Several facts are made obvious in the columns of Table 2.9. A score of 24 deviates $+5$ from the mean; its standard score equivalent is $+1.344$, and 8.9% exhibit greater deviations in the positive direction than the deviation of $X = 24$. A score $X = 14$ deviates -5 from the population mean; its standard score equivalent is -1.344, and deviations greater than this in the negative direction occur in 8.9% of all the frequencies in a normal distribution. These figures are symmetrical around the mean score $X = 19$ which has a standard score equivalent of $.00$, and obviously half the distribution (50%) lies above the mean and half the distribution lies below the mean. Our centour concept, however, regards a deviation of $+5$ in raw score units, or $+1.344$ in standard score units, as equivalent to the same magnitude of deviation in the opposite direction.

A score $X = 24$ is just as close to, and just as far away from, the mean (centroid) of the population as is a score $X = 14$. Consequently we say that 17.8% ($8.9 + 8.9$) are more divergent from the centroid than a score of $X = 24$. The number 17.8 is the centour score equivalent to $X = 24$. The same number 17.8 is also the centour equivalent which describes the divergence of a score $X = 14$. In a normal distribution the centour score is easily calculated. It is given by the sum of the proportions in the positive and negative tails of the normal distribution which are cut off at the computed standard score value. If we deal with absolute values of deviation the centour is twice the percentage in either the positive or the negative tail.

The process of adding frequencies or proportions for two scores of equal absolute deviation is sometimes called "folding the distribution." The analogy can be easily seen by imagining Table 2.9 folded in the middle at $X = 19$. If this is done, the score 18 lies on the same line as the score 20, and the proportion exceeding a deviation of -1 lies on the same line as the proportion exceeding a deviation of $+1$. We will use this concept in the computation of the sample of 93 mechanics.

The centour scores given in the last column of Table 2.9 are the true values; they are the ideal centours for our purposes. They describe the divergence of any score from the centroid of the population. Even though the table is not extended to cover all possible values of outdoor preference scores, it could clearly do so. A score $X = 5$, for example, is not included in the table because it is so divergent that the centour equivalent would be a decimal value much less than 1 (0.01). For practical purposes a divergence so large that it occurs in less than 1 of 10,000 cases is indistinguishable from an even greater divergence that occurs in less than 1 per million instances. Either divergence is very nontypical. This leads to a simple convention for reporting centour scores. We shall eliminate the calculation of centours less than 1.

In Table 2.10 the centours calculated for the ideal model—that is, for the population itself—are compared with the relative frequencies which occur in the actual sample. Columns 7 and 8 appeared in Table 2.9. The percents occurring in the sample (column 9) are obtained by folding the frequency distribution. The two frequencies above and below the mean which are associated with the same absolute deviation may be counted and the sum of the two frequencies converted to a percentage of the sample. Alternatively, the percent exceeding a given divergence may be computed separately for the positive and negative values; these percents are listed in column 6. The percents may be added by folding the table or pairing the positive and negative deviations of the same magnitude. Thus we obtain in column 9 for the scores $X = 24$ and $X = 14$, the percentage value $7 + 11 = 18$. A typical line of the table reads: a score of 22 occurred 6 times in the sample. This score deviates 3 units from $\bar{X} = 19$ and is equivalent to a standard score $z_t = .807$ in the population. In the sample, 17 frequencies lie above $z_t = .807$. This is 18% of the sample. In a normal distribution 21% lie above $z_t = .807$. The true centour is 42. The percent of the sample whose absolute deviations exceed 3 is $18 + 24 = 42$. The difference between columns 6 and 7 reveals the extent to which the sample differs from the population.

It is possible, though not convenient, to calculate centour scores directly from the sample frequencies. It is inconvenient because the deviations of integral raw scores above the average differ in magnitude from the deviations below the average. Interpolation is required to obtain the frequencies which exceed every specified absolute deviation score. We shall not discuss further the arithmetical problems of calculating centour scores by this method.[1]

The pronounced irregularities that are exhibited in the sample frequencies affect the centours computed by counting frequencies. These particular irregularities are not typical of the population as a whole. If we obtained scores for a large number of other members of the population, we would not expect to find twice as many scores at $X = 21$ as we find at $X = 20$. The marked irregularity of the frequencies reading 10, 5, 10, 8, 15 in the middle of the distribution are ascribed to chance accidents of sampling. The chance irregularities that occur in this particular sample are of no intrinsic interest. We are only interested in those aspects of the sample which supply information about the population.

Every apprentice whom we may advise and for whom we would like to

[1] The numerical results labeled "Percent in the Sample" are included for comparison in Table 2.12.

Table 2.10 Centours Calculated for the Ideal Model Compared with Relative Frequencies in a Sample ... Outdoor Activity Score

Population mean = 19.0

1	2	3 Absolute Values Deviation Scores $|X - M|$	4 Absolute Values Standard Scores $|z_t|$	5 Frequency Exceeding z_t	6 Percent of Sample Exceeding z_t	7 Expected Percent in Normal Distribution	8 True Values of Centours in Model	9 Percent Occurring in Sample
X	f							
29	0	10	2.688	0.0	0.0	0.4	0.8	0.0
28	1	9	2.419	0.5	0.5	0.8	1.6	0.5
27	0	8	2.150	1.0	1	1.6	3.2	2
26	0	7	1.882	1.0	1	3.0	6	4
25	3	6	1.613	2.5	3	5.3	10	8
24	5	5	1.344	6.5	7	8.9	17	8
23	5	4	1.075	11.5	12	14.1	28	18
22	6	3	0.807	17.0	18	21.0	42	30
21	10	2	0.538	25.0	27	29.5	59	42
20	5	1	0.269	32.5 ←	36 ←	29.5	79	62
				40	43	39.4 ←		83
19	10*	0	0.000	53	57	50	100	100
				→ 44.0	→ 47	50	79	83
18	8	1	0.269			→ 39.4		
17	15	2	0.538	32.5	35	29.5	59	62
16	5	3	0.807	22.5	24	21.0	42	42
15	7	4	1.075	16.5	18	14.1	28	30
14	6	5	1.344	10.0	11	8.9	17	18
13	4	6	1.613	5.0	5	5.3	10	8
12	1	7	1.882	2.5	3	3.0	6	8
11	2	8	2.150	1.0	1	1.6	3.2	4
10	0	9	2.419	0.0	0	0.8	1.6	2
9	0	10	2.688	0.0	0.0	0.4	0.8	0.0

* This frequency is equally divided between the top half and the bottom half as counted in column 5.

have centour scores is an individual who is not a member of the original sample, nor is he yet a member of the population. He is an individual for whom we seek an answer to the question: Does he appear to be a member of this population? We obtain a more useful and more generally applicable solution if we use the information in the sample to estimate the facts about the population. We choose, therefore, to use the mean and standard deviation of the sample to estimate the mean and standard deviation which describe the frequency distribution of the population. We shall assume, also, unless there is evidence to the contrary, that the population is approximately described by a normal distribution.

The computation of centours by this method is a simple routine parallel to the example of Table 2.9. Standard scores are computed in the usual way using the mean and standard deviation of the sample. The proportion of a normal distribution which exceeds the standard score is determined from a table of the normal distribution. This value is doubled and converted to a percent, that is, the tabled proportion is multiplied by 200. Table 2.11 shows the details of the complete computation for the illustrative group of mechanics.

Table 2.11   *Centours Estimated from the Statistics of a Sample of 93 Mechanics—Outdoor Activity Score (Normality Assumed)*

Raw Score X	$\bar{X} = 18.54$ $(X - \bar{X})$	$SD = 3.54$ z	Percent in Tail	Estimated Centour
28	+9.46	+2.67	0.4	01
27	+8.46	+2.39	0.8	02
26	+7.46	+2.10	1.8	04
25	+6.46	+1.82	3.4	07
24	+5.46	+1.54	6.2	12
23	+4.46	+1.26	10.4	21
22	+3.46	+0.98	16.3	33
21	+2.46	+0.69	24.5	49
20	+1.46	+0.41	34.1	68
19	+0.46	+0.13	44.8	90
18	−0.54	−0.15	44.1	88
17	−1.54	−0.43	33.3	66
16	−2.54	−0.72	23.6	47
15	−3.54	−1.00	15.8	32
14	−4.54	−1.28	10.0	20
13	−5.54	−1.56	5.9	12
12	−6.54	−1.84	3.3	07
11	−7.54	−2.13	1.7	03
10	−8.54	−2.41	0.8	02
9	−9.54	−2.69	0.4	01

The centours computed in Table 2.11 can be compared with the relative frequencies which occur in the actual sample. This comparison can always be performed. In this hypothetical example, because we know the population values, we can also compare the centours computed from the sample statistics with the true values of centours as computed in Table 2.10. These comparisons are presented in Table 2.12. The comparison of the centours

Table 2.12 *Comparison of Centours in the Population and in the Sample Mechanics—Outdoor Activity Score*

Raw Score, X	True Centour	Estimated Centour	Percent in the Sample
29	01	–	0.0
28	02	01	0.5
27	03	02	1
26	06	04	3
25	10	07	6
24	17	12	13
23	28	21	24
22	42	33	37
21	59	49	52
20	79	68	71
19	100	90	91
18	79	88	89
17	59	67	69
16	42	47	50
15	28	32	36
14	17	20	23
13	10	12	12
12	06	07	6
11	03	03	3
10	02	02	0.0
9	01	01	0.0

reveals that the assumption of normality in the distribution is reasonably accurate, that is, the normal distribution fits the sample. The centours estimated by choosing the normal distribution which will best fit the sample (column 3) agree quite closely with the relative frequency in the data (column 4). The table also shows that the differences between the estimated centours and the true centours are larger. In an experiment we should expect the selected distribution to fit the sample better than it fits the population. Since we are interested primarily in population values of the centours, we regard the centours computed from the sample statistics as estimates of the unknown true values. One important consequence of this view is a realization that sampling errors in the mean and standard deviation will affect the values of the centours we obtain.

Samples of occupational groupings selected for determination of centour scores should be sufficiently large to make these sampling errors negligibly small. Table 2.13 compares the true centours for the population

Table 2.13 *Comparison of Centours in the Population and in the Sample. Passenger Agents—Outdoor Activity Score*

Raw Score, X	True Centour	Estimated Centour	Percent in Sample
24	–	01	0.0
23	01	02	0
22	02	04	4
21	04	06	7
20	07	10	11
19	13	15	18
18	20	23	25
17	31	32	33
16	45	45	42
15	61	59	57
14	80	75	79
13	100	93	95
12	80	90	92
11	61	72	74
10	45	56	54
9	31	42	40
8	20	31	32
7	13	21	23
6	07	14	16
5	04	09	10
4	02	05	6
3	01	03	3
2	−0.5	02	1
1	–	01	0.5

of passenger agents with the estimated centours and the percents in the sample. The discrepancies between sample values and true values of the centours are larger for the agent sample because the sample statistics happen, by chance, to contain larger errors. The true statistics for the agent population are $M = 12.0$, $\sigma = 3.92$. Centours estimated for use in counseling and classification of individuals should be derived from samples of several hundred scores.

Summary of the Results for Two Groups

We are now able to assemble the result of our calculations in a form suitable for use in personnel practice. We have extracted from the two frequency distributions all the information the matrices of scores contain for the interpretation of an individual's outdoor activity score. The complete interpretive result is given in the centour scores in Table 2.14.

Table 2.14 *A Practical Table of Centour Scores— Two Groups*

Number of Outdoor Activities	Centour Score	
	Passenger Agents	Mechanics
30	*	*
29	*	*
28	*	01
27	*	02
26	*	04
25	01	07
24	01	12
23	02	21
22	04	33
21	06	49
20	10	68
19	15	90
18	23	88
17	32	66
16	45	47
15	59	32
14	75	20
13	93	12
12	90	07
11	72	03
10	56	02
9	42	01
8	31	*
7	21	*
6	14	*
5	09	*
4	05	*
3	03	*
2	02	*
1	01	*

* Centour < .5

No additional information contained in the data can be extracted to make the interpretation of an apprentice's score easier or better. The centour scores read from the table describe instantly and directly the extent to which any apprentice's outdoor score is typical or atypical of the members of each of two different groups. If greater certainty or greater flexibility of recommendations and assignments is desired, more groups are needed. We therefore proceed to the problems of profile interpretation when the data consist of 3, 4, 5, or any number G of groups.

Passenger Agents, Mechanics, and Operations Control Agents (Three Groups)

In this section we explore the effects upon our analysis of the profile problem of adding a third job, operations control agent (operations men, for short). The data are 66 outdoor activity scores obtained for 66 apprentices who were later identified as satisfactory and satisfied operations control agents. The 66 scores are thought of as a sample representing a population, and the population definition is meaningful in advising an apprentice about his election of a job in World Airlines. These facts, however, become significant only after the method of representing profile data is established. The methodological problem is characteristic of any kind of group contrast or group discrimination. The roster for the new group is given in Table 2.15.

The outdoor activity scores of the 66 operations men form the matrix:

$$\begin{Vmatrix} 19 \\ 17 \\ 8 \\ \vdots \\ 18 \end{Vmatrix} \quad \text{(66 rows)}$$

The total data now available consist of outdoor activity scores for three independent groups. The scores are adequately represented in three matrices denoted X_1, X_2, X_3, where the subscripts identify the group.

$$X_1 = \begin{Vmatrix} 10 \\ 14 \\ 19 \\ \vdots \\ 16 \end{Vmatrix} \quad X_2 = \begin{Vmatrix} 20 \\ 21 \\ 15 \\ \vdots \\ 10 \end{Vmatrix} \quad X_3 = \begin{Vmatrix} 19 \\ 17 \\ 8 \\ \vdots \\ 18 \end{Vmatrix}$$
$$\text{(85 rows)} \qquad \text{(93 rows)} \qquad \text{(66 rows)}$$

Table 2.15 *Roster of Scores. Satisfactory and Satisfied Operations Control Agents*

Apprentice Number	Score	Apprentice Number	Score	Apprentice Number	Score
1	19	23	12	45	14
2	17	24	17	46	25
3	8	25	10	47	18
4	13	26	11	48	14
5	14	27	13	49	13
6	17	28	19	50	20
7	17	29	15	51	12
8	14	30	17	52	16
9	19	31	15	53	21
10	18	32	19	54	18
11	15	33	19	55	19
12	20	34	4	56	17
13	24	35	13	57	4
14	16	36	20	58	17
15	17	37	14	59	14
16	17	38	10	60	15
17	11	39	11	61	20
18	15	40	8	62	20
19	20	41	14	63	16
20	14	42	18	64	9
21	13	43	19	65	15
22	16	44	21	66	18

Obviously the addition of the X_3 matrix has no effect upon the X_1 and X_2 matrices which have been examined in detail previously. The new group of operations men represents an importantly different population, and the basic nature of our profile inquiry demands that its identity as a group be preserved. We therefore deal with the details of the X_3 matrix exactly as we handled the data of the first two groups. The frequency distribution associated with the matrix X_3 is indicated in Fig. 2.14. The sample statistics are: $\overline{X} = 15.58$, $\sigma^2 = 16.65$, and $\sigma = 4.08$. (The scores of this group were obtained by chance sampling from a population in which the mean is 16.0 and the standard deviation is 3.62.) The computation reviewed in detail in the two-group example will not be repeated in this section since the existence of other groups has no effect upon the interpretation of the data for operations men. The computations are identical. The end result (centour scores) is given in column 3 of Table 2.16.

74

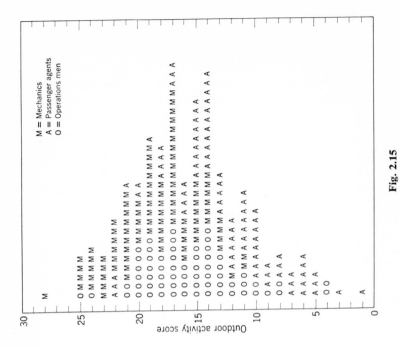

Fig. 2.15

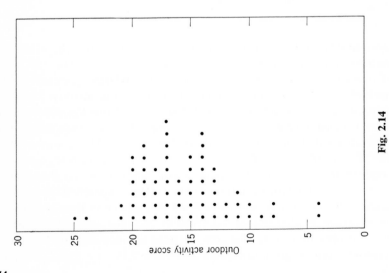

Fig. 2.14

Table 2.16 *Frequency Distribution of 66 Operations men*

$\bar{X}$ = 15.58	SD = 4.08	
Outdoor Activity Score	Frequency	Estimated Centour
27	–	01
26	–	01
25	1	02
24	1	04
23	–	07
22	–	12
21	2	18
20	6	28
19	7	40
18	5	55
17	9	73
16	4	93
15	6	89
14	8	70
13	5	53
12	2	38
11	3	26
10	2	17
9	1	11
8	2	06
7	–	04
6	–	02
5	–	01
4	2	*
	66	

* Centour < .5

Graphic Representation

In the two-group example we were able to find a satisfactory method of representing the two frequency distributions graphically. We were successful in keeping the groups visually separate by plotting the frequencies on the opposite sides of the profile stalk. With three groups, this method is no longer possible. Any other device that we may adopt to represent multiple groups on a single scale is likely to produce visual confusion

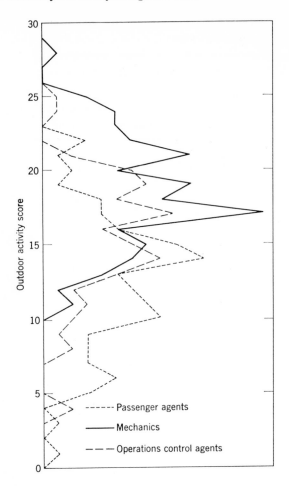

Fig. 2.16 *Frequency polygons—outdoor score—three groups.*

rather than statistical clarity. Figure 2.15 is an example of a frequently recommended device—using different symbols to preserve the identity of the groups. Figure 2.16, which uses the idea of a frequency polygon, is perhaps an improvement. With these examples we have approached the limit of numbers of groups that can be helpfully portrayed by graphic representation. The result of increasing the number of groups to 4, 5, 6, or, in general, any number, *G*, is left to the reader's imagination. Before such a nightmare gets out-of-hand, we turn directly to our method of presenting complete interpretive information in practical form to a personnel adviser.

A practical presentation of centour scores for three groups is given in Table 2.17. With these interpretive data a personnel adviser can advise apprentices regarding their election of jobs in World Airlines.

Joe Armand preferred 22 outdoor activities. Joe's passenger agent centour is 04, his mechanic centour is 33, and his operations man centour

Table 2.17   *A Practical Table of Centour Scores—Three Groups*

Number of Outdoor Activity Preferences	Centour Score		
	Passenger Agents	Mechanics	Operations Control Agents
28	*	01	*
27	*	02	01
26	*	04	01
25	01	07	02
24	01	12	04
23	02	21	07
22	04	33	12
21	06	49	18
20	10	68	28
19	15	90	40
18	23	88	55
17	32	66	73
16	45	47	93
15	59	32	89
14	75	20	70
13	93	12	53
12	90	07	38
11	72	03	26
10	56	02	17
9	42	01	11
8	31	*	06
7	21	*	04
6	14	*	02
5	09	*	01
4	05	*	*
3	03	*	*
2	02	*	*
1	01	*	*

* Centour < .5

is 12. These numbers indicate that only 4% of the passenger agents were as different as Joe. One-third of the mechanics differed more than Joe and 12% of the operations men are more divergent from the mean of that job. Joe's outdoor preferences are most typical of apprentices who became satisfactory and satisfied mechanics; his preferences are least typical of apprentices who became satisfactory and satisfied passenger agents; and his preferences are only moderately typical of apprentices who became satisfactory and satisfied operations men. Taking into account the quotas for these jobs, the personnel adviser suggests mechanic, operations agent, and passenger agent jobs to Joe, in that order.

Tom Baslik preferred 18 outdoor activities. Tom's agent centour is 23, his mechanic centour is 88, and his operations centour is 55. Tom's outdoor activity preferences are most typical of the outdoor activity preferences of satisfactory and satisfied mechanics, least typical of satisfactory and satisfied agents, and reasonably typical of satisfactory and satisfied operations personnel. Therefore, the personnel adviser suggests that Tom consider the jobs, mechanic, operations man, and passenger agent, in that order, *but* he emphasizes that Tom's outdoor activity preferences are really not atypical of those of apprentices in any one of these jobs. As far as Tom's outdoor activity preferences are concerned, he will find a reasonable number of apprentices with a similar number of preferences for outdoor activities in all three jobs.

Bill Flint preferred 20 outdoor activities. His centours are 10 for passenger agent, 68 for mechanic, and 28 for operations control agent. The personnel adviser suggests that Bill consider the jobs, mechanic, operations man, and passenger agent, in that order. He advises Bill that he is not likely to find many apprentices in the job of passenger agent who prefer as many outdoor activities as he does.

Before examining the case of G groups we note that these practical results have been achieved directly from obtained scores—the number of outdoor activity preferences—without reporting to the adviser (1) percentiles, (2) standard scores, or (3) graphic profiles.

The General Univariate Case, G Groups

We have explored systematically the type of data required to advise an apprentice about a job in World Airlines that the apprentice might appropriately choose and in which he is likely to be satisfied. By careful definition of the criterion groups we have also included the airlines' need to have satisfactory employees in each job.

Advising on careers encompasses many jobs besides the three used for illustration. In considering first only two jobs, passenger agent and mechanic, and then introducing a third specialty, operations control agent, we have initiated the process of induction from which we may construct a general system satisfactory for any number of jobs.

Suppose satisfactory and satisfied employees in a fourth job were to be identified by personnel research in World Airlines. The matrix of this new group may be added to the set of matrices for the three previously discussed jobs without influencing any of the former results, and the addition of a fifth, a sixth, and, in fact, any number G of jobs is similarly independent and without effect upon previous findings.

Profile representation of the number of outdoor activity preferences of both agents and mechanics on a common raw score scale was not altered by the introduction of a third job, operations man. The third job was an independent group, and its frequency distribution was independently recorded on the same scale. In the same way, the construction of a fourth frequency distribution on the same axis with the previous three would not alter those three. And we may extend the argument to the last, or Gth job, and say that profile or Cartesian representation of the frequency polygon of the Gth group on the same axis with the other $(G - 1)$ distributions does not alter the representation of any of the data. We have found, however, that the graphic method of examining the data for interpretation fails as a system at about $G = 3$.

The failure of graphic representation is overcome by the numerical computation of centour scores. When the data for each job are treated independently, centours for a first job are not changed by the addition of a second job; centours for two jobs are not changed by the introduction of a third job. Similarly, we may continue the argument and conclude that centours may be determined independently for any number G of jobs.

We have seen that the original data of the group rosters are represented by matrices. The first group was recorded in a matrix X_1. The number of groups was increased by the inclusion of the matrices X_2 and X_3. A fourth group may now be introduced. Its matrix will be

$$X_4 = \begin{Vmatrix} X_{14} \\ X_{24} \\ \vdots \\ X_{n_4 4} \end{Vmatrix} \quad (n_4 \text{ rows})$$

where the first subscript identifies the individual and the second subscript denotes the group. A fifth, sixth, and, in general, a Gth group may be introduced.

The roster for the general or gth group of the G groups will be the following:

Scores of Satisfactory and Satisfied
Apprentices in Specialty g

Apprentice Number	Score
1	X_{1g}
2	X_{2g}
3	X_{3g}
$\vdots$	$\vdots$
n_g	$X_{n_g g}$

There will be G such rosters.

The matrix for the general, or gth, group will be

$$X_g = \begin{Vmatrix} X_{1g} \\ X_{2g} \\ X_{3g} \\ \vdots \\ X_{n_g g} \end{Vmatrix}$$

There will be G such matrices. Each of the G matrices contains the data of a frequency distribution of an independent group. The mean of each group can be computed and, in general, denoted by the symbol $\bar{X}_g$. The matrix of the deviation scores of any one of the groups, for example, the gth group, may be computed. It will be

$$x_g = \begin{Vmatrix} X_{1g} \\ X_{2g} \\ X_{3g} \\ \vdots \\ X_{n_g g} \end{Vmatrix} - \begin{Vmatrix} \bar{X}_g \\ \bar{X}_g \\ \bar{X}_g \\ \vdots \\ \bar{X}_g \end{Vmatrix} = X_g - \bar{X}_g$$

For each group independently, the sum of the squares of the raw scores X may be computed. For any one group, in general for the gth group, the sum of squares is denoted by the matrix product $X'_g X_g$. For each group independently, the scores may be transformed to standard scores and the resulting individual standard scores may be written in a matrix Z. For the gth group the relation between standard scores and raw scores is written

$$Z_g = \frac{1}{\sigma_g}(X_g - \bar{X}_g)'(X_g - \bar{X}_g) = \frac{1}{\sigma_g}(X'_g X_g - \bar{X}'_g \bar{X}_g)$$

where σ_g is the standard deviation of the scores in the gth group. The matrix Z_g is a column of standard scores, one for each individual in the gth specialty group.

Every possible score value is equivalent to a particular standard score in each of the G groups. For every possible standard score in each group independently, we can determine from the table of areas of the normal distribution a centour equivalent. We may therefore prepare a simple interpretive table of centours for every possible score independently for any number of groups. For the general case of G groups there will be G independent centours for every possible raw score.

The centour equivalents in the gth group C_g are defined by

$$C_g = \frac{200}{\sqrt{2\pi}} \int_{|z_g|}^{\infty} \exp\left(-\tfrac{1}{2}z^2\right) dz$$

The equation may be alternatively written

$$C_g = 100 - \frac{100}{\sqrt{2\pi}} \int_{-z_g}^{+z_g} \exp\left(-\tfrac{1}{2}z^2\right) dz$$

There will be as many values C_g as there are different values of scores X or standard scores z. The use of standard scores in the definition of C_g should not be interpreted to mean that standardization of scores of each group is a necessary step. Standard scores are used only to simplify the notation.

The interpretation of the centour equivalents estimated for the gth group depends on the accuracy with which the estimated ideal normal distribution describes the population in the job. The sample data for each group may be examined independently, and if characteristics of the sample data require a different assumption for any group, for example, the gth, a recalculation of centours has no effect upon the centours of the other $(G - 1)$ groups. If personnel research in World Airlines determines that the composition of the ideal specialty group is described by some frequency distribution different from obtained criterion groups, the ideal specifications may be incorporated in the centour tables computed for the use of personnel advisers. If the ideal group is specified by a centroid M_k and a standard deviation σ_k, centours for a normally distributed ideal group may be calculated from

$$C_k = \frac{200}{\sqrt{2\pi}} \int_{|z_k|}^{\infty} \exp\left(-\tfrac{1}{2}z^2\right) dz$$

where $z_k = (X - M_k)/\sigma_k$ is a standard score in the specified ideal distribution. Such centour scores inform a personnel adviser about the frequency distribution by which World Airlines *wishes* to characterize a specialty.

Chapter 3

The Two-Variate Case

Indoor–Outdoor and Solitary–Convivial Scores

The Convivial Score

The Activity Preference Inventory included three sections. The second section contains 35 items. One activity of each pair is a solitary activity, the other convivial. An example is

_____ Solitaire : Bridge _____

The apprentice's score is the number of *convivial* activities he prefers.

Profile Representation

The number of outdoor activities and the number of convivial activities Bill Flint preferred are indicated in a roster:

		Activity Preferences	
Apprentice	Social Security No.	Outdoor	Convivial
Flint, Bill	432-19-8765	20	15

A personnel adviser may tell Bill that he preferred the outdoor activity stated in 20 of the 30 pairs of indoor-outdoor activities and that he preferred the convivial activity stated in 15 of the 35 pairs of solitary-convivial activities. Bill prefers 10 more outdoor than indoor activities and 5 more solitary than convivial activities. These statements exhaust the information in the roster.

The adviser may also indicate this information graphically by constructing *two* profile stalks, one for each score, as in each of the four examples indicated in Fig. 3.1. Bill's outdoor and convivial scores may be indicated as points on these pairs of lines by any convenient symbolic device.

All of the representations in Fig. 3.1 *are* profiles. On most types of profile charts, however, it is customary to draw straight lines connecting

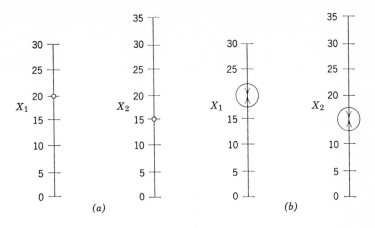

(a)   (b)

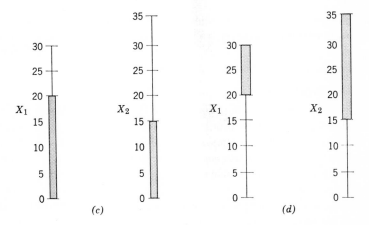

(c)   (d)

Fig. 3.1

the score points on adjacent stalks, as has been done in Fig. 3.2a. When this practice is used the line itself is often loosely referred to as "the profile." The frequently used expression, "shape of the profile," seems to be associated with the impression that the line is the profile.

In Fig. 3.1 all the profiles are presented with the convivial score stalk on the right-hand side. We can ask the question: In what order should the profile stalks be arranged? We do not give this problem the distinction of a number in the series of profile problems because the decision is obviously arbitrary. The order in which the stalks are arranged has no effect on the

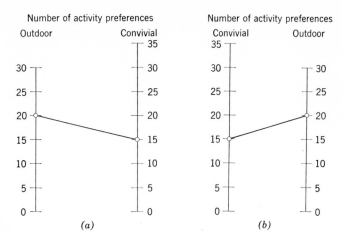

Fig. 3.2   *"The profile" of Bill Flint.*

facts the scores convey concerning the activity preferences of Bill Flint. We draw attention, however, to the visual impression apparent in this example. When the order is changed, the profile "looks" different—it slants in the opposite direction, as seen in Fig. 3.2*b*.

Cartesian Representation

The graphic profiles illustrated so far have all employed the conventional form of vertical profile stalks. The stalks could just as well be, and in psychological test practice frequently are, represented as horizontal axes. We now introduce profile representation in conventional Cartesian axes where, in effect, one profile stalk is horizontal and the other is vertical, as seen in Fig. 3.3. The assignment of tests to the axes is, of course, arbitrary, as was the assignment of order to the arrangement of the profile stalks. We have assigned the outdoor score to the horizontal axis, the convivial score to the vertical axis. It is important to note that the two axes are oriented at right angles to each other. In other respects the axes are like profile stalks. They are marked off in arbitrary units and the numerical values of the conjunction at the intersection are arbitrary. It is convenient to set the origin, or zero point in raw scores, at the point where the axes cross. The device of using orthogonal axes for plotting profile scores is Cartesian representation in two dimensions.

The scores of an apprentice, for example, Tom Baslik, may be graphically indicated on the right-angled profile stalks as they could have been indicated on parallel profile stalks similar to those in Fig. 3.1. The invention of coordinate axes with a common origin has, however, increased the

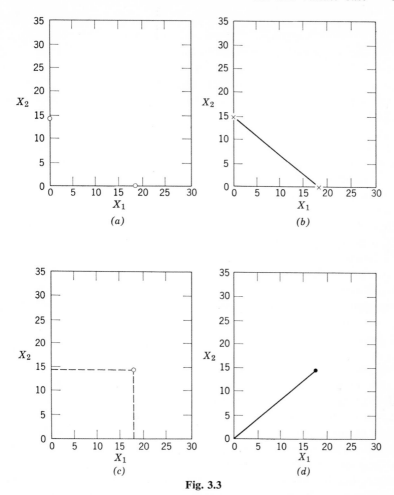

Fig. 3.3

possible variety of graphic devices for visual representation of scores. Some of these are illustrated in the four diagrams of Fig. 3.3. The location of each score on its axis may be marked in the usual profile manner, as in Fig. 3.3*a*. A profile line may be drawn, as in Fig. 3.3*b*, which is merely a reproduction of Fig. 3.2*b* with the outdoor scale rotated 90° and with the two zero points united. The locations on the two stalks may be used to draw a rectangle, as in Fig. 3.3*c*. The most efficient graphic device seems to be the single line in Fig. 3.3*d*, which is drawn from the origin to the point determined by the rectangular method. Such a line is known as a vector. The basic idea of the vector is that any point may be thought of as being located a certain distance in a certain direction from an origin.

The idea of vector representation of a two-score profile is an obvious extension of the basic idea in our representation of the single-score profile. In the univariate case we represented the score as a point on a line. Any point, and thus, any score, is a certain distance along the line in a certain direction from an origin. When zero outdoor preferences was chosen as the origin for profile representation, Tom Baslik's outdoor score $X = 18$ was 18 units of distance in the positive direction. When the centroid of the mechanic group $\bar{X} = 18.59$ was chosen as origin, the location of his score was .41 units of distance in the negative direction. Each score has a definite location on the line; it is located at a point in a space of one dimension.

The same idea of location may be extended to two scores on different tests. In ordinary profile representation the two scores are indicated as points on parallel lines. The two points are locations in two separate unrelated spaces with each of one dimension and with no points in common. In Cartesian representation the two one-dimensional spaces are connected by a common origin. The two axes are said to define a plane and each pair of scores identifies a location in the plane. Any pair of scores on different tests locates points on a pair of axes, and these two points, one in each dimension, locate a single point in a space of two dimensions. The vector representation in Fig. 3.3d shows Tom Baslik's location in the space of the plane. The location is expressed as a distance and direction from the origin.

Because the two axes represent test scores it has become conventional to refer to all of the possible points in the plane as the "test space." The pair of numbers (scores) that determine the location of a point in the space are referred to as coordinates of the point. Figure 3.4 makes use of Bill Flint's scores to illustrate the geometry of vector representation. We first adopt a simple notation to distinguish between the scores. Let X_1 denote the outdoor score axis and X_2 the convivial score axis. Any point in the plane is then located (or defined) by a pair of numbers X_1, X_2, and every pair of numbers locates a point. The coordinates of Bill Flint's point are his two scores $X_1 = 20$, $X_2 = 15$. The point is indicated in Fig. 3.4a by the dot vertically above the location 20 on the X_1 axis and horizontally to the right of 15 on the X_2 axis. A perpendicular line from the point to the X_1 axis meets the X_1 axis at $X_1 = 20$. The vector will be the line from the origin $X_1 = 0$, $X_2 = 0$ to the point. The X_1 axis, the vector, and the perpendicular form a right triangle, as shown in Fig. 3.4b. The length of the base of the triangle is obviously Bill Flint's outdoor score $X_1 = 20$. Bill's convivial score $X_2 = 15$ is the length of the vertical side. The length of the vector is then determined to be $25 = \sqrt{20^2 + 15^2}$.

A second right triangle could be constructed by drawing a perpendicular line from the test score point to the X_2 axis. The length of the vector and

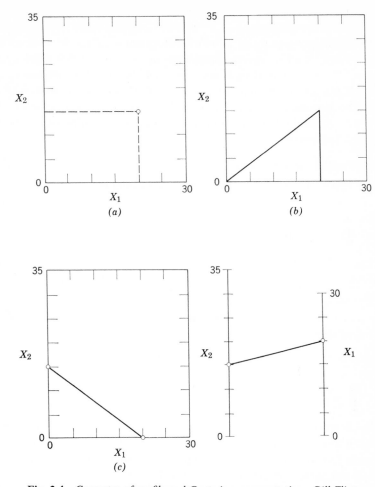

Fig. 3.4 *Geometry of profile and Cartesian representation—Bill Flint.*

the direction of the vector are unchanged. The distance from the origin to the intercept point on an axis is called the projection of the point on the axis. Thus, the projection of Bill's point on the X_1 axis is his score $X_1 = 20$. His projection on the convivial axis is $X_2 = 15$. In these diagrams we see that we have three points of interest, the two score points on the separate axes and the single point in the test space which represents the two scores jointly.

In Fig. 3.4c a profile line is drawn to connect the projections. If we disconnect the X_1 axis at the origin and swing it around to a vertical position, as shown in Fig. 3.4d, we obtain a conventional two-stalk profile chart which is identical to Fig. 3.2b. Profile representation is a special form representing the projections of a point in Cartesian space. A single point in Cartesian space conveys as much information as a pair of points in profile space. Neither representation adds information to that given by the matrix. These graphic devices provide only the visual equivalent of the fact that Bill prefers the outdoor activity in 20 of 30 pairs of indoor-outdoor activities, and the convivial activity in 15 of 35 pairs of solitary-convivial activities. Additional information is obtained for examining similar scores of other apprentices.

Three Profiles for Two Tests

The roster of the three apprentices of our example follows:

	Activity Preferences	
Apprentice	Outdoor	Convivial
Armand, Joe	22	22
Baslik, Tom	18	14
Flint, Bill	20	15

The scores in the roster may be written as a matrix X in which the rows represent men and the columns represent tests.

$$X = \begin{Vmatrix} 22 & 22 \\ 18 & 14 \\ 20 & 15 \end{Vmatrix}$$

The problem of examining groups of profiles and deriving interpretive comparisons of individuals is illustrated in Fig. 3.5a where the three scores on each test are marked on the appropriate profile stalk. Comparisons among the three apprentices are impossible until the scores in adjacent columns are matched. Figure 3.5b identifies the pairs by the usual method of drawing profile lines. The same pairs of scores are represented as points in a plane in Fig. 3.5c. Both profile and Cartesian methods record graphically exactly the same information that the matrix records numerically. The Cartesian method, however, enjoys the advantage of simplicity in both construction and interpretation. All the differences among the apprentices on either test, or on the two tests jointly considered, can be read from the relative distances among three points. To obtain the same comparison information from the profiles requires inspection of three pairs of points. In Cartesian form each apprentice's point can be represented as a vector from any desired origin. In profile representation this simple concept of distance from an origin is not obvious.

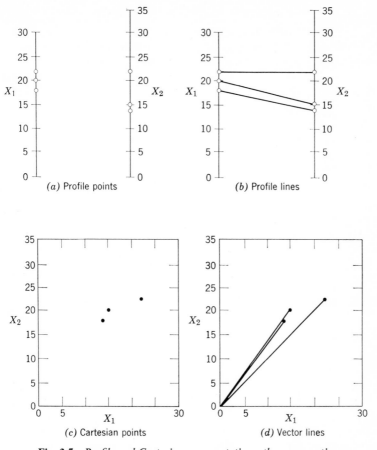

Fig. 3.5   *Profile and Cartesian representation—three apprentices.*

The Group of Apprentices in Two-Space

Roster, Matrix, and Profiles

The number of outdoor *and* convivial activity preferences expressed by each apprentice hired from the group of applicants tested in New York City where our example originated is recorded in Table 3.1. The roster may be written in a matrix of 135 rows and 2 columns:

$$X = \begin{Vmatrix} 21 & 16 \\ 21 & 17 \\ 27 & 20 \\ \vdots & \vdots \\ 21 & 18 \end{Vmatrix} \quad \text{(135 rows)}$$

Table 3.1   *Roster of Scores for Apprentices from New York City*

X_1—Number of outdoor preferençes
X_2—Number of convivial preferençes

Number	X_1	X_2	Number	X_1	X_2	Number	X_1	X_2
1	21	16	46	15	16	91	20	17
2	21	17	47	14	25	92	13	18
3	27	20	48	13	23	93	20	25
4	16	19	49	13	18	94	11	19
5	14	24	50	20	16	95	16	19
6	20	19	51	19	20	96	22	9
7	19	26	52	19	15	97	21	12
8	9	25	53	17	26	98	18	28
9	23	15	54	11	11	99	27	24
10	14	16	55	14	24	100	24	17
11	22	23	56	18	19	101	16	19
12	20	20	57	17	21	102	13	12
13	20	20	58	10	19	103	20	23
14	18	14	59	17	14	104	20	20
15	25	22	60	11	23	105	12	16
16	17	15	61	23	18	106	18	15
17	10	22	62	21	15	107	20	27
18	17	20	63	19	21	108	6	20
19	15	22	64	11	23	109	20	16
20	21	18	65	18	18	110	17	22
21	18	17	66	22	21	111	20	20
22	20	24	67	17	11	112	13	21
23	22	22	68	11	21	113	20	23
24	29	13	69	13	18	114	22	7
25	15	23	70	11	23	115	19	13
26	21	28	71	23	17	116	19	22
27	20	13	72	21	19	117	16	21
28	21	18	73	20	18	118	15	17
29	21	20	74	17	19	119	14	22
30	20	21	75	13	18	120	18	19
31	25	22	76	13	21	121	18	19
32	14	11	77	11	21	122	23	22
33	20	28	78	16	24	123	13	24
34	16	27	79	17	19	124	19	17
35	11	16	80	13	29	125	15	27
36	16	13	81	16	15	126	15	22
37	16	20	82	26	18	127	14	25
38	20	20	83	24	16	128	13	23
39	13	24	84	17	18	129	19	24
40	22	24	85	16	18	130	17	23
41	10	21	86	14	18	131	24	16
42	24	16	87	13	27	132	18	15
43	20	15	88	16	30	133	14	20
44	19	22	89	16	17	134	12	28
45	20	26	90	11	22	135	21	18

Neither roster nor matrix provides a visual impression of the typical scores on either test, the dispersion in the scores, or the relation between the outdoor and convivial activity preferences of the incoming group of apprentices. To ascertain these important interpretive impressions we discuss the profile representation of the matrix. As in the one-variable problem we adopt the idea of a frequency distribution plotted on the profile stalks. Since we have two scores for each apprentice, we must preserve the identity of the pairs of scores. This matching of each outdoor score with its mate is attempted in Fig. 3.6. With this demonstration of graphic absurdity we abandon profile representation as a tool for finding interpretations of the differences among individuals and groups. We therefore turn directly to the problems of extracting from the matrix the desired information by Cartesian representations.

The frequency distribution of the group's scores on each test and the essential descriptive statistics of the distributions are given in Table 3.2. Centour scores could be easily computed for each test and each man's scores could be directly interpreted in terms of his divergence from the centroid of the group. A difficulty is immediately apparent in that the statistical computations result in two centours for each man, one for each test. The facts that the test scores are paired and that the pairing introduces a relationship between scores have not been incorporated in the centour computation. A man who prefers many outdoor activities may prefer many convivial activities, or he may not. The relations among the man's preferences, whatever they may be, have been ignored in the calculations of separate centours for the tests. The double centour approach implies that we should look first at a man's outdoor preferences, then at his convivial preferences, but avoid looking at both simultaneously. This observation introduces: *Profile Problem 3. How may the joint performance of individuals in a group be represented?*

The Joint Distribution of Outdoor and Convivial Scores

The scores of the 135 apprentices hired from New York City are plotted in the two-dimensional test space in Fig. 3.7. A scatter diagram of this kind is usually used for examining the regression of one test score upon another, or for the calculation of the correlation coefficient. The diagram, however, can also be used for examining the dispersion among all the individual score points and for estimating the magnitude of divergence which characterizes any particular pair of scores. The centour concept which we first developed in the one-dimensional test space can be easily extended to include the notion of divergence from a typical point in a two-dimensional test space. It will perhaps be intuitively helpful if we discuss in detail the particular sample represented by the scores for the apprentices

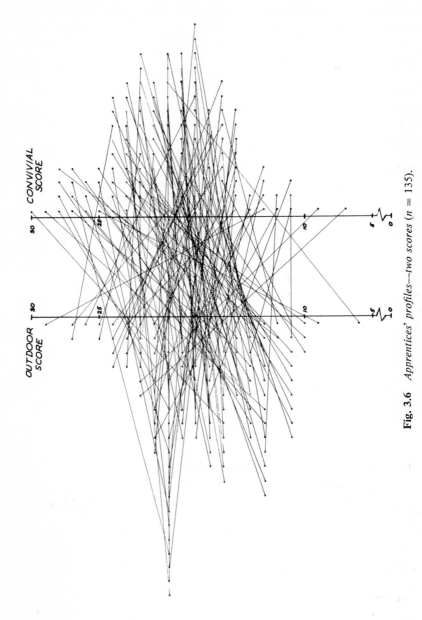

Fig. 3.6 *Apprentices' profiles—two scores* ($n = 135$).

Table 3.2 *Frequency Distributions of the Group*

X_1—Outdoor score $\bar{X}_1 = 17.44$ $\sigma_1 = 4.25$		$n = 135$	X_2—Convivial score $\bar{X}_2 = 19.75$ $\sigma_2 = 4.35$	

	Outdoor		Convivial	
X_1	f		X_2	f
30	–		30	1
29	1		29	1
28	–		28	4
27	2		27	4
26	1		26	3
25	2		25	4
24	4		24	9
23	4		23	10
22	6		22	12
21	10		21	10
20	20		20	12
19	9		19	12
18	9		18	14
17	11		17	8
16	12		16	10
15	6		15	8
14	9		14	2
13	13		13	4
12	2		12	2
11	9		11	3
10	3		10	–
9	1		9	1
8	–		8	
7	–		7	
6	1		6	

from New York City before we proceed to the more general, more abstract, and more precise formulation of the two-dimensional problem.

The frequency distribution of the outdoor scores may be thought of as plotted under the X_1 axis. In Fig. 3.7 the mean outdoor score of the group $\bar{X}_1 = 17.44$ is indicated by the arrow near the scale value 17 on the X_1 axis. We can imagine a vertical line drawn through this mean score value. It divides the test space into two regions; and it divides the score points plotted in the scatter diagram into two sets. All the score points in the right-hand region represent apprentices whose outdoor scores are greater

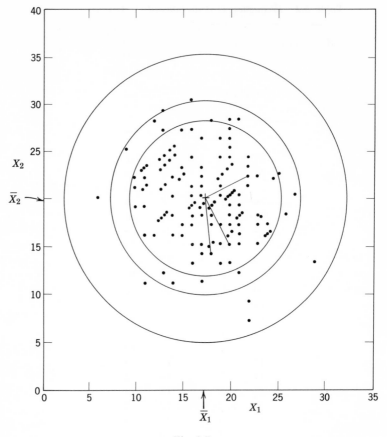

Fig. 3.7

than $\bar{X}_1 = 17.44$. The points to the left of the line identify apprentices whose outdoor scores are less than the mean. The mean score of the convivial preferences is marked on the X_2 axis. A line perpendicular to the X_2 axis and through this point marked by an arrow divides the test space into two regions, each region containing approximately half the score points in the scatter diagram. All the points above the line represent individuals whose convivial scores are greater than the average convivial score $\bar{X}_2 = 19.75$. The intersection of these lines is the centroid of the frequencies in the bivariate distribution. The centroid is marked by a cross $+$ on the diagram. It is obviously a good location to designate as the middle of the many points.

Each individual score point may be represented as a vector from the centroid. The vectors representing Joe, Tom, and Bill are the three lines from the centroid in the figure. Obviously, if an individual is represented by a large vector of this kind (that is, where the origin is the centroid), his score point lies a great distance from the centroid. If his vector is small, his score lies close to the middle of the group.

The usefulness of a vector from the centroid is obvious in the diagram. The generality of the idea and the precision with which it can be used is revealed in the sequence of ideas which follow:

1. Any score on the outdoor activity scale is thought of as a point on an axis.

2. The point is a distance from the origin zero.

3. A distance from an origin is a vector.

4. A raw score is a vector from zero in one dimension (that is, along a line).

5. The same point on the axis is represented by a deviation score where the numerical value is a distance from a mean.

6. A deviation score is a vector from the mean in a space of one dimension (that is, a distance from a mean).

7. A pair of scores may be represented by a point in a space of two dimensions (that is, a plane).

8. A point in a plane is determined by a distance and a direction from a reference point or origin.

Joe Armand's score $X_1 = 22$, $X_2 = 22$, is represented by a vector from the origin zero. The direction is given as $45°$ from the X_1 axis.

The distance along the X_1 axis from zero to Joe's score at 22 is the projection of the vector on that axis. We notice now that Joe's deviation score $X_1 - \bar{X}_1 = 22 - 17.44 = 4.56$ is the projection of his two-dimensional vector from the centroid upon the X_1 axis. The value is identical in magnitude and in direction ($+$) to his one-dimensional vector from the mean of the outdoor scores. Figure 3.8 illustrates the geometry of Joe's vectors and projections. The line from the origin to his score point and the line from the centroid to his point are indicated with their projections upon the X_1 axis in Fig. 3.8a. If we form the right triangle by dropping a perpendicular to the X_1 axis, we see that we can compute the length of Joe's centroid vector, the vertical side of the triangle being Joe's deviation score on the convivial test axis.

We may proceed in exactly the same manner with respect to the convivial score. Each obtained score is thought of as a point on the axis and as a distance from zero. This distance is the projection of Joe's vector in two-space upon the X_2 axis. The projection of Joe's centroid vector upon the X_2 axis is seen to be his deviation score, that is, his deviation from the mean of the convivial scores. The geometry shows that the length of Joe's

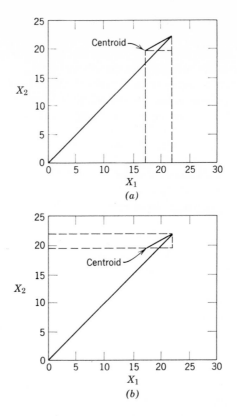

Fig. 3.8 *Geometry of a vector from the centroid—Joe Armand* ($X_1 = 22$, $X_2 = 22$, *centroid* = 17.44, 19.75).

vector is determined by the location of his score point in the test space. If the vector is represented as a distance from zero, the vector length is the square root of the sum of the squared deviation scores. Shifting the origin from zero to the centroid in two dimensions is exactly comparable to the translation of origin that we use in the one-dimensional test space when we compute deviation scores.

With this understanding of vector distances from the centroid we return to considering the concept of regions in the test space. If we choose a distance, say 15 units along the outdoor axis, we may draw a circle with radius 15, using the centroid as the center. This circle is the largest of the three circles drawn in Fig. 3.7. It divides the test space into two regions, the part inside the circle and the space outside. The region inside the circle contains, without exception, every one of the sample points, that is, the individuals in the sample represented by our 135 subjects. Our choice of radius was arbitrary and chosen for illustrative purposes. We may choose any other value.

The middle circle has a radius equal to 10. This circle also divides the test space into two regions, the inside and outside areas, and we see that eight of the sample points lie outside the circle. These sample points represent the individuals who deviate most from the centroid of the group; their vectors are the largest vectors in the group of 135. The inner circle has a radius equal to 8. We find that 20 score points are clearly outside this circle. Twenty is 15% of 135 cases; therefore we could say that any score point that lies on this circle is equivalent to a centour of 15 in this sample. And 15% of the group diverge from the centroid a greater distance than any distance on this circle or within the circle. We could go on drawing circles indefinitely, and by counting the points outside and inside the circles, we could prepare a centour table for the bivariate distribution of this group.

The example serves the purpose of extending the centour concept to a test space of dimensionality two, but the procedure of drawing circles does not provide the precision or the formality that the application of the centour concept generally requires. In the example the standard deviations of the two tests were closely similar. If the standard deviation of one test is much greater than that of the other, satisfactory regions cannot be described by circles. Circles would, of course, describe regions within which all vectors were less than the radius of the circle and outside of which all vector points were larger, but the regions would not be satisfactory if the units of measurement in the two dimensions are unequal. Imagine the frequency scatter diagram of height and weight for a number of airmen. If height is measured in inches and weight in pounds, a deviation score of $+6$ inches has the same effect upon the vector length as a deviation score of $+6$ pounds. We know that 6 inches is an extremely large deviation and that 6 pounds is a small deviation. The absolute value of the vector distance is therefore not always the important measure. We must also consider *Profile Problem 1B* which, adapted to this example, becomes: *Should vectors be represented on a standard score scale or on a raw score scale?* Aside from this technical complication, it is clear that if we can determine the appropriate regions of the test space, we can describe the typicalness of any individual's set of scores by use of the centour concept.

The Bivariate Normal Distribution

Specifications

Certain basic ideas about frequency distributions will recur frequently in our analysis of the problem of interpreting profiles. In this section we introduce the normal distribution in two variates as an extension of the familiar univariate case, and establish concepts and terms that will be useful in the general case of the multivariate distribution.

We begin with the notion of a test space geometrically represented by Cartesian axes. In the one-variate case the test space is the scale on which the scores of individuals may be represented as locations or points. The test space is a line of one dimension. The scores of *N* individuals in a group may then be conceived of as represented by a large group of points in the space. They will, of course, be points distributed on, or scattered along, a line. The manner in which the points are distributed, that is, where in the space (or the line) they are centered and how widely they are dispersed in the space, may be shown by adopting the convention of a unit of area to represent a unit of frequency and constructing a unit of area on the line for each point in the swarm. The result is the familiar histogram. Figure 3.9*a* shows the histogram of the convivial scores of the apprentices from

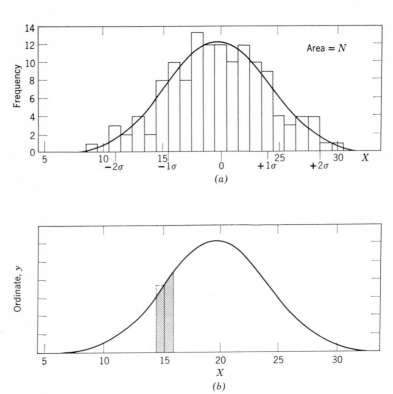

Fig. 3.9 *Histogram and normal distribution—convivial scores—apprentice data.*
($\bar{X} = 19.75$, $N = 135$, $\sigma = 4.35$).

New York City. A scale indicating frequency is shown in the left margin purely as a convenience. The frequency of scores at each point in the test space is actually represented by the size of the rectangular areas constructed on each score interval. The total histogram representing N persons in the group is 135 units of area.

The essential facts about the histogram may be summarized by statistical expressions, and these statistics describe the many points in the test space. The location of the histogram is described by the mean score $\bar{X}$ or, as we shall say, by the centroid of the group of points. The extent of scatter or variation of the individual points around the center is measured by the variance σ^2 or the standard deviation σ. We shall use the term dispersion in referring to the concept of variation around the centroid. The histogram has a form and the problem of describing its form brings us directly to the normal distribution.

The steps in the histogram represent irregular aspects of the 135 scores of the particular group but are of no significance in a general study of apprentices. Experience with test score data indicates that the scores of any other group of apprentices would exhibit similar, but not identical, irregularities. Thus the *details* of the form of the histogram are of little interest or interpretive value, whereas the general characteristic form is of value. We therefore find it convenient to choose a suitable smooth curve to use as an ideal shape to describe the important characteristics of the histogram. In adopting this procedure we follow the same logic that leads us to describe a bicycle wheel as circular, which it is approximately, but not exactly. We use the ideal as a model for studying the practical.

The smooth curve we choose to adopt is the normal distribution defined by the equation

$$y_n = \frac{N}{\sqrt{2\pi}\sigma} \exp\left[-\tfrac{1}{2}\left(\frac{X - \bar{X}}{\sigma}\right)^2\right]$$

The ordinate y_n is then an approximation to the height of the histogram rectangle at the point X. The normal distribution fitted to the group data is plotted in Fig. 3.9. The total area under the smooth curve is exactly $N = 135$ units. Since we shall not usually be concerned with actual values of N, we find it convenient to divide the equation by N so that the total area $= 1.0$, representing one whole distribution of any size. The equation of this unit normal distribution is

$$y = \frac{1}{\sqrt{2\pi}\sigma} \exp\left[-\tfrac{1}{2}\left(\frac{X - \bar{X}}{\sigma}\right)^2\right]$$

The ordinate y is now a relative measure of density of points in the group at the location X in the test space. The frequency on an interval of which

X is the midpoint depends on the size of the interval. The value of y is approximately the height of the average rectangle on whatever small interval is chosen. Figure 3.9b illustrates the ordinate, interval, and area. The concept of density at a point as distinguished from frequency on an interval becomes particularly useful in considering the multivariate distribution.

In the univariate normal distribution there are pairs of points in the test space at which the ordinates are equal. Since the curve is symmetrical, the points are $\pm x = \pm(X - \bar{X})$, one on each side of the centroid. Thus, given any ordinate of the curve, it is possible to find the two corresponding values of X in the test space; or for any choice of $|x| = |X - \bar{X}|$ the value of the ordinate may be found. The two points in the test space for which the ordinates are equal are the loci of equal density. A line parallel to the test space intersects the curve at such points. Although it is not strictly correct, the pairs of points are often referred to as loci of isofrequency. We note that these pairs of points are the loci in a test space of one dimension.

When the individuals in a group are measured by two tests, each pair of scores locates a point in a test space of two dimensions. The scatter diagram is the familiar graphic representation of the frequencies. The dots that represent the individuals obviously form a group of points in the test space. The increase in the dimensionality of the test space requires that the dimensionality of the histogram be extended. In the bivariate distribution, a unit of volume represents a unit of frequency. A graphic model may be constructed, as in Fig. 3.20 (page 123). Figure 3.20 is an illustration of the bivariate histogram of the apprentice data.

The unit normal distribution in one variable is a smooth curve or line, and the relative frequency of any point X is given by the ordinate y. Every point in the test space determines an ordinate y. In the unit normal distribution in two variables there will be an ordinate y for every point in the test space. The equation of the bivariate distribution, therefore, represents a surface. The total volume under the surface is unity for the unit normal case, or is N for the distribution fitted to a sample of N observations. The value or height of the ordinate at any point in the test space is a relative measure of density in the region of the point. The volume built upon any small rectangular interval or cell in the test space represents the frequency in the cell of the bivariate distribution. Figure 3.10 shows this bivariate concept in the same manner as Fig. 3.9b illustrated the idea in the univariate distribution.

Figure 3.11 represents the ideal bivariate frequency distribution in stanine scores for $N = 2500$. Figure 3.12 is an isometric drawing of the frequencies given in Fig. 3.11. Figure 3.13 is a portion of Fig. 3.12. These

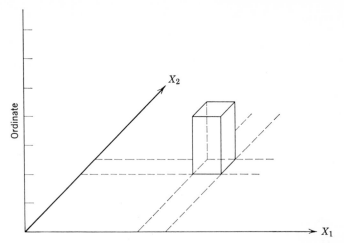

Fig. 3.10   *Construction of a frequency element of volume in a bivariate histogram.*

figures do not represent the mathematical model of the normal distribution exactly. They are histogram-like approximations used in computing stanine scores. The mathematical model defined by the equation for the bivariate normal distribution has a smooth surface. It is more adequately represented in Figs. 3.14, 3.15, and 3.16.

A plane parallel to the test space intersects the frequency (or density) surface. The points of intersection are loci of equidensity. The loci are lines in a space of two dimensions. They can be represented as lines in the test space. Figures 3.17 and 3.18 illustrate isodensity contours. As in

$$N = 2500 \qquad r = .00$$

		100	175	300	425	500	425	300	175	100	(2500)
	9	4	7	12	17	20	17	12	7	4	100
	8	7	12	21	30	35	30	21	12	7	175
	7	12	21	36	51	60	51	36	21	12	300
	6	17	30	51	72	85	72	51	30	17	425
X_2	5	20	35	60	85	100	85	60	35	20	500
	4	17	30	51	72	85	72	51	30	17	425
	3	12	21	36	51	60	51	36	21	12	300
	2	7	12	21	30	35	30	21	12	7	175
	1	4	7	12	17	20	17	12	7	4	100
		1	2	3	4	5	6	7	8	9	

$$X_1$$

Fig. 3.11   *Bivariate cell frequencies–stanine scores. The frequencies in this figure are shown in the isometric drawing of the ideal stanine distribution.*

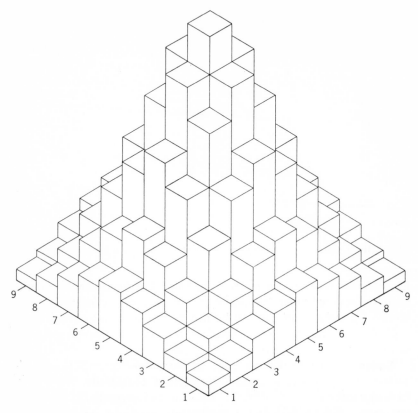

Fig. 3.12 *Ideal bivariate normal distribution approximated for stanine scores with zero correlation (N = 2500, frequency in modal cell = 100).*

the one-variate case, the concept of density and frequency is sometimes used interchangeably and the loci of equal density are often termed isofrequency contours.

In the stanine example illustrated in the figures the contours consist of concentric circles located at the centroid in the test space. Each of these contours divides the test space into two regions, the portion enclosed by the contour and the portion outside. The total frequency of points which lie inside the contour is some fraction or proportion of the whole distribution. We denote this proportion by the symbol q. Then $p = 1 - q$ is the proportion of the total frequency located at points in the test space outside the contour. Thus every contour is associated with a value of p and every proportion p defines a particular contour. Three such contours are illustrated in Fig. 3.7.

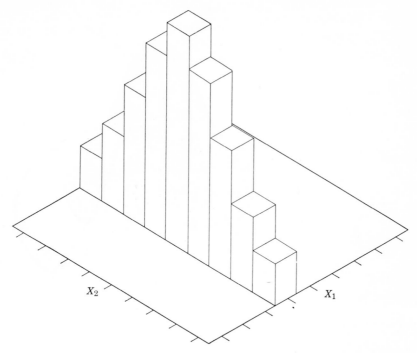

Fig. 3.13 *A section of the ideal stanine distribution* ($X_1 = 4$ *from Fig.* 3.12).

The isodensity contours of the bivariate normal distribution will not usually be circles. If the standard deviations of the two variables X_1, X_2 are unequal, the distribution will be more widely dispersed in one of the dimensions and the contours will be stretched in one direction. They become ellipses. When the correlation is zero, the semiaxes of the ellipses are proportional to the standard deviations of the variables.

The frequency distribution of the scores on one of the variables, say X_1, is a marginal distribution of one variable in the bivariate group of points. Marginal distributions are illustrated for the stanine example in Fig. 3.11. The marginal distributions of any normal bivariate distribution are themselves normal. Furthermore, any linear combination of the test-space variables, such as $Y = aX_1 + bX_2$, is normally distributed. Thus any plane perpendicular to the test space will intersect the bivariate normal frequency surface

$$y = \frac{1}{2\pi\sigma_1\sigma_2 \sqrt{1 - r^2}} \exp\left[-\frac{1}{2(1 - r^2)} \left(\frac{x_1{}^2}{\sigma_1{}^2} - \frac{2rx_1x_2}{\sigma_1\sigma_2} + \frac{x_2{}^2}{\sigma_2{}^2} \right) \right]$$

in a normal distribution (see Figs. 3.15 and 3.16).

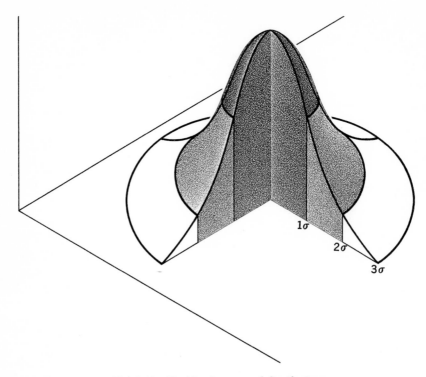

Fig. 3.14   *The bivariate normal distribution.*

In the univariate case the statistics $\bar{X}$ and σ^2 determine the location and dispersion of the group of points. As indicated in the foregoing equation, the addition of a second dimension increases the number of parameters required to describe the central location of the points and the dispersion of the frequencies or the form of the density distribution. Matrix notation proves to be a convenient way to record these facts of location and dispersion in the density distribution. We must, however, take a final step in indicating the procedures of matrix algebra before this correspondence can be shown.

The Two-Dimensional Matrix

All the statistical relations contained in a roster of two-score profiles are contained in the matrix of scores. In this section we extend our review of matrix formulation to include, for the bivariate case, the notation of the sum of squares and cross-products matrix, the variance-covariance matrix, and the correlation coefficient matrix. We begin with a complete numerical

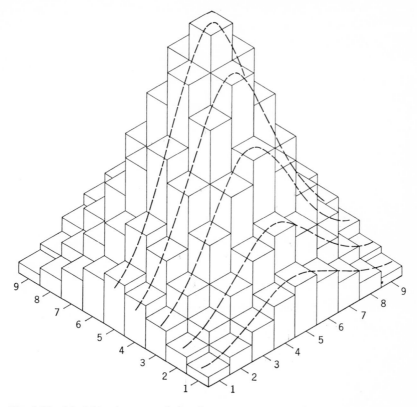

Fig. 3.15 *Ideal bivariate normal distribution approximated for stanine scores with zero correlation (N = 2500, frequency in modal cell = 100).*

example for three profiles and extend the method to all the profiles of the group of apprentices.

The scores of Joe, Tom, and Bill are written in a 3×2 matrix X:

$$X = \begin{Vmatrix} 22 & 22 \\ 18 & 14 \\ 20 & 15 \end{Vmatrix}$$

The transpose of X is the 2×3 matrix X':

$$X' = \begin{Vmatrix} 22 & 18 & 20 \\ 22 & 14 & 15 \end{Vmatrix}$$

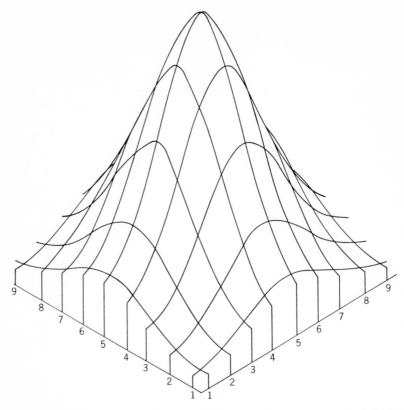

Fig. 3.16   *Ideal bivariate normal distribution approximated for stanine scores with zero correlation—smooth surface.*

Using the rule for matrix multiplication, the product $X'X$ is

$$X'X = \begin{Vmatrix} 22 & 18 & 20 \\ 22 & 14 & 15 \end{Vmatrix} \cdot \begin{Vmatrix} 22 & 22 \\ 18 & 14 \\ 20 & 15 \end{Vmatrix}$$

$$= \begin{Vmatrix} 1208 & 1036 \\ 1036 & 905 \end{Vmatrix}$$

The value 1208 in the upper left-hand corner of the preceding matrix is the sum of squares of the outdoor scores ($22^2 + 18^2 + 20^2$). The value 905 in the lower right-hand corner is the sum of squares of the convivial scores ($22^2 + 14^2 + 15^2$). The value 1036 in the upper right-hand corner is the sum of the cross products of the outdoor and convivial scores

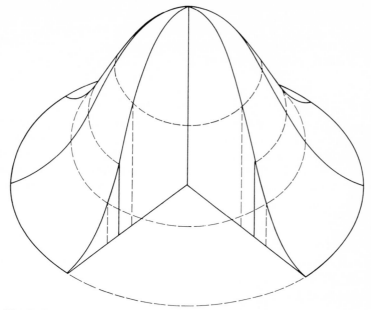

Fig. 3.17   *A view of the bivariate normal distribution and isodensity contours.*

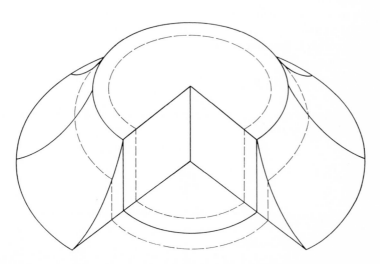

Fig. 3.18   *Isodensity contours in the bivariate normal distribution—in sectioned form.*

$[22(22) + 18(14) + 20(15)]$. The entry in the lower left-hand corner must be the same as in the upper right-hand corner because it comes from the same cross products. In the conventional notation of scalar algebra the $X'X$ matrix may be written as

$$X'X = \begin{Vmatrix} \sum X_1^2 & \sum X_1 X_2 \\ \sum X_2 X_1 & \sum X_2^2 \end{Vmatrix}$$

The matrix product $X'X$ denotes the sum of squares and cross products of the raw scores. For brevity it may be called the cross-product matrix.

The mean of the first column of the X matrix, that is, the mean of the outdoor scores of the three apprentices, is 20; and the mean of the second column, that is, the mean of the convivial scores of the three apprentices, is 17. The $\bar{X}$ matrix is therefore

$$\bar{X} = \begin{Vmatrix} 20 & 17 \\ 20 & 17 \\ 20 & 17 \end{Vmatrix}$$

and

$$\bar{X}'\bar{X} = \begin{Vmatrix} 20 & 20 & 20 \\ 17 & 17 & 17 \end{Vmatrix} \cdot \begin{Vmatrix} 20 & 17 \\ 20 & 17 \\ 20 & 17 \end{Vmatrix}$$

$$= \begin{Vmatrix} 3(20)^2 & 3(20)(17) \\ 3(17)(20) & 3(17)^2 \end{Vmatrix} = \begin{Vmatrix} 1200 & 1020 \\ 1020 & 867 \end{Vmatrix}$$

The element in the upper left-hand column is $3(400) = 1200$, or $n\bar{X}_1^2$. The element in the lower right-hand corner is $3(17)^2 = 867$, which is $n\bar{X}_2^2$. The upper right-hand corner contains $3(20)(17) = 1020$, or $n\bar{X}_1\bar{X}_2$. The lower left-hand corner is the same value, $n\bar{X}_2\bar{X}_1$. In symbolic notation the matrix may be written

$$\bar{X}'\bar{X} = \begin{Vmatrix} n\bar{X}_1^2 & n\bar{X}_1\bar{X}_2 \\ n\bar{X}_2\bar{X}_1 & n\bar{X}_2^2 \end{Vmatrix}$$

The conversion of raw scores X to deviation scores $x = X - \bar{X}$ is achieved by matrix subtraction:

$$X - \bar{X} = \begin{Vmatrix} 22 & 22 \\ 18 & 14 \\ 20 & 15 \end{Vmatrix} - \begin{Vmatrix} 20 & 17 \\ 20 & 17 \\ 20 & 17 \end{Vmatrix} = \begin{Vmatrix} 2 & 5 \\ -2 & -3 \\ 0 & -2 \end{Vmatrix}$$

The sum of squares and cross products of the deviation scores x is

$$x'x = (X - \bar{X})'(X - \bar{X}) = \begin{Vmatrix} 2 & -2 & 0 \\ 5 & -3 & -2 \end{Vmatrix} \cdot \begin{Vmatrix} 2 & 5 \\ -2 & -3 \\ 0 & -2 \end{Vmatrix} = \begin{Vmatrix} 8 & 16 \\ 16 & 38 \end{Vmatrix}$$

This result is identical with $X'X - \bar{X}'\bar{X}$:

$$X'X - \bar{X}'\bar{X} = \begin{Vmatrix} 1208 & 1036 \\ 1036 & 905 \end{Vmatrix} - \begin{Vmatrix} 1200 & 1020 \\ 1020 & 867 \end{Vmatrix}$$

In scalar symbols the values in the matrices are

$$X'X - \bar{X}'\bar{X} = \begin{Vmatrix} \sum X_1{}^2 & \sum X_1 X_2 \\ \sum X_2 X_1 & \sum X_2{}^2 \end{Vmatrix} - \begin{Vmatrix} n\bar{X}_1{}^2 & n\bar{X}_1\bar{X}_2 \\ n\bar{X}_2\bar{X}_1 & n\bar{X}_2{}^2 \end{Vmatrix}$$

$$= \begin{Vmatrix} \sum x_1{}^2 & \sum x_1 x_2 \\ \sum x_2 x_1 & \sum x_2{}^2 \end{Vmatrix}$$

This result is the matrix of the sum of squares and cross products of the deviation scores. If we divide the entries in $x'x$ by n, the result is the variance-covariance matrix, or simply the covariance matrix of the scores in X. The entries in the principal diagonal (upper left to lower right) become the variances

$$\frac{\sum x_1{}^2}{n} = \sigma_1{}^2 \quad \text{and} \quad \frac{\sum x_2{}^2}{n} = \sigma_2{}^2$$

The off-diagonal entries become the covariance

$$\frac{\sum x_1 x_2}{n} = \sigma_1 \sigma_2 r_{12} = \frac{\sum x_2 x_1}{n} = \sigma_2 \sigma_1 r_{21}$$

The result for the numerical example in which $n = 3$ is

$$\text{covariance matrix of } X = \tfrac{1}{3} \begin{Vmatrix} 8 & 16 \\ 16 & 38 \end{Vmatrix} = \begin{Vmatrix} 2.67 & 5.33 \\ 5.33 & 12.67 \end{Vmatrix}$$

The correlation coefficient r_{12} is easily obtained from the elements of the covariance matrix:

$$\text{covariance} = \sigma_1 \sigma_2 r_{12} \quad \text{therefore} \quad r_{12} = \frac{\text{covariance}}{\sigma_1 \sigma_2}$$

or from the elements of the cross-product matrix $x'x$

$$r_{12} = \frac{\sum x_1 x_2}{\sqrt{\sum x_1{}^2}\,\sqrt{\sum x_2{}^2}}$$

In the numerical example,

$$r_{12} = \frac{16}{\sqrt{8}\,\sqrt{38}} = .92$$

The covariance matrix describes the dispersion of the scores around the centroid. We choose, therefore, to denote the covariance matrix by the symbol D. The elements of D are conveniently denoted by d_{ij}. Each d_{ij} is either a variance or a covariance. When the subscripts are the same (that is, when $i = j$), the element lies in the principal diagonal and therefore represents the variance σ_i^2 of the ith variable. When $i \neq j$, the element is the covariance of variables i and j, $d_{ij} = \sigma_i \sigma_j r_{ij}$. In the sample of two tests, the possible values of i, j are 1, 2. The covariance matrix of the numerical example is

$$D = \begin{Vmatrix} d_{11} & d_{12} \\ d_{21} & d_{22} \end{Vmatrix} = \begin{Vmatrix} \sigma_1^2 & \sigma_1\sigma_2 r_{12} \\ \sigma_2\sigma_1 r_{21} & \sigma_2^2 \end{Vmatrix}$$

We note for future use that the number of tests may be 3, 4, 5, or any number T, and that the subscript notation includes these possibilities. Thus, for an example involving three tests, the dispersion matrix would be

$$D = \begin{Vmatrix} d_{11} & d_{12} & d_{13} \\ d_{21} & d_{22} & d_{23} \\ d_{31} & d_{32} & d_{33} \end{Vmatrix} = \begin{Vmatrix} \sigma_1^2 & \sigma_1\sigma_2 r_{12} & \sigma_1\sigma_3 r_{13} \\ \sigma_2\sigma_1 r_{21} & \sigma_2^2 & \sigma_2\sigma_3 r_{23} \\ \sigma_3\sigma_1 r_{31} & \sigma_3\sigma_2 r_{32} & \sigma_3^2 \end{Vmatrix}$$

The extension to any number of tests is accomplished by the inclusion of a row i and a column j for each test. A matrix R containing correlation coefficients r_{ij} may be obtained. For the two-variable example, it is

$$R = \begin{Vmatrix} r_{11} & r_{12} \\ r_{21} & r_{22} \end{Vmatrix} = \begin{Vmatrix} 1 & r_{12} \\ r_{21} & 1 \end{Vmatrix}$$

The value unity appears in the principal diagonal terms because the correlation of a score with itself is $r = 1.00$.

We now observe that the correlation matrix R may be obtained from the dispersion matrix D by a sequence of steps:

1. Divide each element of the first row of D by σ_1.
2. Divide each element of the second row of D by σ_2.
3. Divide the elements of D in the first column by σ_1.
4. Divide the second column by σ_2 (or, in the general case, divide the jth column by σ_j, and the ith row by σ_i).

The result of these operations on the dispersion matrix D is the correlation matrix R:

$$R = \begin{Vmatrix} \dfrac{\sigma_1^2}{\sigma_1\sigma_1} & \dfrac{\sigma_1\sigma_2 r_{12}}{\sigma_1\sigma_2} \\ \dfrac{\sigma_2\sigma_1 r_{21}}{\sigma_2\sigma_1} & \dfrac{\sigma_2^2}{\sigma_2\sigma_2} \end{Vmatrix} = \begin{Vmatrix} 1 & r_{12} \\ r_{21} & 1 \end{Vmatrix}$$

The sequence of multiplications by $1/\sigma$ is accomplished by matrix multiplications with diagonal matrices. Since multiplication of rows and columns by different scalar quantities, and particularly by inverse elements like $\sigma^{-1} = 1/\sigma$, will be useful in further developments, we choose this example to review the special multiplicative characteristics of diagonal matrices and their inverses.

A diagonal matrix contains nonzero elements in the principal diagonal and zero in all off-diagonal cells. We can write the standard deviations of the two test-score distributions in such a matrix and denote it by σ.

$$\sigma = \begin{Vmatrix} \sigma_1 & 0 \\ 0 & \sigma_2 \end{Vmatrix}$$

In scalar algebra the inverse of a number k is written $k^{-1} = 1/k$. A number multiplied by its inverse equals unity, for example $k \cdot k^{-1} = k(1/k) = 1$.

In matrix algebra the inverse is more complicated because a matrix is a set of numbers. Just as the inverse of a number is a number, the inverse of a matrix is a matrix. Although it may be complicated to compute, it is simple to write symbolically. The inverse of the matrix C is written C^{-1}. The inverse of the matrix σ is σ^{-1}. The inverse of a matrix T is another matrix T^{-1} whose elements are such that the matrix product $T \times T^{-1}$ is the unit matrix I, that is, a diagonal matrix in which every diagonal element equals 1 and every other element is zero.

If a matrix T is

$$T = \begin{Vmatrix} 3 & 1 \\ 1 & 2 \end{Vmatrix}$$

then its inverse is

$$T^{-1} = \begin{Vmatrix} .4 & -.2 \\ -.2 & .6 \end{Vmatrix}$$

for

$$T \times T^{-1} = \begin{Vmatrix} 3 & 1 \\ 1 & 2 \end{Vmatrix} \cdot \begin{Vmatrix} .4 & -.2 \\ -.2 & .6 \end{Vmatrix} = \begin{Vmatrix} 1 & 0 \\ 0 & 1 \end{Vmatrix} = I$$

The computation of the inverse of a general matrix is complex and, as a result, somewhat difficult to comprehend. We therefore approach the general concept in two stages. In the first, or special, case of a diagonal matrix the inverse is simple: the elements of the inverse of a diagonal matrix are the inverses of the diagonal elements. Thus if σ is the diagonal matrix of standard deviations

$$\sigma = \begin{Vmatrix} \sigma_1 & 0 \\ 0 & \sigma_2 \end{Vmatrix}$$

then the inverse of σ is

$$\sigma^{-1} = \begin{Vmatrix} \dfrac{1}{\sigma_1} & 0 \\[2ex] 0 & \dfrac{1}{\sigma_2} \end{Vmatrix}$$

We next review the special characteristics of multiplication of a matrix by a diagonal matrix. We note first that the order in which matrices are multiplied must be preserved: the matrix product AB generally is not equal to the same matrices multiplied in the order BA. In the following example, let

$$A = \begin{Vmatrix} 1 & 2 \\ 1 & 3 \end{Vmatrix} \qquad B = \begin{Vmatrix} 2 & 1 \\ 1 & 1 \end{Vmatrix}$$

The product

$$AB = \begin{Vmatrix} 4 & 3 \\ 5 & 4 \end{Vmatrix} \quad \text{is not equal to} \quad BA = \begin{Vmatrix} 3 & 7 \\ 2 & 5 \end{Vmatrix}$$

Because of this characteristic of matrix multiplication we say that the matrix A pre-multiplies the matrix B in the product AB, or that B post-multiplies the matrix A. In the product BA, B pre-multiplies A or is post-multiplied by A.

We can now state the rule describing multiplication by diagonal matrices. Post-multiplication by a diagonal matrix multiplies every element in each column of the matrix by the diagonal element in the corresponding column of the diagonal matrix. If the matrices are

$$A = \begin{Vmatrix} 1 & 2 \\ 3 & 4 \end{Vmatrix} \quad \text{and} \quad W = \begin{Vmatrix} w_1 & 0 \\ 0 & w_2 \end{Vmatrix}$$

the product

$$AW = \begin{Vmatrix} 1 & 2 \\ 3 & 4 \end{Vmatrix} \cdot \begin{Vmatrix} w_1 & 0 \\ 0 & w_2 \end{Vmatrix} = \begin{Vmatrix} 1w_1 & 2w_2 \\ 3w_1 & 4w_2 \end{Vmatrix}$$

The first diagonal element w_1 in W multiplies every element in the first column of A. The element w_2 multiplies the second column of A.

Pre-multiplication by a diagonal matrix multiplies the elements in each row of the matrix by the diagonal element in the corresponding row of the diagonal matrix.

The same matrices provide an example:

$$WA = \begin{Vmatrix} w_1 & 0 \\ 0 & w_2 \end{Vmatrix} \cdot \begin{Vmatrix} 1 & 2 \\ 3 & 4 \end{Vmatrix} = \begin{Vmatrix} 1w_1 & 2w_1 \\ 3w_2 & 4w_2 \end{Vmatrix}$$

With these rules in mind we define the matrix σ:

$$\sigma = \begin{Vmatrix} \sigma_1 & 0 \\ 0 & \sigma_2 \end{Vmatrix} \quad \text{and} \quad \sigma^{-1} = \begin{Vmatrix} \dfrac{1}{\sigma_1} & 0 \\ 0 & \dfrac{1}{\sigma_2} \end{Vmatrix}$$

Then the correlation matrix R may be obtained directly from the covariance matrix D by a combination of pre- and post-multiplication by σ^{-1}.

$$R = \sigma^{-1}D\sigma^{-1} = \begin{Vmatrix} \dfrac{1}{\sigma_1} & 0 \\ 0 & \dfrac{1}{\sigma_2} \end{Vmatrix} \cdot \begin{Vmatrix} \sigma_1^{\,2} & \sigma_1\sigma_2 r_{12} \\ \sigma_2\sigma_1 r_{21} & \sigma_2^{\,2} \end{Vmatrix} \cdot \begin{Vmatrix} \dfrac{1}{\sigma_1} & 0 \\ 0 & \dfrac{1}{\sigma_2} \end{Vmatrix}$$

$$= \begin{Vmatrix} \dfrac{\sigma_1^{\,2}}{\sigma_1} & \dfrac{\sigma_1\sigma_2 r_{12}}{\sigma_1} \\ \dfrac{\sigma_2\sigma_1 r_{21}}{\sigma_2} & \dfrac{\sigma_2^{\,2}}{\sigma_2} \end{Vmatrix} \cdot \begin{Vmatrix} \dfrac{1}{\sigma_1} & 0 \\ 0 & \dfrac{1}{\sigma_2} \end{Vmatrix}$$

$$= \begin{Vmatrix} \dfrac{\sigma_1^{\,2}}{\sigma_1\sigma_1} & \dfrac{\sigma_1\sigma_2 r_{12}}{\sigma_1\sigma_2} \\ \dfrac{\sigma_2\sigma_1 r_{21}}{\sigma_2\sigma_1} & \dfrac{\sigma_2^{\,2}}{\sigma_2\sigma_2} \end{Vmatrix}$$

$$= \begin{Vmatrix} 1 & r_{12} \\ r_{21} & 1 \end{Vmatrix}$$

We complete our study of matrix algebra by taking the second step in specifying the means of computing the inverse of a matrix. We have previously indicated that the inverse of a matrix T defined as

$$T = \begin{Vmatrix} 3 & 1 \\ 1 & 2 \end{Vmatrix}$$

is

$$T^{-1} = \begin{Vmatrix} .4 & -.2 \\ -.2 & .6 \end{Vmatrix}$$

How was T^{-1} computed?

In determining the inverse of a matrix it is necessary to compute a value in the inverse to correspond with each of the elements in the original matrix. Thus if we have the matrix

$$D = \begin{Vmatrix} d_{11} & d_{12} \\ d_{21} & d_{22} \end{Vmatrix}$$

there are four elements in the inverse D^{-1} which we shall designate as

$$D^{-1} = \begin{Vmatrix} d^{11} & d^{12} \\ d^{21} & d^{22} \end{Vmatrix}$$

The element d^{ij} standing in the ith row and jth column of D^{-1} is obtained as follows: (1) Compute the *cofactor* (described below) of the element d_{ji} of matrix D—note that the order of the subscripts i and j is reversed here; then (2) divide this cofactor by the value of the determinant of the original matrix D.

To compute the cofactor of d_{ji}, we delete the jth row and ith column of D and find the value of the determinant of the remaining submatrix. This determinant is called the *minor* associated with the element d_{ji}. (When the matrix to be inverted is of order 2×2, each minor is simply the single element remaining after deletion of the relevant row and column; but for larger matrices the minors will be *bona fide* determinants.) Next, we multiply the minor by $(-1)^{i+j}$ to get the required cofactor of d_{ji}. In other words, the minor is itself the cofactor when $i + j$ is even, but the sign of the minor must be changed to get the cofactor when $i + j$ is odd.

Although each cofactor is to be divided by the determinant of D, it is convenient first to arrange the cofactors themselves into a matrix (remembering to put the cofactor of d_{ji} in the ith row, jth column position—that is, the cofactors from a given *column* of the original matrix go in the corresponding *row* of the new matrix). The resulting matrix is called the *adjoint* (adj) of the original matrix.

Thus, for the matrix T referred to earlier, the adjoint is found to be

$$\begin{Vmatrix} 2 & -1 \\ -1 & 3 \end{Vmatrix} = \|\text{adj } T\|$$

The determinant of T is formed by computing the sum of the products of the elements in any row of T and the elements in the corresponding column of the adjoint of T. Thus

$$|T| = (3)(2) + (1)(-1) = 5$$

if we applied this rule to the first row of T and its adjoint or

$$|T| = (1)(-1) + (2)(3) = 5$$

if we used the second row of T and its adjoint. The $|T|$ is 5 in either instance.

We can now finally complete the computation of the inverse of T. The inverse of a matrix is computed by dividing the adjoint of the matrix by the scalar value of its determinant. Thus

$$T^{-1} = \begin{Vmatrix} \dfrac{2}{5} & \dfrac{-1}{5} \\[2mm] \dfrac{-1}{5} & \dfrac{3}{5} \end{Vmatrix} = \frac{\|\text{adj } T\|}{|T|}$$

It is clear then that T^{-1} is

$$\begin{Vmatrix} .4 & -.2 \\ -.2 & .6 \end{Vmatrix}$$

as we noted when we introduced the concept of the inverse of a matrix. We also indicated that $T \cdot T^{-1} = I$, the identity matrix.

The procedure we have described for the computation of the inverse of a matrix holds for matrices of 3, 4, or more rows and columns. For any square matrix which has an inverse, the latter may be computed by this procedure. Since the procedure involves a division by the value of the determinant of the matrix, it is obvious that only matrices with nonzero determinants have inverses. The computations of the inverse, however, become more difficult fairly rapidly as the size of the square matrix increases. Inverses of matrices are computed readily by electronic data-processing equipment.

The Matrix and the Normal Density Function

We are developing in this section a number of the fundamental relationships inherent in the normal density function. We have already discussed the normal distribution in one dimension and in two dimensions. Before interrupting that development in order to present several aspects of matrix notation we indicated that the ordinate y associated with the point (x_1, x_2) in the bivariate normal frequency surface is

$$y = \frac{1}{2\pi\sigma_1\sigma_2\sqrt{1-r^2}} \exp\left[-\frac{1}{2(1-r^2)} \left(\frac{x_1{}^2}{\sigma_1{}^2} - \frac{2rx_1x_2}{\sigma_1\sigma_2} + \frac{x_2{}^2}{\sigma_2{}^2} \right) \right]$$

It is evident from this equation that several parameters are necessary to specify the location and dispersion of this density function. These parameters are conveniently specified through matrix notation as we will now show by first indicating the algebraic form of the ordinates of equal height in the bivariate distribution of the test space. Such ordinates are called isodensity contours, as indicated in the discussion of Figs. 3.9 through 3.18.

The locus of a particular isodensity contour of any of those suggested in Fig. 3.18 is the set of points in the test space for which the ordinate y is some constant value. Inspection of the foregoing equation for y reveals that the variables $x_1 = (X_1 - \bar{X}_1)$ and $x_2 = (X_2 - \bar{X}_2)$ appear only in the exponent: the other terms in the equation are constants for the particular instance considered. The ordinates y will be equal to some constant number for all values of x_1 and x_2 which make the exponent equal to a constant number. We may therefore write an equation for the iso-density contour, in general. The locus of equal ordinates (or equal density) will be all the points x_1, x_2 for which -2 times the expression in the exponent of y, that is,

$$\frac{1}{1 - r^2}\left(\frac{x_1^2}{\sigma_1^2} - \frac{2rx_1x_2}{\sigma_1\sigma_2} + \frac{x_2^2}{\sigma_2^2}\right) = \chi^2 = \text{constant}$$

We use the symbol χ^2 to denote the constant number for reasons of mnemonic association that will become apparent.

For a fixed value of χ^2, the equation describes an ellipse. We note that x/σ is a standard score and may be conventionally denoted by z. In standard score notation the equation is

$$\frac{1}{1 - r^2}(z_1^2 - 2rz_1z_2 + z_2^2) = \chi^2 \cdot$$

When $r = 0$ the equation describes a circle of radius χ. When $\sigma_1 \neq \sigma_2$ and $r = 0$ the equation

$$\frac{x_1^2}{\sigma_1^2} + \frac{x_2^2}{\sigma_2^2} = \chi^2$$

describes concentric ellipses, one for each value chosen for the constant χ. For convenience a particular ellipse may be chosen to represent the group. If we choose the ellipse defined by $\chi^2 = 1.0$, the equation is written in standard form and the semiaxes for the ellipse are σ_1 and σ_2.

For any chosen value of χ^2 in the general equation for -2 times the value of the exponent of the bivariate frequency surface we may ascertain the deviation score values x_1 and x_2 that lie on the χ^2 contour. Or conversely, for any values x_1, x_2, we may compute the value of χ^2 that defines the contour of which x_1, x_2 is one point. We shall now consider the matrix representation of χ^2.

In the bivariate case two values $\bar{X}_1$ and $\bar{X}_2$ are required to locate the centroid of the distribution of points. The centroid of the group of points is simply written as

$$\bar{X} = \|\bar{X}_1 \quad \bar{X}_2\|$$

The description of the dispersion requires three statistics, σ_1^2, σ_2^2, and r_{12}. Complete specification of the bivariate normal distribution requires the statistics of both of the marginal distributions and one additional statistic

r which describes the relation between the two variables. In the matrix notation the dispersion statistics are conveniently written in the matrix D:

$$D = \begin{Vmatrix} \sigma_1{}^2 & \sigma_1\sigma_2 r \\ \sigma_2\sigma_1 r & \sigma_2{}^2 \end{Vmatrix}$$

The adjoint of D is

$$\begin{Vmatrix} \sigma_2{}^2 & -\sigma_2\sigma_1 r \\ -\sigma_1\sigma_2 r & \sigma_1{}^2 \end{Vmatrix}$$

We may form the row vector x of deviation scores x_1, x_2 for a particular pair of raw scores X_1, X_2 as

$$\|(X_1 - \bar{X}_1) \quad (X_2 - \bar{X}_2)\|$$

The matrix product $x \cdot \text{adj } D \cdot x'$ then has the value

$$\sigma_2{}^2 x_1{}^2 - 2\sigma_1\sigma_2 r x_1 x_2 + \sigma_1{}^2 x_2{}^2$$

The determinant of the dispersion matrix is

$$|D| = \sigma_1{}^2 \sigma_2{}^2 - \sigma_1{}^2 \sigma_2{}^2 r^2 = \sigma_1{}^2 \sigma_2{}^2 (1 - r^2)$$

When we divide $x \cdot \text{adj } D \cdot x'$ by $|D|$, we get

$$\frac{1}{1 - r^2} \left(\frac{x_1{}^2}{\sigma_1{}^2} - \frac{2r x_1 x_2}{\sigma_1 \sigma_2} + \frac{x_2{}^2}{\sigma_2{}^2} \right)$$

This is identical to the value of -2 times the exponent of the bivariate normal density function which has the constant value χ^2 for all the points on an isodensity contour.

We have now demonstrated that

$$x \cdot \text{adj } D \cdot x' = \chi^2 |D|$$

or more simply

$$x \cdot D^{-1} \cdot x' = \chi^2$$

If we note that

$$|D|^{\frac{1}{2}} = \sigma_1 \sigma_2 \sqrt{1 - r^2}$$

we are now in a position to indicate the simplicity in the representation of the ordinate of the bivariate normal distribution in matrix form. We may state that the ordinate y has the form

$$y = \frac{1}{2\pi |D|^{\frac{1}{2}}} \exp \left(-\frac{x D^{-1} x'}{2} \right)$$

A simpler form is

$$y = \frac{1}{2\pi |D|^{\frac{1}{2}}} \exp \left(-\frac{\chi^2}{2} \right)$$

since $\chi^2 = x D^{-1} x'$. This notation is valuable because we have now specified the equation of the normal density function in a manner which is readily generalized to 3, 4, or any number of variables. If the value χ^2 is computed by $xD^{-1}x'$ with x being a row vector of deviation scores for any number of tests T, and with D being the $T \times T$ dispersion matrix for the T tests, then the density of the normal distribution at the point $x_1, x_2, \ldots, x_T$ is

$$y = \frac{1}{(2\pi)^{T/2}|D|^{1/2}} \exp\left(-\frac{\chi^2}{2}\right)$$

Thus, for the normal multivariate frequency surface, the information about the location and dispersion of a particular distribution of scores is carried in the row vector $\bar{X}$ of means for the tests and in the dispersion matrix D.

χ^2 and the Isodensity Contour

The proportion of the bivariate normal distribution which lies outside the isodensity ellipse defined by a fixed value of χ^2 may be determined from the probability table of χ^2. The table gives the value of χ^2 associated with the argument P, the probability of a divergence greater than χ^2 for various degrees of freedom. Each point in the test space is a vector from the centroid. Its divergence from the centroid is measured by the value of χ^2 associated with the isodensity ellipse on which the point lies. Every point outside is characterized by a larger value of χ^2. For a particular value of χ^2 the probability of a greater value P is the proportion of the total distribution which lies outside the χ^2 ellipse in the test space. In a univariate distribution the number of degrees of freedom is one. In the bivariate distribution the test space has dimensionality two and the choice of any point enjoys two degrees of freedom. In the bivariate distribution the value P corresponding to χ^2 is found by entering the table of χ^2 with two degrees of freedom. If interpolation in the table does not yield sufficient accuracy, a more precise result may be computed from Pearson's Table IX in *Tables for Statisticians and Biometricians*, Vol. One (1924).

χ^2 and the Rotation of Axes

We have previously noted that, when $\sigma_1 \neq \sigma_2$ but $r = 0$, the equation

$$\frac{x_1^2}{\sigma_1^2} + \frac{x_2^2}{\sigma_2^2} = \chi^2$$

describes concentric ellipses, one for each value chosen for the constant χ. We do not usually deal with data in which the correlation is zero, and therefore the locus of the isodensity contours is not usually expressed in the simple standard form. The major axis of the ellipses will be oriented at some angle to the axes that define the test space. The dispersion matrix contains all the information required to find the angle. The angle θ illustrated in Fig. 3.19 is found from the equation

$$\tan 2\theta = \frac{2\sigma_1\sigma_2 r}{\sigma_1^2 - \sigma_2^2}$$

The problem of the rotation of axes suggested by the introduction of the angle θ which orients the ellipse in the test space is treated in more detail in Chapter 7 and Appendix A. We note here that (1) the sign of the correlation coefficient identifies the quadrants in which the major axis lies, (2) the angle θ is 45° when $\sigma_1 = \sigma_2$, and (3) the value of χ^2 remains the same (is invariant) as the axes are rotated. The first two points are obvious from the equation for the value of θ in the rotation of axes. The last point should be clear from consideration of figures such as Fig. 3.19 and from the equation for χ^2.

Suppose the X_1 axis in Fig. 3.19 did become coincidental with the designated dotted line after it was rotated through the angle θ. We could (1) think of the ellipse as fixed in the plane and rotated with the plane as

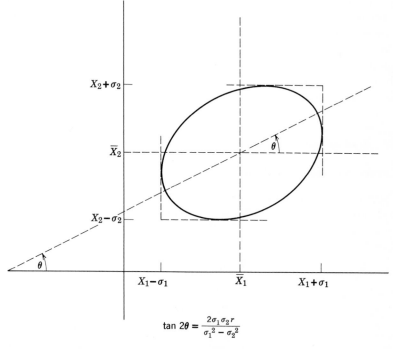

$$\tan 2\theta = \frac{2\sigma_1\sigma_2 r}{\sigma_1^2 - \sigma_2^2}$$

Fig. 3.19   *The orientation of an ellipse in the test space.*

the axis X_1 (and the axis X_2 because it is in the same plane being rotated) assumes the location designated by the dotted line at the end of angle θ, or (2) think of the ellipse as remaining stationary. In the first instance, it is clear that the shape of the ellipse is not changed by the rotation of the plane. In the second instance, the shape of the ellipse is unchanged if we are able to develop a system for making a one to one transformation of the coordinates of each point on the ellipse in terms of original axes into its coordinates in terms of the rotated axes. If such a transformation is an orthogonal one, that is, if both the X_1 and X_2 axes are presumed to be rotated so that they maintain themselves with a 90° angle between them, then the shape of the ellipse is unchanged by the rotation of axes. This instance is similar to the ellipse being stationary and the plane rotating beneath it.

The value of the angle θ in the orthogonal rotation of axes depends upon σ_1, σ_2, and r. These are the same values which specify the dispersion of a matrix and determine χ^2 for every point for which the row vector of deviation scores is available. This correspondence means that the values of σ_1, σ_2, and r have already entered into the determination of χ^2 in terms of the original scores and therefore do not affect the value of χ^2 computed for any other set of coordinates obtained after an orthogonal rotation of the original axes. This point is developed more fully in Appendix A. Here we merely stress that the values of χ^2 as computed by the matrix product $x \cdot D^{-1} \cdot x'$ do not change under orthogonal rotation of the original axes or under any linear rescaling of the original scores. Such rescaling could relocate scores or give them a different variability. It does not modify the densities associated with each original point, however.

The Bivariate Matrix of the Group of Apprentices

Centroid and Dispersion of the Group

Now that we have introduced the concept of the centour score for two dimensions, let us see how it may be applied to the scores for a single group. The 135 pairs of scores for the group of apprentices are written in the matrix X:

$$X = \begin{Vmatrix} 21 & 16 \\ 21 & 17 \\ 27 & 20 \\ \vdots & \vdots \\ 21 & 18 \end{Vmatrix} \quad \text{(135 rows)}$$

The cross-products matrix $X'X$ is

$$X'X = \begin{Vmatrix} \text{(135 columns)} \\ 21 & 21 & 27 & \cdots & 21 \\ 16 & 17 & 20 & \cdots & 18 \end{Vmatrix} \cdot \begin{Vmatrix} 21 & 16 \\ 21 & 17 \\ 27 & 20 \\ \vdots & \vdots \\ 21 & 18 \end{Vmatrix} \quad \text{(135 rows)}$$

$$= \begin{Vmatrix} \sum X_1{}^2 & \sum X_1 X_2 \\ \sum X_2 X_1 & \sum X_2{}^2 \end{Vmatrix} = \begin{Vmatrix} 43,480 & 46,027 \\ 46,027 & 55,202 \end{Vmatrix}$$

The element in the upper left-hand corner of the matrix is $\sum X_1{}^2 = 21^2 + 21^2 + 27^2 + \cdots + 21^2 = 43,480$. It is the sum of squares for the 135 outdoor scores in the first column of X. The sum of squares in the lower right-hand corner is computed from the 135 convivial scores in the second column of X. The cross-product sums in the off-diagonal cells are computed by multiplying each pair of scores in the 135 rows of X and adding the products, namely, $21(16) + 21(17) + 27(20) + \cdots + 21(18) = 46,027 = \sum X_1 X_2$. These computations are easily made from the roster of scores in Table 3.1.

The mean of the outdoor scores is $\bar{X}_1 = 17.4370$, and the mean of the convivial scores is $\bar{X}_2 = 19.7481$. The $\bar{X}'\bar{X}$ matrix is written

$$\bar{X}'\bar{X} = \begin{Vmatrix} n\bar{X}_1{}^2 & n\bar{X}_1\bar{X}_2 \\ n\bar{X}_2\bar{X}_1 & n\bar{X}_2{}^2 \end{Vmatrix}$$

and computed

$$\bar{X}'\bar{X} = \begin{Vmatrix} 135(17.4370)^2 & 135(17.4370)(19.7481) \\ 135(19.7481)(17.4370) & 135(19.7481)^2 \end{Vmatrix}$$

$$= \begin{Vmatrix} 41,046.6112 & 46,486.9287 \\ 46,486.9287 & 52,648.3063 \end{Vmatrix}$$

By subtracting $\bar{X}'\bar{X}$ from $X'X$ the cross-product matrix of deviation scores is

$$X'X - \bar{X}'\bar{X} = \begin{Vmatrix} 43,480 & 46,027 \\ 46,027 & 55,202 \end{Vmatrix} - \begin{Vmatrix} 41,046.6112 & 46,486.9287 \\ 46,486.9287 & 52,648.3063 \end{Vmatrix}$$

$$= \begin{Vmatrix} 2433.3888 & -459.9287 \\ -459.9287 & 2553.6937 \end{Vmatrix}$$

The use of lower-case letters to denote matrices has been found to be unsatisfactory because these symbols are frequently confused with scalar quantities. We therefore abandon the use of $x'x$ to denote the matrix of the sum of squares and cross products of deviation scores. Hereafter the matrix will be denoted by $S = X'X - \bar{X}'\bar{X}$. In the two-variable example the elements of the matrix S will be

$$S = \begin{Vmatrix} \sum x_1^2 & \sum x_1 x_2 \\ \sum x_2 x_1 & \sum x_2^2 \end{Vmatrix}$$

The dispersion matrix D is computed from the matrix S by dividing every element of S by the number of individuals in the group n:

$$D = \frac{1}{n} S$$

In the group of apprentices, $n = 135$ and the dispersion matrix is

$$D = \begin{Vmatrix} 18.0251 & -3.4069 \\ -3.4069 & 18.9162 \end{Vmatrix}$$

The variance of the outdoor scores is $\sigma_1^2 = 18.0251$. The standard deviation is $\sigma_1 = 4.2456$. For the distribution of convivial scores the dispersion matrix values are $\sigma_2^2 = 18.9162$, and $\sigma_2 = 4.3493$.

The reciprocals $1/\sigma_1$ of the standard deviations may be written in the diagonal matrix σ^{-1} and used to calculate the correlation matrix R:

$$R = \sigma^{-1} D \sigma^{-1} = \begin{Vmatrix} 1 & -.1845 \\ -.1845 & 1 \end{Vmatrix}$$

The R matrix can be obtained directly from the S matrix without computing the standard deviations. A diagonal matrix U, the elements of which are computed from the diagonal elements of S, is defined as

$$U = \begin{Vmatrix} \sqrt{n\sigma_1^2} & 0 \\ 0 & \sqrt{n\sigma_2^2} \end{Vmatrix} = \begin{Vmatrix} \sqrt{\sum x_1^2} & 0 \\ 0 & \sqrt{\sum x_2^2} \end{Vmatrix}$$

then

$$R = U^{-1} S U^{-1}$$

This equation is the matrix equivalent of the formula for the correlation coefficient:

$$r_{12} = \frac{\sum x_1 x_2}{\sqrt{\sum x_1^2}\sqrt{\sum x_2^2}}$$

We have now completed the matrix formulation of the bivariate distribution of the outdoor and convivial scores for the apprentices from New York City. The usual descriptive statistics are

	Outdoor X_1	Convivial X_2
N	135	135
Mean	17.44	19.75
SD	4.25	4.35
Correlation	$r_{12} = -0.18$	

The scatter diagram representing these data is illustrated in Fig. 3.7. An isometric representation of the bivariate distribution is shown in Fig. 3.20.

The statistics of a sample provide all the data required to describe the characteristics of a normal bivariate population. When the marginal distributions of X_1 and X_2 in a sample are each reasonably well described by normal distributions with means and standard deviations chosen to fit the sample, the exact mathematical properties of the ideal model provide reasonable descriptions of the characteristics of the particular sample. When the statistics of a sample can be accepted as sufficiently good

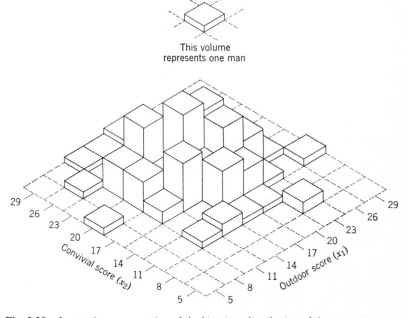

Fig. 3.20 *Isometric representation of the bivariate distribution of the apprentices.*

estimates of the parameters of the population, the exact mathematical properties of the ideal normal model determined by the sample estimates provide reasonable descriptions of the characteristics of the population. We used these ideas in deciding upon a method of computing centours for the single-variate example (see Chapter 2). In the following sections we suggest the same ideas to extend the logic to the calculation of centour equivalents in the two-variate example. We suggest you examine Appendix A from time to time, however, in order to remind yourself of the errors which are present in centour scores because of potential inaccuracy in the estimates provided by the sample, and because the distribution of scores may not be bivariate normal.

Quartile Ellipses for the Group

In our study of the outdoor and convivial activity preferences of the group of apprentices, we reached the point where it was necessary to understand the geometry and algebra of the ellipse in order to apply the concept of centour score used in our study of only the outdoor activity preferences. Our study of the ellipse has associated the dispersion matrix D with the equifrequency ellipses in a normal bivariate surface. We now return to the outdoor and convivial activity preferences for the apprentices and apply our development to these data.

We have already determined that the dispersion matrix for the group is

$$D = \begin{Vmatrix} 18.0251 & -3.4069 \\ -3.4069 & 18.9162 \end{Vmatrix}$$

Therefore, $|D| = 329.3605$, and the adjoint of D is

$$\text{adj } D = \begin{Vmatrix} 18.9162 & 3.4069 \\ 3.4069 & 18.0251 \end{Vmatrix}$$

Thus, for the group data, the equation of the isofrequency ellipses

$$xD^{-1}x' = \chi^2$$

takes the numerical values

$$x \cdot \begin{Vmatrix} .057433 & .010344 \\ .010344 & .054728 \end{Vmatrix} \cdot x' = \chi^2$$

The values of χ^2 exceeded by 25, 50, and 75% of a normal distribution were used to define the three quartile ellipses of the group. The three quartile ellipses are plotted in Fig. 3.21 which is a copy of the basic data provided for Fig. 3.7. Seventy points (52%) lie outside the 50th centour ellipse.

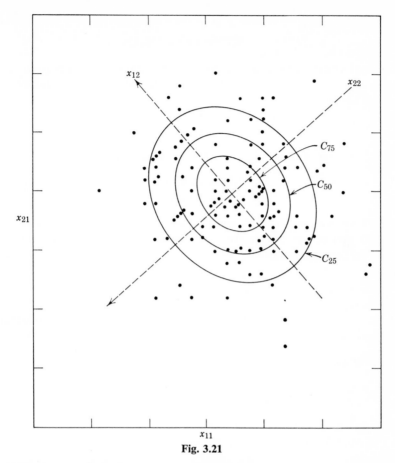

x_{12}

x_{22}

C_{75}

C_{50}

x_{21}

C_{25}

x_{11}

Fig. 3.21

Centours for Advising on Personnel Classification

We now have a framework for interpreting the distance of the point representing the outdoor and convivial activity preferences of any apprentice from the point representing the mean number of outdoor and the mean number of convivial activity preferences of the group. When a normal bivariate distribution of outdoor and convivial activity preferences is assumed for the group, any point representing the preference for both outdoor and convivial activities of any apprentice lies on a particular one of the infinite set of homothetic ellipses possible under this assumption. When the parameters of the set of homothetic ellipses are taken as those of the group, the ellipses are described by the equation

$$x \cdot \begin{Vmatrix} .057433 & .010344 \\ .010344 & .054728 \end{Vmatrix} \cdot x' = \chi^2$$

which is the same as

$$.057433x_1{}^2 + .020688x_1x_2 + .054728x_2{}^2 = \chi^2$$

This is an equation in x_1 and x_2 from which it is possible to determine the value of χ^2 for any set of x_1 and x_2 scores. In the foregoing equation, x_1 and x_2 are given by

$$x_1 = X_1 - \bar{X}_1$$
$$x_2 = X_2 - \bar{X}_2$$

For the data of the group the values of $\bar{X}_1$ and $\bar{X}_2$ are

$$\bar{X}_1 = 17.4370$$
$$\bar{X}_2 = 19.7481$$

We may now compute the centour score for the outdoor and convivial activity preferences of Joe Armand. Joe preferred 22 outdoor and 22 convivial activity preferences. For Joe:

$$x_1 = 22 - 17.4370 = 4.5630$$
$$x_2 = 22 - 19.7481 = 2.2519$$

so that the value of χ^2 for the ellipse on which the point for his outdoor and convivial activity preferences falls is determined from

$$.057433(4.5630)^2 + .020688(4.5630)(2.2519) + .054773(2.2519)^2 = \chi^2$$

This is equal to

$$1.195817 + .212576 + .277527 = \chi^2$$

so that χ^2 is 1.685920 and χ is 1.2984.

Pearson's Table (1924) gives the value of $m_1(\chi)$ for values of χ of 1.2 and 1.3 as

χ	$m_1(\chi)$
1.2	.2047562
1.3	.2275737

Linear interpolation for the χ value associated with Joe Armand's score point gives

$$m_1(1.2984) = .2272086$$

Linear interpolation is employed in this instance because only two significant digits are used for recording centour scores. The value of q is then

$$q = \sqrt{2\pi}m_1(1.2984)$$
$$= 2.5066283 \cdot .2272086$$
$$= .5695$$

and p is

$$p = 1 - .5695 = .4305$$

so that C is

$$C = 100(.4305) = 43 \text{ to two significant figures}$$

Thus Joe Armand's preferences for outdoor and convivial activities lie on an equifrequency ellipse outside of which are the outdoor and convivial activity preferences of about 43% of his fellow apprentices. Many apprentices have both preferences more divergent from the mean numbers of the group's preferences than are Joe's. Joe's preferences are fairly typical of the group.

We now know how to determine centour scores for any pair of outdoor and convivial activity preferences. The determination is not difficult with a calculating machine. However, calculation on the spot is inconvenient and frequently not possible. Therefore, it is best to calculate centour scores for all pairs of scores and to have a table of centour scores available for reference as needed. Such a table of centour scores for every pair of outdoor-convivial activity preferences is Table 3.3.

Joe Armand's preference for 22 outdoor and 22 convivial activities may now be converted to a centour score from this table. Enter the column of "22 outdoor activity preferences" and proceed down this column until it intersects the row of "22 convivial activity preferences." At this inter-section is the number 43, which is the same as the centour number we had computed previously. Bill Flint preferred 20 outdoor and 15 convivial activities. Enter the column of "20 outdoor activity preferences" and proceed down it until it intersects the row of "15 convivial activity preferences." The number at this intersection is 51. Bill's scores are also fairly typical. Thus a table of centour scores provides a ready means for determining the percent of a group that exceeds any given pair of outdoor and convivial activity preferences, provided that the distribution of out-door and convivial activity preferences is reasonably normal, as it is in this instance.

Use of the concept of the centour score requires these answers to the profile problems considered.

Profile Problem 1. On what type of scale should profiles be represented? Answer: On a scale that distributes the scores in each variate approxi-mately normally.

Profile Problem 3. How may the joint performance of all individuals be represented? Answer: By a plane with orthogonal reference axes.

From such representation it is possible to determine the centour ellipses upon which all points in the plane lie.

Table 3.3 Table of Centour Equivalents—Apprentices

	Outdoor																							
Convivial	6	7	8	9	10	11	12	13	14	15	16	17	18	19	20	21	22	23	24	25	26	27	28	29
30	*	01	01	02	03	03	04	05	06	06	06	06	05	04	04	03	02	01	01	*	*	*	*	*
29	01	01	02	03	04	05	07	08	10	10	10	10	09	08	06	05	03	02	01	01	01	*	*	*
28	01	02	03	04	06	08	11	13	15	16	17	16	15	13	10	08	06	04	03	02	01	01	*	*
27	01	02	04	06	08	12	15	19	22	24	25	24	23	20	16	13	09	06	04	03	02	01	01	*
26	02	03	05	08	11	16	21	26	31	34	35	35	33	29	24	19	14	10	07	04	02	01	01	01
25	02	04	06	10	14	20	27	34	40	45	48	48	45	40	34	27	20	14	10	06	04	02	01	01
24	02	04	07	11	17	25	33	42	51	57	61	62	59	53	45	36	27	20	13	08	05	03	02	01
23	03	05	08	13	20	28	38	49	60	69	74	76	73	66	57	46	35	26	17	11	07	04	02	01
22	03	05	08	14	21	31	42	55	67	78	85	87	85	78	68	56	43	31	22	14	09	05	03	01
21	03	05	08	14	22	32	44	58	71	83	92	96	94	88	77	64	50	37	26	17	10	06	03	02
20	02	04	08	13	21	31	43	57	72	85	94	99	99	93	82	69	54	40	28	19	12	07	04	02
19	02	04	07	12	19	29	40	54	68	81	92	98	98	93	83	70	56	42	30	20	13	08	04	02
18	02	03	06	10	16	25	36	48	62	74	84	91	92	88	80	68	55	42	30	20	13	08	05	02
17	01	03	05	08	13	21	30	41	53	64	74	80	82	79	72	62	51	39	28	20	13	08	04	02
16	01	02	04	06	10	16	24	33	42	52	61	67	69	67	62	54	45	35	25	18	12	07	04	02
15	01	01	03	05	08	12	18	25	32	40	47	53	55	54	51	45	37	29	22	15	10	06	04	02
14	*	01	02	03	05	08	13	18	24	30	35	39	41	41	39	35	29	23	17	12	08	05	03	02
13	*	01	01	02	03	06	08	12	16	20	25	28	30	30	28	26	22	17	13	09	06	04	02	01
12	*	*	01	01	02	04	05	08	10	13	16	19	20	20	20	18	15	12	10	07	05	03	02	01
11	*	*	*	*	01	02	03	05	06	08	10	12	13	13	13	12	10	08	06	05	03	02	01	01
10	*	*	*	01	01	01	02	03	04	05	06	07	08	08	08	07	06	05	04	03	02	01	01	01
9	*	*	*	*	*	01	01	01	02	03	03	04	04	05	05	04	04	03	03	02	01	01	01	*
8	*	*	*	*	*	*	01	01	01	01	02	02	02	03	03	02	02	02	01	01	01	01	*	*
7	*	*	*	*	*	*	*	*	01	01	01	01	01	01	01	01	01	01	01	01	*	*	*	*

* Centour <.5

Passenger Agents and Mechanics

Comparison with Two Groups of Employees

We have seen that the outdoor and convivial activity preferences of an apprentice such as Joe Armand can be compared with the preferences for similar activities expressed by other apprentices tested with Joe. The preferences of 43% of these apprentices were more divergent from the centroid of the group than were Joe's.

Suppose that the satisfied and satisfactory employees of World Airlines who are now either passenger agents (85 in number) or mechanics (93) had recorded their preferences for convivial activities as well as outdoor activities when they were tested upon application for apprentice training. The rosters of their outdoor and convivial scores on the Activity Preference Inventory are given in columns 2 and 3 of each panel of Tables B.1 and B.2. These rosters may be represented as matrices X_1 and X_2, where the subscripts 1, 2 identify the two groups:

$$
X_1 = \begin{Vmatrix} 10 & 22 \\ 14 & 17 \\ 19 & 33 \\ \vdots & \vdots \\ 16 & 24 \end{Vmatrix} \quad \text{and} \quad X_2 = \begin{Vmatrix} 20 & 27 \\ 21 & 15 \\ 15 & 27 \\ \vdots & \vdots \\ 19 & 16 \end{Vmatrix}
$$
$$
\text{(85 rows)} \qquad\qquad \text{(93 rows)}
$$

Profile Representation

We have shown in Fig. 3.6 that a confused impression results when the profiles of 135 apprentices are simultaneously represented on even two profile stalks. In general it is not efficient to represent information on profile stalks. One further difficulty with profile representation will be noted in the case of two groups.

The profiles of two groups are sometimes represented as job psychographs, such as the ones for passenger agents and mechanics which are given in Fig. 3.22. The 22 outdoor and 22 convivial preferences of Joe Armand are also noted as the single profile recorded on each of the job psychographs in that figure. Joe's convivial score seems typical of both passenger agents and mechanics. His outdoor score exceeds the outdoor scores of a greater proportion of agents than mechanics, however. How typical of the scores of passenger agents do Joe's outdoor and convivial scores appear to be when they are considered together?

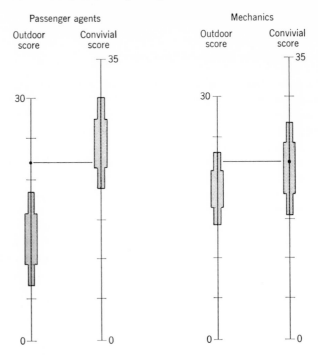

Fig. 3.22   *Profile representation of job psychographs—two groups.*

Representation of the Job Psychograph in the Cartesian Test Space

Consider the possible representation of the percentile demarcations of the job psychograph in the Cartesian test space. One way to represent them is shown in Figs. 3.23 and 3.24. Such figures are constructed by simply connecting equivalent percentile projections from each axis. The point representing the outdoor and convivial activity preferences of Joe Armand is also indicated in these figures. The connected projections of the univariate centours form rectangles in the Cartesian test space. In terms of these rectangles, Joe's outdoor and convivial activity preferences suggest that he prefers a number of activities which seem typical of those who became mechanics but not typical of those who became passenger agents. This result was not apparent in the job psychograph at the left of Fig. 3.22. Is the profile psychograph therefore a good means of interpreting the joint scores of an apprentice on the two sections of the Activity Preference Inventory? Actually the profile psychograph has the drawback of failing to represent the loci of points of equal frequency in the bivariate space. The centour score represents isofrequency points but the profile psychograph does not.

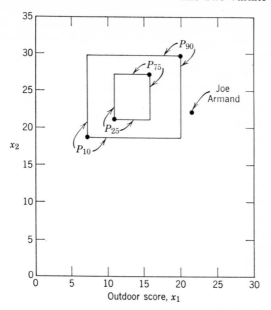

Fig. 3.23 *Profile psychograph regions in the Cartesian test space—passenger agent.*

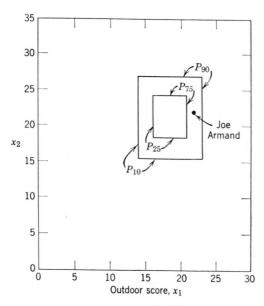

Fig. 3.24 *Profile psychograph regions in the Cartesian test space—mechanic.*

The job psychograph for agents in Fig. 3.22 gives the 10th and 90th percentile points for each type of score. We have already noted in Chapter 2 that in the normal univariate distribution these two percentile points are equivalent to the 20th centour for outdoor activity preferences. The same would be true of those two percentile points for the univariate distribution of convivial activity preferences. Are the percentile demarcations of the job psychograph plotted in two or more dimensions similar to the concept of the centour score as a result? We will explain why they are not.

The 20th and 50th centour ellipses for both passenger agents and mechanics have been constructed in Fig. 3.25. These are two of the ellipses which indicate for a group the points in a bivariate normal distribution which occur with equal frequency when the centroid and dispersion matrix of the group have the values which were computed from the sample.

The inadequacy of the profile psychograph can be seen by comparing the rectangles in Figs. 3.23 and 3.24 with the form of the actual centour locations in Fig. 3.25. The profile psychograph represents rectangles rather

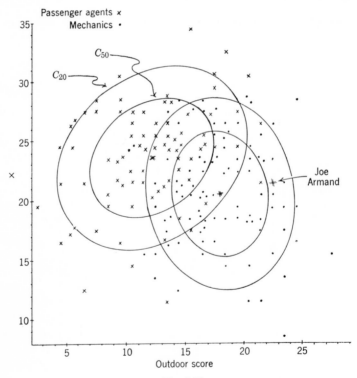

Fig. 3.25

than the ellipses which are expected for two variates. This can have a considerable influence on the interpretation of some of the points representing the scores of employees. For instance, the scores for Joe Armand give the impression of being relatively close to those for passenger agents in Fig. 3.23. The impression of proximity to the scores for passenger agents is modified by Fig. 3.25, however. In Fig. 3.25, it is apparent that Joe's scores are in a region in which the test scores for passenger agents are becoming relatively infrequent.

There is little to recommend the profile as a means of representing information about the probability of group membership. The profile mode of presentation does not record the full facts of simultaneous scores on more than one test. The failure to carry full information in the representation of psychological data has the effect which we have just seen in our discussion of the profile psychograph as a possible substitute for the centour psychograph. The profile psychograph fails to represent the information about the density distribution in an appropriate form.

Centour Score Table

We have already represented the outdoor and convivial activity preferences of the passenger agents and mechanics in the Cartesian test space of Fig. 3.25. We have also used the procedure given in Appendix A to determine and construct the 20th and 50th centour ellipses for each group of employees. We also indicated the 22 outdoor and 22 convivial activity preferences of Joe Armand in Fig. 3.25. The figure suggested that Joe had a centour score less than 20 in relation to apprentices who became agents and a centour less than 50 but greater than 20 in relation to apprentices who became mechanics. We will sketch the computations needed for the construction of a centour table for these two groups in order to provide a means of getting a more definite indication of how similar the activity preferences of an apprentice may be to those of earlier apprentices who fulfilled either job in a satisfying and satisfactory manner. In recording these computations we will, of course, record most of the statistics required for the construction of Fig. 3.25.

The 85 pairs of scores for the group of passenger agents has already been recorded as the matrix X_1. The cross-product matrix $X'X$ for group 1 is

$$
\begin{Vmatrix} 10 & 14 & 19 & \ldots & 16 \\ 22 & 17 & 33 & \ldots & 24 \end{Vmatrix} \cdot \begin{Vmatrix} 10 & 22 \\ 14 & 17 \\ 19 & 33 \\ \vdots & \vdots \\ 16 & 24 \end{Vmatrix}
$$

(85 columns) above left matrix; (85 rows) beside right matrix

and

$$X'X = \begin{Vmatrix} \sum X_1{}^2 & \sum X_1 X_2 \\ \sum X_2 X_1 & \sum X_2{}^2 \end{Vmatrix} = \begin{Vmatrix} 15,170 & 26,307 \\ 26,307 & 51,455 \end{Vmatrix}$$

The mean of the outdoor scores is $\bar{X}_1 = 12.5882$, and the mean of the convivial scores is $\bar{X}_2 = 24.2235$. The $\bar{X}'\bar{X}$ matrix is written

$$\bar{X}'\bar{X} = \begin{Vmatrix} n\bar{X}_1{}^2 & n\bar{X}_1\bar{X}_2 \\ n\bar{X}_2\bar{X}_1 & n\bar{X}_2{}^2 \end{Vmatrix}$$

and computed

$$\bar{X}'\bar{X} = \begin{Vmatrix} 85(12.5882)^2 & 85(12.5882)(24.2235) \\ 85(24.2235)(12.5882) & 85(24.2235)^2 \end{Vmatrix}$$

$$= \begin{Vmatrix} 13,469.3362 & 25,919.0723 \\ 25,919.0723 & 49,876.1259 \end{Vmatrix}$$

By subtracting $\bar{X}'\bar{X}$ from $X'X$ the cross-product matrix S of deviation scores is found to be

$$S = X'X - \bar{X}'\bar{X} = \begin{Vmatrix} 15,170 & 26,307 \\ 26,307 & 51,455 \end{Vmatrix} - \begin{Vmatrix} 13,469.3362 & 25,919.0723 \\ 25,919.0723 & 49,876.1259 \end{Vmatrix}$$

$$= \begin{Vmatrix} 1700.5882 & 387.8235 \\ 387.8235 & 1578.7529 \end{Vmatrix}$$

The dispersion matrix $D = (1/n)S$ is

$$\begin{Vmatrix} 20.0069 & 4.5626 \\ 4.5626 & 18.5736 \end{Vmatrix}$$

The inverse of the matrix D is then

$$D^{-1} = \begin{Vmatrix} .052949 & -.013007 \\ -.013007 & .057035 \end{Vmatrix}$$

Centour scores may be computed for any particular value of raw scores X_1 and X_2 by forming the row vector of deviation scores

$$x = \begin{Vmatrix} (X_1 - \bar{X}_1) & (X_2 - \bar{X}_2) \end{Vmatrix}$$

and evaluating the matrix product $x_1 D_1{}^{-1} x'_1 = \chi_1{}^2$ for any desired pair of scores. The subscript 1 has been added to the row vector of deviation scores, the inverse of D, and χ^2 as a reminder that these values apply to the first group, the passenger agents. Table IX of Pearson's Tables (1924) provides a means of ascertaining the value $q_1 = \sqrt{2\pi}m_1(\chi_1)$ for the value of χ_1 which is obtained for a particular pair of raw scores X_1, X_2. The centour score for this pair of scores is then obtained by the expression

$$C_1 = 100(1 - q_1)$$

The centour scores for passenger agents are given in Table 3.4 for a number of pairs of outdoor and convivial activity preferences of apprentices.

Joe Armand preferred 22 outdoor and 22 convivial activities. His centour score for passenger agent is 06. This is less than the centour 20, which was expected because of the location of Joe's scores in Fig. 3.25. The centour suggests that Joe's preference for outdoor and convivial activities is not very typical of apprentices who later become satisfied and satisfactory passenger agents.

In our calculations so far, we have not considered the X_2 matrix for the 93 mechanics. We may therefore turn to that matrix without concern for its influence on our previous calculations for passenger agents.

The X_2 matrix has already been noted. The mean $\overline{X}_2$ of outdoor activities for mechanics is 18.5376. The mean of the convivial activity preferences of mechanics is 21.1398. Therefore the S matrix is

$$S = X'X - \overline{X}'\overline{X} = \begin{Vmatrix} 33{,}128 & 36{,}300 \\ 36{,}300 & 43{,}466 \end{Vmatrix} - \begin{Vmatrix} 31{,}958.7631 & 36{,}444.9476 \\ 36{,}444.9476 & 41{,}560.8764 \end{Vmatrix}$$

and the dispersion matrix D which is $(1/93)S$ is

$$D = \begin{Vmatrix} 12.5712 & -1.5590 \\ -1.5590 & 20.4858 \end{Vmatrix}$$

The inverse of D is

$$D^{-1} = \begin{Vmatrix} .080305 & .006111 \\ .006111 & .049279 \end{Vmatrix}$$

A row vector of deviation values of raw scores can now be formed for computation of centour scores of mechanics by subtracting the vector of means for mechanics from the matrix of raw scores whose deviations are desired. Centour scores can then be computed by evaluating $x_2 D_2^{-1} x'_2 = \chi_2^2$, ascertaining the values of q_2 from Pearson's Table and computing C_2 by multiplying the complement of q_2 by 100. The centour scores for mechanics have been added to those for passenger agents in Table 3.5.

Table 3.5 indicates that Joe's 22 outdoor and 22 convivial preferences are associated with a centour score of 60 for mechanics as well as with the centour of 06 for agents. Joe's preferences for these types of activities are more typical of apprentices who later became mechanics than they are of apprentices who later became agents.

Table 3.4 *Table of Centour Equivalents—Passenger Agents*

Convivial	Outdoor																														
	0	1	2	3	4	5	6	7	8	9	10	11	12	13	14	15	16	17	18	19	20	21	22	23	24	25	26	27	28	29	30
35	*	*	*	*	*	*	*	*	01	01	02	02	03	03	04	04	04	04	04	03	02	02	01	01	01	*	*	*	*	*	*
34	*	*	*	*	01	01	01	01	02	03	04	05	06	07	07	08	07	07	06	05	04	03	02	01	01	01	*	*	*	*	*
33	*	*	*	01	01	01	02	03	04	05	07	09	10	12	12	13	12	11	09	08	06	04	03	02	01	01	01	01	*	*	*
32	*	*	01	01	02	03	04	06	09	11	14	17	19	20	18	17	14	11	09	06	04	03	02	01	01	01	*	*	*	*	*
31	*	01	01	02	03	05	07	10	14	18	22	25	28	29	29	28	25	22	18	14	10	07	05	03	02	01	01	01	*	*	*
30	*	01	02	03	05	07	11	16	22	27	32	37	40	41	40	37	32	27	21	16	11	08	05	03	02	01	01	01	*	*	*
29	*	01	01	03	04	07	11	16	22	30	37	44	50	53	54	52	47	41	34	26	19	14	09	06	03	02	01	01	*	*	*
28	01	01	02	04	06	10	15	22	30	40	49	58	64	68	68	64	58	49	40	31	22	15	10	06	04	02	01	01	*	*	*
27	01	02	03	05	08	13	20	29	39	50	61	71	78	81	80	75	67	56	45	34	24	17	11	07	04	02	01	01	*	*	*
26	01	02	04	06	11	17	25	35	47	60	72	82	89	92	90	83	73	60	48	36	25	17	11	07	04	02	01	01	*	*	*
25	01	03	05	08	13	20	29	41	54	67	80	90	97	98	95	86	75	61	48	35	25	16	10	06	04	02	01	*	*	*	*
24	02	03	05	09	15	22	32	44	58	72	84	94	99	99	94	85	73	59	45	33	23	15	09	05	03	02	01	*	*	*	*
23	02	03	06	10	16	24	34	46	59	72	84	92	96	95	89	79	67	53	40	29	20	13	08	05	03	01	01	*	*	*	*
22	02	03	06	10	16	24	33	45	57	69	78	85	88	85	79	69	58	46	34	24	16	10	06	04	02	01	01	*	*	*	*
21	02	03	06	10	15	22	31	41	52	61	69	74	76	73	66	58	47	37	27	19	13	08	05	03	01	01	*	*	*	*	*
20	02	03	06	09	14	20	27	36	44	52	58	61	62	59	53	45	37	28	21	14	09	06	03	02	01	01	*	*	*	*	*
19	02	03	05	08	12	17	23	29	36	42	46	48	47	44	40	33	27	20	15	10	06	04	02	01	01	*	*	*	*	*	*
18	01	02	04	06	09	13	18	23	28	32	34	35	34	32	28	23	18	14	10	07	04	03	01	01	*	*	*	*	*	*	*

```
17   01 02 03 05 07  10 13 17 20 22  24 25 24 22 19  15 12 09 06 04  03 02 01  *  *  *  *  *  *  *  *  *  *  *  *
16   01 01 02 04 05  07 09 12 14 15  16 16 15 14 12  10 07 05 04 02  02 01 01  *  *  *  *  *  *  *  *  *  *  *  *
15   01 01 02 02 04  05 06 08 09 10  10 10 09 08 07  06 04 03 02 01  01        *  *  *  *  *  *  *  *  *  *  *  *

14    *  01 01 02 02  03 04 05 05 06  06 06 05 05 04  03 02 02 01 01  01 01     *  *  *  *  *  *  *  *  *  *  *  *
13    *   *  01 01 01  02 02 03 03 03  03 03 03 03 02  02 01 01 01 *   *  01 01  *  *  *  *  *  *  *  *  *  *  *  *
12    *   *   *  01 01  01 01 02 02 02  02 02 02 01 01  01 01 *         01 01     *  *  *  *  *  *  *  *  *  *  *  *
11    *   *   *   *  01  01 01 01 01 01  01 01 01 01 01  01 *                      *  *  *  *  *  *  *  *  *  *  *  *
10    *   *   *   *   *  01 01 01 01 01  01 01 01 *                                *  *  *  *  *  *  *  *  *  *  *  *

 9    *   *   *   *   *   *  *  *  *  *   *  *  *  *  *   *  *  *  *  *   *  *  *   *  *  *  *  *  *  *  *  *  *  *  *
 8    *   *   *   *   *   *  *  *  *  *   *  *  *  *  *   *  *  *  *  *   *  *  *   *  *  *  *  *  *  *  *  *  *  *  *
 7    *   *   *   *   *   *  *  *  *  *   *  *  *  *  *   *  *  *  *  *   *  *  *   *  *  *  *  *  *  *  *  *  *  *  *
 6    *   *   *   *   *   *  *  *  *  *   *  *  *  *  *   *  *  *  *  *   *  *  *   *  *  *  *  *  *  *  *  *  *  *  *
 5    *   *   *   *   *   *  *  *  *  *   *  *  *  *  *   *  *  *  *  *   *  *  *   *  *  *  *  *  *  *  *  *  *  *  *

 4    *   *   *   *   *   *  *  *  *  *   *  *  *  *  *   *  *  *  *  *   *  *  *   *  *  *  *  *  *  *  *  *  *  *  *
 3    *   *   *   *   *   *  *  *  *  *   *  *  *  *  *   *  *  *  *  *   *  *  *   *  *  *  *  *  *  *  *  *  *  *  *
 2    *   *   *   *   *   *  *  *  *  *   *  *  *  *  *   *  *  *  *  *   *  *  *   *  *  *  *  *  *  *  *  *  *  *  *
 1    *   *   *   *   *   *  *  *  *  *   *  *  *  *  *   *  *  *  *  *   *  *  *   *  *  *  *  *  *  *  *  *  *  *  *
 0    *   *   *   *   *   *  *  *  *  *   *  *  *  *  *   *  *  *  *  *   *  *  *   *  *  *  *  *  *  *  *  *  *  *  *
```

* Centour < .5

137

Table 3.5 *Table of Centour Equivalents—Passenger Agents and Mechanics*

Convivial	Spec.	Outdoor																														
		0	1	2	3	4	5	6	7	8	9	10	11	12	13	14	15	16	17	18	19	20	21	22	23	24	25	26	27	28	29	30
35	PA	*	*	*	*	*	*	*	01	01	02	02	03	03	04	04	04	04	04	04	03	02	02	01	01	01	*	*	*	*	*	*
	M	*	*	*	*	*	*	*	*	*	*	*	*	*	01	01	01	01	01	01	01	01	01	01	*	*	*	*	*	*	*	*
34	PA	*	*	*	*	*	01	01	01	02	03	04	05	06	07	07	08	07	07	06	05	04	03	02	01	01	01	*	*	*	*	*
	M	*	*	*	*	*	*	*	*	*	*	*	01	01	01	01	01	01	01	01	01	01	01	01	01	*	*	*	*	*	*	*
33	PA	*	*	*	*	01	01	02	03	04	05	07	09	10	12	12	13	12	11	09	08	06	04	03	02	01	01	*	*	*	*	*
	M	*	*	*	*	*	*	*	*	*	*	*	01	01	01	02	02	02	02	02	02	02	01	01	01	*	*	*	*	*	*	*
32	PA	*	*	01	01	01	02	03	04	06	09	11	14	17	19	20	20	18	17	14	11	09	06	04	03	02	01	01	*	*	*	*
	M	*	*	*	*	*	*	*	*	*	*	01	01	02	03	03	03	03	03	03	02	02	01	01	*	*	*	*	*	*	*	*
31	PA	*	01	01	01	02	03	04	07	10	14	18	22	25	28	29	29	27	24	20	16	12	09	06	04	03	02	01	01	*	*	*
	M	*	*	*	*	*	*	*	*	*	01	01	02	03	04	05	06	06	06	05	05	04	03	02	01	01	01	*	*	*	*	*
30	PA	*	01	02	02	03	05	07	11	16	21	27	32	37	40	41	40	37	32	27	21	16	11	08	05	03	02	01	01	*	*	*
	M	*	*	*	*	*	*	*	*	01	01	02	04	06	08	11	13	14	15	14	12	10	07	05	03	02	01	*	*	*	*	*
29	PA	01	01	02	04	06	10	15	22	30	40	49	58	64	68	68	64	58	49	40	31	22	15	10	06	04	02	01	01	*	*	*
	M	*	*	*	*	*	*	*	*	*	*	02	04	06	11	16	19	22	21	19	15	11	08	05	03	02	01	01	*	*	*	*
28	PA	01	01	02	04	06	10	15	22	30	40	49	58	64	68	68	64	58	49	40	31	22	17	12	08	04	02	01	01	*	*	*
	M	*	*	*	*	*	*	01	01	02	04	08	12	17	22	27	30	32	30	27	22	17	12	08	04	02	01	01	*	*	*	*
27	PA	01	02	03	05	08	13	20	29	39	50	61	71	78	81	80	75	67	56	45	34	24	17	11	07	04	02	01	01	*	*	*
	M	*	*	*	*	*	*	*	01	02	04	08	12	17	23	31	37	41	43	42	37	31	23	16	11	07	04	02	01	01	*	*
26	PA	01	02	04	06	11	17	25	35	47	60	72	82	89	92	90	83	73	60	48	36	25	17	11	07	04	02	01	01	*	*	*
	M	*	*	*	*	*	*	*	*	01	02	06	10	16	24	36	47	53	56	55	49	41	31	22	14	09	05	02	01	01	*	*
25	PA	01	03	05	08	13	20	29	41	54	67	80	90	97	98	95	86	75	61	48	35	25	16	10	06	04	02	01	*	*	*	*
	M	*	*	*	*	*	*	*	*	*	02	05	09	15	23	34	46	57	65	69	68	61	51	39	28	18	11	06	03	02	01	*
24	PA	02	03	05	09	15	22	32	44	58	72	84	94	99	99	94	85	73	59	45	33	23	15	09	05	03	02	01	*	*	*	*
	M	*	*	*	*	*	*	*	*	01	03	05	10	16	26	39	53	66	77	82	80	73	61	48	34	22	14	08	04	02	01	*

23	PA	02	03	06	10	16	24	34	46	59	72	84	92	96	95	89	79	67	53	40	29	20	13	08	05	03	01	01	*	*	*	*
	M	*	*	*	*	*	*	*	*	01	03	05	10	18	29	42	58	73	85	91	91	83	70	55	39	26	16	09	05	02	01	*
22	PA	02	03	06	10	16	24	33	45	57	69	78	85	88	85	79	69	58	46	34	24	16	10	06	04	02	01	01	*	*	*	*
	M	*	*	*	*	*	*	*	*	01	03	06	10	18	30	44	61	77	90	97	97	89	76	60	43	29	18	10	05	03	01	*
21	PA	02	03	06	10	15	22	31	41	52	61	69	74	76	73	66	58	47	37	27	19	13	08	05	03	01	01	*	*	*	*	*
	M	*	*	*	*	*	*	*	*	01	03	05	10	18	29	44	60	77	91	99	99	92	79	62	45	30	19	11	06	03	01	01
20	PA	02	03	06	09	14	20	27	36	44	52	58	61	62	59	53	45	37	28	21	14	09	06	03	02	01	01	*	*	*	*	*
	M	*	*	*	*	*	*	*	*	01	02	05	09	17	27	41	57	73	87	95	96	90	77	61	45	30	19	11	06	03	01	01
19	PA	02	03	05	08	12	17	23	29	36	42	46	48	47	44	40	33	27	20	15	10	06	04	02	01	01	*	*	*	*	*	*
	M	*	*	*	*	*	*	*	*	01	02	04	08	15	24	37	52	67	80	88	89	84	72	58	43	29	18	11	06	03	01	01
18	PA	01	02	04	06	09	13	18	23	28	32	34	35	34	32	28	23	18	14	10	07	04	03	01	01	*	*	*	*	*	*	*
	M	*	*	*	*	*	*	*	*	01	02	04	07	12	21	31	44	58	69	77	78	74	65	52	38	26	17	10	05	03	01	*
17	PA	01	02	03	05	07	10	13	17	20	22	24	25	24	22	19	15	12	09	06	04	03	02	01	*	*	*	*	*	*	*	*
	M	*	*	*	*	*	*	*	*	01	01	03	06	10	17	26	36	47	57	64	66	02	55	44	33	23	14	08	05	02	01	*
16	PA	01	01	02	04	05	07	09	12	14	15	16	16	15	14	12	10	07	05	04	02	02	01	01	*	*	*	*	*	*	*	*
	M	*	*	*	*	*	*	*	*	*	01	02	04	08	13	20	28	37	45	51	52	50	44	36	27	19	12	07	04	02	01	*
15	PA	01	01	02	02	04	05	06	08	09	10	10	10	09	08	07	06	04	03	02	01	01	*	*	*	*	*	*	*	*	*	*
	M	*	*	*	*	*	*	*	*	*	01	02	03	06	09	15	21	28	34	38	40	38	34	28	21	15	09	06	03	02	01	*
14	PA	*	01	01	02	02	03	04	05	05	06	06	06	05	05	04	03	02	02	01	01	*	*	*	*	*	*	*	*	*	*	*
	M	*	*	*	*	*	*	*	*	*	*	01	02	04	07	10	15	20	24	27	29	28	25	20	16	11	07	04	02	01	01	*
13	PA	*	*	01	01	01	02	02	03	03	03	03	03	03	03	02	02	01	01	01	*	*	*	*	*	*	*	*	*	*	*	*
	M	*	*	*	*	*	*	*	*	*	*	01	01	03	04	07	10	13	16	19	20	19	17	14	11	08	05	03	02	01	*	*
12	PA	*	*	*	01	01	01	01	02	02	02	02	02	02	01	01	01	01	*	*	*	*	*	*	*	*	*	*	*	*	*	*
	M	*	*	*	*	*	*	*	*	*	*	*	01	02	03	04	06	09	11	12	13	13	11	10	07	05	03	02	01	01	*	*
11	PA	*	*	*	*	*	01	01	01	01	01	01	01	01	01	01	*	*	*	*	*	*	*	*	*	*	*	*	*	*	*	*
	M	*	*	*	*	*	*	*	*	*	*	*	01	01	02	03	04	05	07	08	08	08	07	06	05	03	02	01	01	*	*	*
10	PA	*	*	*	*	*	*	*	*	*	*	*	*	*	*	*	*	*	*	*	*	*	*	*	*	*	*	*	*	*	*	*
	M	*	*	*	*	*	*	*	*	*	*	*	*	01	01	02	02	03	04	04	05	05	04	04	03	02	01	01	*	*	*	*
9	PA	*	*	*	*	*	*	*	*	*	*	*	*	*	*	*	*	*	*	*	*	*	*	*	*	*	*	*	*	*	*	*
	M	*	*	*	*	*	*	*	*	*	*	*	*	*	01	01	01	02	02	03	03	03	02	02	02	01	01	*	*	*	*	*

Table 3.5 *Table of Centour Equivalents—Passenger Agents and Mechanics—continued*

Convivial	Spec.	Outdoor																														
		0	1	2	3	4	5	6	7	8	9	10	11	12	13	14	15	16	17	18	19	20	21	22	23	24	25	26	27	28	29	30
8	PA	*	*	*	*	*	*	*	*	*	*	*	*	*	*	*	*	*	*	*	*	*	*	*	*	*	*	*	*	*	*	*	*
	M	*	*	*	*	*	*	*	*	*	*	*	*	*	*	*	01	01	01	01	01	01	01	01	01	01	*	*	*	*	*	*	*
7	PA	*	*	*	*	*	*	*	*	*	*	*	*	*	*	*	*	*	*	*	*	*	*	*	*	*	*	*	*	*	*	*	*
	M	*	*	*	*	*	*	*	*	*	*	*	*	*	*	*	*	01	01	01	01	01	01	01	01	01	*	*	*	*	*	*	*
6	PA	*	*	*	*	*	*	*	*	*	*	*	*	*	*	*	*	*	*	*	*	*	*	*	*	*	*	*	*	*	*	*	*
	M	*	*	*	*	*	*	*	*	*	*	*	*	*	*	*	*	*	01	01	01	01	01	p1	*	*	*	*	*	*	*	*	*
5	PA	*	*	*	*	*	*	*	*	*	*	*	*	*	*	*	*	*	*	*	*	*	*	*	*	*	*	*	*	*	*	*	*
	M	*	*	*	*	*	*	*	*	*	*	*	*	*	*	*	*	*	*	*	*	*	*	*	*	*	*	*	*	*	*	*	*
4	PA	*	*	*	*	*	*	*	*	*	*	*	*	*	*	*	*	*	*	*	*	*	*	*	*	*	*	*	*	*	*	*	*
	M	*	*	*	*	*	*	*	*	*	*	*	*	*	*	*	*	*	*	*	*	*	*	*	*	*	*	*	*	*	*	*	*
3	PA	*	*	*	*	*	*	*	*	*	*	*	*	*	*	*	*	*	*	*	*	*	*	*	*	*	*	*	*	*	*	*	*
	M	*	*	*	*	*	*	*	*	*	*	*	*	*	*	*	*	*	*	*	*	*	*	*	*	*	*	*	*	*	*	*	*
2	PA	*	*	*	*	*	*	*	*	*	*	*	*	*	*	*	*	*	*	*	*	*	*	*	*	*	*	*	*	*	*	*	*
	M	*	*	*	*	*	*	*	*	*	*	*	*	*	*	*	*	*	*	*	*	*	*	*	*	*	*	*	*	*	*	*	*
1	PA	*	*	*	*	*	*	*	*	*	*	*	*	*	*	*	*	*	*	*	*	*	*	*	*	*	*	*	*	*	*	*	*
	M	*	*	*	*	*	*	*	*	*	*	*	*	*	*	*	*	*	*	*	*	*	*	*	*	*	*	*	*	*	*	*	*
0	PA	*	*	*	*	*	*	*	*	*	*	*	*	*	*	*	*	*	*	*	*	*	*	*	*	*	*	*	*	*	*	*	*
	M	*	*	*	*	*	*	*	*	*	*	*	*	*	*	*	*	*	*	*	*	*	*	*	*	*	*	*	*	*	*	*	*

* Centour < .5

140

Passenger Agents, Mechanics, and Operations Control Agents

In calculating centours for passenger agents and mechanics we have not yet considered a third group of apprentices who later became operations control agents (operations men). The roster for the 66 apprentices in World Airlines who later became satisfied and satisfactory operations personnel is given in columns 2 and 3 of Table B.3. The matrix X_3 of raw scores for operations personnel is

$$X_3 = \begin{Vmatrix} 19 & 19 \\ 17 & 17 \\ 8 & 17 \\ \vdots & \vdots \\ 18 & 20 \end{Vmatrix} \quad \text{(66 rows)}$$

The mean of the outdoor activities preferred by operations personnel is 15.5758. The mean of the convivial activity preferences for operations personnel is 15.4545. Therefore the S matrix is

$$S = X'X - \bar{X}'\bar{X} = \begin{Vmatrix} 17{,}110 & 15{,}996 \\ 15{,}996 & 16{,}686 \end{Vmatrix} - \begin{Vmatrix} 16{,}011.9660 & 15{,}887.2693 \\ 15{,}887.2693 & 15{,}763.5436 \end{Vmatrix}$$

and the dispersion matrix D which is $(1/66)S$ is

$$D = \begin{Vmatrix} 16.6382 & 1.6474 \\ 1.6474 & 13.9752 \end{Vmatrix}$$

The inverse of D is

$$D^{-1} = \begin{Vmatrix} .060812 & -.007169 \\ -.007169 & .072400 \end{Vmatrix}$$

Centour scores for outdoor and convivial activity preferences of operations men can then be formed for all of the possible scores. This time, however, deviation scores must be computed from the centroid of the operations personnel by evaluation of the expression $x_3 D_3^{-1} x'_3 = \chi_3^2$. The centour scores associated with these new values of χ_3^2 have been added to Table 3.5 to produce Table 3.6.

We now have a third centour score which is associated with the 22 outdoor and 22 convivial activity preferences of Joe Armand. His centour for operations control agent is 08. Joe's activity preferences are still more characteristic of apprentices who became mechanics than of those who became either agents or operations personnel.

Table 3.6 *Table of Centour Equivalents—Passenger Agents, Mechanics, and Operations Personnel*

Convivial	Spec.											Outdoor																				
		0	1	2	3	4	5	6	7	8	9	10	11	12	13	14	15	16	17	18	19	20	21	22	23	24	25	26	27	28	29	30
35	PA	*	*	*	*	*	*	*	01	01	02	02	03	03	04	04	04	04	04	04	03	02	02	01	01	01	*	*	*	*	*	*
	M	*	*	*	*	*	*	*	*	*	*	*	*	*	*	01	01	01	01	01	01	01	01	*	*	*	*	*	*	*	*	*
	OCA	*	*	*	*	*	*	*	*	*	*	*	*	*	*	*	*	*	*	*	*	*	*	*	*	*	*	*	*	*	*	*
34	PA	*	*	*	*	*	01	01	01	02	03	04	05	06	07	07	08	07	07	06	05	04	03	02	01	01	01	*	*	*	*	*
	M	*	*	*	*	*	*	*	*	*	*	01	01	01	01	01	02	02	02	02	02	01	01	01	01	01	*	*	*	*	*	*
	OCA	*	*	*	*	*	*	*	*	*	*	*	*	*	*	*	*	*	*	*	*	*	*	*	*	*	*	*	*	*	*	*
33	PA	*	*	*	01	01	01	02	03	04	05	07	09	10	12	12	13	12	11	09	08	06	04	03	02	01	01	*	*	*	*	*
	M	*	*	*	*	*	*	*	*	*	*	*	01	01	01	02	03	03	04	03	03	02	02	01	01	01	*	*	*	*	*	*
	OCA	*	*	*	*	*	*	*	*	*	*	*	*	*	*	*	*	*	*	*	*	*	*	*	*	*	*	*	*	*	*	*
32	PA	*	*	*	01	01	02	03	04	06	09	11	14	17	19	20	20	18	17	14	11	09	06	04	03	02	01	01	*	*	*	*
	M	*	*	*	*	*	*	*	*	*	*	01	01	02	03	04	05	06	06	05	05	04	03	02	01	01	01	01	*	*	*	*
	OCA	*	*	*	*	*	*	*	*	*	*	*	*	*	*	*	*	*	*	*	*	*	*	*	*	*	*	*	*	*	*	*
31	PA	*	*	01	01	02	03	04	07	10	14	18	22	25	28	29	29	27	24	20	16	12	09	06	04	02	01	01	*	*	*	*
	M	*	*	*	*	*	*	*	*	01	01	02	04	07	08	09	09	09	09	08	06	05	04	02	01	01	01	01	*	*	*	*
	OCA	*	*	*	*	*	*	*	*	*	*	*	*	*	*	*	*	*	*	*	*	*	*	*	*	*	*	*	*	*	*	*
30	PA	*	01	02	03	05	07	11	16	21	27	32	37	40	41	40	37	32	27	21	16	11	08	05	03	02	01	01	*	*	*	*
	M	*	*	*	*	*	*	*	*	*	01	02	04	06	08	11	13	14	15	14	12	10	07	05	03	02	02	01	*	*	*	*
	OCA	*	*	*	*	*	*	*	*	*	*	*	*	*	*	*	*	*	*	*	*	*	*	*	*	*	*	*	*	*	*	*
29	PA	01	01	03	04	07	11	16	22	30	37	44	50	53	54	52	47	41	34	26	19	14	09	06	03	02	02	01	01	*	*	*
	M	*	*	*	*	*	*	*	*	*	01	02	03	05	08	11	15	19	21	22	21	19	15	11	08	05	03	01	01	*	*	*
	OCA	*	*	*	*	*	*	*	*	*	*	*	*	*	*	*	*	*	*	*	*	*	*	*	*	*	01	01	01	*	*	*
28	PA	01	01	02	04	06	10	15	22	30	40	49	58	64	68	68	64	58	49	40	31	22	15	10	06	04	02	01	01	*	*	*
	M	01	01	01	02	04	07	12	17	22	27	30	32	30	27	22	17	11	08	05	04	03	02	17	12	08	04	02	01	01	01	*
	OCA	01	01	01	*	*	*	*	*	*	*	*	*	*	*	*	*	*	*	*	*	*	*	*	*	04	04	01	01	01	01	*

```
         01 02 03 05 08 13 20 29 39 50 61 71 78 81 80 75 67 56 45 34 24 17 11 07 04 02 01 01  *
27  PA
    M    *  *  *  *  *  *  *  03 06 10 15 22 29 36 41 43 42 37 31 23 16 11 06 04 02 01  *
    OCA  *  *  *  *  *  *  *  *  01 01 01 01 01 01 01 01 01 01 01 01  *

         01 02 04 06 11 17 25 35 47 60 72 82 89 92 90 83 73 60 48 36 25 17 11 07 04 02 01 01  *
26  PA
    M    *  *  *  *  *  *  *  04 07 12 19 28 38 47 53 56 55 49 41 31 22 14 09 05 02 01 01  *
    OCA  *  *  *  *  *  *  *  *  01 01 01 02 02 02 02 01 01 01 01 01  *

         01 03 05 08 13 20 29 41 54 67 80 90 97 98 95 86 75 61 48 35 25 16 10 06 04 02 01  *
25  PA
    M    *  *  *  *  *  *  *  05 08 15 23 34 46 57 65 69 68 61 51 39 28 18 11 06 03 02 01  *
    OCA  *  *  *  *  *  *  *  01 01 02 03 03 04 04 04 03 03 02 01 01 01  *

         02 03 05 09 15 22 32 44 58 72 84 94 99 99 94 85 73 59 45 33 23 15 09 05 03 02 01  *
24  PA
    M    *  *  *  *  *  *  *  05 10 16 26 39 53 66 77 82 80 73 61 48 34 22 14 08 04 02 01  *
    OCA  *  *  *  *  *  *  *  01 03 05 06 07 07 07 07 06 05 04 03 02 01 01 01  *

         02 03 06 10 16 24 34 46 59 72 84 92 96 95 89 79 67 53 40 29 20 13 08 05 03 01 01  *
23  PA
    M    *  *  *  *  *  *  *  05 10 18 29 42 58 73 85 91 91 83 70 55 39 26 16 09 05 02 01  *
    OCA  *  *  *  *  *  *  *  01 03 05 07 07 07 07 06 05 04 03 02 01 01 01  *

         02 03 06 10 16 24 33 45 57 69 78 85 88 85 79 69 58 46 34 24 16 10 06 04 02 01  *
22  PA
    M    *  *  *  *  *  *  01 03 06 10 18 30 44 61 77 90 97 97 89 76 60 43 29 18 10 06 04 02 01  *
    OCA  *  *  *  *  *  *  *  01 02 03 04 05 06 06 06 05 05 04 02 02 01 01  *

         02 03 06 10 15 22 31 41 52 61 69 74 76 73 66 58 47 37 27 19 11 08 05 03 01  *
21  PA
    M    *  *  *  *  *  *  01 03 04 07 10 14 19 24 29 44 37 37 33 30 26 21 14 08 05 03 02 01  *
    OCA  *  *  *  *  *  *  01 01 02 04 07 10 14 18 29 45 62 79 91 99 99 92 74 56 39 30 21 14 09 05 03 02 01  *

         02 03 06 09 14 20 27 36 44 52 58 61 62 59 53 45 36 28 21 12 08 05 03 01  *
20  PA
    M    *  *  *  *  *  01 01 02 04 07 09 12 17 22 28 33 33 30 28 21 14 08 05 03 02 01  *
    OCA  *  *  *  *  *  *  01 01 01 02 05 08 12 17 23 30 37 43 47 45 45 41 30 21 14 09 06 03 01  *

         *  01 02 04 06 10 15 22 29 36 42 46 48 47 43 37 30 23 17 11 07 04 02 01 01  *
19  PA
    M    *  *  *  01 02 04 06 10 15 20 23 17 20 27 33 27 20 15 10 07 04 02 01 01  *
    OCA  *  *  *  *  *  01 02 04 08 15 24 37 43 58 72 80 88 89 84 72 58 43 29 18 11 06 03 01  *

         01 02 04 06 09 13 18 23 28 32 34 35 34 32 28 23 18 14 10 07 04 03 01 01  *
18  PA
    M    *  *  01 01 02 03 05 09 14 21 30 39 49 57 62 64 62 56 48 39 30 21 14 09 05 03 02 01  *
    OCA  01 01 02 04 07 12 19 28 38 50 62 71 77 79 76 69 59 47 36 25 17 11 06 04 02 01  *
```

Table 3.6 *Table of Centour Equivalents—Passenger Agents, Mechanics, and Operations Personnel—continued*

Convivial	Spec.															Outdoor															
		0	1	2	3	4	5	6	7	8	9	10	11	12	13	14	15	16	17	18	19	20	21	22	23	24	25	26	27	28	29	30
17	PA	01	02	03	05	07	10	13	17	20	22	24	25	24	22	19	15	12	09	06	04	03	02	01	*	*	*	*	*	*	*	*
	M	*	*	*	*	*	*	*	*	01	01	03	06	10	17	26	36	47	57	64	66	67	55	44	33	23	14	08	05	02	01	*
	OCA	*	*	*	01	01	03	05	09	15	23	34	46	60	73	84	90	92	88	79	67	53	40	28	19	12	07	04	02	01	*	*
16	PA	01	01	02	04	05	07	09	12	14	15	16	16	15	14	12	10	07	05	04	02	02	01	01	*	*	*	*	*	*	*	*
	M	*	*	*	*	*	*	*	*	*	01	02	04	08	13	20	28	37	45	51	52	50	44	36	27	19	12	07	04	02	01	*
	OCA	*	*	*	01	02	04	06	10	17	26	38	51	66	80	91	98	99	94	84	70	56	41	29	19	12	07	04	02	01	*	*
15	PA	01	01	02	03	05	06	08	09	10	10	10	09	09	08	07	06	05	04	03	02	01	01	*	*	*	*	*	*	*	*	*
	M	*	*	*	*	*	*	*	01	01	02	04	07	11	17	24	32	38	40	40	38	34	28	21	15	10	06	04	02	01	*	*
	OCA	*	*	01	02	03	06	09	15	23	30	39	53	68	82	93	98	99	93	82	69	54	40	28	18	11	06	04	02	01	*	*
14	PA	01	01	01	02	03	04	05	06	06	07	07	07	06	06	05	05	04	03	03	02	02	01	01	*	*	*	*	*	*	*	*
	M	*	*	*	*	*	*	*	*	01	02	03	05	08	12	17	22	27	29	28	25	20	16	11	07	04	02	01	*	*	*	*
	OCA	*	01	01	02	03	06	09	15	22	30	38	51	65	78	87	92	92	86	76	63	49	36	25	16	10	06	03	02	01	*	*
13	PA	01	01	01	02	02	03	04	04	05	05	05	05	05	04	04	03	03	02	02	01	01	01	*	*	*	*	*	*	*	*	*
	M	*	*	*	*	*	*	*	01	02	03	05	08	12	17	20	20	19	16	13	10	07	05	03	02	01	*	*	*	*	*	*
	OCA	*	01	01	02	03	05	08	13	19	26	34	46	58	69	77	80	79	74	64	53	41	30	20	13	08	05	03	02	01	*	*
12	PA	01	01	01	01	02	02	03	03	04	04	04	04	04	04	03	03	02	02	01	01	01	01	*	*	*	*	*	*	*	*	*
	M	*	*	*	*	*	*	01	01	02	03	05	07	10	13	13	13	11	09	07	05	04	03	02	01	*	*	*	*	*	*	*
	OCA	*	01	01	02	02	04	06	10	15	22	29	40	50	58	63	65	64	59	51	42	32	23	16	10	06	03	02	01	01	*	*
11	PA	01	01	01	01	01	02	02	03	03	03	04	04	04	03	03	03	02	02	02	01	01	01	01	*	*	*	*	*	*	*	*
	M	*	*	*	*	*	*	01	01	02	03	04	06	07	08	08	08	07	06	05	04	03	02	01	01	*	*	*	*	*	*	*
	OCA	*	01	01	01	02	03	05	08	12	17	23	31	39	45	48	49	48	44	38	31	23	16	11	07	04	03	02	01	*	*	*
10	PA	01	01	01	01	01	01	02	02	02	03	03	03	03	03	03	02	02	02	02	01	01	01	01	01	01	01	*	*	*	*	*
	M	*	*	*	*	*	01	01	02	02	03	04	05	05	05	05	04	04	03	03	02	02	01	01	*	*	*	*	*	*	*	*
	OCA	*	01	01	01	02	02	04	06	09	13	16	22	27	31	33	34	33	30	26	21	16	11	08	05	03	02	01	*	*	*	*

9	PA	*	*	*	*	*	*	*	*	*	*	*	*	*	*	*	*	*	*	*	*	*	*	*	*	*	*	*	*	*	*	*
	M	*	*	*	*	*	*	*	*	*	*	*	*	*	01	01	01	02	02	03	03	03	02	02	02	01	01	*	*	*	*	*
	OCA	*	*	*	*	01	01	02	04	05	08	11	14	18	20	22	23	22	20	17	13	10	07	05	03	02	01	01	*	*	*	*
8	PA	*	*	*	*	*	*	*	*	*	*	*	*	*	*	*	*	*	*	*	*	*	*	*	*	*	*	*	*	*	*	*
	M	*	*	*	*	*	*	*	*	*	*	*	*	*	*	*	01	01	01	01	01	01	01	01	01	01	*	*	*	*	*	*
	OCA	*	*	*	*	*	01	01	02	03	05	07	09	11	13	13	14	13	12	10	08	06	04	03	02	01	01	*	*	*	*	*
7	PA	*	*	*	*	*	*	*	*	*	*	*	*	*	*	*	*	*	*	*	*	*	*	*	*	*	*	*	*	*	*	*
	M	*	*	*	*	*	*	*	*	*	*	*	*	*	*	*	*	*	01	01	01	01	01	01	*	*	*	*	*	*	*	*
	OCA	*	*	*	*	*	*	01	01	02	03	04	05	06	07	08	08	07	06	05	04	03	02	01	01	01	*	*	*	*	*	*
6	PA	*	*	*	*	*	*	*	*	*	*	*	*	*	*	*	*	*	*	*	*	*	*	*	*	*	*	*	*	*	*	*
	M	*	*	*	*	*	*	*	*	*	*	*	*	*	*	*	*	*	*	*	*	*	*	*	*	*	*	*	*	*	*	*
	OCA	*	*	*	*	*	*	*	01	02	02	02	03	03	04	04	04	04	03	03	02	02	01	01	*	*	*	*	*	*	*	*
5	PA	*	*	*	*	*	*	*	*	*	*	*	*	*	*	*	*	*	*	*	*	*	*	*	*	*	*	*	*	*	*	*
	M	*	*	*	*	*	*	*	*	*	*	*	*	*	*	*	*	*	*	*	*	*	*	*	*	*	*	*	*	*	*	*
	OCA	*	*	*	*	*	*	*	*	01	01	01	01	02	02	02	02	02	02	01	01	01	01	*	*	*	*	*	*	*	*	*
4	PA	*	*	*	*	*	*	*	*	*	*	*	*	*	*	*	*	*	*	*	*	*	*	*	*	*	*	*	*	*	*	*
	M	*	*	*	*	*	*	*	*	*	*	*	*	*	*	*	*	*	*	*	*	*	*	*	*	*	*	*	*	*	*	*
	OCA	*	*	*	*	*	*	*	*	*	*	01	01	01	01	01	01	01	01	01	*	*	*	*	*	*	*	*	*	*	*	*
3	PA	*	*	*	*	*	*	*	*	*	*	*	*	*	*	*	*	*	*	*	*	*	*	*	*	*	*	*	*	*	*	*
	M	*	*	*	*	*	*	*	*	*	*	*	*	*	*	*	*	*	*	*	*	*	*	*	*	*	*	*	*	*	*	*
	OCA	*	*	*	*	*	*	*	*	*	*	*	*	*	*	*	*	*	*	*	*	*	*	*	*	*	*	*	*	*	*	*
2	PA	*	*	*	*	*	*	*	*	*	*	*	*	*	*	*	*	*	*	*	*	*	*	*	*	*	*	*	*	*	*	*
	M	*	*	*	*	*	*	*	*	*	*	*	*	*	*	*	*	*	*	*	*	*	*	*	*	*	*	*	*	*	*	*
	OCA	*	*	*	*	*	*	*	*	*	*	*	*	*	*	*	*	*	*	*	*	*	*	*	*	*	*	*	*	*	*	*
1	PA	*	*	*	*	*	*	*	*	*	*	*	*	*	*	*	*	*	*	*	*	*	*	*	*	*	*	*	*	*	*	*
	M	*	*	*	*	*	*	*	*	*	*	*	*	*	*	*	*	*	*	*	*	*	*	*	*	*	*	*	*	*	*	*
	OCA	*	*	*	*	*	*	*	*	*	*	*	*	*	*	*	*	*	*	*	*	*	*	*	*	*	*	*	*	*	*	*
0	PA	*	*	*	*	*	*	*	*	*	*	*	*	*	*	*	*	*	*	*	*	*	*	*	*	*	*	*	*	*	*	*
	M	*	*	*	*	*	*	*	*	*	*	*	*	*	*	*	*	*	*	*	*	*	*	*	*	*	*	*	*	*	*	*
	OCA	*	*	*	*	*	*	*	*	*	*	*	*	*	*	*	*	*	*	*	*	*	*	*	*	*	*	*	*	*	*	*

* Centour <.5

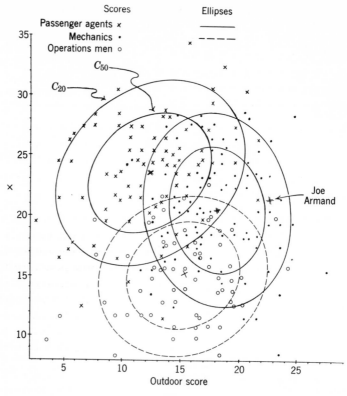

Fig. 3.26

The scores for all 66 apprentices who later became operations personnel can easily be added to Fig. 3.25 as has been done in Fig. 3.26. The addition of the third group does not influence in any way the representation of the data for the former two groups. Figure 3.26 also indicates the 20th and 50th centour ellipses for operations personnel in order to illustrate completely those data. The 20th and 50th centour ellipses were determined and plotted according to the procedure given in Appendix A. As is to be expected, the figure offers much the same information about the meaning of Joe's outdoor and convivial activity preferences as does the centour table. It simply clarifies the data.

The General Bivariate Case

G Groups

Personnel classification encompasses many jobs in addition to the three so far considered. Suppose satisfactory and satisfied employees in a fourth job in World Airlines were identified. Their scores are listed in a separate roster and the score matrix of this new group may be added to the set of rosters and matrices for the three previously discussed jobs without influencing any of them. Each of the four job groups is independent of the others. The selection and addition to the problem of a fifth, a sixth, and, in fact, any number G of jobs are similarly independent.

Profile representation of the outdoor and convivial scores of passenger agents and mechanics was not altered by the introduction of a third job, operations control agent. The data for the third group were included without influencing or modifying any previous representation. The construction of frequency polygons of a fourth group on the same profile axes will not alter the score distributions of the first three groups. Similarly, profile representation of the frequency polygons of job G on the same profile stalks with the previous $G - 1$ groups does not alter the representation of any of the data.

Cartesian representation of the activity scores of two groups was not altered by the introduction of a third job. The bivariate distribution for the third job was included independently. The inclusion of a fourth bivariate distribution independently represented on the same axes would not alter the first three distributions. Similarly, we may say that Cartesian representation of the bivariate distribution of job G in the same test space with the previous $G - 1$ bivariate distributions does not alter the representation of the data.

Profile representation of outdoor and convivial activity preferences for each group emphasizes the central tendency and dispersion for each test independently. Representation of joint preference for outdoor and convivial activities cannot be accomplished by graphic profile methods, and the representation of dispersion in job psychographs becomes graphically impractical when the number of groups is realistically large.

Cartesian representation of the outdoor and convivial scores for each of G jobs in the same test space reveals all the important characteristics of the bivariate density distribution for each job. Each of the density distributions represents the centroid of the job *and* the joint dispersion of outdoor and convivial scores characteristic of the job. Cartesian representation provides an answer to Profile Problem 3.

Profile Problem 3. How may the joint performance of all individuals be represented? Answer: Joint performances of any number of groups may be indicated on Cartesian axes without confusion or elimination of essential information in the empirical data.

If the data for each of G jobs are reasonably well described by normal distributions, the centour job psychograph is analogous to the profile job psychograph. The 10th and 90th percentile points of the profile psychographs of each job are the profile analog of the 20th centour psychograph ellipse. The centour psychograph analogs of the 25th and 75th percentile profile psychographs for each job are the 50th centour ellipses. The 20th and 50th (or any other) centours are readily determined by the appropriate values of χ^2 combined with the dispersion matrix of a job group. The location in the test space of the center of the psychograph ellipses is the centroid of the job. The translation of the origin to the centroid of the group is conveniently expressed as a row matrix. For the general, or gth, job the matrix is

$$x_{.g.} = \|(X_{pg1} - \overline{X}_{.g1})\ (X_{pg2} - \overline{X}_{.g2})\|$$

In this new notation $x_{.g.}$ indicates a row vector of test scores of an unspecified individual represented by the first subscript dot, referred to group g, and tested on an unspecified series of tests represented by the third subscript, a dot.

In a bivariate normal distribution equally probable points in the gth job will lie upon ellipses defined by

$$x_{.g.}D_g^{-1}x'_{.g.} = \chi_g^2$$

The shape and orientation of the ellipses, that is, their appearance in the test space as nearly circular, oval, or long and narrow, and the direction of the axes are completely determined by the group data in the dispersion matrix D_g. The location of the center of the ellipses is determined by the group data in the centroid matrix $\overline{X}_g$. The size of any particular ellipse is determined by the value of χ_g^2. Thus we may choose for any group g a numerical value for χ_g^2 and solve the equation to find the coordinates x which lie on the particular ellipse. The particular ellipse will be the one associated with the assigned value of χ_g^2. There will be G such ellipses, one for each group. Each of these G ellipses will be associated with the same numerical value of χ_g^2 and therefore with the same numerical centour equivalent, but each of the ellipses may be of different shape, location, and orientation in the test space. The numerical value of the centour equivalent may be ascertained from the probability table of χ_g^2 with two degrees of freedom. Thus it is a routine calculation to choose any value of χ_g^2 and construct the equivalent centour psychographs in the test space, one for each job group. A hypothetical illustration of C_{50} for several groups appears as Fig. 3.27. The figure is constructed with extreme variations in shape, size, location, and orientation to emphasize the independence of the group representation.

The same matrix equation for the ellipses may be used to ascertain the centour equivalent in group g of any score point in the test space. In this application the coordinates of the chosen point in the test space take

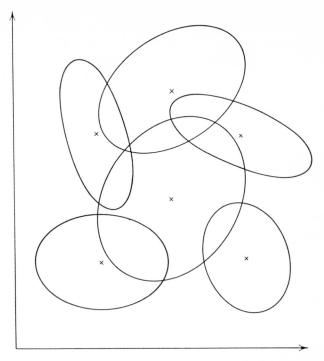

Fig. 3.27 *Equivalent centour psychographs for five hypothetical groups—C_{50} ellipses.*

numerical values in the row matrix $x_{.g}$. The equation (making use of the known numerical values in D_g) may then be solved to find the value of χ_g^2. The particular point in the test space will be identically represented by G different row matrices $x_{.g}$, one for each of the G groups. Therefore for any single point there will be G equations, and G values of χ_g^2, a different value for each group. If there are, say, five groups, the divergence of any point in the test space from the typical central point in each group is described by five different values of χ_g^2 and five different independently determined centour equivalents. The reader may find it instructive to choose a variety of points in the test space of Fig. 3.27 and estimate by visual inspection the centour equivalents of the points for the groups.

Formal Notation

Test scores for satisfactory and satisfied apprentices in each job are grouped by job. There will be G such groups. The roster for the general, or gth, group of the G groups will be

Scores of Satisfactory and Satisfied
Apprentices in Specialty g

Apprentice	Scores	
1	X_{1g1}	X_{1g2}
2	X_{2g1}	X_{2g2}
3	X_{3g1}	X_{3g2}
$\vdots$	$\vdots$	$\vdots$
n_g	$X_{n_g g1}$	$X_{n_g g2}$

The subscript notation identifies, in sequence, person, group, and test. A dot will be used to preserve position when a subscript is suppressed. There will be G such rosters.

The matrix for the general, or gth, group will be

$$X_g = \begin{Vmatrix} X_{1g1} & X_{1g2} \\ X_{2g1} & X_{2g2} \\ X_{3g1} & X_{3g2} \\ \vdots & \vdots \\ X_{n_g g1} & X_{n_g g2} \end{Vmatrix} \quad (n_g \text{ rows})$$

There will be G such matrices.

The centroid for the gth group will be

$$\bar{X}_g = \begin{Vmatrix} \bar{X}_{.g1} & \bar{X}_{.g2} \end{Vmatrix}$$

There will be G such centroids.

The dispersion matrix for the gth group is

$$D_g = \frac{1}{n_g} \begin{Vmatrix} X'_g X_g - \bar{X}'_g \bar{X}_g \end{Vmatrix}$$

There will be G such dispersion matrices.

The deviation scores $x_{pg.}$ for the pth apprentice measured from the centroid of the gth group on tests 1 and 2 are expressed in the row matrix

$$x_{pg.} = \begin{Vmatrix} (X_{pg1} - \bar{X}_{.g1}) & (X_{pg2} - \bar{X}_{.g2}) \end{Vmatrix}$$

There will be G such expressions for each apprentice, that is, any one point in the test space will be represented as vectors from G different centroids.

If the scores for the gth job approximate a bivariate normal distribution, the point $X_{p..}$ will lie on an isofrequency contour ellipse defined by the equation

$$x_{p..} D_g^{-1} x'_{p..} = \chi_g^2$$

There will be G such ellipses for each point in the test space.

For any pair of scores $X_{..1}$ and $X_{..2}$ representing any point in the test space, a matrix variable may be written

$$x_{.g.} = \|(X_{..1} - \bar{X}_{.g1})\ \ (X_{..2} - \bar{X}_{.g2})\|$$

There will be G such row matrices expressing each point as a deviation from a different group centroid. The value of χ_g^2 for any point may be computed for any group. In general there will be G values of χ_g^2 for each point in the test space. For any value of χ_g^2 the centour score associated with χ_g^2 may be ascertained as P in the probability table of χ^2 with two degrees of freedom. For values of χ^2 that are not tabled the centour equivalent may be accurately computed from

$$C_g = 100[1 - \sqrt{2\pi}m_1(\chi_g)]$$

where $m_1(\chi_g)$ is obtained from Pearson's Table IX (1924). There will be G such values of C_g for every point in the test space.

When the raw score distributions for *all* G jobs are approximately normal, the raw score scale is the simplest answer to

Profile Problem 1. On what type of scale should profiles be represented? *Answer:* If the obtained score data in the groups are not acceptably described by normal distributions, a scaling of raw scores to normalize the distributions is necessary. Computation of centour scores solves

Profile Problem 2. On which group should the raw scores be standardized? *Answer:* Raw scores should be standardized upon *each* group in turn. Centour scores solve

Profile Problem 3. How may the joint performance of all individuals be represented? Answer: Centour scores are derived from the dispersion matrix in each job. The dispersion matrix contains all the useful information concerning joint dispersion in the job. Centour scores also provide a solution to

Profile Problem 4. How may the dispersion of job profiles be represented? *Answer:* Centour scores translate the total dispersion characteristic of any group into a directly interpretable statement of individual divergence from the centroid.

This statement of the general case has been introduced with the assumption that apprentices were tested at induction, that test scores were not known when they were advised about the election of a job, and that apprentices were assigned to jobs in the usual manner. Elimination of both unsatisfactory and dissatisfied employees from the empirical selection of groups introduces some guarantee that the centour scores define regions of the test space which are suitable for use in decisions concerning the assignment of men to jobs. However, the assumption also means that use of centour scores preserves a region fixed by present assignment procedures.

The calculation of a table of centour equivalents can be accomplished with *a priori* determination of desired statistical outcomes of assignment procedures. If it is administratively desirable that measures for job *g* be normally distributed with any centroid denoted A_g and with a dispersion matrix B_g, centour tables to be used by assignment personnel may be constructed from

$$C_g = 100[1 - \sqrt{2\pi}m_1(\chi_g)]$$

where $\chi_g{}^2$ is given by

$$\chi_g{}^2 = x_{.g.}B_g{}^{-1}x'_{.g.}$$

in which

$$x_{.g.} = \|(X_{..1} - A_{.g1})\ \ (X_{..2} - A_{.g2})\|$$

Such centour scores will inform personnel advisers of the divergence of individuals from the *desired* centroid in units of measure derived from the *desired* dispersion in the job.

Chapter 4

The Three-Variate Case

The Indoor–Outdoor, Solitary–Convivial, and Liberal– Conservative Scores

The Conservative Score

In Chapters 2 and 3 we noted that the Activity Preference Inventory was in three sections. The third section contains 25 items. One activity of each pair is a liberal activity, the other a conservative activity. An example is

_____ Counseling: Advising _____

The apprentice's score is the number of *conservative* activities he prefers.

Profile Representation

The numbers of outdoor, convivial, and conservative activities Joe Armand preferred are indicated in a roster:

Apprentice	Social Security Number	Number of Activity Preferences		
		Outdoor	Convivial	Conservative
Armand, Joe	123-45-6789	22	22	6

We have noted that each of these numbers represents a statement of preferences in relation to all the preferences of a particular kind which could have been chosen. For instance, Joe prefers 22 of 30 outdoor activities, 22 of 35 convivial ones, and 6 of 25 conservative activities. However, we abandoned this type of interpretation because it contains no information about Joe's activities in relation to those of other apprentices.

We have also indicated in Chapters 2 and 3 that the information for Joe can be represented on a profile such as those constructed in Fig. 3.2. For three tests we must add a third profile stalk to Fig. 3.2. We do so in Fig. 4.1. Actually the new profile stalk could be added in any one of three places in each of the two different ways of noting two profile stalks illustrated in Fig. 3.2. With this method, Joe has not one profile, but six.

153

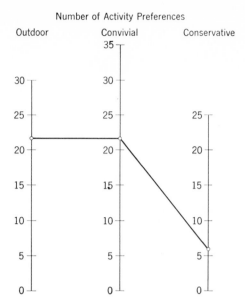

Fig. 4.1   *One of "the profiles" of Joe Armand.*

Fortunately, the fact that Joe has multiple profiles is not important as long as one is being studied independently of all others.

Cartesian Representation

In Chapter 2 we showed that the rotation of one of the stalks of a profile through 90° created a plane after the two zero points of the stalks were united at a single point. The profile of an apprentice was then indicated as a point in the resulting plane.

When three tests are available and it is necessary to create three profile stalks to represent their information for an apprentice, the three stalks can be arranged like a corner of a room in three-dimensional form. Such a three-dimensional space is indicated in Fig. 4.2. The floor of the "room" in Fig. 4.2 is the plane in which the outdoor and convivial activities are represented. The left wall is a plane in which convivial and conservative activity preferences are to be plotted. The supposed wall on the right is a plane in which outdoor and conservative activities are indicated.

In the three-space of the presumed room which we have constructed in Fig. 4.2, the three zero points of the three profile stalks of Fig. 4.1 have been united. The figure is also constructed according to the convention of a *right-handed system*. In the right-handed system, the X_3 axis is drawn vertically, and X_1 and X_2 axes are constructed at right angles to the vertical

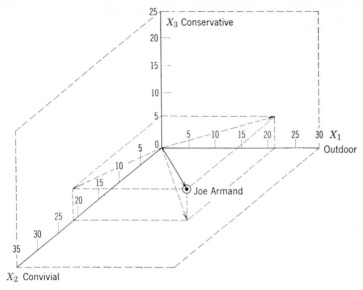

Fig. 4.2 *Profile on Cartesian axes—Joe Armand.*

in a clockwise sequence. Since each of the planes in Fig. 4.2 is at right angles to each of the other two planes, the systems of planes are said to form a Cartesian space. All planes in a Cartesian space are at right angles (that is, orthogonal) to all other planes of the space. The particular Cartesian space of Fig. 4.2 has been labeled according to the scores of our tests. Therefore our test space is a Cartesian space.

We have indicated Joe Armand's test scores, $X_1 = 22$, $X_2 = 22$, $X_3 = 6$, in the Cartesian test space of Fig. 4.2. Since we know that this figure is constructed according to the right-hand convention of labeling the axes we could have reported the location of the point as (22, 22, 6) without indicating the test for which each score stands and still have easily constructed the point. In a right-handed system we understand from the sequence (22, 22, 6) that we measure off 22 units on X_1, construct a vector in the X_1, X_2 plane parallel to the X_2 axis, and measure off 22 units on that vector. From there we construct a vector parallel to X_3 and measure off 6 units on it. The resulting point locates the scores of 22, 22, and 6 for Joe.

The introduction of coordinate axes with a common origin has increased the possible types of visual representations of scores. For instance, in Fig. 4.2 trace the numerous ways to reach the point for Joe Armand. Any three of the united edges of the rectangular solid in that figure offer a route to the point. The rectangular solid represents the various projections of

Joe's point into the planes and parallel planes which are constructed in the three-dimensional test space. We described only the standard right-handed pattern for getting to Joe's point when we first located it. Actually, there are many ways of reaching it.

Though there are various ways to represent the location of Joe's point visually, the most efficient graphic device seems to be the solid line represented as an arrow in Fig. 4.2. The line is drawn from the origin to the point for Joe's scores. In Chapter 3, we called such a line in Fig. 3.3d a vector. The solid arrow in Fig. 4.2 is also a vector. The vector represents both the distance and the direction which Joe's point is from the origin. The distance is $\sqrt{(22)^2 + (22)^2 + (6)^2}$ or $\sqrt{1004}$, which is approximately 31.7 units. It is quite evident in Fig. 4.2 that the vector of Joe's scores is not much longer than is its projection into the X_1 and X_2 planes. The projection has a length of $\sqrt{(22)^2 + (22)^2}$ or $\sqrt{968}$. The projection of a vector into a plane at the origin of the dimension of projection effectively makes the coordinate zero in the dimension from which the projection originates.

The idea of vector representation of the three-score profile is an obvious extension of our basic idea already developed for representing single and double scores for individuals. In the univariate case we represented the score as a point on a line. The vector of the point was then the distance of the point from the origin in the direction of the line. In the bivariate case, we represented the two scores in a plane or two-space. The vector was a line from the origin in the direction of the point and its length was $\sqrt{(X_1)^2 + (X_2)^2}$. Three such planes are indicated in Fig. 4.2. In each of the three planes, the projection of Joe's vector into a particular plane has been indicated by dotted lines with arrow heads at their points of termination. But in the three-dimensional instance in which all scores are considered simultaneously, the scores of a person can be represented in the three-space equivalent of a room. The vector of the scores will be a line from the origin in the direction of the point. The length of the vector will be $\sqrt{(X_1)^2 + (X_2)^2 + (X_3)^2}$.

Three Profiles for Three Tests in Cartesian Space

The roster of the three apprentices in our example is:

	Number of Activity Preferences		
Apprentice	Outdoor	Convivial	Conservative
Armand, Joe	22	22	6
Baslik, Tom	18	14	7
Flint, Bill	20	15	12

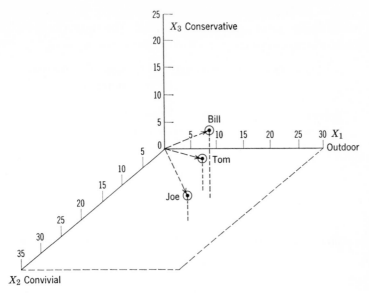

Fig. 4.3 *Three profiles on Cartesian axes.*

The scores in the roster may be written as a matrix X in which the rows represent men and the columns represent tests:

$$X = \begin{Vmatrix} 22 & 22 & 6 \\ 18 & 14 & 7 \\ 20 & 15 & 12 \end{Vmatrix}$$

Cartesian representation in three-space records graphically exactly the same information that the matrix records. We have already noted this for Joe Armand in Fig. 4.2. The scores for the other two apprentices are added in Fig. 4.3. The Cartesian method of vector representation enjoys the advantage of simplicity in both construction and interpretation. All the differences among the apprentices on any test, pairs of tests, or the three tests considered jointly can be read from the distance relations among the three points in Cartesian space. In Cartesian form each apprentice's point can be represented as a vector from any desired origin. In profile representation this simple concept of distance from an origin is not obvious.

The Group of Apprentices in Three-Space

Roster, Matrix, and Profiles

The number of outdoor and convivial activity preferences expressed by each apprentice was reported in Table 3.1. Actually each of those apprentices took the entire Activity Preference Inventory and a third score is available which is not reported in this table. The three scores for each apprentice, which are in a roster such as Table 3.1, take the following form.

Number of Outdoor, Convivial, and Conservative Activity
Preferences of New York City Apprentices

Apprentice	Number of Activity Preferences		
Number	Outdoor	Convivial	Conservative
1	21	16	10
2	21	17	11
3	27	20	14
⋮	⋮	⋮	⋮
135	21	18	13

The roster may be written in a matrix of 135 rows and 3 columns:

$$\begin{Vmatrix} 21 & 16 & 10 \\ 21 & 17 & 11 \\ 27 & 20 & 14 \\ \vdots & \vdots & \vdots \\ 21 & 18 & 13 \end{Vmatrix} \quad \text{(135 rows)}$$

Neither roster nor matrix affords a visual impression of the typical scores on the three tests, the dispersion in the scores, or the joint relation among outdoor, convivial, and conservative activity preferences. We sought these important interpretative impressions from profile representation. In Chapter 2, we found the way in which they could be provided when we were considering only one test.

We noted in Chapter 3 (as we discussed Fig. 3.6) that the problem of examining groups of profiles and deriving interpretative comparisons of individuals becomes confusing for two tests as the number of people increases. Figure 3.6 reminds us why. The problem is even more complex if one attempts to denote the vectors of each person on a profile of three stalks. For instance, in the case of three test scores for each of the apprentices depicted in Fig. 3.6, two more sets of lines would have to be imposed on the already confused representation of the score vectors if the profile depiction were to represent all information available in the matrix for the group. Obviously, the result would no longer have the effect of aiding comprehension through visualization.

The frequency distribution of the group's scores on each test and the essential descriptive statistics of the distribution are given in Table 4.1.

Table 4.1 *Frequency Distributions of the Group* ($N = 135$)

Number of Preferences	Outdoor	Convivial	Conservative
35	–	–	–
34	–	–	–
33	–	–	–
32	–	–	–
31	–	–	–
30	–	1	–
29	1	1	–
28	–	4	–
27	2	4	–
26	1	3	–
25	2	4	–
24	4	9	–
23	4	10	–
22	6	12	–
21	10	10	–
20	20	12	1
19	9	12	3
18	9	14	3
17	11	8	–
16	12	10	2
15	6	8	10
14	9	2	15
13	13	4	20
12	2	2	14
11	9	3	11
10	3	–	16
9	1	1	10
8	–	–	6
7	–	1	11
6	1	–	5
5	–	–	2
4	–	–	4
3	–	–	–
2	–	–	1
1	–	–	1
0	–	–	–
Mean	17.44	19.75	11.16
σ	4.25	4.35	3.56

As was true when only two tests were available, centour scores can be readily computed for each test and each man's score could be directly interpreted in terms of his divergence from the centroid of the group. We abandoned this method in the two-variate case because we sought a single index which would incorporate the information from both tests. We found it possible to extend the concept of the centour score to two variables. We then got a single centour score for each pair of test scores of an apprentice. Of course, we could consider the scores as three pairs for each person and compute the bivariate centour in each instance. This would obviously become more and more impractical as the number of possible pairs multiplied as the number of tests increased. We therefore continue to seek a single index which will present the information about the frequency of an apprentice's score in a group when each apprentice has three, not two, scores.

The Trivariate Normal Distribution

We plotted the outdoor and convivial activity preferences in the two-dimensional test space of Fig. 3.7. The addition of the preference of each apprentice for conservative activities requires a third dimension to depict the three kinds of activities. We have already noted that the preferences can be indicated by the representation of vectors (Fig. 4.3). The data for the group of 135 apprentices would require adding 132 vectors to the three already indicated in Fig. 4.3.

The possible number of activities is: outdoor, 30; convivial, 35; and conservative, 25. There are therefore $31 \times 36 \times 26$, or 29,016, ways in which a set of three scores on the Inventory could be formed. In a group of only 135 apprentices, not many of these combinations will be represented. It is therefore not very likely that any particular set of scores will appear more than once. The empirical probabilities of a single set of scores are therefore not very stable.

We discussed the problem of getting more stable empirical estimates of the probabilities for sets of scores when we considered the two activity preferences of the apprentices in Chapter 3. We noted then that we needed an ideal distribution which represented the empirical facts reasonably well. (We did the same thing with one score in Chapter 2.) The ideal distribution used in Chapters 2 and 3 was the normal distribution.

For one variate, the normal distribution appears as indicated in Fig. 3.9. For two variates, the frequency was represented in three dimensions—one dimension for each of the tests and the third for frequency. In Chapter 3, Fig. 3.10 through 3.18 showed how the concept of frequency for the normal distribution could be represented in three dimensions. That series of diagrams demonstrated representation of frequency for empirical information and for the ideal normal distribution. In Figs. 3.17 and 3.18, we indicated how a contour with the same frequency throughout the test space could be graphed. The contour consisted of all those points which satisfied the matrix equation

$$xD^{-1}x' = \chi^2$$

In that equation x was a row vector of two columns in which were noted the deviations of X_1 and X_2 from their respective means, and D was the dispersion matrix of the group.

When three variables are available, the frequency of the normal distribution must be represented as density, rather than as ordinates. The three dimensions which can be schematized in a plane are all needed for representation of the three test scores themselves. The density of the trivariate normal distribution is schematized in a rough way in Fig. 4.4. The figure depicts a section through four density ellipsoids, those with values of χ of 0.5, 1.0, 1.5, and 2.0.

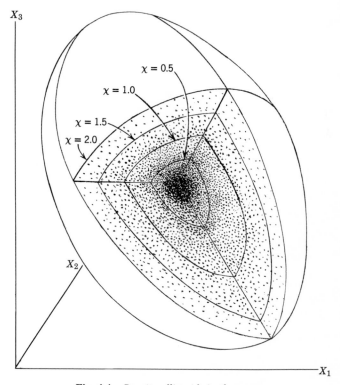

Fig. 4.4 *Density ellipsoids in three-space.*

Four density ellipsoids for the ideal distribution representing a different set of data are indicated in Fig. 4.5. These data represent tests which are also positively intercorrelated. Furthermore, the ratios of standard deviations for the data in Figs. 4.4 and 4.5 are different. The standard deviations of all three tests are about equal in Fig. 4.4 and the isodensity contours approximate the shapes of golf, tennis, beach balls and the like. In Fig. 4.5, however, X_1 is more variable than are X_2 and X_3. The isodensity spheroids are ellipsoidal as a result. The figure resembles a nest of inflated footballs.

The football-like quality of Fig. 4.5 is suggested in Fig. 4.6 where a section through Fig. 4.5 is shown. Figure 4.6 suggests that the particular set of data represented by the ideal normal trivariate distribution yields isodensity contours which are round with regard to X_2 and X_3. The standard deviations of X_2 and X_3 are equal in this instance and are uncorrelated.

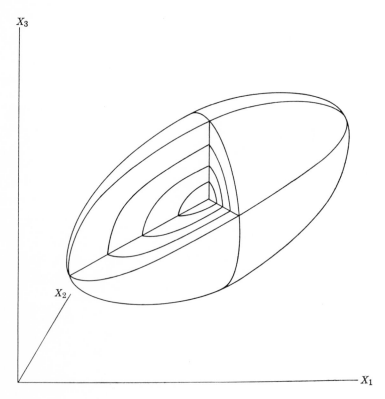

Fig. 4.5   *Contour ellipsoids in three-space.*

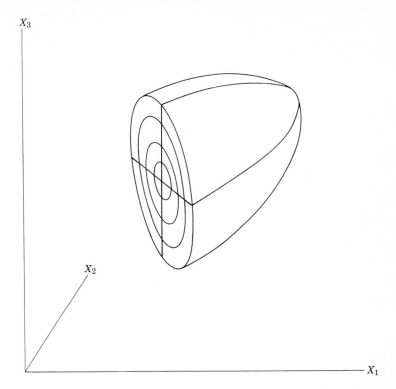

Fig. 4.6 *A section of contour ellipsoids in three-space.*

In Chapter 3, we developed the general form of the normal distribution in terms of matrix notation. The density of the general normal distribution for any number of tests T at the point $(x_1, x_2 \ldots, x_T)$ is

$$y = \frac{1}{(2\pi)^{T/2}|D|^{1/T}} \exp\left(-\frac{\chi^2}{2}\right)$$

Thus in the case of the normal trivariate frequency surface the point (x_1, x_2, x_3) has the density

$$y = \frac{1}{(2\pi)^{3/2}|D|^{1/3}} \exp\left(-\frac{\chi^2}{2}\right)$$

χ^2 in this expression has the value

$$xD^{-1}x' = \chi^2$$

where x is the row vector of deviations of X_1, X_2, X_3 from the mean value of each X, and D is the dispersion matrix of the three variables.

The proportion of the trivariate normal distribution which lies outside the isodensity ellipsoid defined by a fixed value of χ^2 may be determined from the probability table of χ^2. More exact values can be obtained for tabled values of χ in Pearson (1924) which report $m_2(\chi)$ from which it is possible to compute

$$q = 2m_2(\chi)$$

The centour score associated with the particular value of χ is

$$100(1 - q)$$

The centour signifies the percent of the normal density function which lies outside the ellipsoid on which the values of X_1, X_2, and X_3 lie.

The Trivariate Matrix of the Group of Apprentices

Now that we have examined the meaning of centour scores in three dimensions, let us consider their computation for a single group.

The 135 sets of three scores for each apprentice in the New York City group are written in the matrix X:

$$X = \begin{Vmatrix} 21 & 16 & 10 \\ 21 & 17 & 11 \\ 27 & 20 & 14 \\ \vdots & \vdots & \vdots \\ 21 & 18 & 13 \end{Vmatrix} \quad \text{(135 rows)}$$

The cross-product matrix $X'X$ is

$$X'X = \begin{Vmatrix} 43{,}480 & 46{,}027 & 26{,}023 \\ 46{,}027 & 55{,}202 & 29{,}519 \\ 26{,}023 & 29{,}519 & 18{,}516 \end{Vmatrix}$$

which symbolically represents

$$X'X = \begin{Vmatrix} \sum X_1{}^2 & \sum X_1 X_2 & \sum X_1 X_3 \\ \sum X_2 X_1 & \sum X_2{}^2 & \sum X_2 X_3 \\ \sum X_3 X_1 & \sum X_3 X_2 & \sum X_3{}^2 \end{Vmatrix}$$

The mean of the conservative scores is 11.1556. The matrix of means $\overline{X}$ is now

$$\overline{X} = \begin{Vmatrix} 17.4370 & 19.7481 & 11.1556 \\ 17.4370 & 19.7481 & 11.1556 \\ 17.4370 & 19.7481 & 11.1556 \\ \vdots & \vdots & \vdots \\ 17.4370 & 19.7481 & 11.1556 \end{Vmatrix} \quad \text{(135 rows)}$$

Therefore the matrix product $\bar{X}'\bar{X}$ becomes

$$\bar{X}'\bar{X} = \begin{Vmatrix} 41{,}046.6108 & 46{,}486.9287 & 26{,}260.2266 \\ 46{,}486.9287 & 52{,}648.3063 & 29{,}740.7570 \\ 26{,}260.2266 & 29{,}740.7570 & 16{,}800.4005 \end{Vmatrix}$$

which symbolically is equivalent to

$$\bar{X}'\bar{X} = \begin{Vmatrix} n\bar{X}_{.1}^{2} & n\bar{X}_{.1}\bar{X}_{.2} & n\bar{X}_{.1}\bar{X}_{.3} \\ n\bar{X}_{.2}\bar{X}_{.1} & n\bar{X}_{.2}^{2} & n\bar{X}_{.2}\bar{X}_{.3} \\ n\bar{X}_{.3}\bar{X}_{.1} & n\bar{X}_{.3}\bar{X}_{.2} & n\bar{X}_{.3}^{2} \end{Vmatrix}$$

By subtraction of $\bar{X}'\bar{X}$ from $X'X$, the cross-product matrix of deviation scores is found to be

$$X'X - \bar{X}'\bar{X} = \begin{Vmatrix} 2433.3892 & -459.9287 & -237.2266 \\ -459.9287 & 2553.6937 & -221.7570 \\ -237.2266 & -221.7570 & 1715.5995 \end{Vmatrix}$$

There are 135 apprentices in the group and the dispersion matrix therefore is

$$D = \frac{1}{n}\,S = \begin{Vmatrix} 18.0251 & -3.4068 & -1.7572 \\ -3.4068 & 18.9162 & -1.6426 \\ -1.7572 & -1.6426 & 12.7081 \end{Vmatrix}$$

The set of homothetic ellipses for the 135 apprentices are defined by fixed values of χ^2 in the expression

$$xD^{-1}x' = \chi^2$$

where x is the row vector of deviation scores of the point (X_1, X_2, X_3) and D is the dispersion matrix we have just computed. The evaluation of χ^2 for any point in the three-space therefore requires determination of the inverse of the matrix D. We have indicated the rules for computation of the inverse of a matrix in Chapter 3. We compute the inverse of D here to further illustrate the computations in the complex case.

The adjoint of the matrix D is constructed by computing the cofactors of each of the elements in the matrix D. The cofactor of the element in the first row first column is the determinant of

$$D^{11} = (-1)^{1+1} \begin{Vmatrix} 18.9162 & -1.6426 \\ -1.6426 & 12.7081 \end{Vmatrix}$$

The cofactor of the element in the second row first column of D is the determinant of

$$D^{21} = (-1)^{2+1} \begin{Vmatrix} -3.4069 & -1.7572 \\ -1.6426 & 12.7081 \end{Vmatrix}$$

The cofactors of the remaining elements of the matrix D can be constructed similarly. In this instance the adjoint of the matrix D is

$$\text{adj } D = \begin{Vmatrix} 237.6922 & 46.1816 & 38.8366 \\ 46.1816 & 225.9778 & 35.5955 \\ 38.8366 & 35.5955 & 329.3606 \end{Vmatrix}$$

Since we have computed the cofactors of each element of the matrix D in obtaining the adjoint of D, we may compute the determinant of D from the equation

$$|D| = d_{11}D^{11} + d_{21}D^{21} + d_{31}D^{31}$$

We could, of course, have used a similar type of equation for the sum of products of elements and cofactors for any other column or row of D. The value of the determinant is

$$|D| \doteq 4058.8461$$

Thus for the group the inverse of the matrix D is

$$D^{-1} = \begin{Vmatrix} .058562 & .011378 & .009568 \\ .011378 & .055675 & .008770 \\ .009568 & .008770 & .081146 \end{Vmatrix}$$

Consequently, the set of isofrequency ellipses for the group data is specified by the equation

$$x \cdot \begin{Vmatrix} .058562 & .011378 & .009568 \\ .011378 & .055675 & .008770 \\ .009568 & .008770 & .081146 \end{Vmatrix} \cdot x' = \chi^2$$

when χ^2 has a fixed value. We can use this equation to determine the value of χ^2 associated with the preference for outdoor, convivial, and conservative activities of any apprentice in the group. From this value of χ^2 it is possible to determine a centour score by means of Pearson's Tables (1924).

Centour Scores for Individuals

We can compute the actual centour score associated with the activity preferences of Joe Armand by first forming the matrix variable x which is

$$x = \|(22 - 17.4370) \quad (22 - 19.7481) \quad (6 - 11.1556)\|$$

and then computing the triple matrix product:

$$\|4.5360 \quad 2.2519 \quad -5.1556\| \cdot \begin{Vmatrix} .058562 & .011378 & .009568 \\ .011378 & .055675 & .008770 \\ .009568 & .008770 & .081146 \end{Vmatrix} \cdot \begin{Vmatrix} 4.5360 \\ 2.2519 \\ -5.1556 \end{Vmatrix}$$

This triple matrix product is the value of χ^2 for Joe. The value in this instance is 3.2420. By means of Pearson's Tables (1924) we find that .32 is the value of $m_2(\chi)$; thus q, the area within the ellipsoid on which this point falls, is twice this number, or .64. The density outside the ellipsoid on which this point is located is one minus this number, or .36. The centour score is 100 times this, or approximately 36. Thus, 36% of Joe's group have activity preferences more divergent from the centroid of the group than are those of Joe. Joe's activity preferences are reasonably typical of apprentices.

The Tabling of Centour Scores

Since a personnel adviser is likely to advise many apprentices in a single day, it is convenient for him to have a table of centour scores for three variables. It would be most accurate if the table of centour scores provided an entry for each of the possible combinations of outdoor, convivial, and conservative activity preferences. Since there are 29,016 entries in the present instance, complete detail is maintained at the cost of inconvenience. The table becomes impractical. A compromise is frequently made. One such compromise is to table centour scores for every fifth value of each of the variables, as done in Table 4.2. To use Table 4.2, find the panel of the table which most closely approximates the number of conservative activities of an individual. Then enter that panel at the values most closely approximating the outdoor and convivial activity preferences of the individual. For instance, if an apprentice preferred 15 conservative activities, turn to page 168 on which the block corresponding to 15 conservative activity preferences appears. If the apprentice also preferred 20 outdoor and 10 convivial activities, look down the column labeled 20 until it intersects the row labeled 10 in this block of 15 conservative activity preferences. The number 12 is the centour associated with this particular triad of activity preferences. The centour, of course, indicates the fraction of the group expected to have activity preferences more divergent from the group mean (in the χ^2 sense) than is the χ^2 value of this particular point.

Passenger Agents, Mechanics, and Operations Control Agents

We have noted in Chapters 2 and 3 that it is necessary to know the later jobs of apprentices who were tested if we are to provide information for

Table 4.2 *Centour Scores: Outdoor, Convivial, and Conservative Activity Preferences—Apprentice Group*

| Twenty-Five Conservative Activity Preferences | | | | | | |
| | | | Outdoor | | | |
Convivial	0	5	10	15	20	25	30
35	*	*	*	*	*	*	*
30	*	*	*	*	*	*	*
25	*	*	*	*	*	*	*
20	*	*	*	*	*	*	*
15	*	*	*	*	*	*	*
10	*	*	*	*	*	*	*
5	*	*	*	*	*	*	*
0	*	*	*	*	*	*	*

* Centour <.5

| Twenty Conservative Activity Preferences | | | | | | |
| | | | Outdoor | | | |
Convivial	0	5	10	15	20	25	30
35	*	*	*	*	*	*	*
30	*	*	*	*	*	*	*
25	*	*	02	04	02	*	*
20	*	*	04	10	07	01	*
15	*	*	02	07	06	01	*
10	*	*	*	01	02	01	*
5	*	*	*	01	02	01	*
0	*	*	*	*	*	*	*

* Centour <.5

| Fifteen Conservative Activity Preferences | | | | | | |
| | | | Outdoor | | | |
Convivial	0	5	10	15	20	25	30
35	*	*	*	*	*	*	*
30	*	*	03	06	03	*	*
25	*	02	18	40	26	05	*
20	*	03	28	72	61	16	01
15	*	01	13	46	49	16	01
10	*	*	02	09	12	04	*
5	*	*	*	*	01	*	*
0	*	*	*	*	*	*	*

* Centour <.5

Table 4.2 (*continued*)

Ten Conservative Activity Preferences

			Outdoor				
Convivial	0	5	10	15	20	25	30
35	*	*	*	01	*	*	*
30	*	01	06	14	08	01	*
25	*	02	27	65	54	13	01
20	*	02	32	92	93	34	03
15	*	01	13	55	68	28	03
10	*	*	01	09	15	07	01
5	*	*	*	*	01	*	*
0	*	*	*	*	*	*	*

* Centour < .5

Five Conservative Activity Preferences

			Outdoor				
Convivial	0	5	10	15	20	25	30
35	*	*	*	*	*	*	*
30	*	*	02	05	04	01	*
25	*	*	06	22	22	06	*
20	*	*	07	30	37	14	01
15	*	*	02	12	20	09	01
10	*	*	*	01	03	02	*
5	*	*	*	*	*	*	*
0	*	*	*	*	*	*	*

* Centour < .5

Zero Conservative Activity Preferences

			Outdoor				
Convivial	0	5	10	15	20	25	30
35	*	*	*	*	*	*	*
30	*	*	*	*	*	*	*
25	*	*	*	01	01	*	*
20	*	*	*	02	02	01	*
15	*	*	*	*	01	*	*
10	*	*	*	*	*	*	*
5	*	*	*	*	*	*	*
0	*	*	*	*	*	*	*

* Centour < .5

advising incoming apprentices. We have stressed that the employees included in studies of this type should both succeed and be satisfied with their work. We have been referring to passenger agents, mechanics, and operations control agents as reference groups.

In the case of one variable in Chapter 2 and two variables in Chapter 3, we first dealt with two groups and then with three to demonstrate that the centour score procedure is specific to a group. Therefore the addition of the third group did not modify the centour scores for either of the previous two. The additional group only provided another reference group for comparison whenever the scores of a new apprentice were to be interpreted in an advisory session with a personnel head. Because of this independence of centours for groups, we can dispense with the consideration of only two groups before introducing the third. We therefore consider the matrix representation of all three groups simultaneously.

The rosters for the three groups (see Appendix B for full rosters) are

Number of Outdoor, Convivial, and Conservative Activity
Preferences Expressed by Satisfactory and Satisfied:

Apprentice Number	Number of Activity Preferences		
	Outdoor	Convivial	Conservative
Passenger Agents			
1	10	22	5
2	14	17	6
3	19	33	7
⋮	⋮	⋮	⋮
85	16	24	10
Mechanics			
1	20	27	6
2	21	15	10
3	15	27	12
⋮	⋮	⋮	⋮
93	19	16	6
Operations Control Agents			
1	19	19	16
2	17	17	12
3	8	17	14
⋮	⋮	⋮	⋮
66	18	20	10

The rosters may be represented as matrices X_1, X_2, and X_3 where the subscripts 1, 2, and 3, respectively, identify the groups of agents, mechanics, and operations personnel. Thus we have

$$X_1 = \begin{Vmatrix} 10 & 22 & 5 \\ 14 & 17 & 6 \\ 19 & 33 & 7 \\ \vdots & \vdots & \vdots \\ 16 & 24 & 10 \end{Vmatrix} \quad \text{(85 rows)}$$

$$X_2 = \begin{Vmatrix} 20 & 27 & 6 \\ 21 & 15 & 10 \\ 15 & 27 & 12 \\ \vdots & \vdots & \vdots \\ 19 & 16 & 6 \end{Vmatrix} \quad \text{(93 rows)}$$

$$X_3 = \begin{Vmatrix} 19 & 19 & 16 \\ 17 & 17 & 12 \\ 8 & 17 & 14 \\ \vdots & \vdots & \vdots \\ 18 & 20 & 10 \end{Vmatrix} \quad \text{(66 rows)}$$

The average scores for the three variables in each group are

| | Number of Activity. Preferences | | |
Group	Outdoor	Convivial	Conservative
Agents	12.5882	24.2235	9.0235
Mechanics	18.5376	21.1398	10.1398
Operations Men	15.5758	15.4545	13.2424

The matrix of deviations of cross products is formed by computing the matrix product $X'X$ and subtracting the matrix product $\bar{X}'\bar{X}$. The difference between these matrices forms the equivalent of

$$S = \begin{Vmatrix} \sum X_1{}^2 & \sum X_1 X_2 & \sum X_1 X_3 \\ \sum X_2 X_1 & \sum X_2{}^2 & \sum X_2 X_3 \\ \sum X_3 X_1 & \sum X_3 X_2 & \sum X_3{}^2 \end{Vmatrix} - \begin{Vmatrix} n\bar{X}_1{}^2 & n\bar{X}_1\bar{X}_2 & n\bar{X}_1\bar{X}_3 \\ n\bar{X}_2\bar{X}_1 & n\bar{X}_2{}^2 & n\bar{X}_2\bar{X}_3 \\ n\bar{X}_3\bar{X}_1 & n\bar{X}_3\bar{X}_2 & n\bar{X}_3{}^2 \end{Vmatrix}$$

For each group, then, the matrix S of sum of cross products of deviation scores is

$$S_1 = \begin{Vmatrix} 1700.5882 & 387.8235 & -202.1765 \\ 387.8235 & 1578.7529 & 210.5529 \\ -202.1765 & 210.5529 & 829.9529 \end{Vmatrix}$$

$$S_2 = \begin{Vmatrix} 1169.1183 & -144.9892 & 234.0108 \\ -144.9892 & 1905.1828 & 16.1828 \\ 234.0108 & 16.1828 & 967.1828 \end{Vmatrix}$$

$$S_3 = \begin{Vmatrix} 1098.1212 & 108.7273 & 44.7879 \\ 108.7273 & 922.3636 & 8.7273 \\ 44.7879 & 8.7273 & 886.1212 \end{Vmatrix}$$

There are 85 agents, 93 mechanics, and 66 operations men. The dispersion matrix D for each group is formed by computing the product $(1/n)S$. The several dispersion matrices are

$$D_1 = \begin{Vmatrix} 20.0069 & 4.5626 & -2.3787 \\ 4.5626 & 18.5736 & 2.4771 \\ -2.3787 & 2.4771 & 9.7642 \end{Vmatrix}$$

$$D_2 = \begin{Vmatrix} 12.5712 & -1.5590 & 2.5162 \\ -1.5590 & 20.4858 & .1740 \\ 2.5162 & .1740 & 10.3998 \end{Vmatrix}$$

$$D_3 = \begin{Vmatrix} 16.6382 & 1.6474 & .6786 \\ 1.6474 & 13.9752 & .1322 \\ .6786 & .1322 & 13.4261 \end{Vmatrix}$$

Centour scores are computed for a particular set of three raw scores by forming the row vector of deviation scores

$$x = \| (X_1 - \bar{X}_1) \quad (X_2 - \bar{X}_2) \quad (X_3 - \bar{X}_3) \|$$

If the row vector of means used in computation of the deviation vector is for the first group, the row vector is x_1. If the means for group two are used, the row vector of deviation scores is x_2. The means for the third group give x_3 as the row vector of deviation scores.

Centour scores require computation of χ^2 according to

$$x_g D_g^{-1} x'_g = \chi_g^2$$

A particular set of three scores, X_1, X_2, X_3, will then be associated with three values of χ_g^2, that is, with one χ_g^2 for each of the three groups. We can compute χ_g by taking the square root of $\chi_g{}^2$ in each instance. This value may be used to enter Table IX of Pearson's Tables (1924) and to determine the value of $m_2(\chi)$. The proportion of the normal distribution which lies outside the isofrequency ellipsoid corresponding to $\chi_g{}^2$ is then given by

$$q_g = 1 - 2m_2(\chi_g)$$

The percent of the normal distribution outside the ellipsoid is then given by

$$C_g = 100q_g$$

There will be one centour score C_g for each group for which the scores of a particular individual are to be compared.

The centour scores require the inverse of the matrix of a group in the computation of $\chi_g{}^2$. For the three groups under consideration, the inverse of the dispersion matrix of each is

$$D_1{}^{-1} = \begin{Vmatrix} .055741 & -.016047 & .017650 \\ -.016047 & .060345 & -.019218 \\ .017650 & -.019218 & .111591 \end{Vmatrix}$$

$$D_2{}^{-1} = \begin{Vmatrix} .084479 & .006604 & -.020550 \\ .006604 & .049337 & -.002423 \\ -.020550 & -.002423 & .101168 \end{Vmatrix}$$

$$D_3{}^{-1} = \begin{Vmatrix} .060934 & -.007154 & -.003009 \\ -.007154 & .072402 & -.000351 \\ -.003009 & -.000351 & .074637 \end{Vmatrix}$$

An abbreviated table of centour scores has been provided for the three groups in Table 4.3. Table 4.3 has been abbreviated, as was Table 4.2. There are centour scores tabled for only every fifth value of the three scores.

Joe Armand preferred 22 outdoor, 22 convivial, and 6 conservative activities. In the panel for 5 conservative activities, the centours corresponding to 20 outdoor and 20 convivial activities are 15, 37, and 05, respectively, for agents, mechanics, and operations personnel. Joe's preferences are more like those of mechanics than they are of either of the other two groups of apprentices. They are somewhat unusual for those who later become passenger agents and they are quite atypical of those who later become operations personnel. The centours for the exact values of Joe's scores are 13, 33, and 03, respectively. The tabled values are not too different from the exact values.

Table 4.3 *Centour Scores: Outdoor, Convivial, and Conservative Activity Preferences—Passenger Agents (PA), Mechanics (M), and Operations Control Agents (OCA)*

| | | Twenty-Five Conservative Activity Preferences | | | | | | |
| | | Outdoor | | | | | | |
Convivial	Specialty	0	5	10	15	20	25	30
35	PA	*	*	*	*	*	*	*
	M	*	*	*	*	*	*	*
	OCA	*	*	*	*	*	*	*
30	PA	*	*	*	*	*	*	*
	M	*	*	*	*	*	*	*
	OCA	*	*	*	*	*	*	*
25	PA	*	*	*	*	*	*	*
	M	*	*	*	*	*	*	*
	OCA	*	*	*	*	*	*	*
20	PA	*	*	*	*	*	*	*
	M	*	*	*	*	*	*	*
	OCA	*	*	*	01	01	*	*
15	PA	*	*	*	*	*	*	*
	M	*	*	*	*	*	*	*
	OCA	*	*	01	02	01	*	*
10	PA	*	*	*	*	*	*	*
	M	*	*	*	*	*	*	*
	OCA	*	*	*	01	*	*	*
5	PA	*	*	*	*	*	*	*
	M	*	*	*	*	*	*	*
	OCA	*	*	*	*	*	*	*
0	PA	*	*	*	*	*	*	*
	M	*	*	*	*	*	*	*
	OCA	*	*	*	*	*	*	*

* Centour < .5

| | | Twenty Conservative Activity Preferences | | | | | | |
| | | Outdoor | | | | | | |
Convivial	Specialty	0	5	10	15	20	25	30
35	PA	*	*	*	*	*	*	*
	M	*	*	*	*	*	*	*
	OCA	*	*	*	*	*	*	*
30	PA	*	*	*	*	*	*	*
	M	*	*	*	*	*	*	*
	OCA	*	*	*	*	*	*	*
25	PA	*	*	01	*	*	*	*
	M	*	*	*	01	02	01	*
	OCA	*	*	*	02	02	*	*

Table 4.3 (*continued*)

Convivial	Specialty	0	5	10	15	20	25	30
20	PA	*	*	*	*	*	*	*
	M	*	*	*	01	02	01	*
	OCA	*	*	06	17	13	03	*
15	PA	*	*	*	*	*	*	*
	M	*	*	*	*	01	01	*
	OCA	*	01	14	33	22	04	*
10	PA	*	*	*	*	*	*	*
	M	*	*	*	*	*	*	*
	OCA	*	01	06	13	07	01	*
5	PA	*	*	*	*	*	*	*
	M	*	*	*	*	*	*	*
	OCA	*	*	01	01	*	*	*
0	PA	*	*	*	*	*	*	*
	M	*	*	*	*	*	*	*
	OCA	*	*	*	*	*	*	*

* Centour < .5

Fifteen Conservative Activity Preferences

Convivial	Specialty	Outdoor						
		0	5	10	15	20	25	30
35	PA	*	01	03	04	01	*	*
	M	*	*	*	01	01	*	*
	OCA	*	*	*	*	*	*	*
30	PA	*	05	17	17	05	*	*
	M	*	*	*	06	10	02	*
	OCA	*	*	*	*	*	*	*
25	PA	02	13	29	20	04	*	*
	M	*	*	02	20	39	13	01
	OCA	*	*	02	07	06	01	*
20	PA	01	09	14	07	01	*	*
	M	*	*	01	23	50	20	01
	OCA	*	03	26	62	46	19	*
15	PA	*	01	02	01	*	*	*
	M	*	*	*	09	24	11	01
	OCA	*	07	54	97	70	13	*
10	PA	*	*	*	*	*	*	*
	M	*	*	*	01	04	02	*
	OCA	*	04	27	50	27	04	*
5	PA	*	*	*	*	*	*	*
	M	*	*	*	*	*	*	*
	OCA	*	*	02	04	02	*	*
0	PA	*	*	*	*	*	*	*
	M	*	*	*	*	*	*	*
	OCA	*	*	*	*	*	*	*

* Centour < .5

Table 4.3 (*continued*)

Ten Conservative Activity Preferences

Convivial	Specialty	Outdoor						
		0	5	10	15	20	25	30
35	PA	*	01	05	07	06	01	*
	M	*	*	*	02	02	*	*
	OCA	*	*	*	*	*	*	*
30	PA	01	10	45	60	28	03	*
	M	*	*	03	21	24	04	*
	OCA	*	*	*	*	*	*	*
25	PA	03	35	93	93	36	03	*
	M	*	*	09	66	80	20	01
	OCA	*	*	02	06	04	01	*
20	PA	05	35	74	56	13	01	*
	M	*	*	10	77	97	32	01
	OCA	*	02	22	49	35	06	*
15	PA	02	10	16	08	01	*	*
	M	*	*	03	36	59	18	01
	OCA	*	06	47	85	55	09	*
10	PA	*	01	01	*	*	*	*
	M	*	*	*	05	11	03	*
	OCA	*	03	23	41	21	02	*
5	PA	*	*	*	*	*	*	*
	M	*	*	*	*	01	*	*
	OCA	*	*	02	04	01	*	*
0	PA	*	*	*	*	*	*	*
	M	*	*	*	*	*	*	*
	OCA	*	*	*	*	*	*	*

* Centour < .5

Five Conservative Activity Preferences

Convivial	Specialty	Outdoor						
		0	5	10	15	20	25	30
35	PA	*	*	01	02	02	*	*
	M	*	*	*	01	*	*	*
	OCA	*	*	*	*	*	*	*
30	PA	*	02	11	24	15	03	*
	M	*	*	*	08	06	01	*
	OCA	*	*	*	*	*	*	*
25	PA	*	09	43	60	29	04	*
	M	*	*	06	30	25	03	*
	OCA	*	*	*	01	01	*	*
20	PA	01	14	45	47	15	01	*
	M	*	*	07	38	37	06	*
	OCA	*	*	04	08	05	01	*

Table 4.3 (*continued*)

Convivial	Specialty	0	5	10	15	20	25	30
15	PA	01	06	14	10	02	*	*
	M	*	*	02	17	19	03	*
	OCA	*	01	08	17	09	01	*
10	PA	*	01	01	*	*	*	*
	M	*	*	*	03	03	01	*
	OCA	*	01	04	07	03	*	*
5	PA	*	*	*	*	*	*	*
	M	*	*	*	*	*	*	*
	OCA	*	*	*	01	*	*	*
0	PA	*	*	*	*	*	*	*
	M	*	*	*	*	*	*	*
	OCA	*	*	*	*	*	*	*

* Centour < .5

Zero Conservative Activity Preferences
Outdoor

Convivial	Specialty	0	5	10	15	20	25	30
35	PA	*	*	*	*	*	*	*
	M	*	*	*	*	*	*	*
	OCA	*	*	*	*	*	*	*
30	PA	*	*	*	01	01	*	*
	M	*	*	*	*	*	*	*
	OCA	*	*	*	*	*	*	*
25	PA	*	*	01	03	02	*	*
	M	*	*	*	01	01	*	*
	OCA	*	*	*	*	*	*	*
20	PA	*	*	02	04	02	*	*
	M	*	*	*	02	01	*	*
	OCA	*	*	*	*	*	*	*
15	PA	*	*	01	01	*	*	*
	M	*	*	*	01	01	*	*
	OCA	*	*	*	*	*	*	*
10	PA	*	*	*	*	*	*	*
	M	*	*	*	*	*	*	*
	OCA	*	*	*	*	*	*	*
5	PA	*	*	*	*	*	*	*
	M	*	*	*	*	*	*	*
	OCA	*	*	*	*	*	*	*
0	PA	*	*	*	*	*	*	*
	M	*	*	*	*	*	*	*
	OCA	*	*	*	*	*	*	*

* Centour < .5

The General Trivariate Case

G Groups

Personnel classification in a large company encompasses many jobs in addition to the three considered so far. Suppose satisfactory and satisfied employees in a fourth job in World Airlines were identified. Their scores are listed in a separate roster and the score matrix of this new group may be added to the set of rosters and matrices for the three previously discussed jobs without influencing any of them. Each of the four separate job groups is independent of the others. The selection and addition to the problem of a fifth, a sixth, and, in fact, any number of jobs including G of them is similarly independent.

Profile representation quickly becomes confused even for one job when three variables are available for each individual. We have therefore discontinued considering profiles themselves. Cartesian representation of the information for a fourth, fifth, or up to G jobs does not alter the previous representation of information for other jobs. Nevertheless, since construction of Cartesian graphs becomes difficult in three dimensions, it is convenient to think in terms of Cartesian representation but to engage in the analytic specification of the data through matrix representation rather than through geometric representation in Cartesian space.

If the data for each of the G jobs are reasonably well described by normal distributions, the centour job psychograph which was developed in Chapter 3 is applicable, in extension, to three variables. The applicability of the trivariate normal distribution was demonstrated in Figs. 4.4 through 4.6. The location in the test space of the center of the ellipsoidal psychographs is the centroid of the job. The translation of the origin to the centroid of the group is conveniently expressed as a row matrix. For the general, or gth, job the matrix is

$$x_{.g.} = \|(X_{pg1} - \bar{X}_{.g1}) \quad (X_{pg2} - \bar{X}_{.g2}) \quad (X_{pg3} - \bar{X}_{.g3})\|$$

In a trivariate normal distribution equally probable points in the gth job will lie on ellipsoids defined by

$$x_{.g.}D_g^{-1}x'_{.g.} = \chi_g^2$$

The shape and orientation of the family of ellipsoids which have different but constant values of χ_g^2 are completely determined by the group data in the dispersion matrix D_g. The location of the center of the ellipsoid is determined by the group data in the centroid matrix $\bar{X}_g$. The size of any particular ellipsoid is determined by the value of χ_g^2. Thus we may choose for any group g a numerical value for χ_g^2 and solve the equation to find the coordinates $x_{.g.}$ which lie on the particular ellipsoid (see Chapter 6). There will be g such ellipsoids, one for each group. Each of these g ellipsoids will be associated with the same numerical value of χ_g^2 and therefore with the same numerical centour equivalent, but each of the ellipsoids may be of different shape, differently located, and differently oriented in the test space. The numerical value of the centour equivalent may be ascertained from the probability table of χ_g^2 with three degrees of freedom. Thus it is a routine but lengthy calculation to choose any value of χ_g^2 and construct the equivalent centour psychographs in the test space, one for each job group.

The same matrix equation for the ellipsoids may be used to ascertain the centour equivalent in group g of any score points in the test space. In this application the coordinates of the chosen point in the test space take numerical values in the row matrix $x_{.g.}$. The equation (making use of the known numerical values in D_g) then gives the value of χ_g^2. The particular point in the test space is successively represented by g different row matrices $x_{.g.}$, one for each of the g groups. Therefore for any single point there will be G equations and G values of χ_g^2, a different value for each group. If there are, say, seven groups, the divergence of any point in the test space from the typical central point in each group is described by seven different values of χ_g^2 and seven different independently determined centour equivalents.

Formal Notation

Test scores for satisfactory and satisfied apprentices in each job are grouped by job. There are G such groups. The roster for the general, or gth, group of the G groups is

Scores of Satisfactory and Satisfied
Apprentices in Specialty g

Apprentice Number	Scores		
1	X_{1g1}	X_{1g2}	X_{1g3}
2	X_{2g1}	X_{2g2}	X_{2g3}
3	X_{3g1}	X_{3g2}	X_{3g3}
$\vdots$	$\vdots$	$\vdots$	$\vdots$
n_g	$X_{n_g g1}$	$X_{n_g g2}$	$X_{n_g g3}$

As was true in Chapter 3, the subscripts identify, in sequence, person, group, and test. A dot will be used to preserve position. There will be G such rosters.

The matrix for the gth group will be

$$X_g = \begin{Vmatrix} X_{1g1} & X_{1g2} & X_{1g3} \\ X_{2g1} & X_{2g2} & X_{2g3} \\ X_{3g1} & X_{3g2} & X_{3g3} \\ \vdots & \vdots & \vdots \\ X_{n_g g1} & X_{n_g g2} & X_{n_g g3} \end{Vmatrix} \qquad (n_g \text{ rows})$$

There will be G such matrices.

The matrix of means for the gth group will be

$$\bar{X}_g = \begin{Vmatrix} \bar{X}_{.g1} & \bar{X}_{.g2} & \bar{X}_{.g3} \\ \bar{X}_{.g1} & \bar{X}_{.g2} & \bar{X}_{.g3} \\ \bar{X}_{.g1} & \bar{X}_{.g2} & \bar{X}_{.g3} \\ \vdots & \vdots & \vdots \\ \bar{X}_{.g1} & \bar{X}_{.g2} & \bar{X}_{.g3} \end{Vmatrix} \qquad (n_g \text{ rows})$$

There will be G such matrices.

The centroid for the gth group is

$$\bar{X}_g = \begin{Vmatrix} \bar{X}_{.g1} & \bar{X}_{.g2} & \bar{X}_{.g3} \end{Vmatrix}$$

There will be G such centroids.

The dispersion matrix for the gth group is

$$D_g = \frac{1}{n_g} [X'_g X_g - \bar{X}'_g \bar{X}_g]$$

There will be G such dispersion matrices.

The deviation scores x_{pgi} for the pth apprentice measured from the centroid of the gth group are expressed in the row matrix

$$x_{pg.} = \begin{Vmatrix} (X_{pg1} - \bar{X}_{.g1}) & (X_{pg2} - \bar{X}_{.g2}) & (X_{pg3} - \bar{X}_{.g3}) \end{Vmatrix}$$

There will be G such expressions for each apprentice, that is, any one point in the test space will be represented as vectors from G different centroids.

If the scores for the gth job approximate a trivariate normal distribution, the point $X_{p.i}$ will lie on an isofrequency contour ellipsoid defined by the equation

$$x_{p..} D_g^{-1} x'_{p..} = \chi_g^2$$

There will be G such ellipsoids for each point in the test space.

For any triad of scores $X_{..1}$, $X_{..2}$, and $X_{..3}$ representing any point in the test space a matrix variable may be written

$$x_{.g.} = \begin{Vmatrix} (X_{..1} - \bar{X}_{.g1}) & (X_{..2} - \bar{X}_{.g2}) & (X_{..3} - \bar{X}_{.g3}) \end{Vmatrix}$$

There will be G such row matrices expressing each point as a deviation from a different group centroid. The value of $\chi_g{}^2$ for any point may be computed for any group. In general, there will be G values of $\chi_g{}^2$ for each point in the test space. For any value of $\chi_g{}^2$ the centour score associated with $\chi_g{}^2$ may be ascertained as P in the probability table of χ^2 with three degrees of freedom. For values of χ^2 that are not tabled the centour equivalent may be accurately computed from

$$C_g = 100[1 - 2m_2(\chi_g)]$$

where $m_2(\chi_g)$ may be obtained from Pearson's Table IX (1924). There will be G such values of C_g for every point in the test space.

When the raw score distributions for *all* G jobs are approximately normal, the raw score is the most economical answer to the following:

Profile Problem 1. On what type of scale should profiles be represented? *Answer:* If obtained score data in the groups are not acceptably described by normal distributions, a scaling of raw scores to normalize the distributions is necessary. Computation of centour scores solves

Profile Problem 2. On which group should the raw scores be standardized? *Answer:* Raw scores should be standardized upon *each* group in turn. Centour scores solve

Profile Problem 3. How may the joint performance of all individuals be represented? Answer: Centour scores are derived from the dispersion matrix in each job. The dispersion matrix contains all the useful information concerning joint dispersion in the job. Centour scores also provide a solution to

Profile Problem 4. How may the dispersion of profiles of a job be represented? Answer: Centour scores translate the total dispersion characteristic of any group into a directly interpretable statement of individual divergence from the centroid.

This general statement has been introduced with the presumption that apprentices were tested at induction, that test scores were not known during the advising about job selection, and that apprentices were assigned to jobs in the usual manner. Elimination of both unsatisfactory and dissatisfied employees from the empirically selected groups introduces some guarantee that the centour scores define regions of the test space which are suitable for use in decisions concerning the assignment of men to jobs. However, the presumption also means that use of centour scores preserves a region fixed by present assignment procedures. It should be noted also that the calculation of a table of centour equivalents can be accomplished with a priori determination of desired statistical outcomes of assignment procedures. If it is administratively desirable that measures for job g be normally distributed with any centroid denoted A_g and with a dispersion matrix B_g, centour tables to be used by assignment personnel may be constructed from

$$C_g = [1 - 2m_2(\chi_g)]$$

where χ_g is given by

$$\chi_g^2 = x_{.g.}B_g^{-1}x'_{.g.}$$

in which

$$x_{.g.} = \|(X_{..1} - A_{.g1}) \quad (X_{..2} - A_{.g2}) \quad (X_{..3} - A_{.g3})\|$$

Such centour scores will inform personnel advisers of the divergence of individuals from the desired centroid in units of measure derived from the desired dispersion in the job.

Chapter 5

The General Case

T Test Scores

In previous chapters, we have systematically developed the statistical models for the one-, two-, and three-variate profile problem. We have found that Cartesian representation and the centour score concept form a consistent framework for inferring group membership in each of these three instances, and that conventional profile representation cannot reveal some essential characteristics of group data. A similar development may be extended to any number of variates.

Let us suppose that the Activity Preference Inventory has any number T of test sections. The report of Joe Armand's scores will now read

Apprentice	Test One	Test Two	Test Three	...	Test T
Armand, Joe	X_1	X_2	X_3	...	X_T

These scores may be indicated graphically as a profile. In this instance, the profile will consist of T parallel stalks, each with a zero point and each of suitable length to cover the range of possible scores. Points on each stalk will represent the number of activity preferences of a particular kind.

Joe's profile is plotted by placing a point on the first profile stalk corresponding to X_1 activity preferences, a point on the second profile stalk corresponding to X_2 preferences, a point on the third profile stalk corresponding to X_3 preferences, and so on to a point on the Tth profile stalk corresponding to the score X_T on the Tth test. Figure 5.1 represents a typical example. There are many familiar variations of this device, such as the report forms of the Stanford Achievement Test, the Strong Vocational Interest Inventory, and the Differential Aptitude Test.

The indicated points on the profile stalks report identically the information listed in the roster. They indicate graphically the location of the T scores for Joe on T calibrated lines.

183

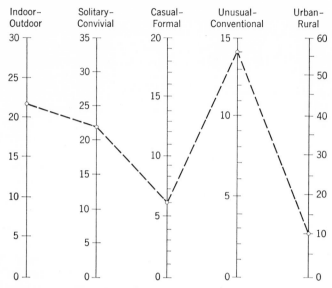

Fig. 5.1   *Activity preference profile chart.*

When lines connecting the score points on adjacent stalks are drawn in the customary manner, the graphic profiles seem to have merit as a simply interpreted representation of complex data. Certain very important facts about such representation are frequently ignored in attempts to develop simple methods of using profiles in practical application. The profile form which the graphic chart suggests is greatly influenced by arbitrary choices of the order in which the stalks are printed and the arbitrary choice of scale intervals. It is obviously essential, and fortunately convenient, to standardize the graphic report form. It is also fortunate that once the printed form has been arbitrarily chosen, it is inconvenient to change the order of the stalks. Thus through repeated experience in handling standardized profile charts a psychologist develops a familiarity with, and a feeling of security in, his visual impressions of the form of a profile. The comfortable security that many psychologists believe they enjoy is illusory. Our experience in the analysis of the one-, two-, and three-variate examples in previous chapters shows that the graphic methods of the profile model cannot adequately summarize the complex data.

We have found that scores of an individual are interpretable principally by evaluation of the individual's location in known frequency distributions and his divergence from the central score values of groups. We have found that graphic methods can be used to incorporate some interpretive information in the profile chart, chiefly the essential facts describing the central location, and the characteristic variation of a single group on a single test. The idea of incorporating group data in graphic devices on profile charts leads directly to the development of some standardization of scale points on the profile stalks; the use of standard scores, percentiles, and other conversions as the scale basis for reporting profiles are examples. As soon as a number of groups are introduced for interpretive reference purposes, graphic methods of presentation and standardized scales break down, in part.

Perhaps the most important fact about profile representation, however, is that the covariation characteristics of any group cannot be represented on graphic profiles and is therefore overlooked entirely in the interpretation of an individual's deviation from a group. When multiple groups are involved in the interpretation of an individual's profile, the complications of graphic representation force the reduction of the interpretive data even further. It becomes impossible to reveal graphically in any practical manner the characteristic variation of the several groups. Customary procedure, therefore, is to represent graphically central tendencies, job psychographs, or group profiles on the individual report form. The idea of variation is abandoned in the representation.

As the number of differentiable groups increases, the complexity of graphic recording of separate group profiles in a single chart representing the profile test space becomes so great that some consolidation of the data is required. It appears desirable to seek the best "grouping of the groups." Thus the limitations of the graphic system lead inevitably to the attempt to single out some typical standardization group to use as reference for interpretation of the individual's test performance. The profile model is thus seen to contain within its basic structure the defect of ignoring the most essential features of the interpretive problem, that is, the variation and the covariation, or, as we term it, the total dispersion of the multivariate measurements on discriminated groups.

In Cartesian representation of the profile data the advantages of profile stalks linked by a common origin are used to develop the concept of a test space defined by coordinate axes. In the Cartesian model the individual data from the roster are represented exactly as they are in the profile model but with conceptual improvements of great practical importance. The variation and covariation within and among groups are explicitly recognized in the Cartesian development and may be analytically examined by algebraic relations paralleling the geometric structure. The only problems in extending the idea of the Cartesian model for any number of variates T are those of finding a suitable notation for recording and analyzing multiple-group data and developing a concept of a test space of more than three dimensions.

The Concept of a Test Space

When scores for only one test are available the single score is represented as a location on a horizontal reference axis denoted X_1. A group of scores is described by the usual statistics of a frequency distribution and the interpretive data for multiple groups are recorded in tabular form for reference. The score of a second test for the same man is a location on a second axis X_2 drawn vertically and intersecting the first axis at an origin zero at an angle of 90°. The pair of axis points representing scores on X_1 and X_2 locate or define a point in the plane of the coordinate axis system. We regard the plane X_1 and X_2 as the test space since every possible pair of test scores X_1 and X_2 is represented by a point in the plane. The familiar scatter diagram is a graphic device for tabulating and inspecting the frequency with which the test space points occur in a sample. The statistics N, $\bar{X}$, σ^2, and r summarize the principal characteristics of the frequency distribution of the observed points. Since there are two tests, or two axes, defining the plane we refer to the test space as a two-space, or as a space of dimensionality two, or as a space of two dimensions.

A third test score may be represented as a location on a third axis X_3 which is constructed at right angles to the plane $X_1 X_2$. The three scores of an individual now locate or define a point in the familiar space of dimensionality three. The graphic device for inspecting the frequency distribution of points in the test space is necessarily a three-dimensional model and the statistical tables for summarizing the principal characteristics of the group data are most conveniently recorded in a matrix.

A fourth test score is regarded as a location on a fourth axis X_4 constructed at right angles to X_1, X_2, and X_3. The combination of any four scores, one on each axis, defines a point in the test space which now has dimensionality four. It is now impossible to construct a model or other graphic device to "look at" the frequency distribution. The system, however, is entirely general. The scores of a group of individuals all measured on four variates are thought of as being represented by a group of points in four-space. The statistics which summarize the frequency distribution may be conveniently recorded in matrices.

In the same way, we may introduce a fifth, a sixth, and so on to the last, or Tth, axis, each time defining the new axis as perpendicular to all other axes. In every instance, any set of scores defines a point in a space of dimensionality equal to the number of axes that span the test space. With the last, or Tth, test, the space will be of dimensionality T. An individual's profile will be a point with T coordinates in this T-space. Though the location of the point cannot be marked with a pencil on a graphic device, it is exactly defined by a row matrix

$$\| X_1 \quad X_2 \quad X_3 \quad \ldots \quad X_T \|$$

The matrix provides a convenient form of Cartesian representation when the number of tests exceeds three. The elements of the matrix are the profile scores. They report the location of the point in the test space in terms of coordinates on the reference axes $X_1, X_2, \ldots, X_T$.

Although activity preferences of Joe Armand may be represented as a matrix (Cartesian representation) or as a profile, neither type of representation adds information to that given by Joe Armand's listing in the roster. Further interpretative information is added only by introducing similar scores of other apprentices.

The General Multivariate Case

G Groups

We have found in previous chapters that test score distributions of an undifferentiated group of apprentices provide no information for personnel classification. Consequently, in this summary of the general case we consider only the situation in which test score distributions are available for men who are validly classified into meaningful job groups. The test score data are assumed to be scores obtained at induction. The meaningful characteristics of the job groups are assumed to derive from the administrative organization of jobs and training in World Airlines. The validity of the grouping is assumed to derive from experimental follow-up. Three facts were ascertained for each apprentice who was tested at induction.

1. The apprentice's present job.
2. Whether the apprentice was performing his duty satisfactorily or not.
3. Whether the apprentice was satisfied with his duty assignment or not.

If we assume that the scores for each of the T tests for all the satisfactory and satisfied apprentices in job 1 have been separated from the entire group of apprentices tested, the roster for these employees is

Satisfactory and Satisfied Apprentices

Job 1

Apprentice Number	Test 1	Test 2	Test 3	...	Test T
1	X_{111}	X_{112}	X_{113}	...	X_{11T}
2	X_{211}	X_{212}	X_{213}	...	X_{21T}
3	X_{311}	X_{312}	X_{313}	...	X_{31T}
⋮	⋮	⋮	⋮	...	⋮
n_1	$X_{n_1 11}$	$X_{n_1 12}$	$X_{n_1 13}$	...	$X_{n_1 1T}$

The multiple subscripts must precisely identify the individual, the particular group of which he is a member, and the test axis which represents the score. Thus the symbol X_{213} stands for the score of individual number 2 in the roster of group 1 on test 3.

Similarly, we may separate satisfactory and satisfied apprentices in job 2 and record their scores in a roster. This roster will be similar in form to the roster of group 1. It will differ in the subscripts; there will be n_2 rows instead of n_1 rows, and the digit 2 will appear in the subscript position which identifies the group.

The process of sorting the entire population of satisfactory and satisfied apprentices into their job groups may be continued through group 3, 4, and so on to the last, or Gth job. A roster of scores on each of the T tests may be prepared separately for each job. The roster for the Gth job will be

Satisfactory and Satisfied Apprentices
Job G

Apprentice Number	Test 1	Test 2	Test 3	...	Test T
1	X_{1G1}	X_{1G2}	X_{1G3}	...	X_{1GT}
2	X_{2G1}	X_{2G2}	X_{2G3}	...	X_{2GT}
3	X_{3G1}	X_{3G2}	X_{3G3}	...	X_{3GT}
⋮	⋮	⋮	⋮	...	⋮
n_G	$X_{n_G G1}$	$X_{n_G G2}$	$X_{n_G G3}$	...	$X_{n_G GT}$

If g stands for the identification of any job, we may write the rosters for all G groups in a general form:

Satisfactory and Satisfied Apprentices
Job g
$(g = 1, 2, 3, \ldots, G)$

Apprentice Number	Test 1	Test 2	Test 3	...	Test T
1	X_{1g1}	X_{1g2}	X_{1g3}	...	X_{1gT}
2	X_{2g1}	X_{2g2}	X_{2g3}	...	X_{2gT}
3	X_{3g1}	X_{3g2}	X_{3g3}	...	X_{3gT}
⋮	⋮	⋮	⋮	...	⋮
n_g	$X_{n_g g1}$	$X_{n_g g2}$	$X_{n_g g3}$	...	$X_{n_g gT}$

Each roster may be written as a matrix. The general matrix will be

$$X_g = \begin{Vmatrix} X_{1g1} & X_{1g2} & X_{1g3} & \cdots & X_{1gT} \\ X_{2g1} & X_{2g2} & X_{2g3} & \cdots & X_{2gT} \\ X_{3g1} & X_{3g2} & X_{3g3} & \cdots & X_{3gT} \\ \vdots & \vdots & \vdots & \cdots & \vdots \\ X_{n_gg1} & X_{n_gg2} & X_{n_gg3} & \cdots & X_{n_ggT} \end{Vmatrix} \qquad (g = 1, 2, \ldots, G)$$

Considerable space is saved by denoting this matrix by its general element:

$$X_g = \|X_{pgi}\| \qquad \begin{matrix} p = 1, 2, \ldots, n_g \\ g = 1, 2, \ldots, G \\ i = 1, 2, \ldots, T \end{matrix}$$

The matrix is defined explicitly. The subscripts identify person, group, and test.

All the information about the scores of the men in job g is stated in the matrix X_g. We need suitable means of summarizing the important characteristics of the groups from the detailed data in the several matrices X_g.

If the matrices X_g each have only one column, that is, only one test score is obtained for each man, profile representation of the matrices X_g will be frequency distributions or frequency polygons similar to Fig. 2.18 in Chapter 2. When each group matrix consists of two columns, profile representation of the matrices X_g will be frequency polygons presented on adjacent but unrelated scales. If any number of test scores are recorded for each man, profile representation of the matrices X_g will be similar. An additional profile stalk will be added for each test and each profile stalk will have G frequency polygons represented on it.

Profile representation of any one of the groups summarizes only the marginal frequency distributions, in the scatter-diagram sense of marginal distribution, of each variate. The data of each column of the group matrix are examined independently. The variation within a column of matrix elements is analyzed, but the significance of the between-columns covariation is ignored.

Representation in the Cartesian model of the single-variate case will be exactly the same as in the profile example for one test. In the two-variate case Cartesian representation of the matrices X_g will be a scatter diagram in which the groups are differentiated by some graphic device, such as varied marks or selected contour ellipses. Cartesian representation of three-variate matrices will be three-dimensional models.

It is particularly noteworthy that the scatter diagram in two-space and the model in three-space contain the explicitly detailed relations existing between columns of the group matrix. The covariation characteristics of the data become, in fact, a principal feature of the analysis of groups and the comparison of an individual's test performance in relation to the groups.

When four or more test scores are considered, Cartesian representation by graphic methods becomes impossible. We may nevertheless continue to conceive of the numbers recorded in each row of the matrix as the co-ordinates of a point in a space spanned by T reference axes, all reference axes being perpendicular to all other axes. That is, we may extend the procedure of defining the locations of points in a test space indefinitely for any number T of tests. Our only problem is that of systematizing the operations on data. This problem is solved by matrix notation and its associated algebra.

The Matrix Notation for the General Case

The matrix of scores of a sample of n_g men in group g observed on T tests contains n_g rows and T columns of scores. Each row represents one individual's performance on as many tests as are involved in the particular analysis; each column represents the details of the frequency distribution of a single group on a single variable (test).

The sum of the scores in one column divided by n_g, the number of rows of the matrix, is the mean score of the group. If this arithmetic operation is performed for each column, it is evident that the T means for group g may be denoted by a row matrix $\bar{X}_g$:

$$\bar{X}_g = \| \bar{X}_{.g1} \quad \bar{X}_{.g2} \quad \bar{X}_{.g3} \quad \ldots \quad \bar{X}_{.gT} \|$$

The dot in the first subscript is a position-preserving notation which indicates that the subscript p is irrelevant in the number $\bar{X}_{.gt}$ because all the n_g individuals in the group are included in the computation of the mean.

The matrix product $X'_g X_g$ is a $T \times T$ matrix of sums of squares and cross products for all pairs of test scores. In the notation of scalar algebra the general element of the matrix is $\sum X_{pgi} X_{pgj}$ $(i, j = 1, 2, \ldots, T)$.

If the origin of the axes is translated from $X_i = 0$ to $\bar{X}_i = 0$, the matrix of sums of squares and cross products is denoted by

$$S = X'_g X_g - \bar{X}'_g \bar{X}_g$$

and when each element is multiplied by the scalar $1/n_g$, we obtain the fundamental dispersion matrix D_g

$$D_g = \frac{1}{n_g} S = \frac{1}{n_g} \| \sum (X_{pgi} - \bar{X}_{.gi})(X_{pgj} - \bar{X}_{.gj}) \|$$

If we drop the group-identifying subscript for simplicity the dispersion matrix is simply the T by T matrix of variances and covariances of T variates for the group:

$$D = \begin{Vmatrix} \sigma_1{}^2 & \sigma_1\sigma_2 r_{12} & \sigma_1\sigma_3 r_{13} & \cdots & \sigma_1\sigma_T r_{1T} \\ \sigma_2\sigma_1 r_{21} & \sigma_2{}^2 & \sigma_2\sigma_3 r_{23} & \cdots & \sigma_2\sigma_T r_{2T} \\ \vdots & \vdots & \vdots & \cdots & \vdots \\ \sigma_T\sigma_1 r_{T1} & \sigma_T\sigma_2 r_{T2} & \sigma_T\sigma_3 r_{T3} & \cdots & \sigma_T{}^2 \end{Vmatrix}$$

In experimental problems where the variables are reasonably approximated by the ideal normal distribution (as they usually are in psychological test data), the dispersion matrix D_g combined with the row matrix of means for each group, defined as

$$\overline{X}_g = \begin{Vmatrix} \overline{X}_{.g1} & \overline{X}_{.g2} & \cdots & \overline{X}_{.gT} \end{Vmatrix}$$

adequately summarize the test scores for the individuals in group g.

The matrix of scores X_g identifies a cluster of individual points in the test space. The row matrix of mean scores locates the centroid of the group of points. The dispersion matrix describes the variation in density of the points in the multivariate frequency distribution; the dispersion matrix describes the size and form of the test space regions enclosed by isofrequency surfaces.

Isodensity Contours in Multivariate Normal Distribution

The locus of points of equal density, sometimes referred to as the locus of equiprobability or isofrequency, in a normal distribution satisfies the equation

$$x_g D_g{}^{-1} x'_g = \chi_g{}^2$$

In this equation $\chi_g{}^2$ is an arbitrary constant. Larger values of χ^2 are associated with loci of lesser density. The matrix x_g is a row matrix of points on the test space axes measured as deviations from the centroid $\overline{X}_g$. When x_g is written in matrices the equation is

$$\chi_g{}^2 = \begin{Vmatrix} (X_{..1} - \overline{X}_{.g1}) & (X_{..2} - \overline{X}_{.g2}) & \cdots & (X_{..T} - \overline{X}_{.gT}) \end{Vmatrix} \cdot D_g{}^{-1} \cdot \begin{Vmatrix} (X_{..1} - \overline{X}_{.g1}) \\ (X_{..2} - \overline{X}_{.g2}) \\ \vdots \\ (X_{..T} - \overline{X}_{.gT}) \end{Vmatrix}$$

By the omission of two subscripts on the $X_{..i}$ in the general term $(X_{..i} - \overline{X}_{.gi})$ we indicate that the row matrix x_g identifies a point in the test space by means of vector representation from the group centroid.

In the one-variate normal distribution the equation reduces to the familiar expression for points of equal density in the normal distribution

$$\|X - \bar{X}_{g1}\| \cdot \left\|\frac{1}{\sigma_1^{2}}\right\| \cdot \|X - \bar{X}_{g1}\| = \chi^2$$

$$\frac{(X - \bar{X}_{g1})^2}{\sigma_1^{2}} = \chi^2$$

$$\pm\frac{x}{\sigma} = \chi$$

$$x = \pm\chi\sigma$$

When χ is chosen as equal to 1.0 the probability of a divergence greater in absolute value than $\chi = 1.0\sigma$ is the familiar value $.32 = (.16 + .16)$. The portion of the normal distribution lying between $\pm 1.0\sigma$ is approximately 68%. These results are found either in the table of the normal distribution or in the probability table of χ^2 for one degree of freedom. From the probability P associated with a greater deviation than a point $|x|$ we obtain $100P$ and refer to this number as a centour score, or as the centour equivalent of the points $+x$ and $-x$ in the test space.

In the case of two variates the x_g matrix contains two elements and the dispersion matrix is 2×2. In the bivariate normal distribution the locus of equal density is an ellipse, and the notion of the form of equal density contours emerges. The orientation and ratio of the major and minor axes of any one of the equal density ellipses for a given group are implicit in the dispersion matrix. Any pair of coordinates defines a point in the test space and, if the values (scores) are substituted in the equation, the quantity χ^2 may be computed. Thus every point in the test space is associated with a value of χ^2. The test space is defined by two axes, and two degrees of freedom are associated with the choice of any point in the test space. The probability associated with a divergence from the centroid greater than any computed value of χ^2 may be located, approximately, in the table of χ^2 for two degrees of freedom. For example, a point in the test space for which $\chi^2 = 4.6$ lies on the density contour ellipse that defines the locus of C_{10}. The centour equivalent of the point is 10. The test space points of 10% of the group described by $\bar{X}_g$ and D_g are characterized by larger values of χ^2.

In the three-variate case the matrices in the equation $\chi^2 = x_g D_g^{-1} x'_g$ are augmented by a third column and a third row representing the third variate.

The row matrix x_g contains values for three axes, and the dispersion matrix is 3×3. Every point in the test space is associated with a value of χ^2 which now enjoys three degrees of freedom. The probability of a greater χ^2 is approximated by referring to the table of χ^2 with three degrees of freedom. The centour equivalent of a value $\chi^2 = 4.6$ in the three-space is 20+. The shape of the equal density contours is ellipsoidal; the locus or boundary of points in the test space for which χ^2 is everywhere constant is an ellipsoid surface. It may be conceived of as a shell containing within its boundaries a proportion $(1 - P)$ of all the frequencies in the group. The proportion P accounts for test space points that lie outside the shell. Large values of χ^2 are associated with large ellipsoids which contain or surround large numbers of the individual test space points in the cluster of the group. Whether the shape of the ellipsoid shell is nearly spherical, egg-shaped, flat like a pancake, or cigar-shaped is described by the numerical elements of the dispersion matrix.

In the general case of T variates the locus of equal density is a surface in T-space, and in the multivariate normal distribution the surface is a hyper-ellipsoid of dimensionality T. The probability P associated with a given point in the T-space (denoted by the row matrix x_g which contains T elements) is found from the value χ^2 with T degrees of freedom (DF):

$$\chi_g{}^2 = x_g D_g{}^{-1} x'_g$$

The size of a particular ellipsoid shell is described by the value χ^2/DF or its associated probability P. The form and angular orientation of the ellipsoid in the test space is described by the matrix D. The central location of the family of ellipsoid shells is described by the row matrix $\bar{X}_g$. The dimensionality of the test space is the number of variates T.

General Application to Personnel Classification

An apprentice whose appropriate job classification is not known is tested at induction. His test performance is recorded in a row matrix of test scores:

$$X_p = \| X_{p.1} \quad X_{p.2} \quad \ldots \quad X_{p.T} \|$$

The matrix X_p is a vector which defines the apprentice's location in the test space. The dot in the subscript indicates that the group designation is irrelevant. We compare the location of this man with the locations of apprentices like him, but who are known to have become satisfactory and satisfied members of each of G jobs. In a probability sense we measure the man's typicalness as a member of each of g groups by computing the centour equivalent of the man's test score vector in each group.

We first compute the g row matrices which describe the man's point as vectors from the centroid of each of the g groups. The man's location in the test space remains the same, but the centroids $\bar{X}_g$ of the groups change. There will therefore be g different row matrices x_p, each one describing the same point in relation to a different origin.

$$x_{pg} = (X_{p.i} - \bar{X}_{.gi}) = \| (X_{p.1} - \bar{X}_{.g1})(X_{p.2} - \bar{X}_{.g2}) \ldots (X_{p.T} - \bar{X}_{.gT}) \|$$
$$(g = 1, 2, \ldots, G)$$

For each row vector x_{pg} we compute $\chi_{pg}{}^2$ by the equation

$$x_{pg}D_g{}^{-1}x'_{pg} = \chi_{pg}{}^2 \qquad (g = 1, 2, \ldots, G)$$

There will be G values of $\chi_{pg}{}^2$, one associated with each specialty group. Each matrix computation involves a different dispersion matrix D_g.

The centour equivalent for each value of χ^2 is determined from tables. The apprentice's observed test performance has now been reduced or converted to directly interpretable form. The Profile Problem has been solved.

Tables Available for Centour Evaluation of χ^2

The value of χ^2 for selected centour equivalents $C = 100P$ may be determined from Fisher and Yates' Tables of χ^2 (1953). The χ^2 values corresponding to the centours 1, 2, 5, 10, 20, 30, 50, 70, 80, 90, 95, 98, and 99 are thus readily available. Intermediate values of P or χ^2 can be roughly approximated by interpolation.

Table II in *The Kelley Statistical Tables* (1938) shows the value P for the argument χ^2/DF. Values of χ^2 equivalent to centours and centours equivalent to values of χ^2 can be similarly approximated by interpolation in this table.

For more precise centour-χ^2 values Table IX in Pearson's Tables (1924) may be used. For the argument χ of 0.0 to 5.0 the function $m_n(\chi)$ is tabled. The probability value $p = 1 - q$ is obtained from the equations

$$q = \sqrt{2\pi}m_{n-1}(\chi) \qquad \text{if } n \text{ is even}$$
$$q = 2m_{n-1}(\chi) \qquad \text{if } n \text{ is odd}$$

The subscript n denotes the number of tests. By interpolation in the table the centour equivalent to a wide range of values of χ^2 or the value of χ^2 equivalent to a selected centour may be computed with precision more than adequate for practical applications.

In the bivariate normal case the centour equivalent to the point X_p in group g is

$$C_{pg} = 100[1 - \sqrt{2\pi}m_1(\chi_{pg})]$$

In the three-variate normal case the centour score is

$$C_{pg} = 100[1 - 2m_2(\chi_{pg})]$$

A similar pattern, depending upon whether the number of variates is even or odd, holds for four, five, or any number T of tests. We write, in general, for T variates

$$C_{pg} = \begin{cases} 100[1 - \sqrt{2\pi}m_{T-1}(\chi_{pg})] & \text{if } T \text{ is even} \\ 100[1 - 2m_{T-1}(\chi_{pg})] & \text{if } T \text{ is odd} \end{cases}$$

The centour model is applicable to any number of variates and any number of groups.

The Profile Problem—A Recapitulation

Test score profiles have frequently been used as a device for studies of intra-individual variation and comparisons of individuals with groups. Cronbach and Gleser have detailed the questions that may be examined by profile comparisons in the following list (1952, page 3).

"1. How similar are persons one and two?
2. How similar is person one to group Y?
3. How homogeneous are the members of group Y?
4. How similar is group Y to group Z?
5. How much more homogeneous is group Y than group Z? Than the combined sample?"

Kogan describes the same purposes of profile comparison in a different way (1953, page 520).

"1. The comparison of the profile of one subject with another.
2. The comparison of profiles for the same subject on different occasions.
3. The comparison of a profile of a subject with one or more standard or reference profiles.
4. The comparison of the 'average' profile of one group with that of another group.
5. The use of profiles for predicting performance on one or more criteria."

The two lists emphasize comparisons of the profile of an individual with that of a group. It is this comparison that is important for the classification and assignment of men. We state this problem formally and concisely in the question: How likely is it that a random point in a test space whose coordinates are T test scores will be a member of (or belong with) a cluster of points which are known to describe a certain group of men? In our consideration of this question we find it helpful to state explicitly certain premises that frequently appear in psychometric problems. These premises are:

I. Points representing a set of T psychological observations on men grouped according to a common designation will be dispersed with centroid as focus in a space of dimensionality T.

II. All the information from which group membership may be inferred is contained in the relations among the points of a homogeneous group. These relations are recounted exactly by the score matrices of homogeneous groups.

III. The centroid of a cluster of points represents the best single statement of the location of the typical point in the cluster.

IV. The most directly interpretable measure of the divergence of a point from the typical is the probability of occurrence of greater divergence in known groups.

When the purpose of profile comparison is to decide appropriate job classifications from an apprentice's profile some measure of propriety is required. A statement of the probability that the profile for the apprentice will belong among the profiles of employees in each of a number of categories is decisive. The following problems arise in the development of such interpretable probability statements:

Profile Problem 1. On what type of scale should profiles be represented?

Since probability calculations for the multivariate normal distributions are preferred, profiles should be represented on scales that approximate normal distributions in each variate of each job group. Strict conditions require, in addition, that the scales produce linear regression among all variates. A raw score scale for each variate may well satisfy these conditions. The conditions should be met separately for every job group.

Profile Problem 2. On which group should the scores be standardized?

A probability-type statement is desired for each group. Consequently scores must be considered for each group in turn. Standardization is accomplished automatically in the computation of probability statements or centour scores.

Profile Problem 3. How may the joint performance of all individuals be represented?

The profile of the centroid of a job group provides no information about either the dispersion or covariation of scores of apprentices in the job. Indication of joint dispersion is graphically impractical. Cartesian representation conveys all information about joint performance. When the number of variates exceeds three, Cartesian representation becomes graphically impossible. The matrix representation of test scores for a job becomes the basic form of recording multivariate data. The dispersion matrix D_g combined with the row matrix of mean scores of the job summarizes all the useful information about joint dispersion of scores within the group.

Profile Problem 4. How may the dispersion of profiles of a job be represented?

The total dispersion of a cluster of points is communicated in interpretable form by centour psychographs which interpret in the probability sense the location, size, and form of isofrequency contours in a multivariate test space.

Profile Problem 5. Is an apprentice's profile characteristic of a particular job?

The resolution of this basic question is found in our procedure of stating in probability terms the typicalness of the man's observed test scores.

Techniques of Profile Comparison

Profile Coding

Several investigators have proposed that test score profiles be coded for convenient sorting. An example is the proposal for coding MMPI Profiles suggested by Hathaway (1947) and discussed by Welsh (1951). The proposed code records the numbers of the MMPI scale in descending order from the highest score to a standard score of 54, and lists the numbers of the MMPI scales in ascending order from the lowest score to a standard score of 46. Variations within the range of the middle nine standard score points are not indicated. Hathaway proposed this system for the purpose of developing a file of cases recorded in a convenient standard form. The file provides a means of finding previous clients whose MMPI scores were reasonably like those of a present client. The criterion behavior ascertained by follow-up studies would· provide norms of codified profile groups for application in personnel classification.

Coefficients of Profile Similarity

Du Mas (1949, 1950) has proposed a coefficient of profile similarity. In our notation Du Mas' coefficient is obtained by the following procedure.

Standardize each test in terms of some general group. Designate these standard scores as z_{pgi}. Name the space between any pair of adjacent profile stalks a profile segment. Plot the profile of the standard scores z_{pgi}. For each profile segment subtract $z_{p,i}$ from $z_{p,j}$. If

$$z_{p,j} - z_{p,i} > 0 \qquad (i = 1, 2, \ldots, T - 1; j = i + 1)$$

call the slope of the profile in that profile segment positive. If

$$z_{p,j} - z_{p,i} < 0 \qquad (i = 1, 2, \ldots, T - 1; j = i + 1)$$

call the slope of the profile in that profile segment negative. Plot the profile of the centroid of the specialty group $\bar{z}_{.gi}$. For each profile segment subtract $\bar{z}_{.gi}$ from $\bar{z}_{.gj}$. If

$$\bar{z}_{.gj} - \bar{z}_{.gi} > 0 \qquad (i = 1, 2, \ldots, T - 1; j = i + 1)$$

call the slope of the profile of the centroid in this profile segment positive. If

$$\bar{z}_{.gj} - \bar{z}_{.gi} < 0 \qquad (i = 1, 2, \ldots, T - 1; j = i + 1)$$

call the slope of the profile of the centroid in this segment negative. When a difference (profile slope) equals zero, flip a coin to determine whether the slope should be called positive or negative. Count the number of segments in which the profile of the apprentice has the same slope as the profile of the centroid. Call this number S. Compute

$$r_{ps} = 2\left(\frac{S}{T-1} - \frac{1}{2}\right)$$

This is the coefficient of profile similarity.

In general, Du Mas' Coefficient of Profile Similarity is inefficient. It is inconsistent with probability statements of similar divergence from the typical and it is derived from an arbitrary choice of only $T - 1$ of the possible $(T - 1)(T - 2)/2$ different profile segments.

Cattell (1949) proposed an index for expressing the similarity of the profile of one individual to that of the profile of another individual. In our notation this coefficient is

$$r_p = \frac{2\chi_{.50}^2 - \displaystyle\sum_{i=1}^{T} (z_{p.i} - z_{q.i})^2}{2\chi_{.50}^2 + \displaystyle\sum_{i=1}^{T} (z_{p.i} - z_{q.i})^2}$$

where p and q identify the pth and qth individuals in the comparison. The scores z are standardized for a general group. When the profile of the centroid of a group is used as the reference profile, the formula must be modified to

$$r_p = \frac{\chi_{.50}^2 - \displaystyle\sum_{i=1}^{T} (z_{pgi} - \bar{z}_{.gi})^2}{\chi_{.50}^2 + \displaystyle\sum_{i=1}^{T} (z_{pgi} - \bar{z}_{.gi})^2}$$

In this case, the standard scores z_{pgi} are standardized for group g. As many standardizations are necessary as there are groups.

In the case of two variates the locus of points with similar profiles in Cattell's modified formula is that of a circle. In the three-variate case the locus of similar profile points is a sphere. In general, the locus of similar profile points in Cattell's modified formula is a hypersphere in a space of dimensionality T. Since, in general, the locus of equiprobable points in a specialty will be an ellipsoid, Cattell's coefficient of profile similarity is inconsistent with probability statements of equivalent divergence.

A correlation-type index of profile similarity patterned after Cattell's index but consistent with probability statements is achieved by the formula

$$r'_p = \frac{\chi_{.50}^2 - \chi_{pg}^2}{\chi_{.50}^2 + \chi_{pg}^2}$$

where

$$\chi_{pg}^2 = x_{pg} D_g^{-1} x'_{pg}$$

This index is difficult to interpret and seems to offer no advantages over direct statements of relative frequency.

Distance Measures

Cronbach and Gleser (1952) discuss a number of distance indices in their consideration of the Profile Problem. They define an index of eccentricity which we write as

$$E_{pg}^2 = \sum_{i=1}^{T} (X_{p.i} - \bar{X}_{.gi})^2 \qquad (i = 1, 2, \ldots, T)$$

The expected value of the index is

$$\overline{E_{pg}^2} = \sum \sigma_i^2$$

Since E_g^2 depends on the number of variates in the set and on the size of their units, this quantity should be standardized. In our notation, Cronbach and Gleser's standardized index is the index divided by its expected value

$$S_{pg}^2 = \frac{E_{pg}^2}{\overline{E_{pg}^2}}$$

In the two-variate case, the locus of points with equal eccentricity is a circle. In the three-variate case, the locus of equal eccentricity is a sphere. In general, the locus of points with equal eccentricity is a hypersphere.

Cronbach and Gleser recognize the inadequacy of their index for correlated variables and propose a modification of Mahalanobis' generalized distance (1936) as a more useful measure with psychological data. In our notation, the measure is

$$\mathbf{E}_{pg}^2 = \sum \sum d_g^{ij} x_{pi} x_{pj}$$

the summation extending over the T tests i, j. The symbol $\mathbf{E}$ is used to identify this quantity because the quantity is more like a generalized eccentricity than a generalized distance. The quantity d_g^{ij} stands for the ijth element of the inverse of the dispersion matrix for specialty g. Therefore the equation is simply a scalar expression for the familiar matrix product

$$x_{pg} D_g^{-1} x'_{pg}$$

where

$$x_{pg} = \|(X_{p.1} - \bar{X}_{.g1}) \quad (X_{p.2} - \bar{X}_{.g2}) \quad \ldots \quad (X_{p.T} - \bar{X}_{.gT})\|$$

Thus $\mathbf{E}^2 = \chi_{pg}^2$. In other words, χ_{pg}^2 is Cronbach and Gleser's generalized eccentricity, or Mahalanobis' generalized distance modified for the comparison of an individual point with a reference point or centroid of a group. And χ_{pg}^2 is a measure that treats as similarly divergent all equally probable points in a Cartesian space.

The size of χ_{pg}^2 depends upon the number of variates. A standardized index may be obtained by dividing χ_{pg}^2 by its expected value. The expected value of χ^2 is the number of variates. Thus a standardized index of distance in the Mahalanobis sense is

$$S_{pg}^2 = \frac{\chi_{pg}^2}{T}$$

This index is consistent with probability statements.

Kelley (1940, pp. 28–30) proposes a distance measure obtained by constructing a profile of principal components for an undifferentiated group. The average profile of the principal component scores of apprentices in a particular group is compared with the principal component profile of an individual. The "misfit variance" is the sum of the squared differences between points on profile stalks. When the principal component scores derived from the undifferentiated group are uncorrelated in the subgroup, Kelley's "misfit variance" is exactly χ_{pg}^2 if the profile scores are standardized.

Centour Score

Pearson's Table IX (1924) provides a method for determining the proportion of a multivariate normal distribution which is contained by any isofrequency contour ellipsoid. The proportion q_g is

$$q_g = \begin{cases} \sqrt{2\pi}m_{(T-1)}(\chi_g) & \text{if } T \text{ is even} \\ 2m_{(T-1)}(\chi_g) & \text{if } T \text{ is odd} \end{cases}$$

The proportion $p_g = 1 - q_g$ is the fraction of the total frequency which lies outside the ellipsoid defined by χ. The centour score of the pth individual in comparison with the gth group is

$$C_{pg} = 100(1 - q_g)$$

The centour is an index to the position of an individual profile in the matrix of a group. Since the relative frequency or probability concept of divergence from the typical is widely understood, centour scores can be simply explained to personnel advisers. The information conveyed by centour score reports can be incorporated in an apprentice's personal evaluation of his decision problem. The centour score is a good index for use in deciding the question: What job classifications are appropriate for this man?

Regions of the Test Space

Chapter 6

Topology of Personnel Classification

Centour scores prove to be a useful index of the similarity of an apprentice's profile to the profiles of employees classified according to later membership in one of several jobs. Centour score equivalents for any combination of individual scores can be made available to personnel advisers in tabular form. We note, however, that even as few as three short tests produce a tremendous number of possible combinations of test scores. As the number of variates and groups increases to satisfy the practical requirements of personnel advising, the physical size of the necessary centour tables grows to impractical dimensions. In Chapter 4, when three variates were considered, the space problem reached such magnitude that it was necessary to approximate the full detail of the computed centours by grouping the scores in multiples of five.

It is amusing to estimate the size of the bookshelf required to store the centour tables required by the eight-group 17-variate air force problem reported by Tiedeman et al. (1953). If the unit for reporting a score is taken in accordance with customary practice as one-tenth of a standard deviation over the useful range of the test, there will be 60 intervals for each test. For each specialty group the total number of score combinations will be 60^{17}. If a 60 by 60 table containing 3600 centours can be printed on one page, there will be 60^{15} pages for each of eight groups. If 480 pages make a one-inch book, the centour tables will require 60^{14} inches or 60^{13} five-foot shelves.

If the centour concept is to have any practical application in counseling, classification, or assignment problems, it is obvious that some reduction in the number of variates used for finding centours is necessary. We must decide which of several methods of reducing the number of variates preserves as much of the information as possible.

The Logic of Topology

One meaning of the word "topology" is "a mnemonic device based on the association of ideas with places." We will use the word in this sense.

Consider a hypothetical classification problem. A group of 200 satisfactory and satisfied employees is known to include 100 fork-lift operators and 100 passenger agents. The 200 employees are listed at random. We set as our problem the task of choosing a rule for naming the job of each employee as accurately as possible by use of the known statistical facts about the groups. We start by examining the efficiency of rules using the available information. Additional information is then supplied, and its effect upon the rules and the efficiency of the new rules is examined.

The known facts are the following.

1. There are 200 men.
2. There are two classes of men: fork-lift operators, FLO's, and passenger agents, PA's.
3. There are 100 FLO's.
4. There are 100 PA's.

A rule will be any procedure adopted for assigning a job title to a man. The efficiency of a rule may be described by the number or proportion of expected errors or misclassifications.

Three simple rules are listed with their efficiencies in Table 6.1.

Table 6.1 *Rules for Classification*

The Rule for Classification	Correct Classifications Expected Number	Proportion	Misclassifications Expected Number	Proportion
1. Classify all men FLO	100	.50	100	.50
2. Classify all men PA	100	.50	100	.50
3. Classify all men by any random process	100	.50	100	.50

The result is the same for all three rules. The frequency or proportion of misclassification is determined entirely by the relative frequency of the two types of jobs in the total group.

The effect of the rules may be analyzed further. The frequency and proportion of correct and incorrect classifications may be determined for each job title separately. Rule 1 correctly classifies every FLO, but this success with FLO's is paid for in the 100% misclassification of the PA's. Rule 2 correctly classifies 100% of the PA's and misclassifies 100% of the FLO's. The exact result of Rule 3 must be expressed in a probability sense: The expectation of misclassification is .50 in both job titles. The idea of incorrect classifications resulting from application of rules is comparable to the psychodiagnostic idea of false-positive and false-negative diagnoses.

We have now exhausted the utility of the known facts about the group. If the efficiency of classification is to be improved, more data are required. The information is increased by the addition of one fact about each man and the summary statistics for the job-title groups. The fact about each man is his answer, yes or no, to the Biographical Inventory item: Did you ever own a motorcycle? The statistics for the job-title groups indicate that 40 FLO's and 5 PA's had owned a motorcycle before being employed by World Airlines.

The frequencies are recorded in conventional statistical form in the two by two arrangement in Table 6.2. The same data may be represented

Table 6.2   *Job Title and Motorcycle Owner-ship*

	Yes	No	
FLO	40	60	100
PA	5	95	100
Total	45	155	200

in topological form, as in Fig. 6.1, where an interval or space on a line has been defined to represent the qualitative variable, yes-no, and frequencies within job-title groups are conventionally indicated. In Fig. 6.2 the topological representation for the two job-title groups has been combined in one yes-no space.

The figures suggest a scheme for distinguishing between fork-lift operators and passenger agents with better than 50% accuracy. The fact that more FLO's than PA's have owned a motorcycle provides an observable taxonomic distinction. Consequently, we formulate a rule for assigning job titles to the 200 men. If he is a "no-motorcycle" man, we will call him a PA; if he is a "yes-motorcycle" man, we will call him an FLO. By this rule we will call 95 + 60 = 155 of these 200 employees agents, and only 40 + 5 = 45 of them fork-lift operators. Of the 155 employees classified PA, 95 will actually be agents; and of the 45 employees classified

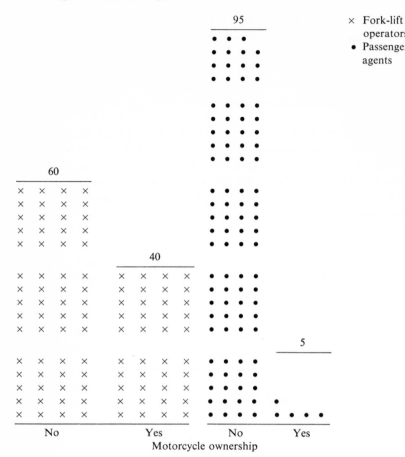

Fig. 6.1   *Frequency of Motorcycle Ownership*

FLO, 40 will actually be fork-lift operators. Thus we will classify correctly 95 + 40 = 135, and misclassify 60 + 5 = 65 of the 200 men. The result is better than we achieved by rules not incorporating the motorcycle facts.

We formalize this classification procedure by identifying two regions of the motorcycle ownership space in Fig. 6.3. This example of the division of a space into two regions by defining a boundary between them is the most rudimentary form of discriminatory topology.

Our method, using a topological space, is identified with probability concepts. We address one employee at random and ask him if he owned a motorcycle before working for World Airlines. On the basis of our knowledge of motorcycle ownership among the fork-lift operators and

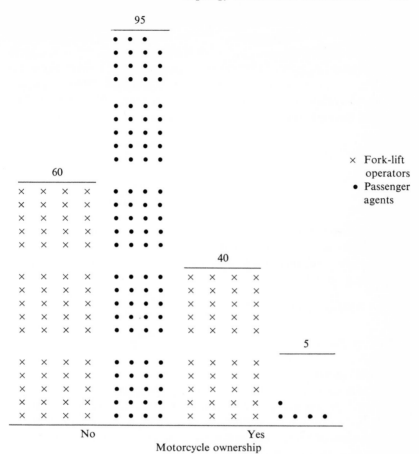

Fig. 6.2 *Frequency of Motorcycle Ownership*

agents in the sample of 200 men, we evaluate the respective probabilities of each of the two alternative possibilities: this man is FLO; or this man is PA. We classify the man questioned according to the larger of the two probabilities.

To make the example specific, let us say that the employee told us he did not own a motorcycle before joining World Airlines. Bayes' theorem can

No	Yes
PA region	FLO region
Motorcycle ownership	

Fig. 6.3 *Regions and Boundaries of the Motorcycle Space.*

be used to evaluate the probabilities. Since there are equal numbers of FLO's and PA's in our population, the *a priori* probability that our sample employee is FLO is equal to the *a priori* probability that he is PA, both probabilities being $p = .50$. If the man questioned is indeed FLO, the probability of his being a no-motorcycle man is 60/100. If he is, in fact, PA, the probability of his being a no-motorcycle man is 95/100. Therefore, by Bayes' theorem, the *a posteriori* probabilities for the alternatives are

$$P\{\text{FLO} \mid \text{no motorcycle}\} = \frac{(.50)(.60)}{(.50)(.60) + (.50)(.95)} = \frac{60}{155}$$

$$P\{\text{PA} \mid \text{no motorcycle}\} = \frac{(.50)(.95)}{(.50)(.60) + (.50)(.95)} = \frac{95}{155}$$

Since the second probability is larger than the first we are likely to designate this employee as a passenger agent.

Conversely, if the man had told us that he had owned a motorcycle, our probabilities would be

$$P\{\text{FLO} \mid \text{motorcycle}\} = \frac{(.50)(.40)}{(.50)(.40) + (.50)(.05)} = \frac{40}{45}$$

$$P\{\text{PA} \mid \text{motorcycle}\} = \frac{(.50)(.05)}{(.50)(.40) + (.50)(.05)} = \frac{5}{45}$$

We would classify the man as a fork-lift operator.

The calculated probabilities hold for any employee we might question at random from the group of 200 men. Therefore every employee replying that he had not owned a motorcycle is assigned a larger probability of being PA than of being FLO, and conversely, every man replying that he had owned a motorcycle is more likely to be FLO than PA. We would adopt the rule: Designate all motorcycle men FLO and designate all others PA. By this rule we misclassify 65 men in all—60 operators are erroneously called agents, and 5 agents are erroneously called operators. The other 135 men are correctly classified.

Probability considerations lead to the same topology of the variate, motorcycle ownership, as was indicated by the graphic frequency distributions in Fig. 6.2. The result may be generalized.

Suppose there are two groups, A and B, occurring in the proportions π_a and π_b such that $\pi_a + \pi_b = 1$. A variate is observed to fall in one of two mutually exclusive categories, X and Y. A man chosen at random is found to belong to the category X. The probability that the man is from group A is

$$P\{A \mid X\} = \frac{\pi_a \cdot P\{X \mid A\}}{\pi_a \cdot P\{X \mid A\} + \pi_b \cdot P\{X \mid B\}} \tag{6.1}$$

The probability that the man is from group B is

$$P\{B \mid X\} = \frac{\pi_b.P\{X \mid B\}}{\pi_a.P\{X \mid A\} + \pi_b.P\{X \mid B\}} \qquad (6.2)$$

If the observation is Y rather than X, the probability that the person is a member of group A is

$$P\{A \mid Y\} = \frac{\pi_a.P\{Y \mid A\}}{\pi_a.P\{Y \mid A\} + \pi_b.P\{Y \mid B\}} \qquad (6.3)$$

The probability that the person is a member of group B is

$$P\{B \mid Y\} = \frac{\pi_b.P\{Y \mid B\}}{\pi_a.P\{Y \mid A\} + \pi_b.P\{Y \mid B\}} \qquad (6.4)$$

In Eqs. 6.1 to 6.4 the notation of conditional probabilities in the form

$$P\{G \mid R\}$$

is read: the probability that the observation lies in the class or group G, given the fact that the observation is in the class R. The notation

$$P\{R \mid G\}$$

denotes the probability that the observation is R, given the fact that it is G.

Since the denominators of Eqs. 6.1 and 6.2 are identical, the rule for classifying an observation depends only on the numerators of these probabilities. If the symbol N denotes frequency, the numerator of Eq. 6.1 is

$$\frac{N_a}{N_a + N_b} \cdot \frac{N_x \text{ in } A}{N_a} = \frac{N_x \text{ in } A}{N_a + N_b}$$

The numerator of Eq. 6.2 is

$$\frac{N_b}{N_a + N_b} \cdot \frac{N_x \text{ in } B}{N_b} = \frac{N_x \text{ in } B}{N_a + N_b}$$

Thus the decision between groups A and B when the observation is known to be X depends only on the contrast of the number of X in group A and the number of X in group B. It was this contrast that we made when we compared the crosses and the dots in the no-motorcycle category in Fig. 6.2. It is the same contrast we achieve in comparing ordinates of two probability distributions.

Similarly it can be shown that the probabilities in Eqs. 6.3 and 6.4 depend only on a comparison of the number of Y in each of the two groups. Thus we arrive at a major principle in discriminatory topology: *The purpose of topology is to define in a test space for each of a series of G groups the regions R in which the frequencies of the test scores are maximal* *for each group.* Assigning individuals of unknown group designation to one of the *G* groups according to this principle accomplishes the classification with the least error. The principle can be written succinctly in the form of inequalities. Before presenting these inequalities, however, we will consider several geometric examples of the general problem of writing the equation of a region.

Suppose we regard the variate *X* as a location on a line:

and that we wish to define the region of this line-space which includes all values of *X* from the score 3 to the score 7 inclusive. The region may be graphically indicated by boundary lines which mark off the interval:

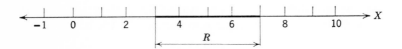

The geometric representation may be algebraically denoted as

$$R \cap 3 \le X \le 7$$

The symbol $\cap$ stands for "is defined by." The symbol *R* stands for region. Thus this expression is read: The region *R* is defined as the space in which *X* is greater than, or equal to, 3 and is less than or equal to 7.

Suppose that we had two variates *X* and *Y* and wished to define the shaded region in algebraic notation:

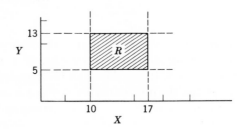

The expression is denoted

$$R \cap \left\{ \begin{array}{l} 10 \le X \le 17 \\ \ 5 \le Y \le 13 \end{array} \right\}$$

Returning to our example, we specify the fork-lift and agent regions in the motorcycle space X. Our principle defines the FLO region as

$$R_{\text{FLO}} \cap P\{\text{FLO} \mid X\} \ge P\{\text{PA} \mid X\}$$

and the passenger agent region as

$$R_{\text{PA}} \cap P\{\text{PA} \mid X\} \ge P\{\text{FLO} \mid X\}$$

We know that when a man has owned a motorcycle before working for World Airlines he is more likely to be a satisfactory operator, whereas if he has not owned a motorcycle before joining World Airlines, he is more likely to be a satisfactory agent. Consequently, these rules result in the following analytic statements of the regions:

$$R_{\text{FLO}} \cap \text{previous ownership of motorcycle}$$
$$R_{\text{PA}} \cap \text{no previous ownership of motorcycle}$$

These statements completely duplicate the geometric representation.

We have purposely developed this example in terms of a previously known job classification in order to avoid certain sampling problems. Obviously, when an employee knows his job classification already, it is more accurate to determine his job classification by asking him what it is than by asking him whether he has owned a motorcycle before joining World Airlines. However, in terms of the variate we are considering, that is, ownership of a motorcycle before being employed, training in the company has had no influence on the variate. Consequently, the data suggest that previous ownership of a motorcycle is more frequent among FLO's than it is among PA's.

If the data proved to characterize real occupational groups, we could form a rational prediction as to whether an individual will later be an operator or an agent by asking him at induction into apprenticeship whether he has owned a motorcycle. Our rule for prediction would be exactly that which has been outlined in Eqs. 6.1 to 6.4. The proportions π_g ($g = 1, 2$) would be determined by the number of FLO's and PA's in World Airlines. Consequently the procedure has merit that is not immediately obvious when stated in our artificial example.

The example can be extended to three job titles. Suppose that a group of 300 employees is known to consist of 100 operators, 100 agents, and 100 mechanics. The problem is to assign the specialty to an individual from a knowledge of his previous ownership of a motorcycle.

We already know the incidence of previous motorcycle ownership among FLO's and PA's. Suppose that among mechanics 20 had owned a motorcycle before being employed, and 80 had not. We now add the information for mechanics to our frequency distribution on the motorcycle space. For convenience in reading, the frequencies are indicated by a scale

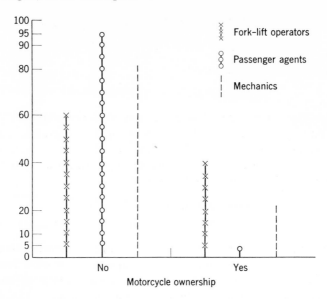

Fig. 6.4   *Frequencies for three specialty groups.*

in Fig. 6.4. The length of the vertical lines are thus comparable to ordinates of a frequency curve. The figure indicates that 60 operators, 95 agents, and 80 mechanics did not own a motorcycle before joining the company. Our problem specifies that we achieve the largest number of correct identifications. The rule we choose is: Classify a man PA whenever we find that he did not own a motorcycle. By this rule 60 operators and 80 mechanics are incorrectly labeled PA. Among those who did own a motorcycle, 40 were operators, 5 agents, and 20 mechanics. To achieve the largest number of correct classifications when we know that a man owned a motorcycle, the rule classifies every man who owned a motorcycle as an operator. By the rule, 5 agents and 20 mechanics are incorrectly called operators. The regions of the motorcycle space are

No	Yes
$\longleftarrow R_{\text{PA}} \longrightarrow$	$\longleftarrow R_{\text{FLO}} \longrightarrow$

These rules result in 165 misclassifications: 5 PA's and 20 M's are called fork-lift operators; 60 FLO's and 80 M's are called passenger agents. The total number of misclassifications has increased by 100, the exact number of mechanics added to the population. Thus when the number of regions is greater than the number of predictive categories, classificatory efficiency drops. If we wish to identify these mechanics, we will have to add more information to the predictive system, the information being chosen so that mechanics will be differentiated from passenger agents and fork-lift operators.

We obtain the same result if we form the rules by probability calculations. Given that an individual owned a motorcycle before entering employment, the probabilities that he is an operator, an agent, and a mechanic are

$$P\{\text{FLO} \mid \text{motorcycle}\} = \frac{(.50)(.40)}{(.50)(.40) + (.50)(.05) + (.50)(.20)} = \frac{8}{13}$$

$$P\{\text{PA} \mid \text{motorcycle}\} = \frac{(.50)(.05)}{(.50)(.40) + (.50)(.05) + (.50)(.20)} = \frac{1}{13}$$

$$P\{\text{M} \mid \text{motorcycle}\} = \frac{(.50)(.20)}{(.50)(.40) + (.50)(.05) + (.50)(.20)} = \frac{4}{13}$$

Thus given the fact that an employee owned a motorcycle, the probability is greatest that he is an operator. Given the fact that an individual did not own a motorcycle, the probabilities are

$$P\{\text{FLO} \mid \text{no motorcycle}\} = \frac{(.50)(.60)}{(.50)(.60) + (.50)(.95) + (.50)(.80)} = \frac{12}{47}$$

$$P\{\text{PA} \mid \text{no motorcycle}\} = \frac{(.50)(.95)}{(.50)(.60) + (.50)(.95) + (.50)(.80)} = \frac{19}{47}$$

$$P\{\text{M} \mid \text{no motorcycle}\} = \frac{(.50)(.80)}{(.50)(.60) + (.50)(.95) + (.50)(.80)} = \frac{16}{47}$$

Given the fact that an individual did not own a motorcycle, the probability is greatest that the man is a passenger agent.

Topologically we wish to define three regions such that:

$$R_{\text{FLO}} \cap \begin{bmatrix} P\{\text{FLO} \mid X\} \geq P\{\text{PA} \mid X\} \\ P\{\text{FLO} \mid X\} \geq P\{\text{M} \mid X\} \end{bmatrix}$$

$$R_{\text{PA}} \cap \begin{bmatrix} P\{\text{PA} \mid X\} \geq P\{\text{FLO} \mid X\} \\ P\{\text{PA} \mid X\} \geq P\{\text{M} \mid X\} \end{bmatrix}$$

$$R_{\text{M}} \cap \begin{bmatrix} P\{\text{M} \mid X\} \geq P\{\text{FLO} \mid X\} \\ P\{\text{M} \mid X\} \geq P\{\text{PA} \mid X\} \end{bmatrix}$$

Because of our previous exploration of probabilities, we know that we can define these regions completely unambiguously in terms of the variable X, motorcycle ownership, as follows:

$R_{\text{FLO}} \cap$ previous ownership of motorcycle
$R_{\text{PA}} \cap$ no previous ownership of motorcycle
$R_{\text{M}} \cap$ nonexistent

This analytic statement is comparable to our graphic representation of two regions on a line separated by a boundary.

Before proceeding further, we note one generalization. When two groups, A and B, are considered, the region for group A is

$$R_A \cap P\{A \mid X\} \geq P\{B \mid X\}$$

and the region for group B is

$$R_B \cap P\{B \mid X\} \geq P\{A \mid X\}$$

When three groups are considered, an additional comparison must be made in each case so that the regions are defined as follows:

$$R_A \cap P\{A \mid X\} \geq P\{B \mid X\}; P\{A \mid X\} \geq P\{C \mid X\}$$
$$R_B \cap P\{B \mid X\} \geq P\{A \mid X\}; P\{B \mid X\} \geq P\{C \mid X\}$$
$$R_C \cap P\{C \mid X\} \geq P\{A \mid X\}; P\{C \mid X\} \geq P\{B \mid X\}$$

A region is defined as the space of the variate X where the probability for a particular group is maximum. This means that the probability must be compared with the probabilities of all other groups.

This general principle must be observed for as many groups as are added. Consequently we may state it very simply as

$$R_g \cap P\{g \mid X\} \geq P\{h \mid X\} \qquad (g, h = 1, 2, \ldots, G; h \neq g) \qquad (6.5)$$

One Continuous Variate

Two Groups

Introduction of a third group into our previous example resulted in a situation in which fewer categories of the predictive variable were available than the number of regions to be defined. One way in which this difficulty may be resolved is by consideration of a single variate with more categories than regions which are to be identified. Since the number of outdoor activity preferences of the Activity Preference Inventory has a range of categories from 0 to 30, we will consider this example next. We consider the same groups that were included in the Activity Preference example in Chapter 2.

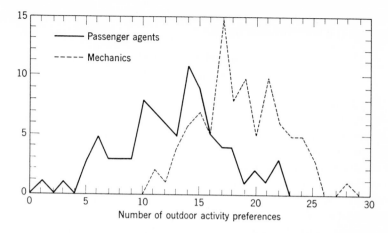

Fig. 6.5 *Frequency polygons for two job groups—passenger agent and mechanic.*

The frequency polygons of outdoor activity preferences of satisfactory and satisfied passenger agents and mechanics are reproduced in Fig. 6.5. With these data, the principle for classification remains exactly the same. We label as the agent region that portion of the horizontal axis in which the ordinate of the frequency polygon for passenger agents is higher than the ordinate for mechanics; we label as the mechanic region that portion of the horizontal axis in which the reverse is true. Comparing the ordinates is the same as comparing the conditional probabilities associated with the score value. We begin at $X = 0$ and inspect the figure to determine which group has the greater ordinate at each score value.

According to the empirical data on the definition of the regions, no agents and no mechanics express preferences for 0, 2, 4, 26, 27, 29, or 30 outdoor activities. In these classes the topology is indeterminate. However, if we note that no mechanics expressed preference for fewer than 11 outdoor activities, whereas some agents did, and that no agent expressed preference for more than 22 outdoor activities, whereas some mechanics did, we might assume that in the long run the frequencies for agents, even though very small, will be greater in the region of scores from 0 to 10, whereas the frequencies of mechanics will be greater in the region from 23 to 30. If we proceed on this basis, the regions are defined without ambiguity. The probability that an individual will be a satisfactory and satisfied agent is greater than the probability that he will be a satisfactory and satisfied mechanic for values of X from 0 to 16 inclusive. The probability favors classification in the mechanic category for values of X from 16 to 30 inclusive. These regions have the ambiguity of sharing the score value

$X = 16$. This ambiguity must be resolved by tossing a coin. The regions we have found are denoted by

$$R_{PA} \cap 0 \le X \le 16$$
$$R_M \cap 16 \le X \le 30$$

The definitions of regions are rules of classification. Application of the rules results in correct classification of 65 of the 85 agents and 68 of the 93 mechanics. Since, in general, the number of misclassifications will be less than the number of correct classifications, we will describe results in terms of misclassification. According to this convention, 15 of the 85 agents and 20 of the 93 mechanics are misclassified by this topology. Five agents and five mechanics, all having the score 16, are not classifiable one way or the other by the definitions. We can do no better than make the decision by the flip of a coin. Among these ten cases, then, the expected number of misclassifications is five. Thus, the total number of misclassifications will be $(15 + 20 + 5) = 40$. This is approximately 22.5% of all 178 men.

We have remarked frequently in Chapters 2, 3, and 4 that the irregularities in the obtained frequency distributions are probably due to sampling errors.

The exact frequencies that characterize the particular sample are not facts that we expect to see identically reproduced in another sample of passenger agents and mechanics. The facts which are more likely to be reproduced in another sample are the central locations of the two distributions, their dispersion, and characteristic form. The statistics we would expect to see approximately reproduced in other samples are the population means and variances and the normal nature of each distribution.

The ordinate of the univariate normal distribution is

$$y = f(X) = \frac{n}{\sigma_x \sqrt{2\pi}} \exp\left[-\frac{1}{2} \left(\frac{X - \mu_x}{\sigma_x} \right)^2 \right]$$

If we choose the sample mean for μ, the sample standard deviation for σ, and the number in the sample for n, the value y will be the ordinate of the normal distribution which best describes the sample. Comparison of the ordinates y_1 and y_2 calculated for two groups is equivalent to the comparison of conditional probabilities estimated for the population. The argument assumes that the n chosen for each sample reflects the population frequency in the specialties. If agents and mechanics are not found in the ratio $n_1 : n_2 = 85 : 93$ in the World Airlines population, the comparison of ordinates is not appropriate for the company population in general. We assume in the example that the values of $n_1 = 85$ and $n_2 = 93$ are appropriate.

The mean outdoor score of agents is 12.59, and the standard deviation is 4.47. Consequently the best fitting normal distribution for agents is

$$y_1 = f_1(X) = \frac{85}{(4.47)\sqrt{2\pi}} \exp\left[-\frac{1}{2}\left(\frac{X - 12.59}{4.47}\right)^2\right]$$

The mean outdoor score of mechanics is 18.54 and the standard deviation 3.55. Consequently, the best fitting normal distribution for mechanics is

$$y_2 = f_2(X) = \frac{93}{(3.55)\sqrt{2\pi}} \exp\left[-\frac{1}{2}\left(\frac{X - 18.54}{3.55}\right)^2\right]$$

These ideal distributions are illustrated in Fig. 6.6. The intersection of the two curves at $X = 15.1$ identifies the boundary point at which the ordinates are equal. Since the ordinate for the agents is always larger at score values less than $X = 15.1$ and the ordinate for the mechanics is larger at score values greater than $X = 15.1$, we choose the point $X = 15.1$ as the boundary between two regions of the test space. The X axis is thus divided into region 1 and region 2. R_1 is the region for agents and R_2 is the region for mechanics. These regions are indicated in Fig. 6.6. (For precision of statement we note that the PA curve in Fig. 6.6 also intersects the M curve at $X = 42$. Since the maximal number of outdoor activity preferences is 30, this outer boundary point has no practical consequence in the problem.)

The shaded area A in Fig. 6.6 represents the portion of the agent distribution which lies on the mechanic region R_2. This area represents the expected frequency with which agents are misclassified. The frequency

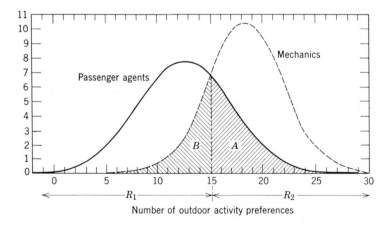

Fig. 6.6 *Normal curves fitted to the observed distributions of outdoor activity preferences—passenger agents and mechanics.*

represented by the area A may be determined from a table of the normal distribution. Similarly, the area marked B in Fig. 6.6 represents the frequency of misclassification of all mechanics when $X = 15.1$ is chosen as the boundary defining classification regions.

We now compute for the example a more precise value of X_b, the boundary point, and use the numerical result to find the estimated number of misclassifications.

Since the required boundary is the point at which the frequency of the agent distribution equals the frequency of the mechanic distribution, the boundary is determined by equating $f_1(X)$ and $f_2(X)$. Thus the boundary is the point that satisfies the equation

$$\frac{85}{(4.47)\sqrt{2\pi}} \exp\left[-\frac{1}{2}\left(\frac{X - 12.59}{4.47}\right)^2\right] = \frac{93}{(3.55)\sqrt{2\pi}} \exp\left[-\frac{1}{2}\left(\frac{X - 18.54}{3.55}\right)^2\right]$$

If we denote the desired boundary as X_b, the equation may be written

$$\left[\frac{1}{(4.47)^2} - \frac{1}{(3.55)^2}\right]X_b{}^2 - 2\left[\frac{12.59}{(4.47)^2} - \frac{18.54}{(3.55)^2}\right]X_b$$

$$+ \frac{(12.59)^2}{(4.47)^2} - \frac{(18.54)^2}{(3.55)^2} + 2\cdot\ln\left[\frac{93(4.47)}{85(3.55)}\right] = 0$$

which reduces to

$$0.296X_b{}^2 - 2(0.8454)X_b + 18.7706 = 0$$

The roots of this equation are 15.08 and 42.04. The second root, 42.04, exceeds the maximum possible outdoor score and may be ignored in the present example. We will use the root 15.08 as the only appropriate boundary. The regions are defined as

$$R_1 \cap 0 \leq X \leq 15.08$$
$$R_2 \cap 15.08 \leq X \leq 30$$

If we choose to apply the theory of the ideal model rigorously by using both roots, the regions will be defined as

$$R_1 \cap -\infty \leq X \leq 15.08; \; 42.04 \leq X \leq \infty$$
$$R_2 \cap 15.08 \leq X \leq 42.04$$

The expected number of misclassifications resulting from our rules and the assumption of normal distributions in the two specialties is determined from the table of areas of the normal distribution. We express $X = 15.08$ as a normal standard score in each of the distributions in turn, find the proportional area beyond this point in each distribution, and multiply each proportion by the number in the specialty. The sum of these areas (frequencies) is $A + B$. In the agent distribution, the standardized deviate is

$$\frac{15.08 - 12.59}{4.47} = .5570$$

The proportion of area of a normal curve beyond this deviate is .2888. The total area of the agent distribution lying on the mechanic region is $85(.2888) = 24.55$. The normalized deviate of the boundary, $X = 15.08$, in the mechanic distribution is

$$\frac{15.08 - 18.54}{3.55} = -.9746$$

The proportion of area of a normal distribution less than this deviate is .1649. The expected frequency of misclassified mechanics is $93(.1649) = 15.34$. Thus the total expected number of misclassifications is $(24.55 + 15.34) = 39.89$. It is notable that the estimate derived from the ideal model is close to the 40 expected misclassifications obtained by counting the observed frequencies in the regions.

When the observed frequency distributions are replaced by continuous theoretical curves as in the foregoing, it becomes a simple matter to prove that the classification rule adopted yields the smallest expected number of misclassifications. We need only compare the number of misclassifications resulting from this rule with the number of misclassifications resulting from another rule represented by a different boundary point. This is demonstrated in Fig. 6.7.

The procedure we have illustrated in the example may be formally stated for the general case. Given one population·distributed as

$$f_1(X) = \frac{n_1}{\sigma_1 \sqrt{2\pi}} \exp\left[-\frac{1}{2}\left(\frac{X - \mu_1}{\sigma_1}\right)^2 \right]$$

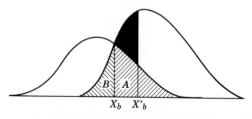

Fig. 6.7   *Demonstration of the effect of changing the boundary point. Choose any other point, say X'_b, as a boundary and erect the ordinate at the point. Inspection of the areas representing misclassification shows that an additional area marked in solid black is added to the original areas A and B, which are not changed by choice of boundary. Any choice of X'_b different from X_b will increase the total area of misclassification.*

and a second population distributed as

$$f_2(X) = \frac{n_2}{\sigma_2 \sqrt{2\pi}} \exp\left[-\frac{1}{2}\left(\frac{X - \mu_2}{\sigma_2}\right)^2\right]$$

we wish to determine regions such that

$$R_1 \cap f_1(X) \geq f_2(X)$$
$$R_2 \cap f_2(X) \geq f_1(X)$$

The boundaries of the regions are the values X_b which satisfy the equation

$$f_1(X) = f_2(X)$$

The equation reduces to the following general equation for the boundary X_b:

$$\left(\frac{1}{\sigma_1^2} - \frac{1}{\sigma_2^2}\right)X_b^2 - 2\left(\frac{\mu_1}{\sigma_1^2} - \frac{\mu_2}{\sigma_2^2}\right)X_b + \left(\frac{\mu_1^2}{\sigma_1^2} - \frac{\mu_2^2}{\sigma_2^2}\right) + 2\ln\frac{n_2\sigma_1}{n_1\sigma_2} = 0 \quad (6.6)$$

The solution yields two boundary points unless σ_1 equals σ_2. Thus, in general, the continuum X will be divided into three subregions defining two regions. If we denote the two roots as X_b and X'_b, the regions are

$$R_1 \cap -\infty \leq X \leq X_b; X'_b \leq X \leq \infty \qquad \begin{bmatrix} \mu_1 < \mu_2 \\ \sigma_1 > \sigma_2 \end{bmatrix}$$
$$R_2 \cap \quad X_b \leq X \leq X'_b$$

when μ_1 is less than μ_2 and σ_1 is greater than σ_2. For different combinations of μ and σ, appropriate modifications of these boundaries are necessary.

If q_1 denotes the proportion of group one frequencies in R_2, and if q_2 denotes the proportion of group two frequencies in R_1, the expected number of misclassifications is $(n_1q_1 + n_2q_2) = A + B$. This number is as small as it can be.

When $\sigma_1 = \sigma_2$ Eq. 6.6 reduces to

$$X_b = \frac{\frac{1}{2}(\mu_1^2 - \mu_2^2) + \sigma^2 \ln(n_2/n_1)}{(\mu_1 - \mu_2)} \qquad (\sigma_1 = \sigma_2 = \sigma) \qquad (6.7)$$

In this instance, the continuum X is divided into two regions by the single point X_b:

$$R_1 \cap -\infty \leq X \leq X_b \qquad \begin{bmatrix} \mu_1 < \mu_2 \\ \sigma_1 = \sigma_2 \end{bmatrix}$$
$$R_2 \cap \quad X_b \leq X \leq \infty$$

Three Groups

We next examine the topology of classificatory regions when three job populations—passenger agent, mechanic, and operations control agents—are considered simultaneously. The three frequency polygons are reproduced in Fig. 6.8. The rules for classification are determined by comparing the three ordinates at each score value. Table 6.3 gives the

Table 6.3 *Frequency and Distribution of Misclassifications Counted in Three-Group Sample*

Actual \ Classified as	Passenger Agent	Mechanic	OCA	Number of Misclassifications	Number of Men
Passenger Agent	65.0	15.5	4.5	20.0	85.0
Mechanic	20.5	65.5	7.0	27.5	93.0
OCA	28.5	27.0	10.5	55.5	66.0
Total	114.0	108.0	22.0	103.0	244.0

result. Of the 244 men, 103 (42%) are misclassified. The irregularities of the frequencies at particular score points, notably $X = 4$ and $X = 20$, favor the OCA group with fewer misclassifications than we expect. The point is made obvious in Fig. 6.9 which shows the effect of using the normal distribution to estimate the long-run result. In Fig. 6.9 the ordinate of the OCA distribution is everywhere smaller than that of either of the other specialties.

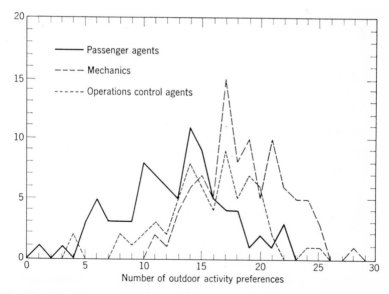

Fig. 6.8 *Cartesian representation: outdoor activity preferences of passenger agents, mechanics, and operations control agents.*

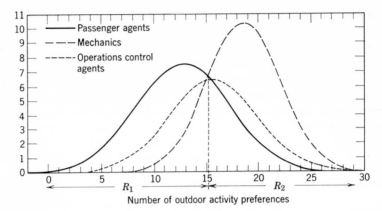

Fig. 6.9 *Normal curves fitted to the observed distributions of outdoor activity preferences of passenger agents, mechanics, and operations control agents.*

The OCA distribution in Fig. 6.9 was obtained by plotting the ordinate given by

$$y = f_3(X) = \frac{66}{4.08\sqrt{2\pi}} \exp\left[-\frac{1}{2}\left(\frac{X - 15.58}{4.08}\right)^2\right]$$

In the figure we see that there is no region assignable to the operations man job-title. All the OCA's are misclassified as either agents or mechanics. The differences among the groups must be larger if we are to achieve success in defining multiple regions. Thus the problem exhibited in this three-group example reduces to the problem of choosing more powerful data. Methodological improvements in the procedure for defining classificatory regions cannot be expected to improve the discrimination observed.

The General Case, G Groups

In general, we seek the boundaries of G regions such that

$$R_g \cap f_g(X) \geq f_h(X) \qquad (g, h = 1, 2, \ldots, G; h \neq g) \qquad (6.8)$$

We assume that each population g is normally distributed with mean μ_g and variance σ_g^2 so that its distribution is given by

$$f_g(X) = \frac{n_g}{\sigma_g\sqrt{2\pi}} \exp\left[-\frac{1}{2}\left(\frac{X - \mu_g}{\sigma_g}\right)^2\right]$$

The boundaries between group g and group h are then determined by solving Eq. 6.6 using n_g, $\bar{X}_g$, and s_g in the sample as estimates of the parameters in the population. This equation is solved for all possible pairs of groups. The test space on the continuum X is then mapped according to the definition, inequality 6.8.

Situations may arise in which $\bar{X}_g$ and s_g are considered good estimates of the population parameters, whereas the sample value of n_g is not considered an appropriate value. If the ratio $\pi_g = n_g/\sum n_g$ can be determined from *a priori* considerations, the proportion π_g may be used for the value n_g in the gth distribution. The region R_g is

$$R_g \cap \pi_g \phi_g(X) \geq \pi_h \phi_h(X) \qquad (g, h = 1, 2, \ldots, G; h \neq g) \qquad (6.9)$$

where $\phi_g(X)$ is

$$\phi_g(X) = \frac{1}{\sigma_g \sqrt{2\pi}} \exp\left[-\frac{1}{2}\left(\frac{X - \mu_g}{\sigma_g}\right)^2\right]$$

The boundary X_b is computed by

$$\left(\frac{1}{\sigma_g^2} - \frac{1}{\sigma_h^2}\right) X_b^2 - 2\left(\frac{\mu_g}{\sigma_g^2} - \frac{\mu_h}{\sigma_h^2}\right) X_b + \left(\frac{\mu_g^2}{\sigma_g^2} - \frac{\mu_h^2}{\sigma_h^2}\right) + 2\ln\frac{\pi_h \sigma_g}{\pi_g \sigma_h} = 0$$
$$(6.10)$$

If p_g is defined as the proportion of the gth population which lies in R_g (correct classifications), $q_g = 1 - p_g$ is the proportion of misclassifications. The expected total number of misclassifications in all groups combined is

$$n_1 q_1 + n_2 q_2 + \cdots + n_G q_G$$

The values n_g can be taken either as the number in the sample or as values estimated from the π_g.

Two Continuous Variates

Two Groups

We consider first the case of two groups, passenger agents and mechanics, when *pairs* of observations are available for each individual of each job. The pairs of observations we will consider are the outdoor and the convivial activity preference scores for each man. The combined scattergram from Chapter 3 of the two groups is shown in Fig. 6.10.

Topological regions in the two-variable case will be areas in the test space of two dimensions. The scatter diagram of the test space is easily divisible into square cells, the center point indicating a pair of score values. The frequencies in each cell show the number of agents and the number of mechanics which occupy the cell. Our principle for defining regions will result in assigning each occupied cell to that job-title which has the greater frequency. Assignments of cellular areas to R_{PA} and R_M are shown in Fig. 6.11, and the frequency of misclassification can be evaluated by counting.

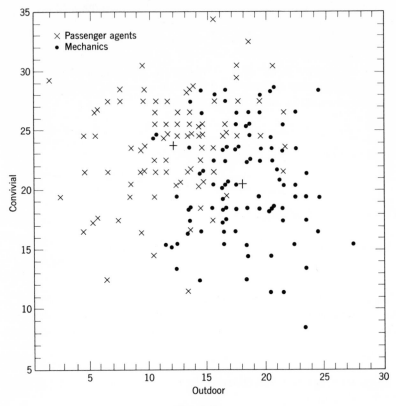

Fig. 6.10

The expected number of misclassifications is 7, or 4%. This startling result is attributable to the fact that only 7 of the 144 occupied cells contain individuals from both populations. By dividing the total test space (30 by 30) into many more cells than we have individuals to occupy them we have capitalized on the chance element in the distribution. It is absurd to expect that future samples would reproduce the observed frequencies in the cells.

Nevertheless, agents occupy mainly the upper left-hand portion of the test space and the density of mechanics is greater in the lower right-hand sector. We therefore choose to adopt an ideal model in order to establish the boundary lines which will be appropriate estimates for the population from which we may draw future samples. We choose the normal distribution as reasonable for these data.

In Chapter 3 we stated that the locus of any specified frequency in a bivariate normal distribution is an ellipse. The ellipse is defined by χ^2

taking a constant value in the expression:

$$\chi^2 = xD^{-1}x'$$

which stands in the exponential function in

$$f(X_1, X_2) = \frac{n}{2\pi|D|^{1/2}} \exp\left(-\frac{\chi^2}{2}\right)$$

where

$$x = \|(X_1 - \mu_1) \quad (X_2 - \mu_2)\|$$

In this instance we find it necessary to use a small x to represent a row matrix of points on the test axes expressed as deviations from μ.

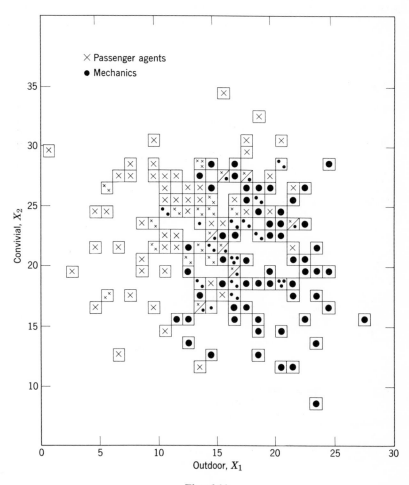

Fig. 6.11

Several centour ellipses for the two idealized models chosen to represent the two samples are shown graphically in Fig. 6.12. The 50th centour ellipses of the two groups intersect at two points. These points identify locations in the test space at which the probability in one population is equal to the probability in the other. There are many possible pairs of equivalent centour ellipses and every pair that intersects identifies two points of equal density or equal probability in the two models. It is important to distinguish the ellipses by equivalent pairing; an observed intersection of C_{50} and C_{20} ellipses does not indicate a point of equal density. The concept of equal density or equal probability we are using here is the two-dimensional extension of the concept of equal ordinates at the point of intersection of two univariate distributions. The locus of the points of intersection of the paired ellipses on the plane of the test space

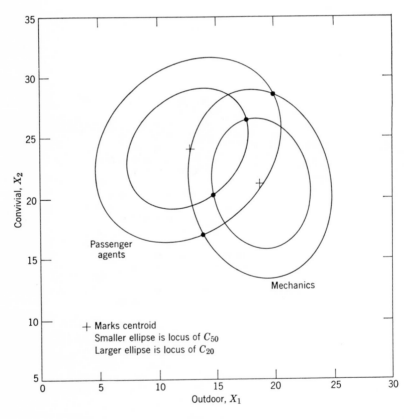

Fig. 6.12

is the line given by the projections on to the plane of the intersection of the two overlapping bivariate frequency surfaces.

This example presents a notation problem, particularly the subscript notation which identifies test space axes and population groups. We shall therefore use a double subscript system in which the first position in the pair identifies the population and the second position identifies the test axis. A dot will be used to preserve order identification of the axis when the population identity is not pertinent. This notation problem develops because we have two groups represented on the same test space. The coordinate axes are the same for both groups, and there will be a density value for each group at every point in the test space. Since we will find the boundary lines between regions by equating density functions in pairs of groups, it is especially necessary to guard against confusion of axes 1 and 2 and populations 1 and 2. Readers who are more familiar with Cartesian axes denoted by x and y will be aided by remembering that we identify the axes by numerical subscripts in preparation for extension of the methods to T tests. For the passenger agent population the frequency at any point X_1, X_2 on the test space is

$$f_1(X_{.1}, X_{.2}) = \frac{n_1}{2\pi |D_1|^{1/2}} \exp\left(-\frac{X_1^2}{2}\right)$$

The subscript in f_1 indicates that we are discussing population 1, the agent group. The subscript in $X_{.1}$ indicates the value of a coordinate point on the first axis, outdoor score, the dot being used to preserve the positional meaning of the numeric subscript which follows it. $X_{.2}$ identifies a value on the second test axis, convivial score. On the right-hand side the subscript 1 is in the first position and therefore refers to the group. The symbol D_1 thus denotes the determinant of the dispersion matrix of group 1.

For the mechanic population (group 2) the frequency at the point $X_{.1}$, $X_{.2}$ in the test space is

$$f_2(X_{.1}, X_{.2}) = \frac{n_2}{2\pi |D_2|^{1/2}} \exp\left(-\frac{X_2^2}{2}\right)$$

The boundary between the passenger agent and mechanic region is then found by solving the equation

$$f_1(X_{.1}, X_{.2}) = f_2(X_{.1}, X_{.2})$$

A systematic computing formula is achieved by equating the logarithms of the sides of this equation, and expressing the result in matrix notation as follows:

$$X(D_1^{-1} - D_2^{-1})X' - 2[(\bar{X}_{1.}D_1^{-1}) - (\bar{X}_{2.}D_2^{-1})]X' + \bar{X}_{1.}D_1^{-1}\bar{X}'_{1.}$$

$$- \bar{X}_{2.}D_2^{-1}\bar{X}'_{2.} - \ln\frac{n_1^2}{|D_1|} + \ln\frac{n_2^2}{|D_2|} = 0 \quad (6.11)$$

where $X = \|X_{.1} \quad X_{.2}\|$, the row vector of raw score axes; $\overline{X}_{1.} = \|\overline{X}_{11} \quad \overline{X}_{12}\|$; and $\overline{X}_{2.} = \|\overline{X}_{21} \quad \overline{X}_{22}\|$. The elements of the matrix X are coordinate values on the Cartesian axes of the test space, whereas the elements of the matrices $\overline{X}_{1.}$, $\overline{X}_{2.}$, and D are statistics characterizing the data of the groups.

For group 1 (agent): $n_1 = 85$

$$\overline{X}_1 = \|12.5882 \quad 24.2235\| \qquad |D_1| = 350.782226$$

$$D_1 = \begin{Vmatrix} 20.0068 & 4.5628 \\ 4.5628 & 18.5735 \end{Vmatrix} \qquad D_1^{-1} = \begin{Vmatrix} .051949 & -.013007 \\ -.013007 & .057035 \end{Vmatrix}$$

For group 2 (mechanic): $n_2 = 93$

$$\overline{X}_2 = \|18.5376 \quad 21.1398\| \qquad |D_2| = 255.100181$$

$$D_2 = \begin{Vmatrix} 12.5713 & -1.5582 \\ -1.5582 & 20.4856 \end{Vmatrix} \qquad D_2^{-1} = \begin{Vmatrix} .080305 & .006111 \\ .006111 & .049279 \end{Vmatrix}$$

Substitution of these values in Eq. 6.11 results in

$$.0274X_{.1}{}^2 - .0077X_{.2}{}^2 + .0382X_{.1}X_{.2} - 2.5330X_{.1} + .1236X_{.2} + 20.0082 = 0$$

as the equation of the boundary between the agent and mechanic regions. The solution for $X_{.2}$ in terms of $X_{.1}$ is

$$X_{.2} = 2.48X_{.1} + 8.03 \pm \sqrt{9.71X_{.1}{}^2 - 289.14X_{.1} + 2662.88}$$

This equation provides a convenient means for finding the boundary between the regions R_{PA} and R_M. A sufficient number of points for plotting the boundary on Fig. 6.10 are listed in Table 6.4.

When the value of $X_{.1}$ is chosen as 5, $X_{.2}$ is found to have two values, -17.8 and 58.6. The two points, 5, -17.8 and 5, 58.6, both lie outside the portion of the plane which we use to represent the test space. All the entries labeled $X'_{.2}$ are values of the convivial scores which cannot occur, and lie outside the effective test space. We are interested only in that portion of the line which divides the test space into regions associated with the population groups. The boundary line in the test space is plotted in Fig. 6.13 on the scatter diagram of Fig. 6.10. We denote the boundary B_{12}. The subscripts identify the job-title regions that are separated by the line B.

The boundary cuts through the outdoor and convivial activity space in such a way that the agent region is above and to the left, and the mechanic region is below and to the right. These are regions in which

$$R_1 \cap f_1(X_{.1}, X_{.2}) \geq f_2(X_{.1}, X_{.2})$$
$$R_2 \cap f_2(X_{.1}, X_{.2}) \geq f_1(X_{.1}, X_{.2})$$

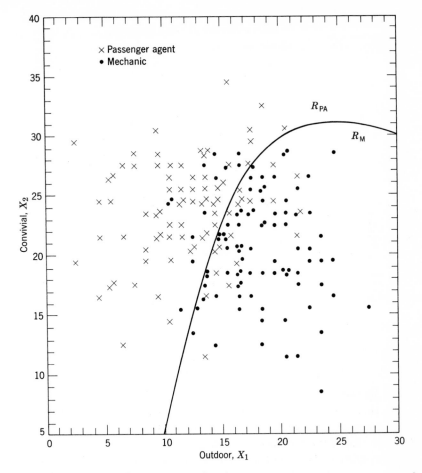

Fig. 6.13 *Boundary line—two groups.*

By counting the number of individuals located in the "wrong" region we obtain a semi-empirical, semitheoretical measure of the expected number of misclassifications. The count gives the following results:

Number of passenger agent points in R_M 18
Number of mechanic points in R_{PA} 12

Total misclassifications   30

Since 40 individuals were misclassified when only their outdoor activity preferences were considered, we see that we have reduced the expected number of misclassifications by 10.

Table 6.4   *Coordinates of the Boundary between Regions for Two Groups*

$X_{.1}$	$X_{.2}$	$X'_{.2}$
5	− 17.8	58.6
7	− 8.0	58.8
8	− 3.3	59.0
9	1.2	59.4
10	5.6	60.1
11	9.7	61.0
12	13.5	62.1
13	16.9	63.6
14	20.0	65.6
15	22.6	67.8
16	24.9	70.6
18	28.1	77.2
20	30.0	85.3
22	30.9	94.2
24	31.3	103.8
26	31.2	113.9
28	30.8	124.2
30	30.2	134.7

Three Groups

We now consider the outdoor and convivial scores of three groups, passenger agents, mechanics, and operations control agents. The scatter diagram (Fig. 6.14) includes the three groups.

Application of the principle of labeling a cell in the test space according to the group of the highest frequency in the cell leads to the disjoint regions indicated in Fig. 6.15. Again the classificatory results appear good on the surface. There are only 21 cells occupied by cases from more than one group. Of these 21 cells, one is occupied by one case from each of the three groups, 15 are occupied by one case from each of two groups, and 5 are occupied by one case from one group and two or three from another group. The resulting total expected number of misclassifications is

$$3 \times \tfrac{1}{3} + 30 \times \tfrac{1}{2} + 5 = 21$$

However, as previously noted, such a determination of group membership on the basis of frequencies in individual cells is extremely unreliable and could not be expected to be repeated in subsequent samples. To determine a more reliable long-run result, we assume that the bivariate distribution

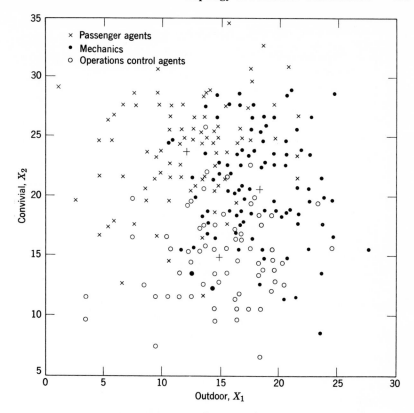

Fig. 6.14   *Scatter diagram—three groups.*

of operations control agents will be normally distributed with parameters of this sample.

In addition to the previous two bivariate normal distributions estimated for agent and mechanic populations we now have a third bivariate distribution for operations control agents. The frequencies for the third distribution are given by

$$f_3(X_{.1}, X_{.2}) = \frac{n_3}{2\pi|D_3|^{1/2}} \exp\left(-\frac{\chi_3^2}{2}\right)$$

We wish to find three regions such that

$$R_1 \cap f_1(X_{.1}, X_{.2}) \geq f_2(X_{.1}, X_{.2}); \quad f_1(X_{.1}, X_{.2}) \geq f_3(X_{.1}, X_{.2})$$
$$R_2 \cap f_2(X_{.1}, X_{.2}) \geq f_1(X_{.1}, X_{.2}); \quad f_2(X_{.1}, X_{.2}) \geq f_3(X_{.1}, X_{.2})$$
$$R_3 \cap f_3(X_{.1}, X_{.2}) \geq f_1(X_{.1}, X_{.2}); \quad f_3(X_{.1}, X_{.2}) \geq f_2(X_{.1}, X_{.2})$$

Specification of these regions requires that the frequencies for operations

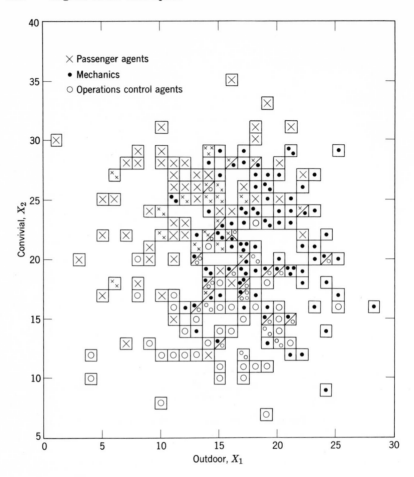

Fig. 6.15 *Frequencies in cellular regions—three groups.*

personnel be compared with the frequencies for *both* agents and mechanics in addition to the previous comparison of the frequencies for agents and mechanics. The boundary B_{12} between agents and mechanics is unchanged by the introduction of operations men into the problem, except that its limits must be determined by the procedure to be outlined. The introduction of operations men requires calculation of two new boundaries, B_{13}, the boundary between agents and operations personnel, and B_{23}, the boundary between mechanics and operations men.

The boundary B_{13} is determined by the equation

$$f_1(X_{.1}, X_{.2}) = f_3(X_{.1}, X_{.2})$$

and a sufficient number of points of B_{13} can be determined by Eq. 6.11 with the subscript identifying group two everywhere changed to 3.

The new expressions for substitution in Eq. 6.11 are

$$\bar{X}_3 = \|15.5758 \quad 15.4545\|$$

$$D_3 = \left\|\begin{matrix} 16.6382 & 1.6468 \\ 1.6468 & 13.9748 \end{matrix}\right\|$$

$$n_3 = 66$$

The equation in the coordinates $X_{.1}$ and $X_{.2}$ becomes

$$.0079 X_{.1}{}^2 + .0154 X_{.2}{}^2 + 2(.0058) X_{.1} X_{.2} - 2(.4847) X_{.1}$$
$$+ 2(.2103) X_{.2} - 5.2415 = 0$$

And the boundary B_{13} is determined by pairs of values which satisfy

$$X_{.2} = -(.3766 X_{.1} + 13.6558)$$
$$\pm (-.3712 X_{.1}{}^2 + 73.2335 X_{.1} + 526.8380)^{\frac{1}{2}}$$

We mention once again that $X_{.2}$ and $X_{.1}$ refer to the axes of the test space. Suitable values of $X_{.1}$ are chosen and the values of $X_{.2}$ computed. The useful range is given in Table 6.5. In Table 6.5 the set of points $(X_{.1}, X'_{.2})$

Table 6.5   *Coordinates of the Boundary B_{13}*

$X_{.1}$	$X_{.2}$	$X'_{.2}$	$X_{.1}$	$X_{.2}$	$X'_{.2}$
0	9.3	−89.	18	21.1	−61.9
5	14.2	−45.	20	21.7	−64.1
8	16.3	−50.	22	22.3	−66.2
10	17.5	−52.4	24	22.8	−68.2
12	18.6	−54.9	26	23.3	−70.1
14	19.5	−57.4	28	23.6	−72.0
16	20.4	−59.7	30	23.9	−73.8

defines a line in the plane but not in the effective test space. This second boundary is a necessary result of the assumed normal distribution. It is the bivariate analogue of the paired points of intersection of two normal distributions which we found in the univariate case.

The boundary between mechanics and operations men B_{23} is determined by the same method. The equation is

$$f_2(X_{.1}, X_{.2}) = f_3(X_{.1}, X_{.2})$$

For computation, the group-identifying subscripts are changed in Eq. 6.11. The equation for the line B_{23} becomes

$$.0195X_{.1}^2 - .0231X_{.2}^2 + 2(.0133)X_{.1}X_{.2} - 2(.7818)X_{.1}$$
$$- 2(.1485)X_{.2} + 25.2497 = 0$$

And the values of the coordinates are tabled from

$$X_{.2} = (.5758X_{.1} - 6.4286) \pm (1.1757X_{.1}^2 - 75.0915X_{.1} + 1134.3875)^{\frac{1}{2}}$$

The boundary can be sketched from the following values given in Table 6.6.

Table 6.6   *Coordinates of the Boundary B_{23}*

$X_{.1}$	$X_{.1}$	$X'_{.2}$	$X_{.1}$	$X_{.2}$	$X'_{.2}$
0	27.3	−40.1	18	16.7	−8.9
5	24.5	−36.6	20	15.2	−5.1
10	21.7	−23.0	22	13.4	−0.9
12	20.5	−19.6	23	12.2	1.4
14	19.3	−16.1	24	10.5	4.3
16	18.1	−12.5	24.5	8.3	7.1

It should be noted that when $X_{.1}$ exceeds 22, the pairs of scores $X_{.1}, X'_{.2}$ enter the region of actual activity preferences. Thus there are two boundaries between OCA's and mechanics. We shall ignore the boundary formed by the points $(X_{.1}, X'_{.2})$ in the example without loss of efficiency.

The three boundaries B_{12}, B_{13}, B_{23} are plotted in Fig. 6.16. In drawing the boundaries for the three regions we have a complication not encountered in the two-group case. In that instance we had only one equation, yielding a boundary between two regions. In the three-group case the three equations yield three lines intersecting at a single point and the T space is divided into six regions. We are generally interested in identifying only as many regions as there are groups, three in this instance. Therefore, we must delete a segment of each of the three curves so that the remaining three segments, all terminating at the point of intersection, will define three regions.

A usually reliable procedure is to inspect the scatter diagram drawn, and decide on the basis of the density of the three groups in the six regions. However, there may be situations in which this method will be ambiguous, or will involve laborious counting, or both.

The logical way to make the decision is to consider the relationship among the group frequencies theoretically holding in each of the six regions. We illustrate the procedure step by step.

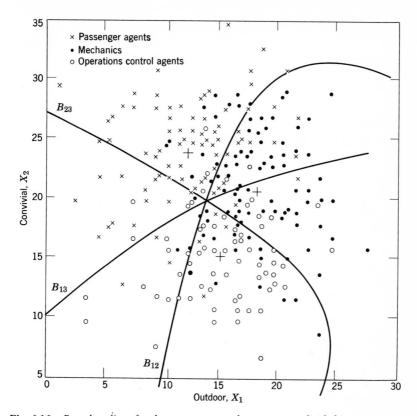

Fig. 6.16 *Boundary lines for three-group example—test space divided into six sectors.*

1. Draw one curve, say B_{12}. The plane is then divided into two regions. In one region the inequality

$$f_1(X_{.1}, X_{.2}) \geq f_2(X_{.1}, X_{.2})$$

holds, and in the other region, the opposite inequality

$$f_2(X_{.1}, X_{.2}) \geq f_1(X_{.1}, X_{.2})$$

is true. Thus we have a line B_{12} and the inequalities that characterize the space in each region.

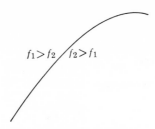

2. Draw a second curve, say B_{13}. The plane is now in four sectors. Before writing in the inequalities holding because of the second curve, write each of the previous inequalities in the appropriate pair of sectors, thus:

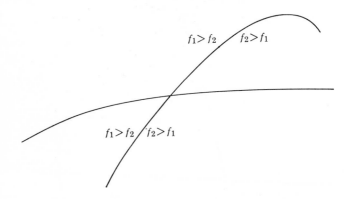

Then write each of the new inequalities in the proper pair of sectors, thus:

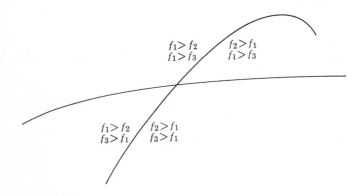

3. Draw the third curve B_{23}. Write the previous statements in their proper sectors. Each of the six sectors now contains two inequalities, thus:

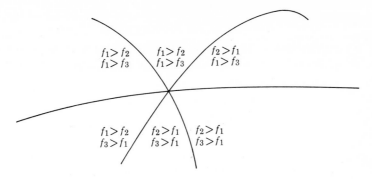

Then write in the new inequality, thus:

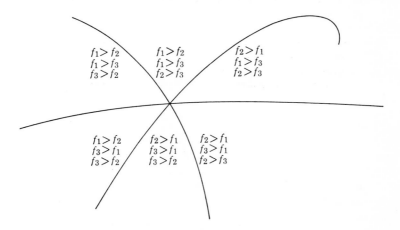

4. Collect the three inequalities in each of the sectors into the single expression

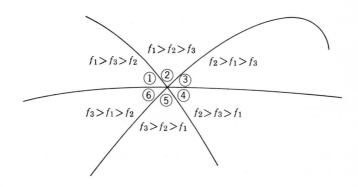

For convenient reference in the next step we have numbered each of the six sectors.

5. We are now able to identify the irrelevant segments of the boundary lines by reference to the definitions of the three regions. Simplified expressions for the regions are

$$R_1 \cap f_1 \geq f_2; \quad f_1 \geq f_3$$
$$R_2 \cap f_2 \geq f_1; \quad f_2 \geq f_3$$
$$R_3 \cap f_3 \geq f_1; \quad f_3 \geq f_2$$

The inequalities holding in sectors 1 and 2 indicate that f_1 is the largest of the frequencies in both sectors and that the regions differ only in the order of the other two frequencies f_2 and f_3. Since we are interested only in identifying the job-title with the greatest frequency, we do not need to retain the distinction between sectors 1 and 2. We therefore erase the

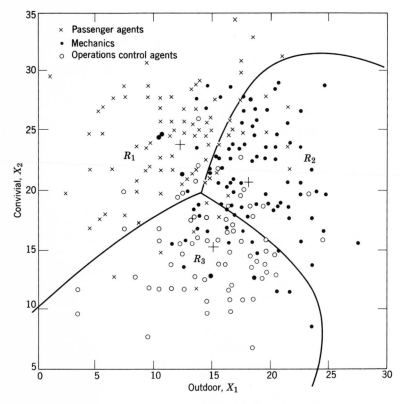

Fig. 6.17 *Regions of the test space for the three-group example—six sectors combined into three regions.*

boundary between these two sectors and denote the combined space, region 1, R_1. R_2 and R_3 are similarly obtained. The final boundaries are shown in Fig. 6.17.

The frequency of misclassification in the sample groups can be counted in Fig. 6.17. The count is shown in Table 6.7. The total number of misclassifications is 67 out of 244. The number of misclassifications in the

Table 6.7 *Frequency of Misclassification—Three Groups*

Actual \ Classified as	Agent	Mechanic	OCA	Number of Misclassifications	Number of Men
Passenger Agent	64	15	6	21	85
Mechanic	10	66	17	27	93
OCA	7	12	47	19	66
Totals	81	93	70	67	244

same three groups was 106 when only the outdoor score was used. We have added 39 to the correct number of classifications by considering joint preference for outdoor and convivial activities. The second variate, taken together with the first, gives us additional information concerning group membership.

The General Case, G Groups

The previous detailed consideration of two and three groups in the two-variate case provides sufficient background for immediate generalization to G groups.

In general, regions defined by comparing cell frequencies in observed data will be disjointed and unreliable. We therefore choose to assume a bivariate normal distribution in each population.

For each group (or population job-title) we write its bivariate normal frequency distribution as

$$f_g(X_{.1}, X_{.2}) = \frac{n_g}{2\pi |D_g|^{1/2}} \exp\left(-\frac{\chi_g^2}{2}\right)$$

where

$$\chi_g^2 = x_g . D_g^{-1} x'_g.$$

and

$$x_g. = \|(X_{.1} - \mu_{g1})(X_{.2} - \mu_{g2})\|$$

We then define the region R_g as

$$R_g \cap f_g(X_{.1}, X_{.2}) \geq f_h(X_{.1}, X_{.2}); \qquad g, h = 1, 2, \ldots, G; \qquad h \neq g$$

Evaluation of the set of inequalities for each group requires that the frequencies of each group be examined in relation to the frequencies in all other groups in turn. This examination is accomplished formally by computation of the $G(G-1)/2$ boundaries B_{gh} defined by the equation

$$f_g(X_{.1}, X_{.2}) = f_h(X_{.1}, X_{.2}); \qquad g, h = 1, 2, \ldots, G; \qquad h > g$$

The boundary B_{gh} may be computed from

$$X(D_g^{-1} - D_h^{-1})X' - 2[(\bar{X}_{g.}D_g^{-1}) - (\bar{X}_{h.}D_h^{-1})]X' + \bar{X}_{g.}D_g^{-1}\bar{X}'_{g.}$$

$$- \bar{X}_{h.}D_h^{-1}\bar{X}'_{h.} - \ln\frac{n_g^2}{|D_g|} + \ln\frac{n_h^2}{|D_h|} = 0 \quad (6.12)$$

where

$$X = \|X_{.1} \quad X_{.2}\|$$
$$\bar{X}_{g.} = \|\mu_{g1} \quad \mu_{g2}\|$$
$$\bar{X}_{h.} = \|\mu_{h1} \quad \mu_{h2}\|$$

and the dispersion matrices D_g and D_h are as defined previously. Sample means are used as estimates of their population parameters. Equation 6.12 differs from Eq. 6.11 only in the subscripts which are now general for any group.

Each of the $G(G-1)/2$ boundaries B_{gh} determined by Eq. 6.12 consists of a pair of lines, one of which usually lies outside the effective test space. There will be $G(G-1)/2$ lines to graph on the plane of the test space, as in Fig. 6.16. These lines divide the test space into sectors. A systematic comparison of the inequalities that describe each sector identifies the one population for which the frequency function f_g is greatest. Every sector may therefore be identified as a portion of one region and there will be, at most, G regions. Segments of the lines B_{gh} which pass through a region may be ignored as irrelevant.

For three groups we determine three lines which divide the plane into six sectors. The inequalities lead to combining three of these sectors with three others in pairs to form three regions. In the case of four groups, we compute six lines which divide the plane into at least 12 sectors. The inequalities lead to combining several sectors with some of the others to form, at most, four regions. For five groups, ten lines produce at least 20 sectors which combine into, at most, five regions.

An estimate of the expected number of misclassifications can be achieved by counting the number of points that are in wrong regions.

It is worth noting that when the dispersion matrices of the groups are identical, Eq. 6.12 reduces to

$$2(\bar{X}_{g.} - \bar{X}_{h.})D^{-1}X' - \bar{X}_{g.}D^{-1}\bar{X}'_{g.} + \bar{X}_{h.}D^{-1}\bar{X}'_{h.} + 2\ln\frac{n_g}{n_h} = 0 \quad (6.13)$$

The boundary B_{gh} becomes a straight line.

Should it be desirable to use *a priori* proportions π_g for the relative sizes of the groups, rather than the numbers n_g of the sample, only slight modifications in the foregoing procedure are necessary. These modifications are

$$R_g \cap \pi_g \phi_g \geq \pi_h \phi_h; \qquad g, h = 1, 2, \ldots, G; \qquad h \neq g$$

where

$$\phi_g = \frac{f_g}{n_g}$$

that is,

$$\phi_g(X_{.1}, X_{.2}) = \frac{1}{2\pi |D_g|^{1/2}} \exp\left(-\frac{X_g^2}{2}\right)$$

The boundary B_{gh} is then defined by the equality

$$\pi_g \phi_g(X_{.1}, X_{.2}) = \pi_h \phi_h(X_{.1}, X_{.2})$$

Equation 6.12 is then changed by the substitution of π_g for n_g in the last term.

Three Continuous Variates

Two Groups

We consider the problems of incorporating a third variable, $X_{.3}$, the conservative activity preferences, in the topological discrimination of the agent and mechanic populations. The three scores of each individual can be represented as a point in three-space. A population group consists of points clustered with greatest density around the centroid of the group of points. The test space may be divided into cubicle cells. Each cell will contain a frequency and if the distributions of the scores are normal in the population, the expected frequency in a cell will decrease as the distance of the cell from the centroid increases. Our problem deals with two such groups of points differently located but occupying the same total test space with overlap.

A familiar physical example of the geometric model is illustrated by a watermelon. Its three-dimensional shape is ellipsoidal. If it is sliced through the center on either axis the seeds will be found distributed over the section but concentrated with greatest density at the center. By measuring and counting, it would be possible to carve the contours of equal density. They would appear as ellipses on the plane surface of the section. If the whole melon were sliced into one-inch cubes the frequency of seeds could be counted in each cube. The cubes in the center would have the greatest number; the cubes between the center and the rind would have fewer seeds; and the frequency of seeds in the rind would be expected to be zero.

The example can be extended to represent precisely the topological problem of two groups in three-space. Consider two watermelons, one with white seeds and one with black seeds, which have grown together in such a fashion that the configuration of each melon can be easily detected even though the two melons have developed a single organic structure.

If we now slice the two-group melon into one-inch cubes and count the seeds in each cube, we shall find a number of cubes containing only black seeds, a number containing only white seeds, and a number of cubes in the volume jointly shared by the melons which contain both white and black seeds. Some contain mostly white, some mostly black, and some have about equal numbers of white and black seeds. Our topological problem is how to determine where to slice the melon once into two parts such that the frequency of white seeds in the black melon plus the frequency of black seeds in the white melon will be as small as possible. We refer to this example as the problem of slicing the Siamese melon.

In the two-variate example we carried to completion the actual comparison of frequencies of agents and mechanics in the cells of the observed scatter diagram. It is obviously absurd to attempt a similar comparison in three dimensions unless we have thousands of individuals in each group. We therefore proceed directly to the use of sample statistics as estimates of the parameters of populations. Our problem is then to find the most efficient classificatory regions for the assumed populations.

We assume for each population a trivariate normal distribution.
The frequency f_1 for any set of three scores in the agent population is

$$f_1(X_{.1}, X_{.2}, X_{.3}) = \frac{n_1}{(2\pi)^{3/2}|D_1|^{1/2}} \exp\left(-\frac{\chi_1^2}{.2}\right)$$

$|D_1|$ is now the determinant of a 3×3 dispersion matrix.
The frequency function for the mechanic population is

$$f_2(X_{.1}, X_{.2}, X_{.3}) = \frac{n_2}{(2\pi)^{3/2}|D_2|^{1/2}} \exp\left(-\frac{\chi_2^2}{2}\right)$$

To simplify the writing we shall denote these functions as f_1 and f_2 without identifying the parenthetical statement of the coordinates $(X_{.1}, X_{.2}, X_{.3})$.

As in all previous cases, the desired topology is defined by

$$R_1 \cap f_1 \geq f_2$$
$$R_2 \cap f_2 \geq f_1$$

The regions will be separated by a boundary on which the frequencies in the groups are equal.

In the two-variate case every isofrequency contour of a single group is an ellipse located in the plane of the test space by the group centroid. The ellipse for any given frequency is determined by χ^2. The numerical value of χ^2 is substituted in a matrix equation $\chi^2 = xD^{-1}x'$ in which x is a 1×2 row vector and D is a 2×2 dispersion matrix. In the three-variate case the test space is three-dimensional and every isofrequency contour is an ellipsoidal surface located in the volume of the test space around the centroid of the group of points. A single isofrequency surface has the shape of a melon. The size of the ellipsoid shell is determined by χ^2. The numerical value of χ^2 is substituted in the same matrix equation $\chi^2 = xD^{-1}x'$, but the order of the matrices is increased by the inclusion of a third variate. The dimensionality of the isofrequency contour is thus seen to be determined by the number of variates.

Two groups in two-space are represented by two sets of isofrequency contours. The intersection of the contour lines of the same frequency in each group defines a locus in the two-space. The locus is a line which may or may not be straight bounding the regions R_1 and R_2. In three-space the intersection of paired isofrequency contours defines the surface such that $f_1 = f_2$. The surface, which may be plane or curved, is the boundary between two regions, R_1 and R_2. These regions are volumes in three-space. In R_1 the frequency of individuals belonging in group 1 is everywhere greater than the frequency of individuals belonging in group 2. The reverse is true in R_2.

In a test space of three dimensions the boundary is obtained by equating the frequency functions, $f_1 = f_2$:

$$f_1 = \frac{n_1}{(2\pi)^{3/2}|D_1|^{1/2}} \exp\left(-\frac{\chi_1^2}{2}\right) = \frac{n_2}{(2\pi)^{3/2}|D_2|^{1/2}} \exp\left(-\frac{\chi_2^2}{2}\right) = f_2$$

Equating the logarithms of $f_1 = f_2$ we obtain

$$\ln\frac{n_1^2}{|D_1|} - \ln\frac{n_2^2}{|D_2|} - \left(\chi_1^2 - \chi_2^2\right) = 0 \tag{6.14}$$

where χ_g^2 stands for the matrix expression $x_g D_g^{-1}x'_g$ which, written in terms of coordinates on the raw score scale X, is

$$\chi_g^2 = \|(X_{.1} - \mu_{g1}) \quad (X_{.2} - \mu_{g2}) \quad (X_{.3} - \mu_{g3})\| \cdot D_g^{-1} \cdot \begin{Vmatrix} (X_{.1} - \mu_{g1}) \\ (X_{.2} - \mu_{g2}) \\ (X_{.3} - \mu_{g3}) \end{Vmatrix}$$

and substituting the matrix of sample means $\overline{X}_g$ for the matrix of the population means μ_g:

$$\chi_g^2 = \|X - \overline{X}_g\| \cdot D_g^{-1} \cdot \|X - \overline{X}_g\|'$$
$$= XD_g^{-1}X' - \overline{X}_g D_g^{-1}X' - XD_g^{-1}\overline{X}_g + \overline{X}_g D_g^{-1}\overline{X}_g'$$

When this expression, with appropriate numerical subscripts 1, 2 replacing g, is substituted in Eq. 6.14 we obtain Eq. 6.15:

$$X(D_1^{-1} - D_2^{-1})X' - 2(\bar{X}_{1.}D_1^{-1} - \bar{X}_{2.}D_2^{-1})X'$$

$$+ (\bar{X}_{1.}D_1^{-1}\bar{X}'_{1.} - \bar{X}_{2.}D_2^{-1}\bar{X}'_{2.}) - \ln \frac{n_1^2}{|D_1|} + \ln \frac{n_2^2}{|D_2|} = 0 \quad (6.15)$$

This equation is the same as Eq. 6.11 (or 6.12) except that the matrices contain three variables:

$$X = \| X_{.1} \quad X_{.2} \quad X_{.3} \| \qquad \text{(the coordinates of } X\text{)}$$

$$\bar{X}_{1.} = \| \mu_{11} \quad \mu_{12} \quad \mu_{13} \| \qquad \text{(group 1 centroid)}$$

$$\bar{X}_{2.} = \| \mu_{21} \quad \mu_{22} \quad \mu_{23} \| \qquad \text{(group 2 centroid)}$$

The numerical equivalents are

$$n_1 = 85$$

$$\bar{X}_{1.} = \| \ 12.5882 \quad 24.2235 \quad 9.0235 \ \|$$

$$D_1 = \begin{Vmatrix} 20.0068 & 4.5628 & -2.3789 \\ 4.5628 & 18.5735 & 2.4766 \\ -2.3789 & 2.4766 & 9.7644 \end{Vmatrix} \qquad \text{(group 1—passenger agents)}$$

$$D_1^{-1} = \begin{Vmatrix} .055741 & -.016047 & .017650 \\ -.016047 & .060345 & -.019218 \\ .017650 & -.019218 & .111591 \end{Vmatrix}$$

$$|D_1| = 3143.470997$$

$$n_2 = 93$$

$$\bar{X}_{2.} = \| 18.5376 \quad 21.1398 \quad 10.1398 \|$$

$$D_2 = \begin{Vmatrix} 12.5713 & -1.5582 & 2.5167 \\ -1.5582 & 20.4856 & .1737 \\ 2.5167 & .1737 & 10.4000 \end{Vmatrix} \qquad \text{(group 2—mechanics)}$$

$$D_2^{-1} = \begin{Vmatrix} .084479 & .006604 & -.020550 \\ .006604 & .049337 & -.002423 \\ -.020550 & -.002423 & .101168 \end{Vmatrix}$$

$$|D_2| = 2521.54407$$

Substitution of these values in Eq. 6.15 gives

$$-.0287X_{.1}^2 + .0110X_{.2}^2 + .0104X_{.3}^2 - 2(.0226)X_{.1}X_{.2}$$
$$+ 2(.0382)X_{.1}X_{.3} - 2(.0168)X_{.2}X_{.3} + 2(1.0249)X_{.1} + 2(.0544)X_{.2}$$
$$- 2(.1700)X_{.3} - 18.3380 = 0$$

as the equation of the boundary B_{12}. The boundary is a continuous surface and cannot be shown in a single graph. We can, however, show the line which the surface makes when it intersects a plane. We may choose several conveniently located planes and obtain a graphic idea of the characteristics and location of the surfaces. This method is suggested in Fig. 6.18. A plane perpendicular to the X_3 (vertical) axis might be passed through the score points $X_3 = 4, 8, 12, 16$. We can "look into" the test space at each of the levels as if we were looking into a multistory building with transparent walls. The line shown on the visible portion of each of the planes (floors) in the figure is the graph of the intersection of each plane and a surface which passes through it. A large round (circular) ventilating duct slanting through the building space is represented in the figure.

To "look at" the boundary B_{12} of the example data we plot the intersection of the B_{12} surface with a plane passing through each conservative preference score. The two axes of the plane will be X_1 and X_2, the outdoor and convivial scores. For each different X_3 score the graph will divide the X_1, X_2 test space into regions R_{PA} and R_M. We can also plot on each plane the points representing agents and mechanics. An individual whose conservative score is $X_3 = 10$ is located on the plane according to his scores on the other tests, say $X_1 = 22$, $X_2 = 19$. By inspection of the boundary line on the appropriate plane we can ascertain whether any coordinate set of scores lies in R_1 or R_2.

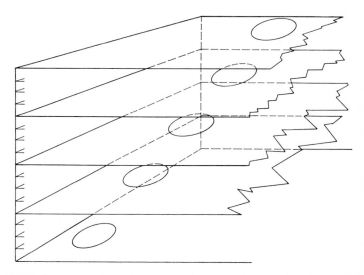

Fig. 6.18 *Illustration of the intersection of a three-dimensional surface with planes passing through.*

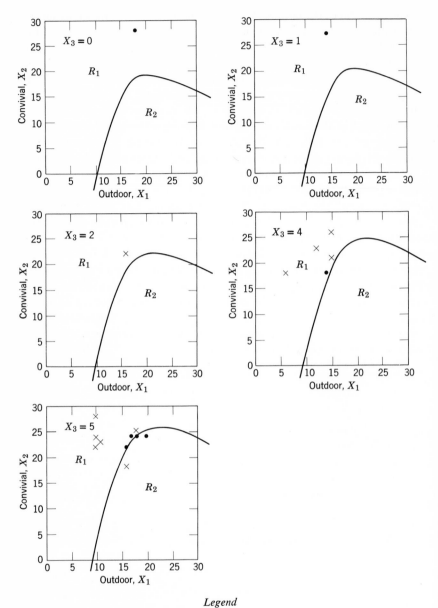

Fig. 6.19   *Regions of the test space for the two-group example.*

To obtain the coordinates of the boundary surface in the $X_{.1}$, $X_{.2}$ plane for a fixed value of $X_{.3}$, we rewrite the boundary equation as

$$X_{.2}^2 - 2(2.0575X_{.1} + 1.5258X_{.3} - 4.9442)X_{.2} - 2.6109X_{.1}^2$$
$$+ (6.9455X_{.3} + 186.3454)X_{.1} + 0.9466X_{.3}^2 - 30.8880X_{.3}$$
$$- 1666.0307 = 0$$

By using the formula for the roots of a quadratic equation of the form $ax^2 + bx + c = 0$, we can express $X_{.2}$ in terms of $X_{.1}$ and $X_{.3}$:

$$X_{.2} = 2.0575X_{.1} + 1.5258X_{.3} - 4.9442$$
$$\pm [6.8442X_{.1}^2 - (.6668X_{.3} + 206.6908)X_{.1}$$
$$+ (1.3815X_{.3}^2 + 15.8003X_{.3} + 1690.4758)]^{\frac{1}{2}}$$

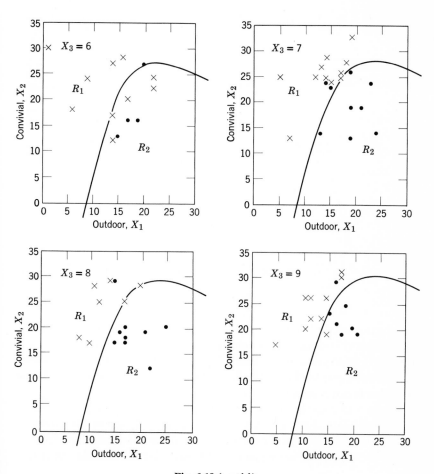

Fig. 6.19 (*cont'd.*)

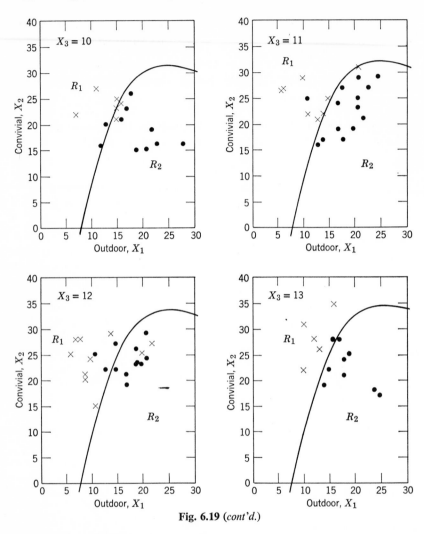

Fig. 6.19 (*cont'd.*)

The section of the boundary surface B_{12} on each of the planes where X_3 is a constant is obtained by substituting the chosen constant for $X_{.3}$ in the above expression and plotting $X_{.2}$ against $X_{.1}$. The results are shown in a series of graphs (Fig. 6.19). Since there were no scores at $X_3 = 3$, that X_3 plane is not represented in Fig. 6.19.

Figure 6.19 consists of a series of 17 graphs, one for each conservative preference score. Each graph shows the X_1 and X_2 scores (outdoor and convivial preferences) of those individuals whose conservative preferences X_3 are the same, and are equal to the X_3 value identified in the upper left-hand corner of the graph. The symbols • and × used to plot the individual locations of the X_1, X_2 pair of scores identify the group to which the man belongs. The dots • represent mechanics, the crosses × represent passenger agents. The line on the graph is the boundary B_{12} between regions R_1 (passenger agent) and R_2 (mechanic) on the X_1X_2 plane for the fixed value X_3. It is the intersection of the B_{12} boundary surface and the plane perpendicular to the X_3 axis at the value of X_3. Inspection of each graph shows how many of each group are misclassified by the boundary B_{12}.

Graph $X_3 = 17$ shows one mechanic and one agent whose conservative

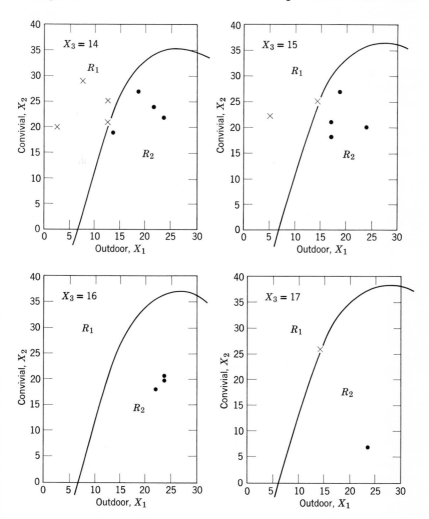

Fig. 6.19 (cont'd.)

score is 17. Their outdoor and convivial scores place them in the correct regions. The cross is in R_1 and the dot is in R_2. Graph $X_3 = 8$ shows the X_1, X_2 score locations of 16 men, of whom nine are mechanics and seven are agents. One of the mechanics and two of the agents are misclassified (one dot in R_1 and two crosses in R_2).

As in the case of two variates, we can estimate the number of misclassifications to be expected in future samples by counting the points in the wrong region on each plane of Fig. 6.19. The number of persons of each type correctly and incorrectly classified by the boundary surface B_{12} is recorded in Table 6.8. The result is disappointing. Thirty-two individuals are misclassified when three variates are used. With two variates for the same groups, only 30 were misclassified. In this example we have an

Table 6.8 *Number of Misclassifications in the Two-Group Three-Variate Example* (*Counted from Fig. 6.19*)

| | Both Specialties: Correctly Classified   146 | | | |
| | | Misclassified | 32 | |

| | Passenger Agents | | Mechanics | |
For $X_{.3}$	Correctly Classified	Misclassified	Correctly Classified	Misclassified
0	–	–	0	1
1	–	–	0	1
2	1	0	–	–
3	–	–	–	–
4	4	0	0	1
5	5	1	2	2
6	5	5	3	1
7	11	0	7	2
8	5	2	8	1
9	9	1	6	1
10	3	3	8	2
11	7	1	13	1
12	8	2	9	3
13	5	0	8	1
14	4	0	4	0
15	2	0	4	0
16	–	–	3	0
17	1	0	1	0
Total	70	15	76	17

illustration of the effect of small numbers in the groups. The irregularities of cell frequencies attributable to sampling are large enough to mask any true superiority of the three-variate topology in the populations. The result emphasizes the importance of two factors in the application of discriminatory systems to personnel problems. First, the samples of job groups must be large in order to obtain acceptable precision in the estimates of the population parameters, and, second, the variates chosen must exhibit validity for discrimination. Topological methods cannot extract from data any more information than the data contain.

Three Groups

The inclusion of a third job-title group, operations control agents, has a negligible effect upon empirically determined probabilities. The number of cells in the test space is so large and the number of individuals in the samples is so small that job regions defined by comparing observed frequencies in the cells result in almost perfect classification of the samples. Only one cell is occupied by individuals from different groups. The cell with coordinates (14, 18, 4) is occupied by one mechanic and one operations man. The necessity of determining classificatory regions by use of stable sample statistics is evident. We assume normal distributions with parameters estimated from the sample.

For the third population, operations control agents, the trivariate distribution is

$$f_3(X_{.1},\, X_{.2},\, X_{.3}) = \frac{n_3}{(2\pi)^{3/2}|D_3|^{1/2}}\, \exp\left(-\frac{X_3{}^2}{2}\right)$$

The desired regions are defined by the inequalities:

$$R_1 \cap f_1 \geq f_2; \qquad f_1 \geq f_3$$
$$R_2 \cap f_2 \geq f_1; \qquad f_2 \geq f_3$$
$$R_3 \cap f_3 \geq f_1; \qquad f_3 \geq f_2$$

Three boundary surfaces are required. The boundaries are obtained by considering separately each of the three contrasts, groups 1 and 2, 1 and 3, 2 and 3. The first of these was determined in the two-group example. The boundaries are defined by the equality:

$$B_{gh} \cap \ln f_g = \ln f_h; \qquad g,\, h = 1,\, 2,\, 3; \qquad g \neq h$$

Computation of the boundary is specified by Eq. 6.12 where

$$X = \|X_{.1} \quad X_{.2} \quad X_{.3}\|$$
$$\overline{X}_{g.} = \|\mu_{g1} \quad \mu_{g2} \quad \mu_{g3}\|$$
$$\overline{X}_{h.} = \|\mu_{h1} \quad \mu_{h2} \quad \mu_{h3}\|$$

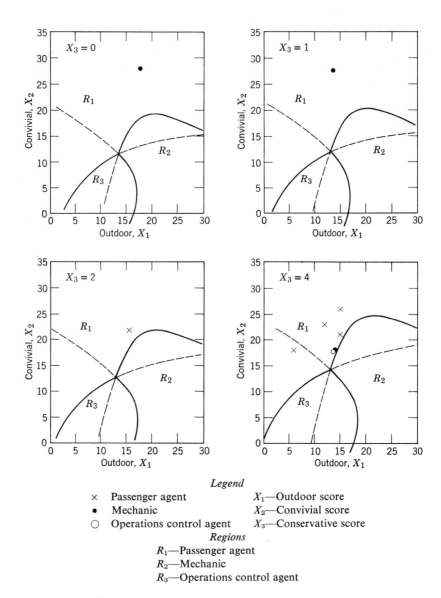

Fig. 6.20 *Regions of the test space for the three-group example.*

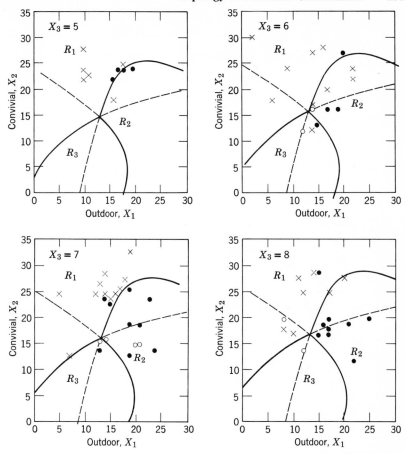

Fig. 6.20 (*cont'd.*)

In this instance g is 3. The numerical equivalents for group 3 are

$$n_3 = 66$$

$$\overline{X}_{3.} = \|15.5758 \quad 15.4545 \quad 13.2424\|$$

$$D_3 = \begin{Vmatrix} 16.6382 & 1.6468 & .6786 \\ 1.6468 & 13.9749 & .1329 \\ .6786 & .1329 & 13.4264 \end{Vmatrix}$$

$$D_3^{-1} = \begin{Vmatrix} .060934 & -.007154 & -.003009 \\ -.007154 & .072402 & -.000351 \\ -.003009 & -.000351 & .074637 \end{Vmatrix}$$

$$|D_3| = 3078.994826$$

Substituting these expressions in Eq. 6.12 gives the following equation for B_{13}, the boundary surface between PA's and OCA's:

$$.005192X_{.1}^2 + .012059X_{.2}^2 - .036951X_{.3}^2 + 2(.008895)X_{.1}X_{.2}$$
$$- 2(.020659)X_{.1}X_{.3} + 2(.018860)X_{.2}X_{.3} - 2(.326474)X_{.1}$$
$$+ 2(.083500)X_{.2} - 2(.172374)X_{.3} + 1.668878 = 0$$

In terms of $X_{.1}$ and $X_{.3}$, the equation for $X_{.2}$ is

$$X_{.2} = -[.7376X_{.1} + (1.5640X_{.3} + 6.9243)]$$
$$\pm [.1136X_{.1}^2 + (5.7335X_{.3} + 64.3608)X_{.1}$$
$$+ (5.5103X_{.3}^2 + 50.2476X_{.3} - 90.4468)]^{\frac{1}{2}}$$

As before, the sections of the boundary surface on the several planes

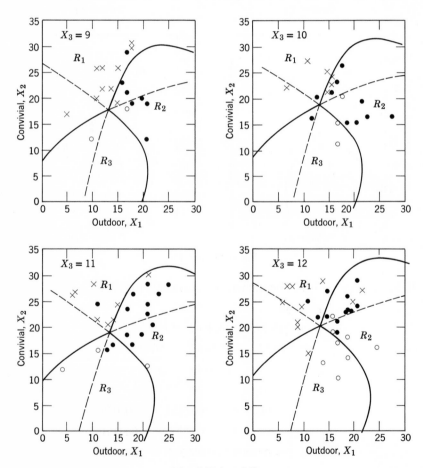

Fig. 6.20 (*cont'd.*)

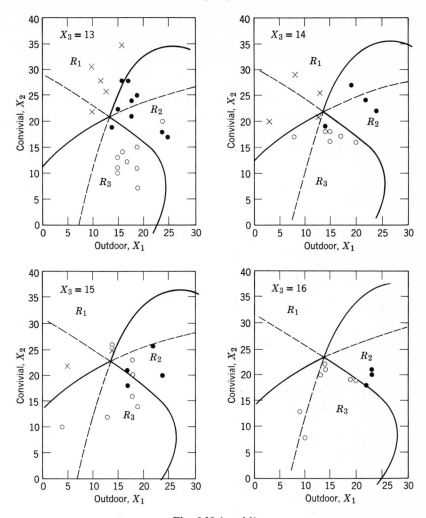

Fig. 6.20 (*cont'd.*)

identified by $X_{.3}$ = constant are obtained by setting $X_{.3} = 0, 1, 2, \ldots, 20$, and plotting $X_{.2}$ against $X_{.1}$ for each value of $X_{.3}$. Results are the lines in Fig. 6.20.

The boundary surface B_{23} which separates R_M from R_{OCA} is given by

$$-.023546X_{.1}{}^2 + .023066X_{.2}{}^2 - .026532X_{.3}{}^2 - 2(.013752)X_{.1}X_{.2}$$
$$+ 2(.017544)X_{.1}X_{.3} + 2(.002066)X_{.2}X_{.3} + 2(.698454)X_{.1}$$
$$+ 2(.137921) - 2(.342366)X_{.3} - 16.669127 = 0$$

In terms of $X_{.1}$ and $X_{.3}$, the equation for $X_{.2}$ becomes

$$X_{.2} = +.5962X_{.1} - (.0896X_{.3} + 5.9795)$$
$$\pm\ [1.3762X_{.1}^2 - (1.6280X_{.3} + 67.6911)X_{.1}$$
$$+ (1.1583X_{.3}^2 + 30.7573X_{.3} + 758.4241)]^{1/2}$$

This equation is used to determine the values of $X_{.2}$ and $X_{.1}$ on each plane of $X_{.3}$. The intersections of the three boundary surfaces B_{12}, B_{13}, and B_{23} and the $X_{.3}$ planes are plotted together in Fig. 6.20. It is apparent in Fig. 6.20 that the boundary surfaces section the three-space into more sectors

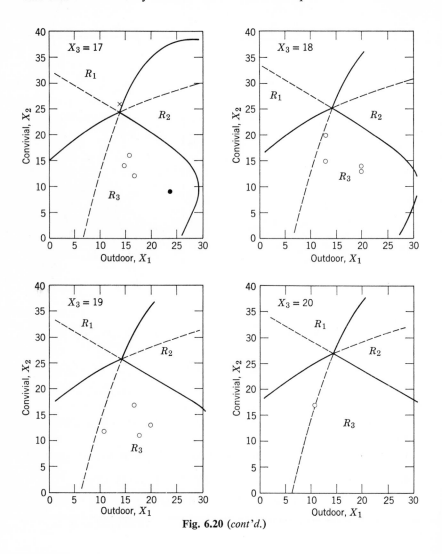

Fig. 6.20 (*cont'd.*)

than are desired. The sectors are chosen for combination into the appropriate regions by identifying the largest f_g in the series of inequalities associated with each sector.

Table 6.9 *Misclassifications Counted in Three-Group Three-Variate Example* (*Counted from Fig. 6.20*)

$X_{.3}$	Actual	PA	M	OCA	Error	$X_{.3}$	Actual	PA	M	OCA	Error
		Classified as						Classified as			
0	PA	–	–	–	–	11	PA	7	1	0	1
	M	1	0	0	1		M	1	11	2	3
	OCA	–	–	–	–		OCA	0	1	2	1
1	PA	–	–	–	–	12	PA	7	2	1	3
	M	1	0	0	1		M	3	9	0	3
	OCA	–	–	–	–		OCA	0	4	4	4
2	PA	1	0	0	0	13	PA	5	0	0	0
	M	–	–	–	–		M	1	7	1	2
	OCA	–	–	–	–		OCA	0	1	8	1
3	PA	–	–	–	–	14	PA	3	0	1	1
	M	–	–	–	–		M	0	3	1	1
	OCA	–	–	–	–		OCA	0	0	6	0
4	PA	4	0	0	0	15	PA	2	0	0	0
	M	1	0	0	1		M	0	3	1	1
	OCA	1	0	0	1		OCA	1	2	4	3
5	PA	5	1	0	1	16	PA	–	–	–	–
	M	2	2	0	2		M	·0	2½	½	½
	OCA	–	–	–	–		OCA	0	0	7	0
6	PA	5	4	1	5	17	PA	1	0	0	0
	M	1	2	1	2		M	0	0	1	1
	OCA	0	1	1	1		OCA	0	0	3	0
7	PA	11	0	0	0	18	PA	–	–	–	–
	M	2	6	1	3		M	–	–	–	–
	OCA	0	3	1	3		OCA	0	0	4	0
8	PA	5	2	0	2	19	PA	–	–	–	–
	M	1	8	0	1		M	–	–	–	–
	OCA	1	0	1	1		OCA	0	0	4	0
9	PA	9	1	0	1	20	PA	–	–	–	–
	M	1	6	0	1		M	–	–	–	–
	OCA	0	1	1	1		OCA	0	0	1	0
10	PA	3	3	0	3						
	M	1	8	1	2			Total misclassifications: 59½			
	OCA	0	1	2	1						

The series of 20 graphs which constitute Fig. 6.20 show for the three-group–three-region example the same kind of graphic tabulation that Fig. 6.19 showed for the two-group–two-region example.

Each graph shows the location of the X_1X_2 scores for all the individuals whose X_3 score is the value indicated in the upper left-hand corner of the graph. The lines on each sheet are the intersections of the three boundary surfaces B_{12}, B_{13}, B_{23} and the plane perpendicular to the X_3 axis. The dotted portion of each line is the segment eliminated in combining the six sectors into three regions. The three job-title categories are symbolically differentiated as indicated in the legend.

The misclassifications occurring in Fig. 6.20 are given in Table 6.9.

The estimated number of misclassifications in the three-group example is $59\frac{1}{2}$. When only the outdoor preferences of the three types of specialists were used, the estimated number of misclassifications was 105.89. When the outdoor and convivial preferences were used, there were 67 misclassifications. The introduction of a third variable has improved the discrimination among groups.

The General Case, G Groups

Extension of the three-variate case to any number of groups follows immediately.

The trivariate distribution for each group is assumed to be normal. The frequency of any point $(X_{.1}, X_{.2}, X_{.3})$ in the test space is

$$f_g(X_{.1}, X_{.2}, X_{.3}) = \frac{n_g}{(2\pi)^{3/2}|D|^{1/2}} \exp\left(-\frac{\chi_g^2}{2}\right)$$

where

$$\chi_g^2 = x_g.D_g^{-1}x_g'.$$

and

$$x_g. = \|(X_{.1} - \mu_{g1})\ (X_{.2} - \mu_{g2})\ (X_{.3} - \mu_{g3})\|$$

we want to define G regions such that

$$R_g \cap f_g \geq f_h; \qquad [g, h = 1, 2, \ldots, G;\ \ h \neq g]$$

These regions are determined by computing the $G(G-1)/2$ surfaces B_{gh} defined by the equation

$$B_{gh} \cap \ln f_g = \ln f_h$$

Each boundary is determined by evaluation of Eq. 6.12, where

$$X = \|X_{.1}\ \ X_{.2}\ \ X_{.3}\|$$
$$\bar{X}_{g.} = \|\bar{X}_{g1}\ \ \bar{X}_{g2}\ \ \bar{X}_{g3}\|$$
$$\bar{X}_{h.} = \|\bar{X}_{h1}\ \ \bar{X}_{h2}\ \ \bar{X}_{h3}\|$$

The equations of the boundary surfaces may be solved for $X_{.2}$ in terms of $X_{.1}$ and $X_{.3}$ and graphed on the required planes. The sectors of the test space are combined into at most G regions by reference to the leading term in the extended series of inequalities that define each sector.

An estimate of the number of misclassifications to be expected in applications of the system can be obtained by counting the number of misclassifications observed on the two-dimensional planes which lie in the three-dimensional test space.

If it is more appropriate in the application to use *a priori* estimates of the proportion of individuals in each specialty than the number of men in the sample, only slight modifications are necessary. In this instance, the region R_g is defined as

$$R_g \cap \pi_g \phi_g \geq \pi_h \phi_h; \qquad [g, h = 1, 2, \ldots, G; \quad h \neq g]$$

where

$$\phi_g = \frac{1}{(2\pi)^{3/2} |D_g|^{1/2}} \exp\left(-\frac{\chi_g^2}{2}\right); \qquad [g = 1, 2, \ldots, G]$$

T Continuous Variates

The General Case, G Groups

The general case of G groups observed on T variates is an obvious extension. As T increases, the number n in the sample of each population must increase rapidly if the topology calculated from observed frequencies of profile configurations is to have reasonable statistical stability. It will usually be necessary to derive the topology from an assumed distribution function using the sample statistics as estimates of the required parameters. The only theoretical model we consider is the multivariate normal distribution.

The multivariate normal distribution for group g is

$$f_g(X_{.1}, X_{.2}, \ldots, X_{.T}) = \frac{n_g}{(2\pi)^{T/2} |D_g|^{1/2}} \exp\left(-\frac{\chi_g^2}{2}\right); \quad [g = 1, 2, \ldots, G]$$

(6.16)

where

$$\chi_g^2 = x_{g.} D_g^{-1} x'_{g.} \qquad g = 1, 2, \ldots, G$$

and

$$x_{g.} = \|(X_{.1} - \bar{X}_{g1}) \quad (X_{.2} - \bar{X}_{g2}) \quad \cdots \quad (X_{.T} - \bar{X}_{gT})\|; \quad [g = 1, 2, \ldots G]$$

The T space is to be sectioned into G regions, defined as

$$R_g \cap f_g(X_{.1}, X_{.2}, \ldots, X_{.T}) \geq f_h(X_{.1}, X_{.2}, \ldots, X_{.T});$$
$$[g, h = 1, 2, \ldots, G; \quad h \neq g] \quad (6.17)$$

Evaluation of the $(G - 1)$ inequalities for group g requires the comparison of that group with each of the other $(G - 1)$ groups. The necessary comparisons of each group with all other groups is accomplished by computing the $G(G - 1)/2$ boundary hypersurfaces B_{gh} defined by the equality

$$B_{gh} \cap \ln f_g(X_{.1}, X_{.2}, \ldots, X_{.T}) = \ln f_h(X_{.1}, X_{.2}, \ldots, X_{.T})$$
$$[g, h = 1, 2, \ldots, G; \quad h > g] \quad (6.18)$$

This equality reduces to the matrix equation

$$X(D_g^{-1} - D_h^{-1})X' - 2[\bar{X}_{g.}D_g^{-1} - \bar{X}_{h.}D_h^{-1}]X' + \bar{X}_{g.}D_g^{-1}\bar{X}'_{g.}$$

$$- \bar{X}_{h.}D_{.h}^{-1}\bar{X}'_{h.} - \ln \frac{n_g^2}{|D_g|} + \ln \frac{n_h^2}{|D_h|} = 0$$

$$[g, h = 1, 2, \ldots, G; \quad h > g] \quad (6.19)$$

where

$$X = \| X_{.1} \quad X_{.2} \quad \ldots \quad X_{.T} \|$$
$$\bar{X}_{g.} = \| \bar{X}_{g1} \quad \bar{X}_{g2} \quad \ldots \quad \bar{X}_{gT} \| \quad [g = 1, 2, \ldots, G]$$
$$\bar{X}_{h.} = \| \bar{X}_{h1} \quad \bar{X}_{h2} \quad \ldots \quad \bar{X}_{hT} \| \quad [h = g + 1, g + 2, \ldots, G]$$

Should it be desirable to use *a priori*-determined values of the proportion of men in each job π_g rather than the number of men in the sample, the procedure may be easily modified. Regions R_g can be defined as

$$R_g \cap \pi_g \phi_g(X_{.i}) \geq \pi_h \phi_h(X_{.i}); \quad g, h = 1, 2, \ldots, G; h \neq g$$
$$i = 1, 2, \ldots, T \quad (6.20)$$

where $\phi_g(X_{.i})$ is

$$\phi_g(X_{.i}) = \frac{1}{(2\pi)^{T/2}|D_g|^{\frac{1}{2}}} \exp \left(-\frac{\chi_g^2}{2} \right); \quad \begin{array}{l} g = 1, 2, \ldots, G \\ i = 1, 2, \ldots, T \end{array} \quad (6.21)$$

Topology and the Centour Score

In the opening paragraphs of this chapter we observed that the sheer volume of calculations required for centour scores in multivariable situations and the bulk and impracticality of the resulting tables require some reduction if the obvious advantages of the centour concept are to be realized in practice. We then embarked upon the analysis of the geometry of topological regions in test space as an approach to the classification problem. The objective of inquiring into applications of topological concepts was to find ways of simplifying the computations and the tabular results for practical test-score interpretation. The result appears to indicate that, with any practical number of tests, the problem of calculating, and then using, geometric definitions of classificatory regions is just as complicated, and perhaps less interpretable, than centour calculations.

The development, however, has a purpose. It clearly establishes the logical foundations of classification and group discrimination. The topological system extracts from the data, whatever they may be, the maximum information that bears upon the problem. Though an approximation to the ideal represented in our topological system is not readily apparent, we will be able to find a reasonable approximation for practical use by combining the topological notions of regions in the test space with the concept of the centour score as a measure of divergence from the typical in a group. As an introduction to the following chapters, we shall connect the centour concept with the formal topological regions we have discussed.

The classificatory regions R_g are defined by

$$R_g \cap \ln \pi_g \phi_g(X_{.i}) \geq \ln \pi_h \phi_h(X_{.i}) \qquad \begin{array}{l} g, h = 1, 2, \ldots, G \\ i = 1, 2, \ldots, T \end{array} \qquad (6.22)$$

When we substitute the multivariate normal distribution for the density function $\phi(X_{.i})$ in Eq. 6.22, the regions are written

$$R_g \cap \ln \frac{\pi_g}{(2\pi)^{T/2} |D_g|^{1/2}} \exp\left(-\frac{\chi_g^2}{2}\right) \geq \ln \frac{\pi_h}{(2\pi)^{T/2} |D_h|^{1/2}} \exp\left(-\frac{\chi_h^2}{2}\right)$$

These inequalities simplify to

$$R_g \cap \chi_g^2 \leq \chi_h^2 - \ln \frac{|D_g|}{|D_h|} + 2 \ln \frac{\pi_g}{\pi_h} \qquad g, h = 1, 2, \ldots, G; \quad h \neq g \quad (6.23)$$

The scalar number χ^2 is given by the matrix product

$$\chi^2 = xD^{-1}x'$$

Equation 6.23 shows that boundaries developed from frequency considerations may be described in terms of density functions which are closely related to centour expressions. Any set of scores representing a point in the test space lies on an ellipsoid surface of a group, and the density in the group which is more divergent is determined by the value of χ^2 with T degrees of freedom. This is the centour concept, and classificatory regions may be bounded by lines or surfaces of centour equivalence.

If we assume for simplicity that the sizes of the populations are the same ($\pi_g = \pi_h$) and that the dispersions of the groups are essentially the same ($D_g = D_h$), the two logarithmic terms in Eq. 6.23 vanish and the regions are associated with the smallest χ^2 value of the points in it. For example, any point given by the T coordinates $X_{.i}$ will lie on a different ellipsoid for each group; the point will be classified in that group for which χ^2 is least (and the centour is greatest). The two logarithmic terms express constants which the practitioner of classification and assignment may use to adjust supply to demand and adapt to the variations in size and dispersion of job-title populations. The term $2 \ln \pi_g/\pi_h$ reflects the effect of differences in population size. When one job group is significantly smaller than another group, the logarithmic term operates to move the boundary away from the centroid of the larger group. This movement favors classifications in the larger group.

Topological methods define regions in the test space which classify men into job specialties with minimum error. The centour development expresses the regions in directly interpretable form. Both developments involve unmanageable calculations and impractical tabulations in real problems where the number of groups and the number of tests are usually greater than 3 or 4. A desirable approximation procedure will preserve the identity of important groups, tolerate the use of many measurements, and reduce the volume of calculations with as little loss of efficiency as possible. The test of any approximation will be comparison with the ideal topological model.

The Problem of Reducing Dimensionality

Chapter 7

Factor Analysis

The Concept of a Reduced Dimensionality

Suppose we have two points located as follows in the (X_{11}, X_{21}) reference frame:

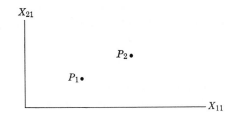

If we rotate the axis X_{11} through the angle θ to the position X_{12} thus:

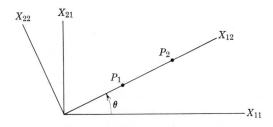

and at the same time we rotate the axis X_{21} so that it always forms a right angle with the axis X_{11}, we can achieve a new axis system X_{12}, X_{22} such that the X_{22} coordinates of both points will be 0. Points that were formerly located by means of *two* coordinates are now specified exactly by only *one* coordinate. All the information in the old variates (X_{11}, X_{21}) is now in the single new variate (X_{12}). *By rotation of axes we have reduced the number of dimensions* from two to one.

265

In Appendix A, we note that we may consider points in Cartesian space as fixed and describe them in terms of either an original axis system (X_{11}, X_{21}) or an orthogonal axis system (X_{12}, X_{22}) rotated through the angle θ. The matrix of points in the new system, for example, $X_{.2}$, is related to the matrix of points in the original system, say $X_{.1}$, by the transformation equation

$$X_{.2} = X_{.1}\Gamma \qquad (7.1)$$

where Γ is a matrix of cosines of the four angles involved in the transformation; θ_{11}, the angle between the old first and new first axis; θ_{12}, the angle between the old first and new second axis; θ_{21}, the angle between the old second and the new first axis; and θ_{22}, the angle between the old second and new second axis.

If we write Γ as

$$\Gamma = \left\| \begin{matrix} \gamma_{11} & \gamma_{12} \\ \gamma_{21} & \gamma_{22} \end{matrix} \right\|$$

where γ_{st} is the cosine of the angle between axis s in system 1 and axis t in system 2, we see from Eq. 7.1 that the matrix $X_{.2}$ is a series of N rows, the number in each row being of the forms

$$(\gamma_{11}X_{11} + \gamma_{21}X_{21}) \quad \text{and} \quad (\gamma_{12}X_{11} + \gamma_{22}X_{22})$$

Thus scores expressed in terms of rotated axes are *linear combinations* of the original scores. The new score X_{12} is the *linear combination*

$$X_{12} = \gamma_{11}X_{11} + \gamma_{21}X_{21}$$

and the new score X_{22} is the *linear combination*

$$X_{22} = \gamma_{12}X_{11} + \gamma_{22}X_{22}$$

The concept of linear combinations is not new to psychologists. If Joe Armand runs 100 yards in 15 seconds on one occasion and in 13 seconds on another, we say his average time for these two runs is $(15 + 13)/2 = 14$ seconds. In general, the average of two scores is $(X_1 + X_2)/2$, which may also be written as $\frac{1}{2}X_1 + \frac{1}{2}X_2$. When we write the mean of two observations in this form, we specify a vector in the X_1, X_2 space, the space in which we represent the two observations for each person. The mean $\bar{X}$ of any two observations (X_1, X_2) can be represented by a vector whose end-point has the coordinates $(X_1 + X_2)/2, (X_1 + X_2)/2$. The *direction cosines* of this vector are proportional to the elements of the vector

$$\left\| \begin{matrix} \frac{1}{2} \\ \frac{1}{2} \end{matrix} \right\|$$

the vector of the coefficients of X_1 and X_2 in the expression $\bar{X}$. A vector is *normalized* by dividing each element by the square root of the sum of the squares of its elements, in this instance:

$$\sqrt{(\tfrac{1}{2})^2 + (\tfrac{1}{2})^2} = \frac{1}{\sqrt{2}}$$

The normalized transformation vector is therefore

$$\Gamma = \sqrt{2} \cdot \left\| \begin{matrix} \tfrac{1}{2} \\ \tfrac{1}{2} \end{matrix} \right\| = \left\| \begin{matrix} \dfrac{1}{\sqrt{2}} \\ \dfrac{1}{\sqrt{2}} \end{matrix} \right\|$$

The sum of the squares of the elements of Γ is one. Such a vector is said to be *normalized to unity*, or, alternatively, to have a *unit length*. The elements of Γ are then *direction cosines* of the vector $\bar{X}$. Since these two direction cosines are equal, the vector $\bar{X}$ bisects the angle $X_2\,0\,X_1$ in this instance.

The *length* of any vector v is given by the positive square root of $v'v$. In this instance, denoting the length of $\bar{X}$ by $|\bar{X}|$ we have, using Eq. 7.1:

$$|\bar{X}|^2 = \bar{X}'\bar{X} = (X_{.1}\Gamma)'(X_{.1}\Gamma)$$

$$= \Gamma'X'_{.1}X_{.1}\Gamma$$

$$= \left\| \begin{matrix} \dfrac{1}{\sqrt{2}} & \dfrac{1}{\sqrt{2}} \end{matrix} \right\| \cdot \left\| \begin{matrix} X_1 \\ X_2 \end{matrix} \right\| \cdot \| X_1 \quad X_2 \| \cdot \left\| \begin{matrix} \dfrac{1}{\sqrt{2}} \\ \dfrac{1}{\sqrt{2}} \end{matrix} \right\|$$

$$= \left(\frac{X_1 + X_2}{\sqrt{2}} \right)\left(\frac{X_1 + X_2}{\sqrt{2}} \right) = \left(\frac{X_1 + X_2}{\sqrt{2}} \right)^2$$

Therefore

$$|\bar{X}| = \frac{X_1 + X_2}{\sqrt{2}} = \frac{1}{\sqrt{2}} X_1 + \frac{1}{\sqrt{2}} X_2$$

In other words, the projections of the point $P(X_1, X_2)$, to the line bisecting the angle $X_2\,0\,X_1$, define a point with coordinates $(\bar{X}, \bar{X})$ in terms of the original ones in this way:

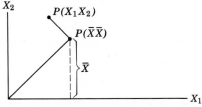

A perpendicular from the point $P(\bar{X}, \bar{X})$ to either the axis X_1 or X_2 forms a right triangle with equal sides $\bar{X}$ and $\bar{X}$. By the Pythagorean theorem, the length of the hypotenuse of this right triangle, in this instance the vector $\overline{X}$, is

$$\sqrt{\overline{X}^2 + \overline{X}^2} = \overline{X}\sqrt{2}$$

Thus

$$X_{.2} = \overline{X}\sqrt{2} \quad \text{or} \quad \overline{X} = \frac{1}{\sqrt{2}} X_{.2}$$

Pairs of observations on other individuals may also be plotted on the X_1, X_2 plane and each point may be projected to the line bisecting the angle $X_2 \, 0 \, X_1$. All these vectors from the origin to the point of intersection of the projection of the point, although probably of differing lengths, will have the same direction Γ. Thus the vector Γ specifies the *direction* of the axis along which the projections are to be measured. The lengths ($X_{.2}$) of the mean vectors corresponding to each point (X_1, X_2) are given by

$$X_{.2} = X_{.1}\Gamma \tag{7.2}$$

where

$$X_{.1} = \| X_1 \quad X_2 \|$$

The coefficients, both $\frac{1}{2}$ in the foregoing example, are called *combination weights*, or simply *weights*. In the illustration so far we have started with a linear combination familiar to all psychologists, the mean. The space in which the mean vector is represented is somewhat different from the test space we have been considering. The space in which the mean vector has been represented is a space in which the axes represent observations of the same person on the *same test* at two different times. Usually we observe the same person on two different tests. Thus X_1 and X_2 ordinarily refer to two different tests rather than two observations on the same test. The logic of linear combinations and axis rotation is the same for this latter case as it is for the former. Generally speaking,

$$aX_1 + (1 - a)X_2$$

in which $0 < a < 1$ and the two coefficients add up to 1, is a *weighted average* of X_1 and X_2. A weighted average may be represented as a vector in the X_1, X_2 space. The direction of the vector will be

$$\left\| \begin{matrix} a \\ (1 - a) \end{matrix} \right\|$$

Psychologists are accustomed to predicting a standardized criterion score from the linear combination

$$\beta_1 z_1 + \beta_2 z_2$$

β coefficients specify a vector in the standardized test space z_1, z_2. The vector has the direction given by

$$\left\| \begin{matrix} \beta_1 \\ \beta_2 \end{matrix} \right\|$$

Generally, using any two numbers a_1 and a_2 as weights, we call

$$y = a_1 X_1 + a_2 X_2$$

a linear combination of X_1 and X_2. The linear combination is the projection of the point X_1, X_2 to a vector with direction numbers specified by

$$\left\| \begin{array}{c} a_1 \\ a_2 \end{array} \right\|$$

in the X_1, X_2 test space.

With any number of variates $X_1, X_2, \ldots, X_T$ we can write a linear combination

$$y = a_1 X_1 + a_2 X_2 + \cdots + a_T X_T$$

with any set of numbers $a_1, a_2, \ldots, a_T$ as the combination weights. The linear combination is the projection of the point $(X_1, X_2 \ldots, X_T)$ to the vector whose direction is specified by

$$\left\| \begin{array}{c} a_1 \\ a_2 \\ \vdots \\ a_T \end{array} \right\|$$

in the test space.

In general, in reducing the number of dimensions necessary for description of a set of data, we start with the variates $X_1, X_2, \ldots, X_T$. The essence of most available statistical methods of reducing the dimensionality is to determine a certain number of, say, $r < T$ linear combinations of the T variates which, in some sense, contain most of the information inherent in the original variates. For instance, we might wish to have those linear combinations of the original variates that reproduce essentially all of the dispersion in the original variates. On the other hand, the purpose might be to have that linear combination which correlates most highly with a criterion variable, and so forth.

From a geometric standpoint, the problem of reducing the number of variates is a matter of rotating the axis system through a certain angle, whose magnitude is determined by the properties that we wish to confer on one or more of the new axes. What the properties are will depend on the particular purpose.

Before discussing one of these purposes, we note explicitly something about linear combinations or rotated axes that has only been implicit.

Although we speak of "reducing the number of variates," we do not mean simply *discarding* or ignoring some of the original variates. Rather, we use all of the original T variates and *newly define* a smaller set of derived variables, that is, the linear combinations of the T original variates.

Thus, what is reduced is the number of *concepts* pertinent to the final advising process. The number of tests administered is still the original T and, to reiterate, all (or most) of the information thereby obtained is utilized even though we *handle* only the reduced set of variables or, geometrically speaking, deal with a *reduced space*.

The Principal Component Method of Factor Analysis

Factor analysis has been used frequently as a method for reducing the number of variates. We choose to consider only Kelley's method of principal components (1935) because this method is directly expressed in the raw score test space model. Hotelling's method (1933) is similar to that of Kelley; it expresses the relations in a standard score test space.

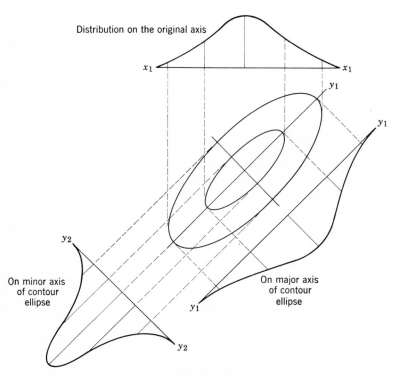

Fig. 7.1 *Illustration of marginal distributions on rotated axes (points shown are 0, ±1σ, ±2σ). In original axes x_1, x_2 the correlation is r = .707, $\sigma_1 = \sigma_2$. When the axes are rotated 45° the correlation between the y_1, y_2 scores is 0.00, Σ_1 is greater than σ_1, and Σ_2 less than σ_2. Σ_1 is maximized by a rotation through $\theta = 45°$. The contours shown are the 1 and 2 sigma ellipses.*

We found in Chapter 3 that the loci of equifrequency points in the normal bivariate distribution were ellipses. The dispersion of the scores (X_{11}, X_{21}) is indicated by the dispersion matrix

$$D_{.1} = \frac{1}{n} x'_{.1} x_{.1} \qquad (7.3)$$

where

$$x_{.1} = \|(X_{11} - \bar{X}_{11}) \quad (X_{21} - \bar{X}_{21})\|$$

In general, the symmetric dispersion matrix $D_{.1}$ has the elements $d_{ij(1)}$, $(i, j = 1, 2; d_{ij} = d_{ji})$.

The axes x_{11}, x_{21} can be rotated through the angle θ to the position x_{12}, x_{22} so that the new axes coincide with the major and minor axes of the set of homothetic isofrequency contour ellipses. As is apparent in Fig. 7.1, for the major and minor axes of the homothetic ellipses, dispersion of the projections of the points on the axis x_{12} has a maximum value, and dispersion of the projections of the points on the axis x_{22} has a minimum value. Also, the two principal components are uncorrelated, that is, $d_{21(2)} = d_{12(2)} = 0$. Since we are considering two different axis systems for the terms in the matrices, we here indicate the particular axis system by a number in parentheses ( ).

Actually the *principal components* (x_{12}, x_{22}) have other properties which are general for all orthogonal transformations: $d_{11(1)} + d_{22(1)} = d_{11(2)} + d_{22(2)}$, that is, the sum of the variances is invariant for the transformation; and $|D_{.1}| = |D_{.2}|$, that is, the determinant of the original dispersion matrix equals the determinant of the dispersion matrix of the principal components. We will develop these ideas gradually. First, let us examine what happens to the dispersion matrix when axes are rotated.

Consider two points, each of whose coordinates are written in a row of the matrix

$$\begin{Vmatrix} 2 & 4 \\ 4 & 5 \end{Vmatrix}$$

The points may, of course, be represented in the Cartesian space X_{11}, X_{21}, as in Fig. 7.2a.

The matrix of means $\bar{X}_{.1}$ for these data is

$$\bar{X}_{.1} = \begin{Vmatrix} 3.0 & 4.5 \\ 3.0 & 4.5 \end{Vmatrix}$$

and the deviation score matrix $x_{.1}$ is

$$x_{.1} = X_{.1} - \bar{X}_{.1} = \begin{Vmatrix} -1.0 & -.5 \\ 1.0 & .5 \end{Vmatrix}$$

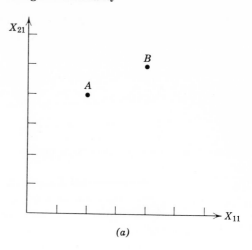

(a)

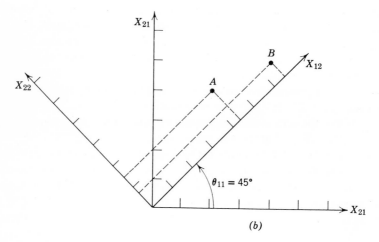

(b)

Fig. 7.2 *Projections on a rotated axis.*

The dispersion matrix of original scores is then

$$D_{.1} = \frac{1}{n} x'_{.1} x_{.1}$$

$$= \frac{1}{2} \begin{Vmatrix} 2.0 & 1.0 \\ 1.0 & .5 \end{Vmatrix} = \begin{Vmatrix} 1.00 & .50 \\ .50 & .25 \end{Vmatrix}$$

Suppose that we rotate X_{11} through the angle of 45° to the position X_{12} while keeping X_{22} perpendicular to X_{12}. Our points may then be referred to the rotated axes, as in Fig. 7.2b. The transformation matrix Γ for this rotation is

$$\Gamma = \begin{Vmatrix} \cos\theta_{11} & \cos\theta_{12} \\ \cos\theta_{21} & \cos\theta_{22} \end{Vmatrix} = \begin{Vmatrix} \dfrac{1}{\sqrt{2}} & -\dfrac{1}{\sqrt{2}} \\ \dfrac{1}{\sqrt{2}} & \dfrac{1}{\sqrt{2}} \end{Vmatrix}$$

Equation 7.1 gives the coordinates of the points in terms of $X_{.2}$. They are

$$X_{.2} = X_{.1}\Gamma = \begin{Vmatrix} 2 & 4 \\ 4 & 5 \end{Vmatrix} \cdot \begin{Vmatrix} .7071 & -.7071 \\ .7071 & .7071 \end{Vmatrix} = \begin{Vmatrix} 4.23 & 1.41 \\ 6.35 & .71 \end{Vmatrix}$$

Similarly, the centroid in the new axis system is related to the centroid in the old axis system by the equation

$$\bar{X}_{.2} = \bar{X}_{.1}\Gamma \tag{7.4}$$

For these data

$$\bar{X}_{.2} = \begin{Vmatrix} 3.0 & 4.5 \\ 3.0 & 4.5 \end{Vmatrix} \cdot \begin{Vmatrix} .7071 & -.7071 \\ .7071 & .7071 \end{Vmatrix} = \begin{Vmatrix} 5.29 & 1.06 \\ 5.29 & 1.06 \end{Vmatrix}$$

Consequently,

$$x_{.2} = X_{.2} - \bar{X}_{.2} = \begin{Vmatrix} -1.06 & .35 \\ 1.06 & -.35 \end{Vmatrix}$$

We note for further reference that Eqs. 7.1 and 7.4 imply that

$$x_{.2} = x_{.1}\Gamma \tag{7.5}$$

In other words, we could have obtained $x_{.2}$ directly by the matrix multiplication $x_{.1}\Gamma$ rather than by taking the difference of the two matrix products $X_{.1}\Gamma$ and $\bar{X}_{.1}\Gamma$, as we did.

We may now compute the dispersion matrix in terms of the rotated scores. It is

$$D_{.2} = \frac{1}{n}x'_{.2}x_{.2} = \frac{1}{2}\begin{Vmatrix} -1.06 & 1.06 \\ .35 & -.35 \end{Vmatrix} \cdot \begin{Vmatrix} -1.06 & .35 \\ 1.06 & -.35 \end{Vmatrix}$$

$$D_{.2} = \frac{1}{2}\begin{Vmatrix} 2.25 & -.74 \\ -.74 & .25 \end{Vmatrix}$$

We have done a great deal of matrix multiplication in computing this dispersion matrix. If we note that

$$D_{.2} = \frac{1}{n}x'_{.2}x_{.2} = \frac{1}{n}[(x_{.1}\Gamma)'(x_{.1}\Gamma)]$$

we have a shorter method for the computation of $D_{.2}$. Since the transpose of a matrix product equals the product of the transposes in reverse order, we can rewrite $D_{.2}$ as

$$D_{.2} = \frac{1}{n} \left[\Gamma' x'_{.1} x_{.1} \Gamma \right]$$

This is, of course, equivalent to

$$D_{.2} = \Gamma' \left[\frac{1}{n} x'_{.1} x_{.1} \right] \Gamma$$

because the $1/n$ is a scalar quantity. Consequently, we have

$$D_{.2} = \Gamma' D_{.1} \Gamma \tag{7.6}$$

The dispersion matrix of the rotated scores can be obtained directly from the dispersion of the original scores.

For our illustration, Eq. 7.6 gives

$$D_{.2} = \left\| \begin{array}{cc} \dfrac{1}{\sqrt{2}} & \dfrac{1}{\sqrt{2}} \\ -\dfrac{1}{\sqrt{2}} & \dfrac{1}{\sqrt{2}} \end{array} \right\| \cdot \left\| \begin{array}{cc} 1.00 & .50 \\ .50 & .25 \end{array} \right\| \cdot \left\| \begin{array}{cc} \dfrac{1}{\sqrt{2}} & -\dfrac{1}{\sqrt{2}} \\ \dfrac{1}{\sqrt{2}} & \dfrac{1}{\sqrt{2}} \end{array} \right\|$$

$$= \frac{1}{2} \left\| \begin{array}{cc} 2.25 & -.75 \\ -.75 & .25 \end{array} \right\|$$

This result differs from our computation of $D_{.2}$ by $(1/n)x'_{.2}x_{.2}$ only in the accuracy of the numbers computed for $x_{.2}$.

There are several facts about $D_{.2}$ and $D_{.1}$ worth nothing. The first is that

$$d_{11(1)} + d_{22(1)} = 1.00 + .25 = 1.25$$

and

$$d_{11(2)} + d_{22(2)} = \tfrac{1}{2}(2.25 + .25) = \tfrac{1}{2}(2.50) = 1.25$$

The sums of the variances are the same. The second is that

$$|D_{.1}| = |D_{.2}|$$

The determinant of a dispersion matrix is invariant under an orthogonal rotation.

However, concerning $D_{.2}$, we should notice that $d_{21} = d_{12} = -.75/2 \neq 0$. The correlation between the rotated scores is *not* zero. The axes X_{12} and X_{22} are not the principal components of these data.

In this illustration we arbitrarily chose $45°$ as the angle of rotation. In principal component factor analysis we want to find the angle that will make the variance of one of the linear combinations along one of the new axes, say, the first, a maximum.

We will first solve the problem by continuing the trial-and-error process we have initiated. We rotate the axes through various angles and each time compute the variance along the new first axis, that is, the upper left-hand element of the new dispersion matrix. For various values, we obtain Table 7.1. Since the angle of rotation which makes the variance

Table 7.1 *Effect of Angle of Rotation on the Variance of x_{12}*

θ_{11}	Variance along New First Axis
10°	1.149
20°	1.234
30°	1.245
40°	1.182
50°	1.053
60°	.870

along the new first axis a maximum is seen, in Table 7.1, to be in the neighborhood of 30°, let us compute the variances for finer steps of the angle in this vicinity.

With $\theta_{11} = 31°$, the variance is 1.242; thus the variance is decreasing when the angle exceeds 30°. The variances for $\theta_{11} = 29°, 28°, \ldots, 25°$ are

θ_{11}	Variance along New First Axis
29°	1.2486
28°	1.2490
27°	1.2499
26°	1.2499
25°	1.2486

The desired angle must lie between 27° and 26°. If we continued with the foregoing procedure of successive approximation by computing the variance for finer steps of the angle between 27° and 26°, we would eventually obtain $\theta = 26° 34'$ as the required angle, with 1.2500 as the maximum variance along the new first axis. A more rational method than trial and error can be found for determining the maximizing angle. We may write the variance along the new first axis in its general form, that is, denoting the angle of rotation by θ_{11} instead of specifying it as 10°, 20°, etc., as we have done in the example, or using a better approach we may write the whole dispersion matrix in general form, and pay attention to the upper left-hand element, which is the variance in question. Then, using Eq. 7.6, the new dispersion matrix is

$$D_{.2} = \Gamma' D_{.1} \Gamma = \begin{Vmatrix} \gamma_{11} & \gamma_{21} \\ \gamma_{12} & \gamma_{22} \end{Vmatrix} \cdot \begin{Vmatrix} 1.00 & .50 \\ .50 & .25 \end{Vmatrix} \cdot \begin{Vmatrix} \gamma_{11} & \gamma_{21} \\ \gamma_{21} & \gamma_{22} \end{Vmatrix}$$

The variance along any "new first axis" for this example is

$$d_{11(2)} = (1.00)\gamma_{11}^2 + 2(.50)\gamma_{21}\gamma_{11} + (.25)\gamma_{21}^2$$
$$= \gamma_{11}^2 + \gamma_{21}\gamma_{11} + .25\gamma_{21}^2$$

Since $\gamma_{ij} = \cos \theta_{ij}$, we see that

$$\gamma_{11} = \cos \theta_{11}, \quad \gamma_{12} = -\sin \theta_{11}, \quad \gamma_{21} = \sin \theta_{11}, \quad \text{and} \quad \gamma_{22} = \cos \theta_{11}$$

and we may rewrite the foregoing expression as

$$d_{11(2)}(\theta_{11}) = \cos^2 \theta_{11} + \cos \theta_{11} \sin \theta_{11} + .25 \sin^2 \theta_{11}$$

where we have written θ_{11} in parentheses after $d_{11(2)}$ to denote explicitly that it is a function of θ_{11}. The problem thus becomes one of finding the value of θ_{11} which maximizes the function $d_{11(2)}(\theta_{11})$.

Such a problem is best solved by means of differential calculus. We equate the derivative of $d_{11(2)}(\theta_{11})$ with respect to θ_{11} to 0. Dropping the subscripts from $\theta_{11(2)}$ and writing simply θ:

$$\frac{d}{d\theta} d_{11(2)}(\theta) = -2 \cos \theta \sin \theta - \sin^2 \theta + \cos^2 \theta + .5 \sin \theta \cos \theta$$
$$= (\cos^2 \theta - \sin^2 \theta) - 1.5 \cos \theta \sin \theta$$
$$= \cos 2\theta - .75 \sin 2\theta = 0$$

or $$\sin 2\theta(\cot 2\theta - .75) = 0$$

Therefore $2\theta = 0$ or $\cot 2\theta = .75$. Thus $\theta = 0$ or $26° 34'$, as determined from a table of trigonometric functions. We then take the second derivative to see which of these values of θ gives the maximum value of $d_{11(2)}\theta$:

$$\frac{d^2}{d\theta^2} d_{11(2)}(\theta) = -2 \sin 2\theta - 1.5 \cos 2\theta$$
$$= -(1.5) \sin 2\theta(\tfrac{4}{3} + \cot 2\theta)$$

so that $\theta = 0$ makes the second derivative zero and $\theta = 26° 34'$ makes the second derivative negative.

The conditions for a maximum are that the first derivative vanish and the second derivative be negative, so $26° 34'$ is the required angle.

In the foregoing, we have found it convenient to use the conventional transformation equation represented in the matrix

$$\begin{Vmatrix} \cos\theta & -\sin\theta \\ \sin\theta & \cos\theta \end{Vmatrix}$$

instead of using the matrix of direction cosines

$$\Gamma = \begin{Vmatrix} \gamma_{11} & \gamma_{12} \\ \gamma_{21} & \gamma_{22} \end{Vmatrix}$$

which could be generalized to T variables. Because of this, we turn to a solution of the factor analysis problem which utilizes the latter form of the transformation matrix and which is therefore directly applicable to more than two variables.

We first note, from Eq. 7.6, that the variance along *any* new first axis is given by

$$\begin{Vmatrix} \gamma_{11} & \gamma_{21} \end{Vmatrix} \ D_{.1} \begin{Vmatrix} \gamma_{11} \\ \gamma_{21} \end{Vmatrix} \tag{7.7}$$

the column matrix $\begin{Vmatrix} \gamma_{11} \\ \gamma_{21} \end{Vmatrix}$ being the first column of the transformation matrix Γ.

We will write the original dispersion matrix as

$$D_{.1} = \begin{Vmatrix} d_{11} & d_{12} \\ d_{21} & d_{22} \end{Vmatrix}$$

in which the third subscript of each element, indicating the system of axes, has been omitted since there is no danger of confusion. Then, Eq. 7.7 can be "spelled out" as

$$d_{11(2)} = d_{11}\gamma_{11}{}^2 + d_{12}\gamma_{21}\gamma_{11} + d_{21}\gamma_{11}\gamma_{21} + d_{22}\gamma_{21}{}^2 \tag{7.8}$$

Thus $d_{11(2)}$ now appears to be a function of two variables γ_{11} and γ_{21}. However, these variables are not independent of each other because one property of the orthogonal transformation matrix is that the squares of the elements of each column (and row) sum to unity. That is, in the present two-variable case:

$$\gamma_{11}{}^2 + \gamma_{21}{}^2 = 1 \tag{7.9}$$

We could use this relationship to eliminate one of the variables, that is, to express, say, γ_{21} in terms of γ_{11}, and substitute in Eq. 7.8, whereupon $d_{11(2)}$ will become a function of γ_{11} alone. But this would be equivalent to using the second procedure just described, and would not be general in the sense of immediate applicability to more than two variables.

There exists an elegant mathematical solution to problems of this type, which are called problems of conditional maximization. In the present instance, the problem is to maximize $d_{11(2)}$ as given by Eq. 7.8, subject to the condition expressed in Eq. 7.9. The principle of the solution is as follows: Write the conditional Eq. 7.9 in the form

$$\gamma_{11}{}^2 + \gamma_{21}{}^2 - 1 = 0 \tag{7.9a}$$

Multiply the left number of the equation by the symbol λ, called the *Lagrangian multiplier* (Sokolnikoff and Sokolnikoff, 1941), and subtract the product from $d_{11(2)}$, as defined by Eq. 7.8, obtaining

$$F = d_{11(2)} - \lambda(\gamma_{11}{}^2 + \gamma_{21}{}^2 - 1)$$
$$= d_{11}\gamma_{11}{}^2 + d_{12}\gamma_{21}\gamma_{11} + d_{21}\gamma_{11}\gamma_{21} + d_{22}\gamma_{21}{}^2 - \lambda(\gamma_{11}{}^2 + \gamma_{21}{}^2 - 1) \tag{7.10}$$

This new function F can be treated as though the two variables γ_{11} and γ_{21} are independent of each other in finding the values of γ_{11} and γ_{21} which maximize it, and which therefore maximize $d_{11(2)}$, subject to the condition in Eq. 7.9. This means that we can take the partial derivatives of F with respect to γ_{11} and γ_{21}, and equate them to zero, obtaining two equations with three unknowns γ_{11}, γ_{21}, and λ. With a third equation supplied by Eq. 7.9, we can solve for the three unknowns.

Before substituting the values of d_{11}, d_{12}, d_{21}, and d_{22} appropriate to the present example, we will carry out the solution in its general form. Taking the partial derivatives of F and equating them to zero, we get

$$\begin{cases} \dfrac{\partial F}{\partial \gamma_{11}} = 2d_{11}\gamma_{11} + d_{12}\gamma_{21} + d_{21}\gamma_{21} - 2\lambda\gamma_{11} = 0 \\[2mm] \dfrac{\partial F}{\partial \gamma_{21}} = d_{12}\gamma_{11} + d_{21}\gamma_{11} + 2d_{22}\gamma_{21} - 2\lambda\gamma_{21} = 0 \end{cases}$$

But, since any dispersion matrix is symmetrical, $d_{12} = d_{21}$; thus the middle two terms in the first equation and the first two terms in the second can be collected as $2d_{12}\gamma_{21}$ and $2d_{21}\gamma_{11}$, respectively. Therefore, dividing both equations through by 2, we have

$$\begin{cases} d_{11}\gamma_{11} + d_{12}\gamma_{21} - \lambda\gamma_{11} = 0 \\ d_{21}\gamma_{11} + d_{22}\gamma_{21} - \lambda\gamma_{21} = 0 \end{cases}$$

or

$$\begin{cases} (d_{11} - \lambda)\gamma_{11} + d_{12}\gamma_{21} = 0 & (7.11) \\ d_{21}\gamma_{11} + (d_{22} - \lambda)\gamma_{21} = 0 & (7.12) \end{cases}$$

These, together with

$$\gamma_{11}{}^2 + \gamma_{21}{}^2 = 1 \tag{7.9}$$

constitute a set of three simultaneous equations in three unknowns and can be solved.

We will first solve these in an ordinary algebraic way, and then develop a schematic solution in matrix notation which can be generally applied to any number of variables.

$$(\text{Eq. } 7.11) \cdot d_{21} : d_{21}(d_{11} - \lambda)\gamma_{11} + d_{12}d_{21}\gamma_{21} = 0 \qquad (7.13)$$

$$(\text{Eq. } 7.12) \cdot (d_{11} - \lambda_1) : (d_{11} - \lambda) d_{21}\gamma_{11} + (d_{11} - \lambda)(d_{22} - \lambda)\gamma_{21} = 0$$
$$(7.14)$$

$$(\text{Eq. } 7.14) - (\text{Eq. } 7.13) : [(d_{11} - \lambda)(d_{22} - \lambda) - d_{12}d_{21}]\gamma_{21} = 0$$

Therefore

$$(d_{11} - \lambda)(d_{22} - \lambda) - d_{12}d_{21} = 0 \qquad (7.15)$$

or

$$\gamma_{21} = 0 \qquad (7.16)$$

The second alternative $\gamma_{21} = 0$ corresponds to the previous $\sin 2\theta_{11} = 0$ and leads to $\theta_{11} = 0$, which implies no rotation.

In the previous solution, the second derivative of $d_{11(2)}(\theta_{11})$ with respect to θ_{11} was taken to show that $\theta_{11} = 0$ is not the desired angle. In general, it can be said that, unless all the off-diagonal elements of the original dispersion matrix are zeros, $\theta_{11} = 0$ is *not* the angle that maximizes the variance along the new first axis. So we may call it a general rule, in factor analysis problems, that we are to seek a solution of the set of simultaneous equations analogous to (7.9), (7.11), (7.12), such that $\theta_{11} \neq 0$. It therefore follows, in the present instance, that the first alternative, Eq. 7.15, must be the one leading to the proper angle of rotation.

Equation 7.15 is a quadratic in λ, so it can be solved by use of the familiar formula for the roots of any quadratic. We could write out the solution in its general form, but nothing is gained by doing so. Let us, at this point, substitute the values of d_{11}, $d_{12} = d_{21}$, and d_{22} in our example to make further discussion concrete. Then, Eqs. 7.11, 7.12, and 7.15 become, respectively,

$$(1.00 - \lambda)\gamma_{11} + .50\gamma_{21} = 0 \qquad (7.11a)$$

$$.50\gamma_{11} + (.25 - \lambda)\gamma_{21} = 0 \qquad (7.12a)$$

and

$$(1.00 - \lambda)(.25 - \lambda) - (.50)^2 = 0 \qquad (7.15a)$$

Simplifying Eq. 7.15a, we have

$$\lambda(\lambda - 1.25) = 0$$

where $\lambda = 0$ or $\lambda = 1.25$. We will follow through with the solution for both these alternatives.

I. $\lambda = 0$. Substituting this in Eq. 7.11a and expressing γ_{21} in terms of γ_{11}, we have

$$\gamma_{21} = 2\gamma_{11}$$

Therefore, by virtue of Eq. 7.9,

$$\gamma_{11}{}^2 + (2\gamma_{11})^2 = 1, \qquad \text{or} \quad 5\gamma_{11}{}^2 = 1$$

Therefore

$$\gamma_{11} = \cos\theta_{11} = \pm\sqrt{.20} = \pm.4472$$

From the table of trigonometric functions, we find that

$$\theta_{11} = 116°\ 34' \qquad \text{or} \quad 296°\ 34'$$

But since these are just 180° apart, it is conventional to take the smaller of the two

$$\theta_{11} = 116°\ 34' \qquad \text{as solution I.}$$

II. $\lambda = 1.25$. Equation 7.11a leads to

$$\gamma_{21} = -.50\gamma_{11}$$

from which, by Eq. 7.9, we obtain

$$\gamma_{11}{}^2 + (-.50\gamma_{11})^2 = 1, \qquad \text{or} \quad 1.25\gamma_{11}{}^2 = 1$$

Therefore

$$\gamma_{11} = \cos\theta_{11} = \pm\frac{1}{\sqrt{1.25}} = \pm.8944$$

from which

$$\theta_{11} = 26°\ 34' \qquad \text{or} \quad 206°\ 34'$$

Again taking the *smaller* angle,

$$\theta_{11} = 26°\ 34' \qquad \text{is solution II.}$$

Comparing solutions I and II, we see that they are just 90° apart. That is, if we take II as the desired solution which, in this example, we know from our previous solutions to be the case, I is none other than the angle θ_{12} between the old first axis and the new second axis. Conversely, if we took I as our solution, we would be making the variance along the new second axis rather than the new first axis a maximum. Thus both these solutions are correct in a certain sense, that is, if we did not specify *which* new axis should have the maximum variance. But it is evident that such ambiguity could lead to much confusion. How are we to decide which of the solutions is best?

In the current example, we knew the answer from other solutions performed previously. Without this knowledge, we could have referred to the scatter diagram to decide on the best solution. But this procedure would be difficult in problems involving more than two variables. Actually, there is a simple way to make this decision, which is best seen in the fourth, and last, solution we will give of this example—the general solution in matrix notation, which is immediately applicable to any number of variables.

To discuss this general solution, we will return to the general forms (7.11), (7.12), and (7.9) of the basic equations. We notice that Eqs. 7.11 and 7.13 can be expressed, in matrix notation, as

$$\begin{Vmatrix} d_{11} - \lambda & d_{12} \\ d_{21} & d_{22} - \lambda \end{Vmatrix} \cdot \begin{Vmatrix} \gamma_{11} \\ \gamma_{21} \end{Vmatrix} = \begin{Vmatrix} 0 \\ 0 \end{Vmatrix} \tag{7.17}$$

Using the symbol Γ_1 to denote the first column of Γ which is

$$\begin{Vmatrix} \gamma_{11} \\ \gamma_{21} \end{Vmatrix}$$

and noting that

$$\begin{Vmatrix} d_{11} - \lambda & d_{12} \\ d_{21} & d_{22} - \lambda \end{Vmatrix} = \begin{Vmatrix} d_{11} & d_{12} \\ d_{21} & d_{22} \end{Vmatrix} - \lambda \begin{Vmatrix} 1 & 0 \\ 0 & 1 \end{Vmatrix}$$
$$= D_{.1} - \lambda I$$

we can rewrite Eq. 7.17 as

$$(D_{.1} - \lambda I)\Gamma_1 = 0 \tag{7.18}$$

where the 0 on the right-hand side represents a column vector of zeros. Equation 7.9 may also be written in matrix notation thus:

$$\Gamma'_1 \Gamma_1 = 1 \tag{7.19}$$

Written in these forms, our basic equations are perfectly general with regard to number of variables. If we symbolically regard Γ'_1 and Γ_1 as two variates, we can write the function

$$F = \Gamma'_1 D_{.1} \Gamma_1 - \lambda(\Gamma'_1 \Gamma_1 - 1)$$

where λ is the Lagrange multiplier. We now take the *symbolic* partial derivative with respect to Γ'_1 and obtain

$$\frac{\partial F}{\partial \Gamma'_1} = 2D_{.1}\Gamma_1 - 2\lambda\Gamma_1$$

Set this equal to 0, remembering that zero stands for a column vector of as many zeros as there are variates T in our notation. Dividing through by 2, we get

$$D_{.1}\Gamma_1 - \lambda\Gamma_1 = 0$$

This reduces to

$$(D_{.1} - \lambda I)\Gamma_1 = 0 \tag{7.20}$$

It is known from the theory of equations (Uspensky, 1948) that a set of homogeneous linear equations, such as Eq. 7.20, has no nonvanishing root unless the determinant of its coefficients is equal to zero. That is,

$$|(D_{.1} - \lambda I)| = 0 \tag{7.21}$$

is a necessary condition for the existence of any nonzero root to Eq. 7.20. It is readily seen that $\gamma_{11} = \gamma_{21} = \cdots = \gamma_{T1} = 0$ does not satisfy the conditions stated in Eq. 7.19. In the two-variate case, Eq. 7.20 reads

$$\begin{vmatrix} (d_{11} - \lambda) & d_{12} \\ d_{21} & (d_{22} - \lambda) \end{vmatrix} = (d_{11} - \lambda)(d_{22} - \lambda) - d_{12}d_{21} = 0$$

With three original variates Eq. 7.21 would mean

$$\begin{vmatrix} (d_{11} - \lambda) & d_{12} & d_{13} \\ d_{21} & (d_{22} - \lambda) & d_{23} \\ d_{31} & d_{32} & (d_{33} - \lambda) \end{vmatrix} = 0$$

In general, Eq. 7.21 stands for a Tth degree equation in λ, T being the number of variates involved. This is known as the *characteristic equation* of the dispersion matrix $D_{.1}$.

The first step is to solve the characteristic equation for the appropriate values of λ. These values are called the *latent roots* of $D_{.1}$. The following steps are repeated for each latent root obtained except for 0 roots, or roots that are not of significant magnitude.

With any one latent root substituted for λ in the left-hand side of Eq. 7.20 we can solve for the column vector Γ_1 by means of Laplace's theorem on the expansion of determinants (Schreier and Sperner, 1951). This theorem states that the algebraic sum of cross products between elements of any row and the corresponding cofactors is equal to the value of the determinant, whereas the algebraic sum of cross products between elements of any row and cofactors of corresponding elements of any other row is equal to zero. This also holds when "row" is replaced by "column."

Thus, for example, if we consider the determinant

$$\begin{vmatrix} 5 & 6 & 7 \\ 2 & -3 & -5 \\ 6 & 7 & 2 \end{vmatrix}$$

the cofactors of the element 5, 6, and 7 of the first row are, respectively,

$$\begin{vmatrix} -3 & -5 \\ 7 & 2 \end{vmatrix} = 29$$

$$-\begin{vmatrix} 2 & -5 \\ 6 & 2 \end{vmatrix} = -34 \quad \text{and}$$

$$\begin{vmatrix} 2 & -3 \\ 6 & 7 \end{vmatrix} = 32$$

The algebraic sum of the indicated cross products is

$$5(29) + 6(-34) + 7(32) = 145 - 204 + 224 = 165$$

which is the value of the determinant. On the other hand, if the foregoing cofactors are multiplied by the corresponding elements of the second row, the algebraic sum of the cross products is

$$2(29) + (-3)(-34) + (-5)(32) = 58 + 102 - 160 = 0$$

Similarly, the cross products with the third row elements and the first row cofactors add to

$$6(29) + 7(-34) + 2(32) = 174 - 238 + 64 = 0$$

Similar results are obtained for the algebraic sum of cross products of the cofactors of any other row.

In applying Laplace's theorem to the present problem, we note that the value of the determinant in Eq. 7.20 is itself zero, since we have substituted one of the latent roots of $D_{.1}$ for λ. This means that, if we take as each element of Γ_1, that is, the column vector to be determined, the cofactor of the corresponding element of any, say, the first, row of Eq. 7.20, the column vector will satisfy Eq. 7.19. The first element of the matrix product specified by Eq. 7.19 will be equal to the value of the determinant specified by Eq. 7.20, that is, zero in this instance, whereas all other elements will vanish regardless of the value of the determinant. This is because all other elements are the sums of cross products between the second, third, and so on, to the Tth rows, respectively, and the cofactors of the elements of the *first* row. Likewise, the column vector whose elements are cofactors of any row will serve just as well for Γ_1 to satisfy Eq. 7.20.

In Chapters 3 and 4 we encountered the concept of the adjoint of a matrix, the matrix whose *columns* consist of the cofactors of the *rows* of the original matrix. Therefore we may say that any column of the adjoint of

$$\| D_{.1} - \lambda I \|$$

satisfies Eq. 7.20 and thus will serve as Γ_1.

It appears that Γ_1 is so indeterminate that *any column* of the adjoint will do. Actually, however, the situation is not so indeterminate as it seems. All the columns of the adjoint of any matrix of the form

$$\| D_{.1} - \lambda I \|$$

where λ is one of the latent roots of $D_{.1}$, are proportional. Thus Eq. 7.20 determines Γ_1 uniquely except for an arbitrary factor. Any Γ_1 which satisfies Eq. 7.20 is called a *latent vector* corresponding to the latent root λ_1 of $D_{.1}$.

The Γ_1 we seek must satisfy not only Eq. 7.18, but also Eq. 7.19. Since 7.19 translated into scalar algebra means that the sum of the squares of the elements of Γ_1 must be unity, this determines the arbitrary factor involved in Γ_1. That is to say, if, in the previous step,

$$v_1 = \left\| \begin{matrix} v_{11} \\ v_{21} \\ \vdots \\ v_{T1} \end{matrix} \right\|$$

was found to satisfy Eq. 7.20, then the appropriate factor by which each element v_{i1} should be multiplied is

$$\frac{1}{(v_{11}{}^2 + v_{21}{}^2 + \cdots + v_{T1}{}^2)^{\frac{1}{2}}}$$

That is,

$$\Gamma_1 = \frac{1}{\left(\sum_{i=1}^{T} v_{i1}{}^2 \right)^{\frac{1}{2}}} \cdot \left\| \begin{matrix} v_{11} \\ v_{21} \\ \vdots \\ v_{T1} \end{matrix} \right\|$$

will satisfy both Eqs. 7.18 and 7.19. The procedure of multiplying v_1 by

$$\frac{1}{\left(\sum_{i=1}^{T} v_{i1}{}^2 \right)^{\frac{1}{2}}}$$

is called *normalizing* v to unity.

This is a complete description of the general matrix-algebraic solution of the principal component factor analysis problem except for the problem of which roots of the characteristic equation are sought.

Let λ_t be any one of the latent roots of $D_{.1}$ and Γ_t be the latent vector corresponding to λ_t normalized to unity. Then, by Eq. 7.20,

$$(D_{.1} - \lambda_t I)\Gamma_t = 0$$

or

$$D_{.1}\Gamma_t = \lambda_t \Gamma_t$$

Therefore premultiplying both sides by Γ'_t we have

$$\Gamma'_t D_{.1} \Gamma_t = \lambda_t \Gamma'_t \Gamma_t$$
$$= \lambda_t$$

because of Eq. 7.19. But, according to Eq. 7.18, the left-hand side of this equation is $d_{11(2)}$, resulting from the rotation indicated by Γ_t. Thus we see that any *latent root* of the dispersion matrix is equal to the variance along the new first axis resulting from a rotation specified by a transformation matrix whose *first* column is the corresponding latent vector normalized to unity. Therefore if we want to find the one axis that gives the largest variance, we take the new first axis as defined by the latent vector corresponding to the largest latent root.

However, in problems involving many original variates, we generally want not one but several axes along which the variances are largest, second largest, third largest, and so on. It may be anticipated that the desired result can be achieved by taking the largest, second largest, third largest, and so on, latent roots and their corresponding latent vectors, each normalized to unity. This is true, but one other fact has to be proved before this procedure can be justified. Although it has been demonstrated that the variance along the new *first* axis will equal the value of the latent root whose corresponding latent vector is taken as the *first* column of the transformation matrix, it does not automatically follow that the normalized latent vectors corresponding to successively smaller latent roots, starting from the largest, can be taken as the first, second, third, etc., columns of the transformation matrix. For this to be possible, we also must know that the several latent vectors are mutually orthogonal, that is, the sum of cross products between corresponding elements of any two latent vectors is zero. That this is true may be seen from the following:

If λ_t and λ_u are two latent roots, and Γ_t and Γ_u the corresponding normalized latent vectors, we have, from Eq. 7.20,

$$D_{.1}\Gamma_t = \lambda_t \Gamma_t$$

and

$$D_{.1}\Gamma_u = \lambda_u \Gamma_u$$

Consequently we may write

$$\Gamma'_u D_{.1}\Gamma_t = \lambda_t \Gamma'_u \Gamma_t$$

and

$$\Gamma'_t D_{.1}\Gamma_u = \lambda_u \Gamma'_t \Gamma_u$$

Take the transpose of both sides of the first of these equations and obtain

$$\Gamma'_t D'_{.1}\Gamma_u = \lambda_t \Gamma'_t \Gamma_u$$

Since $D_{.1}$ is symmetrical, $D'_{.1}$ equals $D_{.1}$ so that

$$\Gamma'_t D_{.1}\Gamma_u = \lambda_t \Gamma'_t \Gamma_u$$

Since quantities equal to the same quantity are equal to each other, we have

$$\lambda_t \Gamma'_t \Gamma_u = \lambda_u \Gamma'_t \Gamma_u$$

which may be written as

$$(\lambda_t - \lambda_u)\Gamma'_t\Gamma_u = 0$$

Consequently

$$\Gamma'_t\Gamma_u = 0$$

provided λ_t is not equal to λ_u. This indicates that the transformation is orthogonal.

We can now summarize the principal component factor method.

Given a $(T \times T)$ dispersion matrix $D_{.1}$, we compute a $(T \times T)$ orthogonal transformation matrix Γ whose first r columns are

$$\Gamma_1, \Gamma_2, \ldots, \Gamma_r$$

such that the variances along the first r new axes

$$d_{11(2)} = \Gamma'_1 D_{.1}\Gamma_1, \qquad d_{22(2)} = \Gamma'_2 D_{.1}\Gamma_2, \qquad \ldots, \qquad d_{rr(2)} = \Gamma'_r D_{.1}\Gamma_r$$

will account for most of the dispersion in the original variates. That is,

$$d_{11(2)} + d_{22(2)} + \cdots + d_{rr(2)}$$

will be nearly equal to

$$d_{11} + d_{22} + \cdots + d_{TT}$$

How closely the sum is required to approximate the original total variance depends upon considerations of statistical significance.

Step 1.   The basic equations are immediately written down as

$$(D_{.1} - \lambda I)\Gamma_t = 0 \qquad t = 1, 2, \ldots, r \qquad (7.20)$$
$$\Gamma'_t\Gamma_t = 1 \qquad t = 1, 2, \ldots, r \qquad (7.19)$$

where the 0 on the right-hand side of Eq. 7.20 stands for a column vector of T zeros.

Step 2.   Solve the characteristic equation

$$\|D_{.1} - \lambda I\| = 0 \qquad (7.21)$$

which is an algebraic equation of the Tth degree. Let the r largest roots of this equation, that is, the r largest latent roots of $D_{.1}$, be

$$\lambda_1, \lambda_2, \ldots, \lambda_r$$

Step 3.   Substitute the value λ_1 for the λ in the matrix

$$\|D_{.1} - \lambda I\|$$

Obtain the first column of the adjoint of this matrix. This is the latent vector of $D_{.1}$ corresponding to the largest latent root λ_1. It satisfies Eq. 7.20 but not Eq. 7.19. Call it

$$v_1 = \begin{Vmatrix} v_{11} \\ v_{21} \\ \vdots \\ v_{T1} \end{Vmatrix}$$

Step 4. Normalize v_1 so that the resulting vector will satisfy Eq. 7.19 as well as Eq. 7.20. That is, multiply each element of v_1 by

$$\pm \frac{1}{(v_{11}{}^2 + v_{21}{}^2 + \cdots + v_{T1}{}^2)^{\frac{1}{2}}}$$

The sign of the multiplier is to be chosen so that the diagonal element γ_{ii} in Γ is positive. The resulting vector is Γ_1, the *normalized* latent vector corresponding to the largest latent root. It satisfies both Eqs. 7.20 and 7.19.

Steps 3 and 4 are repeated with each latent root $\lambda_2, \lambda_3, \ldots, \lambda_r$. The results are $\Gamma_2, \Gamma_3, \ldots, \Gamma_r$, the normalized latent vectors of $D_{.1}$ corresponding to the second, third, $\ldots$, rth largest latent root of $D_{.1}$.

As previously demonstrated, the set of vectors $\Gamma_1, \Gamma_2, \ldots, \Gamma_r$ are mutually orthogonal. Therefore they meet the conditions for being the first r columns of the orthogonal transformation matrix Γ which rotates the axis system into such a position that the variance along the first r new axes accounts for almost all of the dispersion in the original variates. These axes are the principal components.

Returning to the present numerical example:

Step 1. The basic equations are

$$\begin{bmatrix} 1.00 - \lambda & .50 \\ .50 & .25 - \lambda \end{bmatrix} \cdot \begin{bmatrix} \gamma_{11} \\ \gamma_{21} \end{bmatrix} = \begin{bmatrix} 0 \\ 0 \end{bmatrix}$$

and

$$\begin{bmatrix} \gamma_{11} & \gamma_{21} \end{bmatrix} \begin{bmatrix} \gamma_{11} \\ \gamma_{21} \end{bmatrix} = 1$$

Step 2. We have already solved the characteristic equation

$$(1.00 - \lambda)(.25 - \lambda) - (.50)(.50) = 0 \qquad (7.15a)$$

obtaining the latent roots

$$\lambda = 1.25, \quad 0$$

In this example, then, the variance along the new first axis actually accounts for the *whole* total variance in the original variables, so we will obviously need only the axis specified by the latent vector corresponding to $\lambda_1 = 1.25$.

Step 3.   With $\lambda_1 = 1.25$ substituted, the matrix $\| D_{.1} - \lambda_1 I \|$ becomes

$$\begin{bmatrix} -.25 & .50 \\ .50 & -1.00 \end{bmatrix}$$

Its adjoint is

$$\begin{bmatrix} -1.00 & -.50 \\ -.50 & -.25 \end{bmatrix}$$

so that

$$v_1 = \begin{bmatrix} -1.00 \\ -.50 \end{bmatrix}$$

is a latent vector.

Step 4.

$$v_{11}{}^2 + v_{21}{}^2 = (-1.00)^2 + (-.50)^2 = 1.25$$

Therefore

$$\pm \sqrt{v_1{}^2 + v_2{}^2} = \pm \sqrt{1.25} = \pm 1.1180$$

Choosing the sign that makes γ_{11} positive, we obtain

$$\Gamma_1 = \frac{-1}{1.1180} \begin{bmatrix} -1.00 \\ -.50 \end{bmatrix} = \begin{bmatrix} .8944 \\ .4472 \end{bmatrix}$$

Therefore

$$\gamma_{11} = \cos \theta_{11} = .8944.$$

Therefore $\theta_{11} = 26° 34'$, as found before.

The linear combination of the two variates which is the first and, in this example, the only, principal component is

$$.8944 X_{11} + .4472 X_{21}$$

The weights .8944 and .4472 are called the *factor loadings* of test 1 and test 2, respectively, on the principal component (or factor). The factor scores of the two individuals are

$$(.8944) \cdot 2 + (.4472) \cdot 4 = 3.5816$$
$$(.8944) \cdot 4 + (.4472) \cdot 5 = 5.8136$$

The fact that the first principal component accounts for all the variance in the original variables is merely an artifact because there are only two individuals, which necessarily implies a perfect correlation between the two variables within this group. This is tantamount to saying that with only two cases there is only one "effective variable" in the test space of two dimensions. A single linear combination of the test space variables describes the situation completely. With actual data, of course, we could not expect such complete reduction of multivariate dispersion to a single linear combination of the test scores. We may, however, search for the best approximation.

We can always find the one linear combination which accounts for the maximum portion of the dispersion in the test space. If the combination accounts for a large portion, say, 95%, of the total dispersion, we may decide that for practical purposes the test space has been reduced; practically all of the dispersion is found in a principal component score space of one dimension. If the first principal component accounts for only 60% of the total dispersion, we may decide that one dimension is not sufficient. A second linear combination may then be found which will account for the maximum portion of the residual dispersion. If the two principal components account for a sufficiently large portion of the total dispersion in the test space, we can use a component space of dimensionality two to account for most of the dispersion observed in the original test space of dimensionality T. Thus the dimensions required for understanding the covariation in the test scores have been reduced in number, and the number T of original variates has been combined into a lesser number r of component scores—the number of variates has been reduced.

Principal Component Analysis—Other Examples

Two Variates

In order to illustrate the procedure further, we compute the principal components of the data on the outdoor and convivial activity preferences of the 135 members of the group of apprentices from New York City. The dispersion matrix for the group is

$$D_{.1} = \begin{Vmatrix} 18.0234 & -3.4084 \\ -3.4084 & 18.9147 \end{Vmatrix}$$

Step 1. The basic equations are

$$\begin{Vmatrix} 18.0234 - \lambda & -3.4084 \\ -3.4084 & 18.9147 - \lambda \end{Vmatrix} \cdot \begin{Vmatrix} \gamma_{11} \\ \gamma_{21} \end{Vmatrix} = \begin{Vmatrix} 0 \\ 0 \end{Vmatrix}$$

and

$$\begin{Vmatrix} \gamma_{11} & \gamma_{21} \end{Vmatrix} \cdot \begin{Vmatrix} \gamma_{11} \\ \gamma_{21} \end{Vmatrix} = 1$$

Step 2. The characteristic equation is

$$\lambda^2 - 36.9381\lambda + 329.2899 = 0$$

and the roots of this equation are

$$\lambda_1 = 21.9064$$

and

$$\lambda_2 = 15.0317$$

Step 3. With $\lambda_1 = 21.9064$,

$$\|D_{.1} - \lambda_1 I\| = \begin{Vmatrix} -3.8830 & -3.4084 \\ -3.4084 & -2.9917 \end{Vmatrix}$$

the adjoint of this matrix is

$$\begin{Vmatrix} -2.9917 & 3.4084 \\ 3.4084 & -3.8830 \end{Vmatrix}$$

Therefore

$$v_1 = \begin{Vmatrix} -2.9917 \\ 3.4084 \end{Vmatrix}$$

is a latent vector corresponding to latent root λ_1.

Step 4. Since

$$v_{11}{}^2 + v_{21}{}^2 = 20.5674$$

$$\pm \sqrt{v_{11}{}^2 + v_{21}{}^2} = \pm 4.5351$$

the normalized latent vector is

$$\Gamma_1 = -\frac{1}{4.5351} \begin{Vmatrix} -2.9917 \\ 3.4084 \end{Vmatrix} = \begin{Vmatrix} .6597 \\ -.7516 \end{Vmatrix}$$

The negative sign is attached to the multiplier in order to make γ_{11} positive.

The elements of Γ_1 indicate that $\gamma_{11} = \cos\theta_{11} = .6597$ and $\gamma_{21} = \cos\theta_{21} = -.7516$. Since $\gamma_{21} < 0$, the new axis X_{12} must lie in the fourth

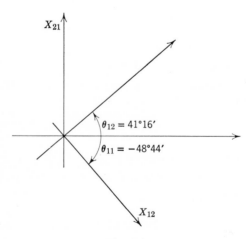

Fig. 7.3

quadrant. Consequently, of the two angles whose cosine is .6597, namely, $\pm 48°\ 44'$, the angle $-48°\ 44'$ is the proper value for θ_{11}. Axis X_{12} therefore has the orientation illustrated in Fig. 7.3.

Step 3.   repeated with $\lambda_2 = 15.0317$,

$$\| D_1 - \lambda_2 I \| = \left\|\begin{matrix} 2.9917 & -3.4084 \\ -3.4084 & 3.8830 \end{matrix}\right\|$$

and the adjoint is

$$\left\|\begin{matrix} 3.8830 & 3.4084 \\ 3.4084 & 2.9917 \end{matrix}\right\|$$

Therefore

$$v_2 = \left\|\begin{matrix} 3.8830 \\ 3.4084 \end{matrix}\right\|$$

is a latent vector corresponding to latent root λ_2.

Step 4.   (repeated for the second root). Since

$$v_{12}{}^2 + v_{22}{}^2 = 26.6949$$

$$\pm \sqrt{v_{12}{}^2 + v_{22}{}^2} = \pm 5.1667$$

the second principal component Γ_2 is

$$\Gamma_2 = \frac{1}{5.1667} \cdot \left\|\begin{matrix} 3.8830 \\ 3.4084 \end{matrix}\right\| = \left\|\begin{matrix} .7516 \\ .6597 \end{matrix}\right\|$$

The positive value of $\sqrt{\sum v^2}$ is chosen to make γ_{22} positive.

The elements of Γ_2 indicate that $\gamma_{12} = \cos \theta_{12} = .7516$ and $\gamma_{22} = \cos \theta_{22} = .6597$. Since $\gamma_{12} > 0$, the new axis X_{22} must lie in the first quadrant. Consequently, of the two angles whose cosine is .7516, namely, $\pm 41°\ 16'$, we take $+41°\ 16'$ as the proper value for θ_{12}, the angle between the old first and new second axis. The axis X_{12} therefore has the orientation indicated in Fig. 7.3.

It should be noted that, whenever there are only two variates involved, a second principal component automatically follows from the first by virtue of the orthogonal relationship stated previously. In this example,

$$\theta_{11} + \theta_{12} = 48°\ 44' + 41°\ 16' = 90°$$

the two latent roots are of the same order of magnitude, so that neither of the two principal components absorbs a sufficient proportion of the original total variance to allow a parsimonious description of the original dispersion in terms of one factor alone. This resulted because the off-diagonal term of $D_{.1}$ was low relative to the square root of the product of the diagonal term; that is, X_{11} and X_{21} had a low correlation.

Three Variates

The matrix solution involves computing the adjoint of a matrix whose order is equal to the number of variates. Computation of an adjoint becomes increasingly complex as the number of variates increases. An alternative method which dispenses with the detailed calculation of the adjoint is presented in detail by Tiedeman et al. (1953). Although such calculations are now almost routinely done by data-processing systems, we illustrate Bryan's procedure by computing the principal components of the outdoor, convivial, and conservative activity scores of the 135 apprentices from New York City. The *steps* referred to are references to the report cited.

The three-variate dispersion matrix of which we seek the characteristic equation is

$$D_{.1} = \begin{Vmatrix} 18.0234 & -3.4084 & -1.7572 \\ -3.4084 & 18.9147 & -1.6497 \\ -1.7572 & -1.6497 & 12.7092 \end{Vmatrix}$$

We compute the coefficients of the characteristic equation of this dispersion matrix according to Step 10 (Tiedeman et al., 1953, pp. 283–293). The matrix vector sequence for this problem is

$$f_1 = \begin{Vmatrix} -1 & 18.0234 \end{Vmatrix}$$

$$B_2 = \begin{Vmatrix} 0 & 3.4084 \\ -1 & 18.0234 \end{Vmatrix}$$

$$f_2 = \begin{Vmatrix} 1 & -36.9381 & 329.2900 \end{Vmatrix}$$

$$B_3 = \begin{Vmatrix} 0 & -1.7572 & 38.8597 \\ 0 & -1.6497 & 35.7224 \\ 1 & -36.9381 & 329.2900 \end{Vmatrix}$$

$$f_3 = \begin{Vmatrix} -1 & 49.6473 & -792.9344 & 4057.7970 \end{Vmatrix}$$

Consequently, the characteristic equation of $D_{.1}$ is

$$\lambda^3 - 49.6473\lambda^2 + 792.9344\lambda - 4057.7970 = 0$$

The latent roots may be found by the procedure outlined in Step 11 (Tiedeman et al., 1953, pp. 291–294). For these data, the latent roots are

$$\lambda_1 = 21.9073$$
$$\lambda_2 = 16.5442$$
$$\lambda_3 = 11.1958$$

The matrix L is then constructed according to Step 12 (Tiedeman et al., 1953, p. 295). In this instance, L is

$$L = \begin{Vmatrix} \lambda_1^2 & \lambda_2^2 & \lambda_3^2 \\ \lambda_1 & \lambda_2 & \lambda_3 \\ 1 & 1 & 1 \end{Vmatrix}$$

$$= \begin{Vmatrix} 479.9298 & 273.7106 & 125.3459 \\ 21.9073 & 16.5442 & 11.1958 \\ 1 & 1 & 1 \end{Vmatrix}$$

The latent vectors of $D_{.1}$ are defined by the matrix product B_3L as given in Step 13 (Tiedeman et al., 1953, p. 295). For these data the product is

$$v = B_3L = \begin{Vmatrix} .364192 & 9.7882 & 19.1864 \\ -.418073 & 8.4294 & 17.2527 \\ .005762 & -8.1107 & 41.0843 \end{Vmatrix}$$

$$\sum_{i=1}^{3} v_{iu}^2 = [.307454 \quad 232.64710 \quad 2353.69331]$$

$$\pm\sqrt{\sum_{i=1}^{3} v_{iu}^2} = [\pm.554485 \quad \pm 15.2528 \quad \pm 48.5149]$$

The normalizing factor for each column is recorded in the last row of the foregoing data. If the elements of each column are divided by this factor, choosing the sign so that γ_{ii} is positive, the resulting quotients are the coefficients of the transformation matrix Γ. In this instance,

$$\Gamma = \begin{Vmatrix} .6568 & .6417 & .3955 \\ -.7540 & .5526 & .3556 \\ .0104 & -.5318 & .8468 \end{Vmatrix}$$

As a check we compute the product

$$\Gamma'\Gamma = \begin{Vmatrix} 1.0000 & -.0007 & .0004 \\ -.0007 & 1.0000 & .0000 \\ .0004 & .0000 & 1.0000 \end{Vmatrix}$$

which is the identity matrix within the accuracy of the number of figures carried. The elements of the matrix Γ are ordinarily referred to as *factor loadings*.

In this example we find that the three latent roots are roughly of the same order of magnitude, so that the latent vectors corresponding to no one of them can be ignored without losing a rather considerable amount of the original dispersion of the scores. We are accustomed to this result when the variates are not highly intercorrelated, as in this example.

Topology and Factor Analysis—An Example

Establishing a topology requires the comparison of at least two groups. Consequently, in considering topology in the factor space we will use the simplest example of two jobs, namely, our agent and mechanic example. We consider the outdoor and convivial activity preferences of these two types of employees.

In factor analysis, it is customary to avoid the question of what group to use for the determination of principal components in the test space. In our example, we will follow the customary practice of using an occupationally undifferentiated group for which we have already reported the principal components in the two-variable example, that of the apprentices from New York City.

We obtain the dispersion matrices for the agent and mechanic groups, respectively, by the equations

$$D_{1.2} = \Gamma' D_{1.1} \Gamma \qquad \text{(group 1—passenger agents)}$$

and

$$D_{2.2} = \Gamma' D_{2.2} \Gamma \qquad \text{(group 2—mechanics)}$$

where

$$D_{1.1} = \begin{Vmatrix} 20.0068 & 4.5628 \\ 4.5628 & 18.5735 \end{Vmatrix}$$

is the original dispersion matrix for agents,

$$D_{2.1} = \begin{Vmatrix} 12.5713 & -1.5582 \\ -1.5582 & 20.4856 \end{Vmatrix}$$

is the original dispersion matrix for mechanics, and

$$\Gamma = \begin{Vmatrix} .6597 & .7516 \\ -.7516 & .6597 \end{Vmatrix}$$

is the transformation matrix derived for the apprentice data. We have added another subscript to the dispersion matrices in the original and new axes in order to designate the group. The dispersion matrix for agents in this factor space is

$$D_{1.2} = \begin{Vmatrix} 14.6745 & .1189 \\ .1189 & 23.9099 \end{Vmatrix}$$

and the dispersion matrix for the mechanics in this factor space is

$$D_{2.2} = \left\| \begin{array}{cc} 18.5886 & -3.7221 \\ -3.7221 & 14.4717 \end{array} \right\|$$

By a similar transformation of the centroid in the test space we determine that the centroids for the two groups in the factor space are

$$\bar{X}_{1.2} = \left\| -9.9019 \quad 25.4415 \right\|$$

and

$$\bar{X}_{2.2} = \left\| -3.6594 \quad 27.8788 \right\|$$

By the methods of Chapter 6 we write the equation

$$B'_{12} \cap X_{22} = (29.345 - .480X_{12}) \pm (.598X_{12}{}^2 + 28.664X_{12} + 216.656)^{\frac{1}{2}}$$

as the boundary between the first, or agent group, and the second, or mechanic group, in the *factor space defined by the New York City data.* We employ the convention of using a prime to denote the boundary in the rotated space.

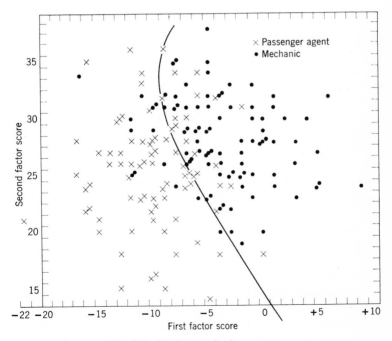

Fig. 7.4 *Regions in the factor space.*

From Fig. 7.4 we obtain the following results for the *factor space* data:

Actual \ Classified as	Passenger Agents	Mechanics	Number Misclassified
Passenger Agents	66	19	19
Mechanics	13	80	13
Total	79	99	32

In the original test space the results were (as recorded in Chapter 6)

Actual \ Classified as	Passenger Agents	Mechanics	Number Misclassified
Passenger Agents	67	18	18
Mechanics	12	81	12
Total	79	99	30

The two results are almost identical. Indeed, they should be identical, for all that we have done is rotate the reference axes through a certain angle, keeping the points in their original positions. The increase of one misclassified case in each group is due simply to rounding errors in computing the factor scores.

Thus we see in this example that we have accomplished nothing by applying the factor transformation to the test space data for agents and mechanics. We started with a two-variate test space and a topology that misclassified 30 of these 178 agents and mechanics, and ended up with a two-variate factor space topology which misclassified 32 of these same agents and mechanics. There has been no decrease in the number of misclassifications. Of course, we do not expect a decrease because preserving the number of misclassifications in the test space is the best that we can do by any rule for classification.

We next examine the result obtained when we reduce the number of variates by classification rules using only the first principal component score.

Figure 7.5 shows the frequency distributions of the two groups on the first factor score. Empirically determined rules result in 39 misclassifications. The distributions for the second factor score are represented in Fig. 7.6. The empirically determined number of misclassifications is 63. Reducing the two-variate test space to the first factor score results in a material

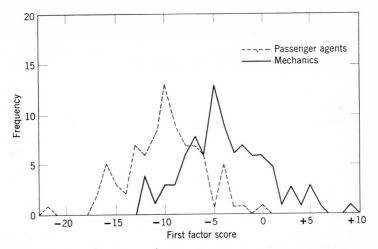

Fig. 7.5 *Frequency distributions of first factor score for passenger agents and mechanics.*

increase in the expected number of misclassifications and use of the second factor alone more than doubles the misclassifications in the particular example.

The factor procedure itself provides little or no information for choice between the two factors. The classificatory results obtained for each factor have to be investigated separately if a factor is to be used as a substitute for the two original test variates. There is no guarantee in the factor

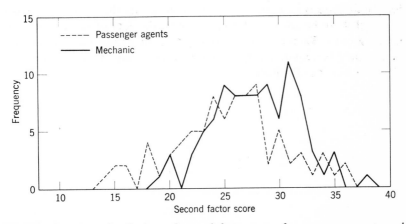

Fig. 7.6 *Frequency distributions of second factor score for passenger agents and mechanics.*

procedure that the regions of reduced dimensionality will be "best" in any sense of achieving an approximation with minimum error.

Theory of Topology and Factor Analysis

We have seen that principal components are the vectors in the test space that transform the matrix $D_{.1}$ to the matrix $D_{.2}$. The dispersion matrix of factor scores has several desirable properties. (1) It is diagonal; the projections of the points in the test space to the principal component vectors (factor scores) are uncorrelated in the sample on which the principal components are determined. (2) The determinant of the dispersion matrix for the principal components is equal to the determinant of the dispersion matrix for the original test variates. (3) The principal component vectors are arranged in decreasing order of importance. The first principal component accounts for the largest portion of the total dispersion, the second principal component for the second largest portion, and so on. Finally (4) The sum of the diagonal elements of the dispersion matrix of principal components is equal to the sum of the diagonal elements of the dispersion matrix of the original test variates. This guarantees that all the variation present in the original test space is carried over to the principal component space.

Desirable as these properties are, they do *not* include the property of achieving a transformation which yields the *smallest* space in which multiple groups are efficiently classified by topological regions as they were in the original test space. The derivation of principal components does *not* incorporate information about group membership. Even when factor methods successfully reduce the dimensionality required to account for the dispersion in a single heterogeneous group the same factor space is not likely to be adequate for representing the data of several homogeneous groups. Factor analysis does not result in the smallest number of dimensions required for the purpose of group discrimination and classification of individuals.

Chapter 8

Discriminant Analysis

Topology and Axis Rotation

The boundary B_{AB} between two groups A and B is a *straight line* when the dispersion matrices D_A and D_B are equal. When $D_A = D_B$, in the three-variate case, B_{AB} is a plane. In general, in the multivariate case the boundary surface B_{AB} is a hyperplane when $D_A = D_B$. These facts have some interesting consequences for reducing the number of dimensions required to represent classification regions originally determined in the T space.

If the scores in groups A and B are bivariate normal we know that isofrequency points in the test space form two families of similar concentric ellipses. If, in addition, we assume that the dispersion matrices of the two

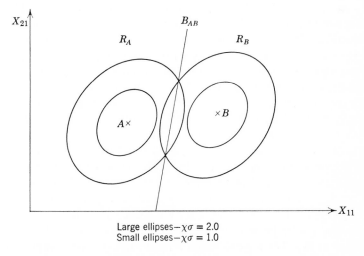

Large ellipses—$\chi\sigma = 2.0$
Small ellipses—$\chi\sigma = 1.0$

Fig. 8.1 *Boundary between overlapping groups in two-space.*

299

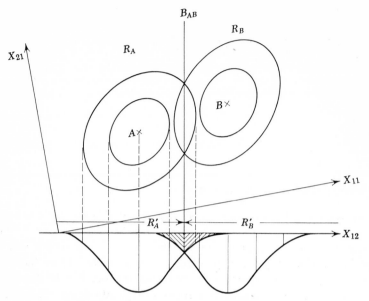

Fig. 8.2 *Projections on the best discriminant line.*

groups are equal, that is, $D_A = D_B$, both families of ellipses will be *similarly oriented*; their principal axes will be parallel. Some of the corresponding contour ellipses of these families will intersect, as illustrated for a particular case in Fig. 8.1. The points of intersection define a straight line. It is apparent that this line divides the test space into two regions. Most of the group of points constituting group A lie on one side of the boundary, and most of the group B points lie on the other side.

If we rotate the axis system through an angle θ so that the axis X_{12} makes a right angle with the boundary line we have a new axis system in which the axes are X_{12}, B_{AB}. (The old axis X_{21} may be disregarded for the example. It will be parallel to B_{AB}.) The score points in the test space project on the X_{12} axis. The projections are "new" scores, one for each point, obtained by the linear combination determined by the angle θ. Each group A and B is described by frequency distributions on the line X_{12} which we shall call the discriminant line. Figure 8.2 illustrates the line and the distributions of the projections of the groups on it. It is apparent from the figure that every point in the test space which lies in R_B (region B in the test space) projects to a point on the segment of X_{12} which is indicated as R'_B. The regions A and B on the line X_{12} are separated at the origin where the test space boundary line intersects the X_{12} axis. Thus it is clear that every point in the test space which would be misclassified by the boundary line of R_A and R_B would also be misclassified by regions R'_A and R'_B on the discriminant line. The properly classified points in the test space are all classified by their projections on the discriminant line. This example shows that when $D_A = D_B$, points classified into regions of a two-dimensional test space may sometimes be grouped or classified in exactly the same way by regions in an appropriately chosen one-dimensional discriminant space.

The boundary line chosen for the illustration was defined by the points at which corresponding ellipses intersect. Any number of other boundaries might have been chosen, as is indicated in Fig. 8.3.

It is apparent that some basis of choice is needed. One basis is the number of misclassified points. The procedure defining the discriminant line in Fig. 8.2 kept misclassifications constant. Do other lines? We will consider this question in Fig. 8.4. Figure 8.4 shows the new axis system obtained by drawing the boundary through the test space so that it bisects and is perpendicular to the line connecting the two group centroids. The

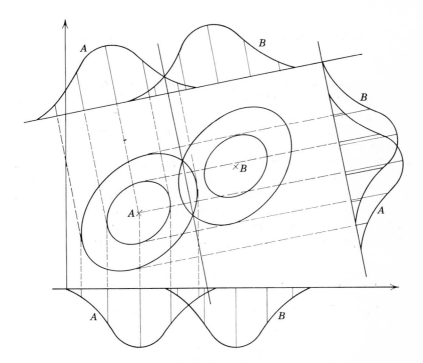

Fig. 8.3 *Projections on sundry axes.*

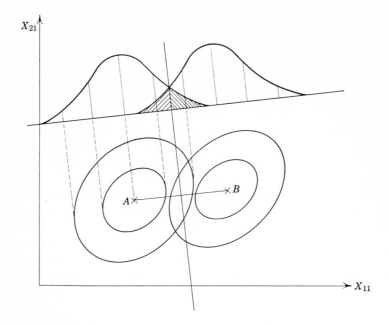

Fig. 8.4   *Projections of two groups on a proposed discriminant line.*

axis perpendicular to the boundary and, of course, parallel to the line connecting the centroids will be a discriminant line. The points in the test space may be projected upon it and the frequency distributions of the groups calculated. Figure 8.4 shows clearly that this choice of line is less satisfactory. The overlap of the groups is greater; $\alpha_{12} + \alpha_{21}$ is greater. By choosing this line we have reduced the two-dimensional test space regions to one-dimensional discriminant space regions but we have increased the number of errors of classification. We use these examples to introduce the discriminant criterion and the general method of choosing among all possible discriminant lines the one which is best for reproducing the ideal test space regions in a discriminant space of fewer dimensions.

The Discriminant Criterion

In Chapter 7 we showed that the projections of the N points $(X_{p.11},$ $X_{p.21}, \ldots, X_{p.T1})$ to the vector $X_{..12}$ are determined by

$$X_{..12} = X_{...1}\gamma_1 \qquad (8.1)$$
$$(N,1) \quad (N,T)(T,1)$$

where

$$\gamma_1 = \|\gamma_{i1}\| \qquad (\gamma_{i1} = \cos\theta_{i1}; \qquad i = 1, 2, \ldots, T)$$
$$(T,1)$$

is the transformation matrix. Here we again adopt the convention of subscripts which has been used throughout. We portray in subscripts individual p, group g, and test i in that order. We now need a fourth subscript, however, a subscript to denote the original axis system (1) and the axis system following rotation of the original axes (2).

In this chapter it will be essential to keep clear the four concepts denoted by subscripts. We shall therefore continue to use a dot (.) to replace a subscript not needing specific consideration at the time. The dot therefore maintains the order of subscripts and makes clear which values are to be considered general for a particular subscript and which are to be given specific treatment during that development. Finally, we introduce an additional convention of matrix notation, namely, specification of the order of the matrix beneath its symbol. Thus the notation $X_{\ldots 1}$ indicates
$$(N,T)$$
a matrix of values in the original (1) axis system. The matrix is of N rows and T columns. The group is not important in this particular illustration. It will be later.

We demonstrated in Chapter 7 that the relationship specified by Eq. 8.1 holds for the projections of means and deviations. Thus the matrix of the mean of the projections to the vector $X_{..12}$ is

$$\overline{X}_{..12} = \overline{X}_{...1}\gamma_1 \qquad\qquad (8.2)$$
$$(N,1) \quad\ (N,T)(T,1)$$

and the deviation vector of projections is

$$x_{..12} = x_{...1}\gamma_1 \qquad\qquad (8.3)$$
$$(N,1) \quad (N,T)(T,1)$$

We also demonstrated that the dispersion matrix of the projections is

$$D_{.2} = \gamma'_1 D_{.1}\gamma_1 \qquad\qquad (8.4)$$
$$(1,1) \quad (1,T)(T,T)(T,1)$$

Now suppose that the N projections to the vector $X_{..12}$ can be separated according to the group membership of individuals. Let there be G groups, with n_g of the projections belonging to the gth group ($g = 1, 2, \ldots, G$). We may apply the ordinary analysis of variance procedure to the coordinates of the points along this vector. In scalar notation, the sums of squared deviations of the coordinate of the projections are partitioned in the following way:

Source of Variation	Sum of Squares
Among groups	$\displaystyle\sum_{g=1}^{G} n_g(\overline{X}_{.g12} - \overline{X}_{..12})^2$
Within groups	$\displaystyle\sum_{g=1}^{G} \sum_{p=1}^{n_g} (X_{pg12} - \overline{X}_{.g12})^2$
Total	$\displaystyle\sum_{q=1}^{G} \sum_{p=1}^{n_g} (X_{pg12} - \overline{X}_{..12})^2$

In the reduction of dimensionality, the original axes are rotated to a position which maintains the information desired in terms of a smaller number of variates than was originally available. In discriminant analysis, the rotation is defined by finding the transformation γ_1 of the original scores which will provide for the projections to the rotated vector the largest value of the ratio of the among-groups sum of squares to the within-groups sum of squares. The ratio is the value of the two scalar quantities

$$\frac{\displaystyle\sum_{g=1}^{G} n_g(\overline{X}_{.g12} - \overline{X}_{..12})^2}{\displaystyle\sum_{g=1}^{G} \sum_{p=1}^{n_g} (X_{pg12} - \overline{X}_{.g12})^2} \tag{8.5}$$

In order to describe the needed rotation we must first express the ratio of these projections in terms both of their analogous values in the original axis system and of the transformation vector γ_1. We will now establish this association.

We form the (N,T) matrix of means for groups as these means hold for the original tests. We write n_1 rows of $\overline{X}_{.1.1}$ for the individuals in group 1, n_2 rows of $\overline{X}_{.2.1}$ for the individuals in group 2, and continue in this way until we write n_G rows of $\overline{X}_{.G.1}$ for the individuals in the last, or G, group. Of course, $n_1 + n_2 + \cdots + n_G = N$. We then form the (N,T) matrix of values $\overline{X}_{...1}$, that is, the (N,T) matrix of means for all individuals for each of the variables. If we then form the matrix of deviation scores $\bar{x}_{.g.1}$ of the group means by the operation $\overline{X}_{.g.1} - \overline{X}_{...1}$, we can compute

$$\underset{(N,T)}{} \qquad \underset{(N,T)}{}$$

the among-groups sum of squares for the original variates by

$$\underset{(T,N)(N,T)}{\bar{x}'_{.g.1}\bar{x}_{.g.1}} = \underset{(T,T)}{A}$$

It is true, from Eq. 8.4, that

$$\begin{array}{cc} \gamma'_1 A \gamma_1 \\ (1,T)(T,T)(T,1) \end{array} = \begin{array}{c} \bar{x}'_{.g.2}\bar{x}_{.g.2} \\ (1,1) \end{array} = \sum_{g=1}^{G} n_g(\bar{X}_{.g12} - \bar{X}_{..12})^2$$

Similarly, if we subtract the matrix $\bar{X}_{.g.1}$ from the (N,T) matrix X_{pgi1} of original scores, we can compute the cross-product matrix of within-group deviation scores $x_{.g.1}$ by

$$\begin{array}{cc} x'_{.g.1}x_{.g.1} & = & W \\ (T,N)(N,T) & & (T,T) \end{array}$$

This matrix is related to the within-group dispersion of projections to a new axis by the equation

$$\begin{array}{cc} \gamma'_1 W \gamma_1 \\ (1,T)(T,T)(T,1) \end{array} = \begin{array}{c} x'_{.g.2}x_{.g.2} \\ (1,1) \end{array} = \sum_{g=1}^{G} \sum_{p=1}^{n_g} (X_{pgi2} - \bar{X}_{.g12})^2$$

A similar relationship holds for the total dispersion T which is $x'_{...1}x_{...1}$. The three relationships can be summarized as follows:
$(T,N)(N,T)$

Source of Variation	Defined	In terms of $X_{11}, X_{21}, \ldots, X_{T1}$
Among groups	$\sum_{g=1}^{G} n_g(\bar{X}_{.g.2} - \bar{X}_{...2})^2$	$\gamma'_1 A \gamma_1$
Within groups	$\sum_{g=1}^{G} \sum_{p=1}^{n_g} (X_{pg.2} - \bar{X}_{.g.2})^2$	$\gamma'_1 W \gamma_1$
Total	$\sum_{g=1}^{G} \sum_{p=1}^{n_g} (X_{pg.2} - \bar{X}_{...2})^2$	$\gamma'_1 T \gamma_1$

Thus we note that the equations of the two scalar quantities indicated as 8.5 can be written as

$$\lambda_1 = \frac{\gamma'_1 A \gamma_1}{\gamma'_1 W \gamma_1}$$

This is the discriminant criterion.

It is customary to represent the discriminant criterion as

$$\lambda = \frac{v'Av}{v'Wv} \tag{8.6}$$

This equation is identical in meaning to the previous one. The vector **v** replaces the vector **γ** in our notation at this time merely because discriminant vectors prove to be uncorrelated but not necessarily orthogonal. We have employed the symbol Γ to denote a matrix which provides an orthogonal transformation of the original axes. We shall denote the matrix of uncorrelated, but not necessarily orthogonal, transformations as V. A vector of Γ is **γ**; a vector of V is **v**.

The Rao–Tukey–Bryan Multiple Discriminant Function

In Chapter 7 we showed how, in factor analysis, the equations necessary for specification of the vector with maximum dispersion can be derived by taking partial derivatives for each of the coefficients of the vector which is being specified. In discriminant analysis we determine the value of v_1 which will provide a maximum value of the discriminant criterion indicated in Eq. 8.6.

In order to find the v_1 associated with the maximum value of λ_1, we take the symbolic partial derivative for v_1 and get

$$\frac{\partial \lambda_1}{\partial v_1} = \frac{2[(v'_1 W v_1) A v_1 - (v'_1 A v_1) W v_1]}{(v'_1 W v_1)^2}$$

Set this equal to 0, remembering that zero stands for a column vector of as many zeros as there are variates T in our notation. We simplify to

$$(A - \lambda_1 W)v_1 = 0$$

Premultiplication by W^{-1} and replacement of $W^{-1}A$ by R finally gives

$$(R - \lambda_1 I)v_1 = 0 \tag{8.7}$$

where I is the unit matrix with which we are now familiar.

Equation 8.7 has the same form as Eq. 7.20. We stated for Eq. 7.20 that the set of homogeneous linear equations represented did not have a nonvanishing root unless the determinant of its coefficients is equal to zero. The same condition holds for Eq. 8.7. That is,

$$|R - \lambda_1 I| = 0 \tag{8.8}$$

is a necessary condition for the existence of any nonzero root in the set of Eqs. 8.7. In general Eq. 8.8 stands for a Tth degree equation in λ_1, T being the number of variates involved. This is known as the characteristic equation of the matrix R. The characteristic equation may have up to T roots which are nonzero. The largest of these roots is the value λ_1 which we seek.

We have so far indicated that the vector v_1 is defined by maximizing the ratio λ_1 in Eq. 8.6. Maximizing is accomplished by ascertaining the largest root of the characteristic equation indicated as Eq. 8.8. The discriminant function ratio λ which we are considering here is the G group extension of Fisher's (1936) two-group criterion of discriminant analysis. Actually, in the G group case, the ratio λ has several extrema, each of which is indicative of a distinct dimension of the subspace defined by the group means. All discriminant functions are obtained from the same initial ratio λ (Bryan, 1950, pp. 132–138).

The coefficients of the discriminant functions are determined by the latent vectors of R, and the corresponding latent roots of R equal the respective ratios of among-groups to within-groups sums of squares along the discriminant vectors. By considering the rank of the matrix A, Bryan (1950, pp. 138–139) showed that the number of solutions of Eq. 8.8 for which λ is not equal to 0 is at most equal to the smaller of the two integers, $G - 1$ and T. Consequently, letting r stand for the smaller of those two numbers, the total discriminative power of the variates is exhausted by r linear functions defined in this manner. Among these, all functions corresponding to distinct values of λ are uncorrelated as they stand. Repeated roots other than 0 are possible but unlikely to occur.

If one or more multiple roots should occur, however, the vectors corresponding to any one of them are already uncorrelated with the vectors corresponding to all different roots, and can be chosen in such a way as to be uncorrelated among themselves. The numerical values of these functions are independent of the origin of coordinates, the units of measurement, and, in fact, any nonsingular linear transformation of the variates (Bryan, pp. 138–139). Detailed directions for computation of multiple discriminant functions are available in Tiedeman et al. (1953, Chapters 2 and 4, and Appendix C).

The Bryan computational procedure used in Chapter 7 provides all the latent vectors (discriminant functions) corresponding to nonzero latent roots in the same operation. Consequently, instead of defining only the single vector v_1 that we have been discussing, the Bryan procedure defines the discriminant function transformation matrix

$$V = \|v_{iu}\|; \qquad (i = 1, 2, \ldots, T; \qquad u = 1, 2, \ldots, r)$$

This matrix is similar to the transformation Γ discussed in Chapter 7. However, transformation matrix V is different from the transformation matrix Γ in that the successive axes of the discriminant function transformation are not necessarily orthogonal, whereas the successive axes of the transformation Γ are always defined as orthogonal.

The coefficients of the matrix V are the coefficients of the multiple discriminant function. If only one root of the matrix R is significant, only one discriminant vector need be used in accounting for the stable variation of the data. If two of the latent roots of the matrix R are significant, the two discriminant functions corresponding to these latent roots span the plane necessary for description of the stable variation among the groups. The projections of the points in the original space to these vectors in the reduced space are uncorrelated but the vectors are not necessarily orthogonal. In general, the vectors of the matrix V span the space of dimensionality not greater than r which is necessary for description of the stable variation among the groups.

Rao gives an approximate test for dimensionality that can be applied quite readily once the latent roots $(\lambda_1, \lambda_2, \ldots, \lambda_r)$ of the matrix R are computed by the Bryan procedure. Rao (1952, pp. 372–373) indicates that when the dispersion matrix W is estimated on a large number of degrees of freedom, the total variation is approximately distributed as χ^2 with $T(G - 1)$ degrees of freedom. The total variation is apportioned to the various roots as follows:

Source of Variation	χ^2	ndf
v_1 corresponding to λ_1	$(N - G)\lambda_1$	$(T + G - 2)$
v_2 corresponding to λ_2	$(N - G)\lambda_2$	$(T + G - 4)$
$\vdots$	$\vdots$	$\vdots$
v_r corresponding to λ_r	$(N - G)\lambda_r$	$(T + G - 2r)$
Total	$(N - G)\sum_{n=1}^{r} \lambda_u$	$T(G - 1)$

Since these chi-squares and their degrees of freedom can be added in the usual manner, their sum to χ_n^2 provides a test of the dimensionality of the discriminant space. Only those discriminants are necessary which have a residual variation ascribable to the least roots of λ that may be attributable to chance at some previously specified level of significance.

Rao indicates further (p. 373) that the χ^2 approximation can be improved slightly by using

$$[N - \tfrac{1}{2}(T + G)] \ln (1 + \lambda)$$

instead of

$$\chi^2 = (N - G)\lambda$$

itself. N is the sum of the individuals in all groups. Thus an alternative test of dimensionality is provided by partitioning this approximation of χ^2 in this manner:

Source of Variation	χ^2 Approximation	*ndf*
v_1 corresponding to λ_1	$[N - \frac{1}{2}(T + G)] \ln (1 + \lambda_1)$	$(T + G - 2)$
v_2 corresponding to λ_2	$[N - \frac{1}{2}(T + G)] \ln (1 + \lambda_2)$	$(T + G - 4)$
$\vdots$	$\vdots \qquad \vdots$	$\vdots$
v_r corresponding to λ_r	$[N - \frac{1}{2}(T + G)] \ln (1 + \lambda_r)$	$(T + G - 2r)$
Total	$[N - \frac{1}{2}(T + G)] \sum_{u=1}^{r} \ln (1 + \lambda_u)$	$T(G - 1)$

Illustrations of both tests of dimensionality can be found in Rao (pp. 370–373) and Tiedeman and Bryan (1954).

Topology and Discriminant Analysis—An Example

Three illustrations of the Bryan procedure are available in Tiedeman et al. (1953). Consequently, we will not consider the details of computing multiple discriminant functions. We have, however, already used the procedure in Chapter 7. Here we shall go further and illustrate the general process of reducing the number of variates by means of discriminant analysis. We will also relate topology in the discriminant space to topology in the test space because the latter topology is the one we want to preserve in the reduced space. Therefore we consider the outdoor, convivial, and conservative activity preferences of passenger agents, mechanics, and operations control agents.

Partitioning the Total Dispersion Matrix

Essentially we have a 244 × 3 matrix X_{pgi1} defined as

$$X_{...1} = \|X_{pgi1}\|; \quad \begin{pmatrix} p = 1, 2, \ldots, n_g \\ g = 1, 2, 3 \\ i = 1, 2, 3 \end{pmatrix}$$

If we compute the mean of each variate without regard to group and form the matrix of 244 rows and 3 columns with the mean of each variate in each of the 3 columns, we have the new matrix

$$\bar{X}_{...1} = \|\bar{X}_{..i1}\|; \quad (i = 1, 2, 3)$$

We then define the deviation score matrix as

$$x_{...1} = X_{...1} - \bar{X}_{...1}$$

The total dispersion matrix T is the matrix product

$$T = x'_{...1}x_{...1}$$

In general, the total dispersion matrix is

$$\begin{array}{ccc} T & \equiv x'_{...1} & x_{...1} \; ; \\ (T,T) & (T,N) & (N,T) \end{array}$$

where N is the sum of the number of cases in each group.

For these data the matrix T is

$$T = \begin{Vmatrix} 5540.5742 & -421.4364 & 350.2556 \\ -421.4364 & 7295.5710 & -1170.5590 \\ 350.2556 & -1170.5590 & 3374.9232 \end{Vmatrix}$$

We next compute the mean of each variate for each group. This new matrix of means is

$$\bar{X}_{.g,1} \equiv \| \bar{X}_{.gi1} \| ; \qquad (g = 1, 2, 3; \quad i = 1, 2, 3)$$

where the row on which the mean of each group is written is dictated by the group subscript in the raw score matrix. We may then compute the within-group deviation scores as

$$x_{.g,1} = X_{.g,1} - \bar{X}_{.g,1}$$

The within-group dispersion matrix is the matrix product

$$W = x'_{.g,1}x_{.g,1}$$

In general, the within-group dispersion matrix is

$$\begin{array}{ccc} W & = x'_{.g,1} & x_{.g,1} \; ; \\ (T,T) & (T,N) & (N,T) \end{array}$$

For these data the within-group dispersion matrix is

$$W = \begin{Vmatrix} 3967.8301 & 351.6142 & 76.6342 \\ 351.6142 & 4406.2517 & 235.4365 \\ 76.6342 & 235.4365 & 2683.3164 \end{Vmatrix}$$

The third deviation score matrix is formed by the equation

$$\bar{x}_{...1} = \bar{X}_{.g,1} - \bar{X}_{...1}$$

This will be the 244 × 3 matrix of deviations of the group means from the grand mean. The among-group dispersion matrix is then computed from the matrix product

$$A = \bar{x}'_{...1}\bar{x}_{...1}$$

In general, the among-group dispersion matrix is

$$A \equiv \bar{x}'_{...1} \quad \bar{x}_{...1}$$
$$(T,T) \quad (T,N) \quad (N,T)$$

For these data the among-group dispersion matrix is

$$A = \begin{Vmatrix} 1572.7441 & -773.0506 & 273.6214 \\ -773.0506 & 2889.3193 & -1405.9955 \\ 273.6214 & -1405.9955 & 691.6068 \end{Vmatrix}$$

As a check it is useful to ascertain that

$$\mathsf{T} = W + A$$
$$(T,T) \quad (T,T) \quad (T,T)$$

Multiple Discriminant Function

For these data we wish to obtain the two roots $[G - 1 = 2$, which is less than $T = 3]$ of the matrix

$$R = W^{-1}A$$

and their corresponding discriminant functions v_1 and v_2 which satisfy Eq. 8.8. These roots are the relative maxima of the discriminant criterion given as Eq. 8.6. The modified Crout procedure described by Tiedeman et al. (1953, Appendix C) gives

$$\begin{Vmatrix} .396374 & -.194830 & .068960 \\ -.208549 & .676060 & -.326906 \\ .108967 & -.578917 & .285056 \end{Vmatrix}$$

as the matrix R. The characteristic equation of R is

$$\lambda^3 - 1.404626\lambda^2 + .350182\lambda + .000024 = 0$$

Since there are at most $G - 1$, or T, discriminants, whichever is smaller, and $G - 1$ or 2 is less than $T = 3$ in this instance, the last term of this equation is actually 0 within the number of significant digits carried. Therefore the third root λ_3 is taken to be 0 and the characteristic equation is rewritten as

$$\lambda^2 - 1.404626\lambda^2 + .350182 = 0$$

The roots of this equation are

$$\lambda_1 = 1.080548$$
$$\lambda_2 = .324078$$

Consequently the matrix of unconventionalized vectors satisfying Eq. 8.8 is

$$V(\text{unconventionalized}) = \begin{Vmatrix} .099824 & -.212791 \\ -.207675 & -.045605 \\ .164809 & .082378 \end{Vmatrix}$$

If each element of a column is divided by the largest element of the column, we have the *conventionalized* matrix V of discriminant coefficients. This matrix is

$$V(\text{conventionalized}) = \begin{Vmatrix} -.480674 & 1.000000 \\ 1.000000 & .214318 \\ -.793591 & -.387131 \end{Vmatrix}$$

Discriminant coefficients are ordinarily reported in this conventionalized form. The matrix V is a matrix defining the rotation of two axes in the original test space. Rotation of the third axis is ignored because all of the information about group separation pertinent to the ratio λ is contained in the two rotations specified by V.

If each of the elements in the columns of unconventionalized V is divided by the square root of the sum of the squares of the elements, we convert the rotation matrix stated to normalized form. For these data the normalized transformation matrix is

$$V(\text{normalized}) = \begin{Vmatrix} .352368 & .914472 \\ -.733071 & .195988 \\ .581759 & -.354020 \end{Vmatrix}$$

In this form the transformation matrix of discriminant coefficients is analogous to the matrix Γ that we discussed in Chapter 7 except that v_1 and v_2 are not necessarily orthogonal. Consequently, each element in V (normalized) is the cosine of the angle between the discriminant vector and the original test axis. For instance, .352368 is the cosine of the angle between test axis 1 and discriminant vector 1; $-.733071$ is the cosine of the angle between the second test axis and the first discriminant vector; and .581759 is the cosine of the angle between the third test axis and the first discriminant vector.

The matrix product V' (normalized) V (normalized) proves to be

$$\begin{Vmatrix} 1.000000 & -.027397 \\ -.027397 & 1.000000 \end{Vmatrix}$$

Since this is not a unit or identity matrix, the discriminant transformation is not orthogonal in this instance.

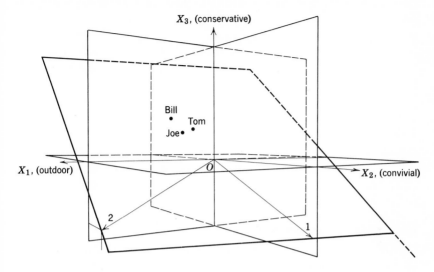

Fig. 8.5 *Normalized discriminant vectors for three-group case.*

Discriminants in Test Space

From the discriminant matrix V (normalized) it is possible to plot the two normalized discriminant vectors v_1 and v_2. This is done in Fig. 8.5.

Unless coincidental, any two vectors will span a plane. The plane spanned by the discriminant vectors v_1 and v_2 is the thin sheet whose extremities are outlined in bold relief in Fig. 8.5. Points representing the test scores of all individuals considered will project to this plane. The coordinates of such projections are the two discriminant scores of each person. The projections of the points for Joe, Tom, and Bill are depicted in the discriminant plane in the figure.

Significance of Discriminants

The application of Rao's (1952) first approximation to a test of dimensionality gives the following values for these data:

Discriminant	Approximate χ^2	*ndf*	*P*
v_1	260.412	4	< .001
v_2	78.103	2	< .001
Total	338.515	6	< .001

Data for Rao's second approximation to a test of dimensionality are

Discriminant	Approximate χ^2	*ndf*	*P*
v_1	176.564	4	$<.001$
v_2	67.654	2	$<.001$
Total	244.217	6	$<.001$

Both of these tests indicate that dispersion along both discriminant vectors is significant. Consequently, significant information about group separation with regard to the ratio λ would be ignored if either discriminant vector were to be ignored. Discriminant vector 2 is needed in this problem.

Topology in Discriminant Space

Since it is necessary to consider both discriminant vectors, let us see what happens when we project all points in the test space to the discriminant plane outlined in bold relief in Fig. 8.5. We will depict this discriminant plane as we have in previous chapters. In order to do this it is necessary to determine the two discriminant coordinates of each point in the test space of Fig. 8.5. We do this by Eq. 8.1 in this way:

$$X_{pgi2} = X_{pgi1} V \text{ (conventionalized)}$$
$$(N,2) \quad (N,T)(T,2)$$

For this transformation we arbitrarily choose the transformation matrix of conventionalized discriminant coefficients. The points representing the results of this transformation are indicated in Fig. 8.6.

Figure 8.6 indicates that the ×, •, and ○ points overlap to a considerable extent but that each type of point tends to be concentrated in a distinguishable region of the discriminant plane.

If we are to reach decisions about the later job classification of these apprentices from a knowledge of the discriminant transformation of their activity preferences, we apply the logic of topology described in Chapter 6 to the discriminant space. However, in this instance, we forgo consideration of the problem from the standpoint of the observed frequencies in each class of discriminant scores and move directly to the bivariate normal assumption for each group, as we have found we generally have to do. Actually, the bivariate normal assumption is more likely to hold for discriminant scores than it is for the test scores themselves because of the Central Limit Theorem. This theorem indicates that the sums of scores originally distributed in any fashion tend toward the normal distribution

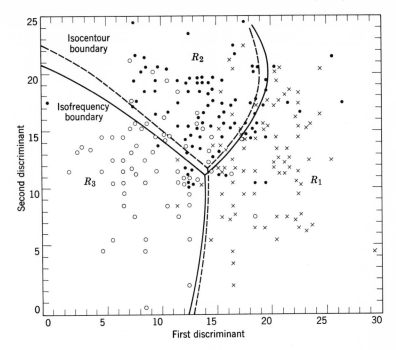

Fig. 8.6 *Three groups in the discriminant space.*

as the number of variates included in the sum increases. Since we know that the trivariate distribution in test space was reasonably normal, we know that the bivariate distribution in discriminant space must also be reasonably normal because the discriminants are nothing but linear combinations of the original test scores.

We now develop the topology for the discriminant space. As indicated in Chapter 6, the topology requires computation of the boundaries B_{12}, B_{13}, and B_{23}. However, it is first necessary to compute the dispersion matrix of the discriminant scores for each group. We do this by adapting Eq. 8.4 which for two vectors is

$$
\begin{array}{cccc}
D_{.2} = & V' & D_{.1} & V \\
(2,2) & (2,T) & (T,T) & (T,2)
\end{array}
$$

We also must find the centroid in the discriminant space which is computed by the more general statement of Eq. 8.2 as

$$
\begin{array}{ccc}
\bar{X}_{.g.2} = & \bar{X}_{.g.1} V \\
(N,r) & (N,T)(T,r)
\end{array}
$$

For these data the discriminant space dispersion matrix and centroid for group 1 is

$$D_{1.2} = \begin{Vmatrix} 19.4417 & 1.5391 \\ 1.5391 & 26.0158 \end{Vmatrix}$$

$$\bar{X}_{.1.2} = \begin{Vmatrix} 11.0117 & 14.2865 \end{Vmatrix}$$

For group 2

$$D_{2.2} = \begin{Vmatrix} 33.4418 & -1.4971 \\ -1.4971 & 12.5605 \end{Vmatrix}$$

$$\bar{X}_{.2.2} = \begin{Vmatrix} 4.1825 & 19.1429 \end{Vmatrix}$$

For group 3

$$D_{3.2} = \begin{Vmatrix} 25.3837 & .1159 \\ .1159 & 19.7503 \end{Vmatrix}$$

$$\bar{X}_{.3.2} = \begin{Vmatrix} -2.5414 & 13.7614 \end{Vmatrix}$$

The boundaries are then determined by Eq. 6.18. For these data, the boundary equations are

$$B_{12} \cap X_{..12} = (.2469X_{..22} + 22.9954)$$
$$\pm [1.2883X_{..22}{}^2 - 50.2845X_{..22} + 544.3396]^{\frac{1}{2}}$$

$$B_{13} \cap X_{..12} = (.1875X_{..22} + 49.6938)$$
$$\pm [.6800X_{..22}{}^2 - 3.0330X_{..22} + 1308.4652]^{\frac{1}{2}}$$

$$B_{23} \cap X_{..12} = (.3229X_{..22} - 11.1458)$$
$$\pm [2.0765X_{..22}{}^2 - 119.9550X_{..22} + 1644.3306]^{\frac{1}{2}}$$

The topology defined by these boundaries is indicated in Fig. 8.6.

It is worth looking at Figs. 8.5 and 8.6 together. Figure 8.6 is actually a plane from Fig. 8.5 where the original test space is indicated. Consequently, in terms of the original test space the boundaries indicated in Fig. 8.6 are actually solid figures cutting through the entire test space perpendicular to the discriminant plane in Fig. 8.5.

From Fig. 8.6 it is possible to count the number of points of each type of specialist that is misclassified by this topology. The counts are

Actual \\ Classified as	Passenger Agent	Mechanic	Operations Personnel	Number Misclassified
Passenger Agent	71	11	3	14
Mechanic	16	69	8	24
Operations Personnel	4	17	45	21
Total				59

The discriminant space topology results in the semiempirical, semi-theoretical estimate of 59 misclassifications. This number can be contrasted with the estimated number of misclassifications using the test space topology for the three variates. That number was 59.5. Actually, the improvement in accuracy in the discriminant space topology is not guaranteed. It is more likely a chance result of these data. If the original dispersion matrices of all the groups are reasonably similar, the number of misclassifications from the discriminant space topology should closely approximate the number of misclassifications from the test space topology.

Centour Scores in Discriminant Space

Quotas for jobs in a company fluctuate from time to time. Consequently, personnel officers often cannot use a topology based on isofrequency boundaries such as that shown in Fig. 8.6. That topology results in a minimum number of misclassifications only when agents, mechanics, and operations men are in the ratio 85:93:66. However, personnel officers must be familiar with the general logic of topology. They can then develop a topology clinically as quotas vary.

We noted in the last section of Chapter 6 that a topology could be defined in terms of centour scores or in terms of chi-squares. In order to avoid computation of a new topology every time job quotas are changed, a table of centour scores can be provided for personnel advisers. With proper understanding of principles of topology and with centour scores available, advisers can do a reasonable job of approaching the statistically desirable topology clinically.

We developed the concept of the centour score for the test space in Chapters 2–5. The concept of centour score is just as useful when we know the two-discriminant equivalents of the outdoor, convivial, and conservative activity preferences of an individual. However, with centours in discriminant space it is first necessary to make the discriminant conversion of the raw scores according to the general version of Eq. 8.1. Once these conversions are made, it is possible to indicate the discriminant scores in Cartesian space as in Fig. 8.6. Since we know that there is greater likelihood that discriminant scores are distributed in a multivariate normal manner than that test scores are distributed normally, the normality assumption made in centour scores is more likely to be appropriate in the case of discriminant scores than in the case of test scores.

If we make the normality assumption for the bivariate discriminant scores of the individuals in each job, and use the discriminant scores as our arguments, we can construct a table of centour scores based on discriminant scores rather than original test scores. The tables of centour scores will look like other tables of centour scores already illustrated in

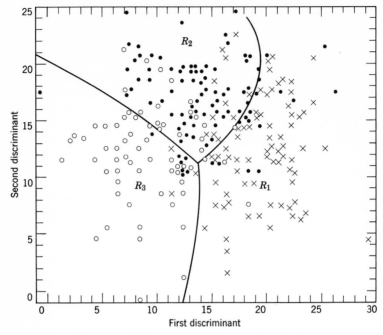

Fig. 8.7 *Isofrequency and isocentour boundaries.*

Chapters 2–4. The only difference in this instance is that the argument for entry will be discriminant, not original, scores.

How is the concept of topology related to the centour scores in the discriminant space? As can be seen in Fig. 8.7, the equicentour topology is not very different from the isofrequency topology *when the ratios in the three groups approximate the ratio 85:93:66*. The isocentour boundaries (dashed lines) in Fig. 8.7 are reasonably close to the isofrequency boundaries (solid lines) of that figure. The isocentour topology in the figure results in the following semiempirical, semitheoretical numbers of misclassifications:

Actual \ Classified as	Passenger Agent	Mechanic	Operations Personnel	Number Misclassified
Passenger Agent	72	10	3	13
Mechanic	19	64	10	29
Operations Personnel	4	14	48	18
Total				60

More mechanics are misclassified by the isocentour boundaries than by the isofrequency boundaries, but fewer agents and operations men are misclassified by the isocentour boundaries. The net effect is to increase the total number of misclassifications from 59 to 60. This is true, however, only when the numbers of apprentices in each job are of the same general magnitude. When the numbers in the groups are not approximately the same, the isocentour frame of reference will generally over-supply jobs requiring a small number of men and under-supply jobs needing a large number of men.

In this chapter we have presented the case for the discriminant function as a means of reducing the dimensionality of the test space without loss to the power of the topology in the test space. There is no loss of power in the discriminant space when the group dispersion matrices are identical in the test space (Tatsuoka, 1953). In this event, a point in the discriminant space will be in the same region of the topology as it was in the test space. When the group dispersion matrices are different from group to group in the test space, the discriminant topology only approximates the topology of the test space. The approximation in the discriminant space approaches that in the test space as the group dispersion matrices become more nearly equal.

Although the topology in the discriminant space will be the same as it is in the test space when the within-group dispersion matrices are equal for all the groups, the centour score of an individual is not necessarily the same in the discriminant space as it was in the test space. This is particularly true when the number of stable discriminant functions r is less than the number of tests T. For instance, a point that has a very low centour score in the test space of Fig. 8.5 may project to the discriminant plane of that figure through the centroid of one of the jobs. In this instance, the centour score associated with the discriminant score coordinates of that point would be 100. This means that the direction in which the point differs from the centroid is perpendicular to the discriminant plane, a dimension that is immaterial for separating the groups, but which could be of importance for some other purpose.

The issue of difference of centour score in test space and discriminant space is not important for a topology provided the points stay in the same job region in the discriminant space as they were in the test space. However, the difference of the centours in the two spaces could be of importance if the question at issue is different from the question of classification. The question of classification leads to the concept of topology. Other uses of test scores may not.

Chapter 9

Regression Analysis

The prediction of a single criterion from a linear combination of T predictor variates is a familiar procedure in selection and classification practice. The linear combination of the predictors is a regression equation obtained by minimizing the sum of squared differences between the

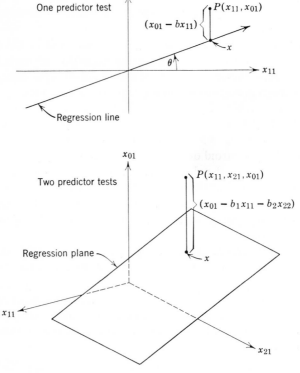

Fig. 9.1 *Deviations from regression equations—$(x_{01} - \hat{x}_{01})$ = error of estimate.*

observed criterion scores and the estimated criterion scores computed by the linear combination.

The regression equation describes a choice of axis rotation in the predictor test space that results in the reduction of the predictor test space to a one-dimensional space. For instance, in the familiar single-predictor case, the regression of the criterion variable (x_{01}) on the predictor variable (x_{11}) is illustrated in Fig. 9.1 by the line x_{11} rotated through the angle θ, so that the sum of the squared differences $\sum(x_{01} - bx_{11})^2$ is a minimum. In the two-predictor deviation score space the x_{11}, x_{21} plane is rotated so that the sum of squared differences $\sum(x_{01} - b_1x_{11} - b_2x_{21})^2$ is a minimum.

The Regression Equation

Given a matrix of predictor scores $X_{...1}$ defined as

$$X_{...1} \equiv \|X_{p.i1}\|; \quad (p = 1, 2, \ldots, N; \quad i = 1, 2, \ldots, T)$$

we want to find the column vector of estimated criterion scores $\hat{X}_{..0}$ defined as

$$\hat{X}_{..0} \equiv \|\hat{X}_{p.0}\|; \quad (p = 1, 2, \ldots, N)$$

We wish to determine the matrix of coefficients b_i

$$B = \begin{Vmatrix} b_1 \\ b_2 \\ \vdots \\ b_T \end{Vmatrix}$$

which may be used to obtain $\hat{X}_{p.0}$ so that the sum of squared differences $\sum(X_{p.01} - \hat{X}_{p.0})^2$ is a minimum.

We first translate the origin of our predictor-criterion space from the point with the $T + 1$ coordinates $(0, 0, \ldots, 0)$ to the point with coordinates $(\bar{X}_{..11}, \bar{X}_{..21}, \ldots, \bar{X}_{..T1}, \bar{X}_{..01})$. This corresponds to treating the deviation scores

$$\begin{array}{cccc} x_{..i1} &=& X_{..i1} &-& \bar{X}_{..i1} \\ (N,T) && (N,T) && (N,T) \end{array} \quad \text{(predictor variables)}$$

$$\begin{array}{cccc} x_{..01} &=& X_{..01} &-& \bar{X}_{..01} \\ (N,1) && (N,1) && (N,1) \end{array} \quad \text{(criterion variable)}$$

The estimated criterion score as a deviation from $\bar{X}_{..01}$ is $\hat{x}_{..0} = b_1x_{..11} + b_2x_{..21} + \cdots + b_Tx_{..T1}$. In matrix notation the column of N estimated deviation scores is

$$\begin{array}{ccc} \hat{x}_{..0} &=& x_{...1}B \\ (N,1) && (N,T)(T,1) \end{array}$$

The vector B is derived by minimizing the sum of the squares of the differences $(x_{..01} - \hat{x}_{..0})$ which are the deviations of the estimated criterion scores from the observed criterion scores of the N individuals in the sample. The individual values form an $N \times 1$ matrix. The sum of squares of the differences is obtained by multiplying the transpose of the matrix by the matrix itself. Thus we define the quantity Q as

$$Q = (x_{..01} - \hat{x}_{..0})'(x_{..01} - \hat{x}_{..0})$$

Since the transpose of the difference between two matrices is the difference between the transposes, we may write Q as

$$Q = (x'_{..01} - \hat{x}'_{..0})(x_{..01} - \hat{x}_{..0})$$

This matrix product may then be expanded to

$$Q \;=\; \underset{(1,1)}{x'_{..01}x_{..01}} \;-\; \underset{(1,N)(N,1)}{x'_{..01}\hat{x}_{..0}} \;-\; \underset{(1,N)(N,1)}{\hat{x}'_{..0}x_{..01}} \;+\; \underset{(1,N)(N,1)}{\hat{x}'_{..0}\hat{x}_{..0}}$$

Each one of the four matrix products is a scalar and the second and third terms are equal:

$$Q \;=\; \underset{(1,1)}{x'_{..01}x_{..01}} \;-\; \underset{(1,N)(N,1)}{2\hat{x}'_{..0}x_{..01}} \;+\; \underset{(1,N)(N,1)}{\hat{x}'_{..0}\hat{x}_{..0}}$$

By substitution of $x_{...1}B$ for $\hat{x}_{..0}$ we obtain

$$Q \;=\; \underset{(1,1)}{x'_{..01}x_{..01}} \;-\; \underset{(1,T)(T,N)(N,1)}{2B'x'_{...1}x_{..01}} \;+\; \underset{(1,T)(T,N)(N,T)(T,1)}{B'x'_{...1}x_{...1}B}$$

This expression is minimized by differentiating with respect to b_1, b_2, and so on to b_T. We indicate the T partial derivatives that result by the symbolic matrix differentiation

$$\frac{\partial Q}{\partial B'} = -2x'_{...1}x_{..01} + 2x'_{...1}x_{...1}B$$

When these expressions are equated to the null vector (a column vector of T zeros), we obtain

$$x'_{...1}x_{...1}B = x'_{...1}x_{..01}$$

When multiplied by the scalar $1/N$, the equation becomes

$$\underset{(T,T)(T,1)}{D_{1...}B} \;=\; \underset{(T,1)}{C_{..0i}}$$

where D is the dispersion matrix of the T predictor variables, B is a column of regression coefficients, and $C_{..0i}$ is the column vector of the T values of the covariance of each variate i and the criterion 0.

If we premultiply both sides of the equation by the inverse of the dispersion matrix, we obtain the matrix equation for the vector B

$$B = D_{\ldots 1}^{-1} C_{..0i} \tag{9.1}$$

This equation is the familiar solution for regression coefficients expressed in matrix notation. Psychologists have usually computed the coefficients in B by the Doolittle method. The matrix B may also be computed by Bryan's modified Crout procedure described by Tiedeman et al. (1953, pp. 268–276). The initial matrix is

$$M = \begin{Vmatrix} D_{\ldots 1} & C_{..0i} \\ \hline I & 0 \end{Vmatrix}$$

where I is a $T \times T$ identity matrix and 0 is a $T \times 1$ matrix of zeros. The desired matrix B will emerge in the lower right-hand panel of the modified auxiliary matrix.

Classification by Regression Equations

The aptitude index used by personnel advisers is an estimate of an individual's future success in the aptitude area. The index for a job is determined by administering tests to a sample of apprentices at induction, determining a criterion score for each apprentice at a later time, sorting together all persons of this sample whose criterion score belongs in a particular job, and determining the regression of the criterion score for the job on the test scores of the apprentices. An equation is thus derived for each of several jobs. Thereafter the several indices may be computed for any newly inducted apprentice as soon as his scores on the battery of tests are available.

Two assumptions underlie the use of such a job index. The first is that the experience on which the job index is based holds for the current group of inductees. The second and more dubious assumption is that any one and all of the regression equations may be validly used for any and all apprentices. The assumption that the job indexes are unbiased estimates in every job for every apprentice has not received the serious attention it deserves.

Dunn (1955) reports the regression of sophomore grade average on antecedent data of college students concentrating in one of 13 fields of instruction offered at Brown University. Her regression equations were obtained by the Wherry–Doolittle method. The equation for predicting the grade average of chemistry majors gives zero weight to mathematics ability and the equation for history majors gives zero weight to verbal ability. It seems clear that the students who became chemistry majors have recognized the importance of mathematics in their selection of chemistry as a field of concentration. The samples available for the calculation of regression weights are homogeneous at a high level of mathematics ability. As a consequence, mathematics aptitude is not importantly related to grade average for those who chose chemistry as their major. However, if students at Brown University chose to concentrate in chemistry in some random manner, without receiving advice and without self-selection incorporating antecedent knowledge of interests and abilities, the regression equations would surely have a different character.

On the other hand, history majors at Brown University are a homogeneous group at a relatively high level of verbal aptitude. Distinctions within the homogeneous distribution of verbal scores do not forecast differences in grade average. However, the heterogeneity in mathematics within the history group is sufficient to make the mathematics score useful in predicting grade average in history. It seems clear that the members of these two groups are essentially different before their selection of a major. The groups may occupy different regions of test space.

The possibility of examining the distinguishing characteristics before the use of a regression equation has received little attention in the literature of psychology. The emphasis has been upon correlation studies and criterion score estimation. Perhaps too little attention has been given to the effects of choice and assignment on the centroids and dispersion which characterize the jobs. As a result, very little is known about the regions of the test space from which satisfactory and satisfied apprentices are drawn.

In selection and placement problems regression equations are used to predict the success a man may be expected to achieve if he were to enter a particular job. When several jobs are compared, the estimates of success in these jobs may not be expressed on a common scale. In order to permit comparison of a success estimate in one job with a success estimate in another job, the estimates may be standardized. The customary procedure is to standardize the criterion scores for the men in each specialty independently. Such standardization permits a comparison of relative success in one job with relative success in another job, each measure of success being a deviation above or below the mean of the actual job group. The many different criterion scores are thus reduced to a single numerical scale. The data for each specialty may now be treated as if they were in the same $(T + 1)$ space. We may examine this test space in search of boundaries which separate the groups into regions.

It is customary to estimate relative success in each of the jobs that are to be considered for a man, and to place or guide him in terms of these estimates. The natural tendency of personnel advisers is to ignore estimates that are low and to pay attention to estimates that are relatively high. It is usually thought desirable to guide or allocate individuals into the job in which the estimate of relative success is greatest. If this procedure is followed consistently the resulting classification system is

$$R_g \cap \hat{z}_{.g0} \geq \hat{z}_{.h0}; \quad \begin{aligned} &(g = 1, 2, \ldots, G) \\ &(h = 1, 2, \ldots, g - 1, g + 1, \ldots, G) \end{aligned} \quad (9.2)$$

where $\hat{z}_{.g0}$ is the predicted standardized criterion score in the gth job group. This definition of R_g is, of course, different from R_g as defined in Chapter 6. In Chapter 6, R_g was defined as the sector of the test space in which the frequencies in the gth group exceeded the frequencies in any other group. Here we define R_g as the sector in the test space in which the predicted standard score in group g exceeds the predicted standard score in any other group. We now examine the regions that develop from this definition in the case of regression on a single predictor test.

Classification Regions Derived from Regression Analysis

One Variate

The regression equation in the one-variate case is

$$\hat{Y} = \bar{Y} + \left(\frac{\sigma_y}{\sigma_x}\right) r_{xy}(X - \bar{X})$$

where Y is the criterion score and X is the predictor score. In our notation this equation is

$$\hat{X}_{pg0} = \bar{X}_{.g01} + \frac{\sigma_{x.g01}}{\sigma_{x.g11}} r_{x.g11, x.g01}(X_{pg11} - \bar{X}_{.g11})$$

We will have such a regression equation for each of the G groups.

When the criterion scores are standardized, the mean of the criterion scores in any specialty is arbitrarily set at zero, and the standard deviation of the criterion scores in any specialty is arbitrarily defined as 1. With these modifications the equation becomes

$$\hat{z}_{pg0} = \frac{r_{x.g11z.g01}}{\sigma_{x.g11}} (X_{pg11} - \bar{X}_{.g11})$$

An equation of this nature can be computed for group g and group h. When this is done, the inequality defined by Eq. 9.2 will become

$$R_g \cap \left(\frac{r_g}{\sigma_g} - \frac{r_h}{\sigma_h}\right) X - \left(\frac{r_g \bar{X}_g}{\sigma_g} - \frac{r_h \bar{X}_h}{\sigma_h}\right) \geq 0$$

$$\begin{aligned} &(g = 1, 2, \ldots, G) \\ &(h = 1, 2, \ldots, g - 1, g + 1, \ldots, G) \quad (9.3) \end{aligned}$$

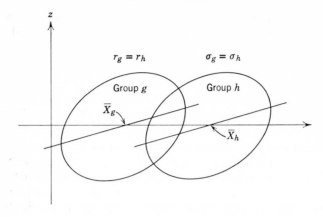

Fig. 9.2 *Case I. The conditions $r_g = r_h$ and $\sigma_g = \sigma_h$ indicate that the regression line in group g is parallel to the regression in group h. For every value of X the estimated criterion score z_g will be higher on the z scale than will the estimated criterion score z_h.*

where for convenience we have adopted a simplified system of subscripts. In this system r_g stands for the correlation between standardized criterion scores and the predictor scores X in group g, σ_g stands for the standard deviation of the predictor scores in group g, and $\bar{X}_g$ stands for the mean of the predictor scores in group g.

Case I. $r_g = r_h > 0;$ $\sigma_g = \sigma_h$
Under these conditions, the inequalities (9.3) reduce to

$$R_g \cap (\bar{X}_g - \bar{X}_h) \leq 0 \tag{9.4}$$

Any one of these inequalities *always holds* if $\bar{X}_g < \bar{X}_h$ and *never holds* if $\bar{X}_g > \bar{X}_h$. Therefore in Case I all individuals will be classified as members of the group with the smaller predictor mean. If there is no difference between the means, the classification will be by chance alone.

Case I, in which group g has a lower mean score on the predictor variable than group h, is illustrated in Fig. 9.2. All members of group h will be misclassified.

Case II. $r_g = r_h > 0;$ $\sigma_g < \sigma_h$
The inequalities (9.3) now reduce to

$$\left(\frac{1}{\sigma_g} - \frac{1}{\sigma_h}\right)X - \left(\frac{\bar{X}_g}{\sigma_g} - \frac{\bar{X}_h}{\sigma_h}\right) \geq 0$$

which may be rewritten as

$$(\sigma_h - \sigma_g)X \geq \sigma_h \bar{X}_g - \sigma_g \bar{X}_h \tag{9.5}$$

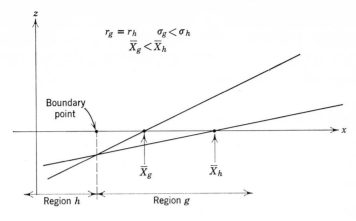

Fig. 9.3   *Case IIA.*

Case IIA. $\overline{X}_g < \overline{X}_h$

Under this condition,

$$\overline{X}_h = \overline{X}_g + k, \qquad k > 0$$

so that (9.5) becomes

$$(\sigma_h - \sigma_g)X \geq (\sigma_h - \sigma_g)\overline{X}_g - \sigma_g k$$

Therefore, R_g is

$$R_g \cap X \geq \overline{X}_g - \frac{\sigma_g k}{\sigma_h - \sigma_g}$$

The regions are indicated in Fig. 9.3.

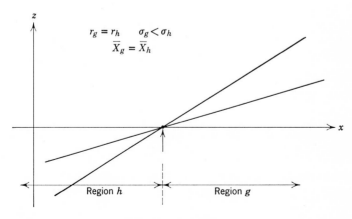

Fig. 9.4   *Case IIB.*

Case IIB. $\overline{X}_g = \overline{X}_h = \overline{X}$

Under this condition, R_g becomes

$$R_g \cap X \geq \overline{X}$$

Figure 9.4 illustrates the condition.

Case IIC. $\overline{X}_g > \overline{X}_h$

Under this condition, we write

$$\overline{X}_g = \overline{X}_h + k, \qquad k > 0$$

and as a consequence (9.5) becomes

$$(\sigma_h - \sigma_g)X \geq (\sigma_h - \sigma_g)\overline{X}_h + \sigma_h k$$

and the regions (Fig. 9.5) are

$$R_g \cap X \geq \overline{X}_h + \frac{\sigma_h k}{(\sigma_h - \sigma_g)}$$

Case III. $r_g < r_h; \qquad \sigma_g = \sigma_h$

In this case (9.3) becomes

$$R_g \cap (r_g - r_h)X \geq r_g\overline{X}_g - r_h\overline{X}_h \tag{9.6}$$

Case IIIA. $\overline{X}_g < \overline{X}_h$

Under this condition we may write

$$\overline{X}_h = \overline{X}_g + k, \qquad k > 0$$

so that (9.6) becomes

$$(r_g - r_h)X \geq [r_g\overline{X}_g - r_h(\overline{X}_g + k)]$$

which may be rewritten as

$$(r_g - r_h)X \geq (r_g - r_h)\overline{X}_g - kr_h$$

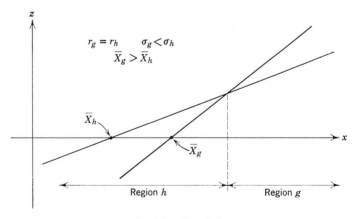

Fig. 9.5 *Case IIC.*

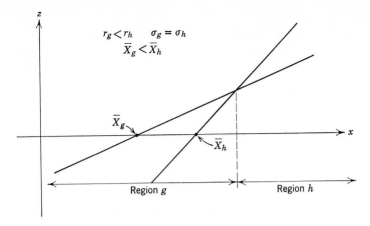

Fig. 9.6   *Case IIIA.*

from which we obtain the boundary in Fig. 9.6:

$$R_g \cap X \le \overline{X}_g + \frac{kr_h}{r_h - r_g}$$

Case IIIB. $\overline{X}_g = \overline{X}_h = \overline{X}$

Under this condition (9.6) becomes

$$(r_g - r_h)X \ge (r_g - r_h)\overline{X}$$

from which we obtain R_g (Fig. 9.7):

$$R_g \cap X \le \overline{X}$$

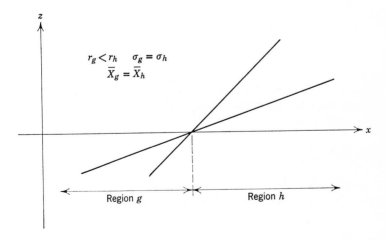

Fig. 9.7   *Case IIIB.*

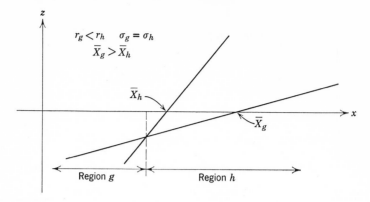

Fig. 9.8 *Case IIIC.*

Case IIIC. $\overline{X}_g > \overline{X}_h$

This condition may be rewritten as

$$\overline{X}_g = \overline{X}_h + k, \qquad k > 0$$

so that (9.6) becomes

$$(r_g - r_h)X \ge r_g(\overline{X}_h + k) - r_h\overline{X}_h$$

The region R_g is (Fig. 9.8)

$$R_g \cap X \ge \overline{X}_h - \frac{r_g k}{r_h - r_g}$$

Case IV. $r_g < r_h; \qquad \sigma_g < \sigma_h$

In general, the regression of the standardized criterion score on the predictor variate is (for group g and group h)

$$b_{zx_g} = \frac{r_g}{\sigma_g}$$

$$b_{zx_h} = \frac{r_h}{\sigma_h}$$

Consequently, Case IV does not specify which, if any, of the two group regression lines has the largest slope. Therefore, Case IV has to be subdivided further into

Case IVA. $\dfrac{r_g}{\sigma_g} = \dfrac{r_h}{\sigma_h}$

Case IVB. $\dfrac{r_g}{\sigma_g} > \dfrac{r_h}{\sigma_h}$

and

Case IVC. $\dfrac{r_g}{\sigma_g} < \dfrac{r_h}{\sigma_h}$

All the essential possibilities in Case IV have been exhausted in the previous cases. Case IVA is essentially the same as Case I; Case IVB corresponds to Case II; and Case IVC corresponds to Case III.

Case V. $r_g < r_h;$ $\quad\sigma_g > \sigma_h$
These conditions imply that

$$\frac{r_g}{\sigma_g} < \frac{r_h}{\sigma_h}$$

which has been explored in Case III. We have now exhausted all the possible combinations of means, standard deviations, and correlation coefficients of the one-predictor case.

A common feature of all of the foregoing examples is that the centroids of the predictor variables for the two groups both lie in the same classificatory region, or on the boundary point if the means are equal. Therefore we conclude that in all instances one or the other of the two centroids is misclassified. Consequently, since we expect a fairly high concentration of cases in the vicinity of the mean, a fairly large number of cases of one group are erroneously misclassified as members of the other. This conclusion holds regardless of the combinations of the several entering statistics. In Cases IIA and IIIC the specialty requiring a lesser ability in the talent X receives most of the talented candidates, whereas the specialty requiring a greater talent receives the less able. In Cases IIC and IIIA only highly qualified men are assigned to the group requiring the higher talent, whereas the group requiring less talent receives a large number of men from the higher talented brackets who would do at least an average job in this more demanding occupation.

Two Variates

In our notation the standard criterion score predicted from the multiple regression equation in two predictor variables is

$$\hat{z}_{pg0} = \beta_{g1}\left(\frac{X_{pg11} - \overline{X}_{.g11}}{\sigma_{g1}}\right) + \beta_{g2}\left(\frac{X_{pg21} - \overline{X}_{.g21}}{\sigma_{g2}}\right)$$

There are too many combinations of the β's, means, and standard deviations in this equation to record a complete exploration of the classificatory regions similar to the preceding one-variate exposition. There *are* combinations of statistics for which the centroids of two compared groups lie in different classificatory regions and other combinations for which the centroids of the two groups lie in a single classificatory region. The centroids lie in the *same* region in the following cases:

1. When the coefficients in two groups for one variate are of like sign, and the two coefficients of the other variate are proportional to the

standard deviations of that variate in their respective groups. In this instance the magnitude relations among the group means are immaterial.

2. When the raw score regression coefficients of the two groups are in approximately the same ratio for both variates. In this instance the two centroids lie in the same region for most values of the ratio of the difference between the two group means on the two variates.

3. When the β coefficients of one variate in both groups are of like sign, and the β coefficients of the second variate in both groups are also of like sign. In this instance the centroids lie in the same region when the group with the larger mean on one variate also has the larger mean on the other variate.

4. When the β coefficients of one variate for the two groups are of unlike sign, and the β coefficients of the other variate are of like sign. In this instance the centroids lie in the same region when the difference between the means on the variate which has the β's of unlike signs is much smaller, in absolute value, than the difference between the means on the variate which has β's of like sign in the two groups.

Although we cannot make as precise a statement in the two-predictor case as we can in the one-predictor instance, it is apparent that there is ample scope for situations in which a multiple regression method of classification will lead to little separation of group centroids and will result in a considerable number of misclassifications. Existence of these possibilities indicates that a classification system based on comparisons of predicted standardized criterion scores should not be applied indiscriminately.

The fact that the two-predictor case does not always result in locating the centroids in the same region suggests that a test space of greater dimensionality might yield more favorable results. Nevertheless, in a test space of any dimensions there will always be at least one case in which the centroids lie in the same region. The one instance will arise when the regression planes in the two groups are oriented identically. In this case there will be only one classificatory region no matter how different the centroids of the groups may be.

We conclude that regression analysis is a poor means for reducing the number of the dimensions of a classification system. Regression methods always reduce the T-space to a one-space. The derivation of the regression equation does not guarantee that it will be a suitable single variate for locating points in or bounding topological regions in a reduced space. Regression methods involve a separate rotation of the *predictor* test space for each of the G groups. The score distributions of the groups may exhibit different effects of selection with the result that some important determinants of proficiency in a job may have inappropriate regression weights. Development of rules for classification on the basis of the group in which the predicted standardized score is maximum rests on the dubious assumption that all criteria may be represented on a single numerical scale, and that the distributions of criterion scores describe the same utilitarian values in all groups. We conclude that decisions on the problem of personnel assignments based on regression methods alone are inadequate.

The Productivity Criterion

Brogden (1946) discussed the problem of assigning N men to n mutually exclusive job categories by rules which maximize over-all productivity of the assigned groups. The requirement of a common criterion scale for this problem was recognized. Brogden considered the problem for two categories ($n = 2$). Thorndike (1950) restated the problem and discussed the issues involved in obtaining a criterion comparable for all of the n categories.

General solutions to the personnel assignment problem were published by Votaw and Bailey (1952), Votaw (1952), Lord (1952), and Rao (1952). Each of these papers represented a general procedure for allocating the N men to G jobs so that the over-all efficiency is a maximum. In all of these developments the problem of comparable criterion scores which appeared in the work of Brogden and Thorndike was skirted by assuming the existence of productivity criterion scores for each man on each job. The startling effects of accepting predicted standardized criterion scores for the productivity measure are revealed in the following example.

We return to Tiedeman and Sternberg's (1952) Chapter 1 data on the college preparatory and business curriculum pupils at Waltham High School. The distribution of verbal scores is given in Table 9.1.

Following Votaw's method (1952) we have $m = 37$ personnel categories, that is, 37 nonzero categories of verbal reasoning score. We have $G = 2$ job categories, that is, two curricula. We wish to determine the allocation of the $75 + 132$, or 207, pupils which will maximize the average "productivity" in the school. We must assign 75 pupils to the college preparatory curriculum and 132 to the business curriculum.

Associated with each one of the 37 personnel categories ($i = 1, 2, \ldots, 37$) there is a productivity measure for each job category ($g = 1, 2$). If the predicted standardized grade average in each curriculum is used as this productivity measure (c_{ig}), there are 37 possible scores for the college curriculum C_{i1}, and 37 different values C_{i2}. These values are listed in Table 9.2.

We make a trial allocation of pupils to curriculum categories. We designate the allocations x'_{ig}. We allocate the 75 pupils with highest

Table 9.1 *Frequency of Verbal Reasoning Scores in Two Curriculum Groups*

Verbal Reasoning Score	Curriculum	
	College Preparatory	Business
42	1	–
41	2	–
40	2	–
39	1	–
38	4	–
37	3	–
36	1	–
35	4	1
34	3	1
33	5	–
32	1	1
31	4	3
30	4	2
29	1	1
28	2	1
27	6	2
26	4	2
25	1	4
24	3	10
23	6	6
22	2	9
21	3	9
20	3	6
19	1	4
18	2	5
17	2	8
16	1	10
15	1	8
14	1	5
13	1	6
12	–	6
11	–	9
10	–	4
9	–	3
8	–	1
7	–	4
6	–	–
5	–	1
Total	75	132

Table 9.2 *List of C_{ij} Productivity Criteria Scores Corresponding to X_i*

Score	C_{i1}	C_{i2}
$x_i = 42$	.520	1.118
41	.482	1.071
40	.443	1.024
39	.405	.977
38	.367	.930
37	.329	.882
36	.291	.835
35	.253	.788
34	.215	.741
33	.177	.694
32	.139	.647
31	.101	.600
30	.062	.553
29	.024	.506
28	−.014	.459
27	−.052	.411
26	−.090	.364
25	−.128	.317
24	−.166	.270
23	−.204	.223
22	−.242	.176
21	−.281	.129
20	−.319	.082
19	−.357	.035
18	−.395	−.013
17	−.433	−.060
16	−.471	−.107
15	−.509	−.154
14	−.547	−.201
13	−.585	−.248
12	−.623	−.295
11	−.662	−.342
10	−.700	−.389
9	−.738	−.436
8	−.776	−.484
7	−.814	−.531
6	–	–
$x_i = 5$	−.890	−.625

verbal reasoning scores to the college curriculum and the 132 pupils with lowest verbal reasoning scores to the business curriculum.

For this rule of assignment the over-all efficiency of the school is

$$\sum_{i=1}^{37} \sum_{g=1}^{2} c_{ig} x'_{ig} = -.0071$$

We made this allocation x'_{ig} only for the purpose of comparison. It illustrates the usual rule recommended for the selection of candidates or applicants for admission to college or a job. The allocation of these 207 pupils, which is optimal by Votaw's criterion, increases the over-all efficiency of the school to the value

$$\sum_{i=1}^{37} \sum_{g=1}^{2} c_{ig} x'_{ig} = .0495$$

This result is achieved by assigning the pupils with the *highest* verbal reasoning scores to the *business* curriculum and the pupils with *lowest* verbal scores to the *college* preparatory curriculum. Criteria derived from regression equations appear to be inadequate for multigroup assignment problems.

Statistical Procedures and Personnel Procedures

Chapter 10

Discriminant Analysis and Regression Analysis Combined: Joint Probability of Membership and Success in a Group

It was emphasized in Chapter 1 that group membership, rather than success in a group, should constitute the *primary* datum in classification. Some undesirable consequences of misguidedly using an individual's predicted success (or productivity) score in each of several groups as the sole basis for assigning him to one of the groups were discussed in Chapter 9.

In certain situations, however, a combination of the information concerning group membership and that concerning probable degree of success in a group may provide a more efficient basis for guidance or allocation than the former alone. We turn now to a method for effecting such a combination: a union, as it were, of discriminant analysis and regression analysis for obtaining the joint probability of membership and success in a group (Tatsuoka, 1956).

Probability of Group Membership

Up to now, the centour score was used as the best single index for answering the question: What job classifications are appropriate for a given individual? This index, it will be recalled, gives, with respect to each group, the conditional probability that the point in T-space (or in the discriminant space) representing an individual's predictor-score combination will lie as far as (or farther than) it does from the centroid of that group, *given* that the individual is indeed a member of that group.

To combine the information from discriminant and regression analyses in the manner to be described, it is necessary to obtain conditional

339

probabilities that are, in a certain sense, the probabilistic "inverses" of centour scores; namely, the conditional probability that an individual is a member of each of the groups, *given* that he has a particular combination of predictor scores. These conditional probabilities can be computed from a formula known as Bayes' theorem, provided the *a priori* probabilities of group membership are known or can be estimated, that is, the probabilities of group membership before knowledge of the predictor scores is obtained.

Bayes' theorem was long viewed with skepticism by many statisticians so far as its applications to statistical inference were concerned [see Fisher (1930)]. Recently, however, a new school of thought known as the neo-Bayesian school has developed and given Bayes' theorem a prominent position in its approach to problems of statistical inference and hypothesis testing. [For a discussion of this approach, see Edwards, Lindman, and Savage (1963).]

To state Bayes' theorem in a form suited to hypothesis testing, we use the following notation. Let $H_1, H_2, \ldots, H_G$ denote G mutually exclusive and together exhaustive hypotheses; in the problem of our immediate concern, H_g will stand for the hypothesis that a given individual is a member of group g, there being G groups to only one of which any individual must belong.

For each $g(= 1, 2, \ldots, G)$ let $p(H_g)$ be the *a priori* probability that hypothesis H_g is true. In our problem this may be taken as P_g, the proportion of individuals among our total sample who belong to group g. Or, if the corresponding population proportion π_g is known, or an estimate $\hat{\pi}_g$ better than P_g can be obtained, these may be used for $p(H_g)$.

Next, letting x designate a particular observation, that is, a combination of predictor-variable scores (or discriminant-function scores), we denote by $p(x \mid H_g)$ the conditional probability of observing x, given that H_g is true. In other words, $p(x \mid H_g)$ is the probability that an individual drawn at random from group g will have the particular combination x of scores; it is, therefore, closely related to the centour score, except that the latter corresponds to the probability that a random member of group g will have a score combination x *or one that is farther* (in the generalized-distance sense) from the centroid of group g.

Finally, we denote by $p(H_g \mid x)$ the conditional probability that H_g is true given that observation x was made. This is the "probabilistic inverse" of $p(x \mid H_g)$ that we need for computing our joint-probability index, and Bayes' theorem enables us to determine $p(H_g \mid x)$ for each g when all the $p(H_g)$ and $p(x \mid H_g)$ are known. The formula is

$$p(H_g \mid x) = \frac{p(H_g)p(x \mid H_g)}{\sum\limits_{j=1}^{G} p(H_j)p(x \mid H_j)}; \qquad g = 1, 2, \ldots, G \qquad (10.1)$$

We have already indicated how the $p(H_g)$ in Eq. 10.1 may be evaluated in applying this equation to our problem of determining the probability of group membership. How do we evaluate the $p(x \mid H_g)$, the other ingredients of Eq. 10.1? As usual, we resort to the assumption that the predictor variables follow, at least approximately, a multivariate normal distribution. This assumption, in general, will be more nearly valid for the discriminant functions, provided the number of original predictor variables is much larger than the number of groups. Then the central limit theorem assures us that each discriminant function, being a linear combination of many variables, at least individually follows an approximate normal distribution.[1] Therefore it is fairly likely that their joint distribution will not be very far from a multivariate normal distribution.

In this section, we will let x represent a combination of discriminant-function scores. More specifically, let

$$x = \|x_1, x_2, \ldots, x_r\|$$

be the r-dimensional row vector of discriminant scores, where r is the number of statistically significant discriminant functions. Similarly, we let

$$\bar{x}_g = \|\bar{x}_{1g}, \bar{x}_{2g}, \ldots, \bar{x}_{rg}\|$$

be the discriminant-function centroid for group g. Then, denoting by D_g the dispersion matrix of the discriminant functions for group g, we introduce the usual abbreviation,

$$\chi_g^2 = (x - \bar{x}_g)D_g^{-1}(x - \bar{x}_g)' \qquad (10.2)$$

With the foregoing notation and the assumption of multivariate normality of the joint distribution of the discriminant scores, we may evaluate $p(x \mid H_g)$ as follows:

$$p(x \mid H_g) = (2\pi)^{-r/2}\,|D_g|^{-1/2}\exp\left(-\chi_g^2/2\right)dx, \qquad (10.3)$$

where dx is the volume element $dx_1, dx_2, \ldots, dx_r$ in the r-dimensional space spanned by the significant discriminant functions. (It should be noted that the indicated probability is not that of a random observation being exactly equal to x, but that it lie within a small rectangular parallelepiped of dimensions $dx_1, dx_2, \ldots, dx_r$ surrounding the point x in the r-dimensional space.)

---

[1] Strictly speaking, the central limit theorem does not apply unless the variables being linearly combined are independently distributed. However, if we have a large *variety* of original predictor variables, most of these will tend to have low intercorrelations, and the condition for applicability of the theorem will at least approximately be satisfied.

We have seen how each of the quantities involved in Eq. 10.1 for $p(H_g \mid x)$ may be evaluated. Tentatively using the simplest option of taking

$$p(H_g) = n_g \bigg/ \sum_{j=1}^{G} n_j \qquad (10.4)$$

as the *a priori* probability of membership in group g, we substitute this and Eq. 10.3 in Eq. 10.1 and obtain

$$p(H_g \mid x) = \frac{(n_g/\sum n_j)(2\pi)^{-r/2} \mid D_g \mid^{-1/2} \exp\left(-X_g{}^2/2\right) dx}{\displaystyle\sum_{j=1}^{G} \left[(n_j/\sum n_i)(2\pi)^{-r/2} \mid D_j \mid^{-1/2} \exp\left(-X_j{}^2/2\right) dx\right]}$$

Upon cancellation of common factors in numerator and denominator, it reduces to

$$p(H_g \mid x) = \frac{n_g \mid D_g \mid^{-1/2} \exp\left(-X_g{}^2/2\right)}{\displaystyle\sum_{j=1}^{G} \left[n_j \mid D_j \mid^{-1/2} \exp\left(-X_j{}^2/2\right)\right]} ; \qquad g = 1, 2, \ldots, G \quad (10.5)$$

This, then, gives the probability that an individual *with a particular discriminant-score combination*, selected at random from the entire sample, will turn out to be a member of group g.

Probability of Success

We now turn to the other component in our combination of information from discriminant and regression analyses: the probability that a member of a certain group having a particular combination x of predictor scores will be "successful" in the sense of exceeding some cutting point on the criterion variable. Thus these probabilities are essentially the entries of a theoretical expectancy table for each group.

For actual computation of these probabilities we again invoke the assumption of multivariate normality of the joint distribution of the predictors and the criterion variable y_g for each group. We then construct a multiple regression equation

$$\tilde{y}_g = a_g + \sum_{j=1}^{p} b_{jg} x_j$$

for each group; and the probability that a member of group g who has a particular combination x of predictor scores will obtain a criterion score exceeding some critical point $y_g{}^*$ may be estimated as follows:

$$p(y_g(x) > y_g{}^* \mid H_g \;\&\; x) = (2\pi)^{-1/2} \int_{t_g{}^*}^{\infty} \exp\left(-t^2/2\right) dt \qquad (10.6)$$

with

$$t_g{}^* = \frac{y_g{}^* - \tilde{y}_g(x)}{\sigma_{yg}\sqrt{1 - R_g{}^2}}$$

where $\tilde{y}_g(x)$ is the value of the linear combination $\tilde{y}_g$ for the particular predictor-score combination $x = (x_1, x_2, \ldots, x_p)$, σ_{yg} is the standard deviation of y_g, and R_g is the coefficient of multiple correlation between y_g and $x_1, x_2, \ldots, x_p$. The presence of an integration sign in this equation need not discourage readers who are unfamiliar with calculus. This is just a convenient way of indicating that we are to use a table of normal-curve areas to find the area to the right of the point $z = t_g{}^*$. The only actual calculations needed are those involved in determining $t_g{}^*$ for the given predictor-score combination.

Joint Probability of Membership and Success in a Group

We have seen how, given a particular predictor-score combination, we may compute the probability of group membership and the probability of "success" in a group given membership therein. We now proceed to apply the general multiplication theorem of probability theory in order to obtain the desired probability: the probability of the joint event, membership *and* success in a group, given a particular predictor-score combination. The multiplication theorem may be written, in general form, as follows:

$$p(A \ \& \ B \mid C) = p(A \mid C)p(B \mid A \ \& \ C)$$

For our problem, we let A stand for membership in a certain group, B for "success" in that group, and C for the observation of a particular predictor-score combination. Thus the desired joint probability may be computed as

$$p[H_g \ \& \ y_g(x) > y_g{}^* \mid x] = p(H_g \mid x)p[y_g(x) > y_g{}^* \mid H_g \ \& \ x] \quad (10.7)$$

where the two factors on the right are given by Eqs. 10.5 and 10.6, respectively.

At this point the reader may be perplexed by the fact that in Eq. 10.5 x stood for a set of scores on the significant discriminant functions, whereas in Eq. 10.6 x stands for a set of scores on the original predictor variables. How, then, are we justified in using $p(H_g \mid x)$ from the one equation and $p[y_g(x) > y_g{}^* \mid H_g \ \& \ x]$ from the other as two factors in the right-hand side of Eq. 10.7? And what does the x to the right of the vertical bar on the left-hand side of this equation denote? Actually, Eq. 10.7 is only approximately valid when the x in $p(H_g \mid x)$ refers to the set comprising only the *significant* discriminant functions. However, it can be proved, as shown by Tatsuoka (1956, Appendix), that when the entire set of discriminant functions $z = (z_1, z_2, \ldots, z_n)$ is taken, the $p(H_g \mid z)$ computed from the discriminant space is equal to the $p(H_g \mid x)$ computed from the original test space, provided the original predictor variables have multivariate normal distributions with identical dispersion matrices in the G groups.

It is reasonable to assume, then, that even if we use only the significant discriminant functions, the conditional probability of membership in group g will not be very far off from the $p(H_g \mid x)$ computed from the original test space. In fact, it could even be argued that using only the significant discriminant functions may give us better estimates of what the true conditional probabilities are in the populations than using the entire set of discriminant functions (or, equivalently, all the original predictors). This is because, by using only the significant functions, we are deliberately ignoring information concerning group differentiation that is most likely peculiar to our particular sample and irrelevant for the populations.

Thus a satisfactory interpretation of the "hybrid" usage of x in Eq. 10.7 would be as follows. Logically (that is, for strict validity of the equation), every occurrence of x stands for a set of scores on the original predictors. It is merely that, for computational purposes, we are *estimating* $p(H_g \mid x)$ by the corresponding quantity computed in terms of the significant discriminant functions alone.

Illustrative Example

To apply the joint-probability index for guiding or allocating a new applicant to one of several job categories, we need all the information on previous groups of applicants that we needed when applying the centour score approach; and in addition, we need a criterion measure of success or productivity for members of each job category.

Let us therefore assume that, for each of our passenger agents, mechanics, and operations control agents for whom we had scores on the three activity-preference scales, we also have a score on a criterion variable measuring his subsequent success. The rosters for our three groups, augmented by the criterion scores, are shown in part in Table 10.1. (The entire rosters of the criterion scores are given in Appendix B.)

Probability of Group Membership

We have already obtained in Chapter 8 the basic quantities needed for computing the $p(H_g \mid x)$ from Eq. 10.5, namely the dispersion matrices of the three groups in the two-dimensional discriminant space. These are reproduced here, together with the values of their determinants, the inverse matrices, and the group means on the discriminant functions—all of which are needed in computing the $p(H_g \mid x)$. The passenger agents, mechanics, and operations control agents groups are denoted by subscripts 1, 2, and 3, respectively:

$$D_1 = \begin{Vmatrix} 19.4417 & 1.5391 \\ 1.5391 & 26.0158 \end{Vmatrix} \qquad D_1^{-1} = \begin{Vmatrix} 51.6779 & -3.0572 \\ -3.0572 & 38.6191 \end{Vmatrix} \cdot 10^{-3}$$

$$|D_1| = 503.4209 \qquad \bar{X}_{1.2} = \begin{Vmatrix} 11.0117 & 14.2865 \end{Vmatrix}$$

$$D_2 = \begin{Vmatrix} 33.4418 & -1.4971 \\ -1.4971 & 12.5605 \end{Vmatrix} \qquad D_2^{-1} = \begin{Vmatrix} 30.0631 & 3.5833 \\ 3.5833 & 80.0418 \end{Vmatrix} \cdot 10^{-3}$$

$$|D_2| = 417.8044 \qquad \bar{X}_{2.2} = \begin{Vmatrix} 4.1825 & 19.1429 \end{Vmatrix}$$

$$D_3 = \begin{Vmatrix} 25.3837 & .1159 \\ .1159 & 19.7503 \end{Vmatrix} \qquad D_3^{-1} = \begin{Vmatrix} 39.3964 & -.2312 \\ -.2312 & 50.6335 \end{Vmatrix} \cdot 10^{-3}$$

$$|D_3| = 501.3225 \qquad \bar{X}_{3.2} = \begin{Vmatrix} -2.5414 & 13.7614 \end{Vmatrix}$$

(A factor of 10^{-3} has been factored out of every element of each inverse matrix in order to save space for recording a larger number of significant digits.)

In terms of the quantities just displayed, the χ_g^2 (with $g = 1, 2, 3$) for an individual with any pair of discriminant scores (x_1, x_2) may be computed in accordance with Eq. 10.2, as follows:

$$\chi_1^2 = \begin{Vmatrix} x_1 - 11.01 & x_2 - 14.29 \end{Vmatrix}$$
$$\cdot \begin{Vmatrix} 51.68 & -3.06 \\ -3.06 & 38.62 \end{Vmatrix} \cdot \begin{Vmatrix} x_1 - 11.01 \\ x_2 - 14.29 \end{Vmatrix} \cdot 10^{-3} \qquad (10.8a)$$

$$\chi_2^2 = \begin{Vmatrix} x_1 - 4.18 & x_2 - 19.14 \end{Vmatrix}$$
$$\cdot \begin{Vmatrix} 30.06 & 3.58 \\ 3.58 & 80.04 \end{Vmatrix} \cdot \begin{Vmatrix} x_1 - 4.18 \\ x_2 - 19.14 \end{Vmatrix} \cdot 10^{-3} \qquad (10.8b)$$

$$\chi_3^2 = \begin{Vmatrix} x_1 + 2.54 & x_2 - 13.76 \end{Vmatrix}$$
$$\cdot \begin{Vmatrix} 39.40 & -.23 \\ -.23 & 50.63 \end{Vmatrix} \cdot \begin{Vmatrix} x_1 + 2.54 \\ x_2 - 13.76 \end{Vmatrix} \cdot 10^{-3} \qquad (10.8c)$$

(Numerical values have been rounded off to two decimal places here, but subsequent calculations are based on five decimal places.)

To illustrate, suppose that a new applicant had, as his outdoor, convivial, and conservative activity preference scores, 20, 27, and 6, respectively. Then, applying the conventionalized discriminant coefficients

$$\begin{Vmatrix} -.48067 & 1.00000 \\ 1.00000 & .21432 \\ -.79359 & -.38713 \end{Vmatrix}$$

Table 10.1 *Scores on Outdoor, Convivial, and Conservative Activity Preference Scales and Criterion Score Measuring Success*

| Apprentice Number | Group 1. Passenger Agents | | | Criterion Score |
	Outdoor	Convivial	Conservative	
1	10	22	5	.7
2	14	17	6	5.5
3	19	33	7	7.5
⋮	⋮	⋮	⋮	⋮
85	16	24	10	6.2
Mean	12.59	24.22	9.02	5.4529*
SD	4.50	4.34	3.14	1.9402*

| Apprentice Number | Group 2. Mechanics | | | Criterion Score |
	Outdoor	Convivial	Conservative	
1	20	27	6	5.3
2	21	15	10	7.5
3	15	27	12	5.4
⋮	⋮	⋮	⋮	⋮
93	19	16	6	4.6
Mean	18.54	21.14	10.13	5.7011*
SD	3.56	4.55	3.24	1.8437*

| Apprentice Number | Group 3. Operations Control Agents | | | Criterion Score |
	Outdoor	Convivial	Conservative	
1	19	19	16	2.4
2	17	17	12	8.5
3	8	17	14	2.6
⋮	⋮	⋮	⋮	⋮
66	18	20	10	6.7
Mean	15.58	15.45	13.24	5.2485*
SD	4.11	3.77	3.69	1.9421*

* Means and standard deviations are shown to four decimal places only for the criterion variable because they are presented here for the first time.

obtained in Chapter 8 (p. 312), his two discriminant-function scores are

$$x_1 = (-.48067)(20) + (1)(27) + (-.79359)(6) = 12.62506$$

and

$$x_2 = (1)(20) + (.21432)(27) + (-.38713)(6) = 23.46386$$

Therefore his χ_g^2 values with respect to the three groups are, in accordance with Eqs. 10.8a, b, and c, as follows:

$$\chi_1^2 = \|12.63 - 11.01 \quad 23.46 - 14.29\|$$

$$\cdot \left\| \begin{matrix} 51.68 & -3.06 \\ -3.06 & 38.62 \end{matrix} \right\| \cdot \left\| \begin{matrix} 12.63 - 11.01 \\ 23.46 - 14.29 \end{matrix} \right\| \cdot 10^{-3}$$

$$= \|1.61 \quad 9.18\| \cdot \left\| \begin{matrix} 51.68 & -3.06 \\ -3.06 & 38.62 \end{matrix} \right\| \cdot \left\| \begin{matrix} 1.61 \\ 9.18 \end{matrix} \right\| \cdot 10^{-3}$$

$$= 3296.7 \times 10^{-3} = 3.297$$

$$\chi_2^2 = \|8.44 \quad 4.32\| \cdot \left\| \begin{matrix} 30.06 & 3.58 \\ 3.58 & 80.04 \end{matrix} \right\| \cdot \left\| \begin{matrix} 8.44 \\ 4.32 \end{matrix} \right\| \cdot 10^{-3}$$

$$= 3899.1 \times 10^{-3} = 3.899$$

$$\chi_3^2 = \|15.17 \quad 9.70\| \cdot \left\| \begin{matrix} 39.39 & -.23 \\ -.23 & 50.63 \end{matrix} \right\| \cdot \left\| \begin{matrix} 15.17 \\ 9.70 \end{matrix} \right\| \cdot 10^{-3}$$

$$= 13760.5 \times 10^{-3} = 13.760$$

We are now ready to compute the $p(H_g \mid x)$ for this applicant in accordance with Eq. 10.5. For this purpose, we first calculate the three (in general, G) terms in the common denominator for $p(H_1 \mid x)$, $p(H_2 \mid x)$, and $p(H_3 \mid x)$. Using the values of the determinants $|D_g|$ given earlier, and recalling that $n_1 = 85$, $n_2 = 93$, $n_3 = 66$, the three denominator terms are

$$n_1 |D_1|^{-\frac{1}{2}} \exp(-\chi_1^2/2) = (85)(503.42)^{-\frac{1}{2}} e^{-3.297/2} = .72866$$
$$n_2 |D_2|^{-\frac{1}{2}} \exp(-\chi_2^2/2) = (93)(417.80)^{-\frac{1}{2}} e^{-3.899/2} = .64766$$
$$n_3 |D_3|^{-\frac{1}{2}} \exp(-\chi_3^2/2) = (66)(501.32)^{-\frac{1}{2}} e^{-13.76/2} = .00303$$

Therefore

$$\sum n_g |D_g|^{-\frac{1}{2}} \exp(-\chi_g^2/2) = .72866 + .64766 + .00303 = 1.37935$$

Dividing each of the terms by this sum, we obtain

$$p(H_1 \mid x) = \frac{.72866}{1.37935} = .5283 \tag{10.9a}$$

$$p(H_2 \mid x) = \frac{.64766}{1.37935} = .4695 \tag{10.9b}$$

$$p(H_3 \mid x) = \frac{.00303}{1.37935} = .0022 \tag{10.9c}$$

for an applicant whose scores on the three activity preference scales are $X = (20, 27, 6)$.

Thus if we were to allocate this applicant solely on the basis of his probability of group membership, a rational decision would be to allocate him to group 1 (passenger agents), for the probability is maximal for this group. But the proposal in this chapter is to advise any applicant to enter that job specialty for which his joint probability of membership *and* success is the greatest. Our next step, therefore, is to compute for each $g(= 1, 2, 3)$ the probability of success, conditioned by an applicant's being a member of group g *and* having the particular score combination that was observed.

Probability of Success

The first step toward computing the probability of success for a randomly selected member of a given group having a particular combination of predictor scores, is to construct for each group the multiple regression equation of a criterion variable (measuring success) on the predictors. This is accomplished by applying Eq. 9.1 to compute a vector B_g of regression coefficients for each group, and forming a linear function

$$\tilde{y}_g = a_g + \sum_{i=1}^{p} b_{ig} x_i \tag{10.10}$$

where the coefficients in the sum are given by the elements of B_g. We illustrate the details in constructing the regression equation for group 1, and record the results for the other two groups.

The group 1 dispersion matrix for the original predictor variables is, as modified by a factor of $n/(n - 1) = 85/84$ from that shown on page 172,

$$D_1 = \begin{Vmatrix} 20.2451 & 4.6170 & -2.4069 \\ 4.6170 & 18.7947 & 2.5066 \\ -2.4069 & 2.5066 & 9.8804 \end{Vmatrix}$$

The vector of covariances between the criterion variable and the predictors, computed from the complete roster for group 1 as given in Appendix B, is

$$C'_1 = \begin{Vmatrix} -1.18398 & 3.17126 & 2.04157 \end{Vmatrix}$$

In accordance with Eq. 9.1, we compute

$$B_1 = D_1^{-1} C_1 = (10^{-2}) \begin{Vmatrix} 5.50844 & -1.58578 & 1.74416 \\ -1.58578 & 5.96352 & -1.89923 \\ 1.74416 & -1.89923 & 11.02771 \end{Vmatrix} \cdot \begin{Vmatrix} -1.18398 \\ 3.17126 \\ 2.04157 \end{Vmatrix}$$

$$= \begin{Vmatrix} -.07990 \\ .16912 \\ .14426 \end{Vmatrix}$$

whose elements are the coefficients of the linear combination in Eq. 10.10.

The constant term a_1 is computed as

$$a_1 = \bar{y}_1 - b_{11}\bar{x}_1 - b_{12}\bar{x}_2 - b_{13}\bar{x}_3$$
$$= 5.4529 - (-.07990)(12.5882) - (.16912)(24.2235) - (.14426)(9.0235)$$
$$= 1.06029$$

Thus the complete raw score regression equation for predicting success in group 1 from the three activity preference scores of any member of that group is

$$y_1 = 1.06029 - .07990x_1 + .16912x_2 + .14426x_3 \qquad (10.11a)$$

Next, the coefficient of multiple correlation is computed from the equation

$$R_g{}^2 = \left(\frac{1}{\sigma_{yg}{}^2}\right)C_g B_g \qquad (g = 1, 2, 3) \qquad (10.12)$$

where σ_{yg} is the standard deviation of the criterion variable for group g. Thus for group 1, with the vectors C_1 and B_1 just given, and the value of σ_{yg} as shown in Table 10.1, we find

$$R_1{}^2 = \left(\frac{1}{1.9402}\right)^2 \|-1.18398 \quad 3.17126 \quad 2.04157\| \cdot \begin{Vmatrix} -.07990 \\ .16912 \\ .14426 \end{Vmatrix}$$

$$= \left(\frac{1}{3.7644}\right)(.92544) = .24584$$

(when $R_1 = .49583$ if we want the coefficient of multiple correlation itself; but for our purposes we are more interested in the squared coefficient $R_1{}^2$). From this we compute the standard error of estimate

$$\sigma_{yg}\sqrt{1 - R_g{}^2} = 1.9402\sqrt{1 - .24584} = 1.6849 \qquad (10.13a)$$

We now have all the quantities needed for computing the probability that a randomly selected member of group 1, with a given combination of predictor scores, will earn a criterion score equal to, or greater than, any specified critical value. For the purposes of this illustration, we arbitrarily take $y_g{}^* = 6.00$ as the cutting score defining "success" in each job specialty.

Going back to the applicant whose activity preference scores were 20, 27, and 6, let us compute his probability of success in group 1, under the assumption that he is indeed a member of group 1. Substituting his scores in Eq. 10.11a, we find

$$y_1(20, 27, 6) = 1.06029 - (.07990)(20) + (.16912)(27) + (.14426)(6)$$
$$= 4.8941$$

which is less than the critical value 6.00. Therefore if this applicant comes from the same population as the present passenger agents' group does, his chances of success in this job specialty are less than 50%. To estimate what his actual chances might be, we use Eq. 10.6 to determine

$$p[y_1(x) > 6.00 \mid H_1 \ \& \ x = (20, 27, 6)]$$

The abscissa value with which to enter the normal-curve table is

$$t_1{}^* = \frac{6.00 - 4.8941}{1.6849} = .6564$$

By referring to any table of unit normal-curve areas, the area under the curve to the right of this abscissa value is found to be .2558.

We thus conclude that, for an applicant with the predictor-score combination (20, 27, 6), the probability of success in group 1, *on condition that* this applicant is a member of the population corresponding to group 1, is equal to

$$p[y_1(x) > y_1{}^* \mid H_1 \ \& \ x] = .2558 \tag{10.14a}$$

We similarly construct regression equations for predicting success for group 2 and group 3. The results are[1]

$$y_2 = -.75871 + .25061x_1 + .12323x_2 - .07809x_3 \tag{10.11b}$$

and

$$y_3 = 2.34259 + .16429x_1 - .14399x_2 + .19424x_3 \tag{10.11c}$$

The squares of the coefficients of multiple correlation for groups 2 and 3 are, respectively,

$$R_2{}^2 = .28803 \quad \text{and} \quad R_3{}^2 = .32397$$

From these values and the criterion-variable standard deviations $\sigma_{y2} = 1.8437$ and $\sigma_{y3} = 1.9421$, shown in Table 10.1, we compute the standard errors of estimate. The results are

$$\sigma_{y2}\sqrt{1 - R_2{}^2} = 1.5557 \tag{10.13b}$$

$$\sigma_{y3}\sqrt{1 - R_3{}^2} = 1.5968 \tag{10.13c}$$

Using Eq. 10.11b in conjunction with the standard error, Eq. 10.13b, we may compute the probability of success for any member of group 2

[1] Readers who wish to carry out the calculations for practice, following the steps that led to Eq. 10.11a, may obtain the dispersion matrices D_2 and D_3 of the predictor variables from page 172. The vectors of covariances between the criterion variable and the predictors, not shown there, are

$$C_2 = \begin{Vmatrix} 2.79398 \\ 2.14984 \\ -.17840 \end{Vmatrix} \qquad C_3 = \begin{Vmatrix} 2.66858 \\ -1.74238 \\ 2.74191 \end{Vmatrix}$$

having a given combination of predictor scores. Similarly, Eqs. 10.11c and 10.13c enable the corresponding computation for group 3 members. Thus for our applicant with the predictor-score combination (20, 27, 6), we successively find—under the two alternative assumptions that he is a member of the group 2 population and that he comes from the group 3 population—the following results.

Assuming group 2 membership:

$$y_2(20, 27, 6) = 7.1122$$
$$t^* = -.7149$$

and thus

$$p[y_2(x) > y_2^* \mid H_2 \ \& \ x] = .7627 \tag{10.14b}$$

Assuming group 3 membership:

$$y(20, 27, 6) = 2.9061$$
$$t^* = 1.9376$$

and thus

$$p[y_3(x) > y_3^* \mid H_3 \ \& \ x] = .0263 \tag{10.14c}$$

The probability values stated in Eqs. 10.14a, b, and c, then, represent the probabilities that an applicant with the predictor-score combination $x = (20, 27, 6)$ will "succeed" (that is, obtain a criterion score not less than 6.00) in the three job specialty groups, respectively, *under the successive assumptions* that he is a member of the group 1 population, the group 2 population, and the group 3 population. The fact that each of the computed probabilities of success is conditioned on the assumption that the applicant is indeed a member of the particular group cannot be over-emphasized. For each of the regression equations (Eqs. 10.11a, b, and c) is valid only for members of the population from which the particular group was drawn. This is why a plan of allocation based on the relative magnitudes of these three (in general, g) probabilities cannot be entertained.

Joint Probability of Membership and Success in a Group

It now remains only to put together the probabilities exemplified in Eqs. 10.9a, b, and c and those in Eqs. 10.14a, b, and c, respectively, to compute the desired joint probability in accordance with Eq. 10.7. We collect the relevant probability values for our applicant with the predictor-score combination (20, 27, 6) in Table 10.2 which follows, and obtain his joint probability of membership and success in each of the three job specialties.

As seen in Table 10.2, the joint probabilities that our applicant is a member of group 1 and will be successful, that he is a member of group 2 and will be successful, and that he is a member of group 3 and will be successful are equal to .1351, .3581, and .0001, respectively. (Each of these values is obtained in accordance with Eq. 10.7 by multiplying the first two entries in the relevant column.)

Table 10.2 *Probability of Group Membership, Probability of Success Given Group Membership, and Joint Probability of Membership and Success in Each Group for an Applicant with Predictor-Score Combination $x = (20, 27, 6)$*

Type of Probability	Group (g)		
	1	2	3
$p(H_g \mid x)$	.5283	.4695	.0022
$p(y > y^* \mid H_g \& x)$	.2558	.7627	.0263
$p(H_g \& y > y^* \mid x)$	.1351	.3581	.0001

Allocation of Members of Entire Groups by the Joint-Probability Index

By applying the procedures illustrated for a single applicant, in the preceding section, to every member of a large group and examining the percentage of "correct classifications," we may assess the merits of the proposed scheme. Ideally, as in validating any actuarial method, we should apply the proposed allocation scheme to a new cross-validation sample. This would require that we compute the joint-probability index (based on the discriminant functions and regression equations constructed for our normative sample) for each member of a group of applicants, assign each applicant to the job specialty for which his index is the largest, and subsequently obtain measures of his satisfaction and success in that job.

This approach obviously poses grave difficulties in practice. The employing firm would have to be willing to carry through such an experimental allocation of employees in the face of a possible loss in over-all productivity if the system does not work. The applicants, too, would have to be cooperative enough to work in the job specialties prescribed for them by the index even if the assignments are at variance with what they would have chosen for themselves (perhaps out of inadequate insight into their own aptitudes and genuine interests, perhaps due to social prestige factors, and so forth).

An alternative approach to the validation of the proposed scheme is one which was used by Tatsuoka (1956) in the context of curricular "allocation" at an institute of technology. In this approach, the cross-validation sample consists of individuals who already have entered various specialty groups (curricula or job categories, as the case may be) without reference to the joint-probability index. The index is computed (on the basis of equations determined for a separate, normative group) for each member of this sample. The sample is then subdivided into a group consisting of those individuals whose actual specialty coincides with the specialty prescribed for them by the index, and a complementary group comprising individuals whose actual and prescribed specialties are not the same. Comparisons are then made between these two groups in terms of a measure of success and of some measure of satisfaction, if available. If it is found that the "positive" group (where the actual and prescribed specialties agree) is superior, on the average, to the "negative" group (where the actual and prescribed specialties differ) with respect to these measures, we may infer that the proposed allocation scheme would have been a good one to use.

In the context of the World Airlines example (in which the data were artificially contrived), however, even this alternative method for cross validation is infeasible. There is no way to assign success measures to the applicants without biasing the results in one way or another—except, of course, the meaningless method of random assignment. Therefore for this example we will content ourselves with applying the joint-probability classification scheme to members of the normative sample (that is, the "satisfied and successful" passenger agents, mechanics, and operations control agents for whom the discriminant functions and regression equations were constructed), and examining the percentage of correct classifications. It must be emphasized, however, that we would not be surprised if this percentage of "hits" is not exceedingly high. For the joint-probability method does not purport to accurately "predict" what the actual group affiliations are, but rather to indicate to each applicant what specialty he *should* enter if he wishes to maximize the chances of being successful and satisfied—satisfied, that is, to the extent that being affiliated with a group whose modal member he most resembles leads to satisfaction.

Although the percentage of "correct classifications," for reasons discussed previously, can be examined only in the normative sample itself, it is, of course, possible to apply the method to a separate sample (that is, the group of applicants) and to investigate certain characteristics of the resulting classification. We use these two methods of assessing the proposed method in the next two subsections.

Classification of Normative-Sample Members

The results of allocating each member of the normative sample to that group for which his joint-probability value is the largest, and comparing this allocation with his actual group membership, are summarized in

Table 10.3. We see that 180 of the 244 employees (about 74%) are correctly classified by the proposed classification scheme.

Table 10.3 *Classification of Normative-Sample Members in Accordance with Joint-Probability Index*

Actual / Classified as	Passenger Agents	Mechanics	Operations Control Agents
Passenger Agents	64	19	2
Mechanics	13	68	12
Operations Control Agents	4	14	48

In contrast, a classification of the normative-sample members by use of the criterion of maximal probability of group membership (discriminant analysis) achieves a 77% rate of correct classification—188 out of the 244 employees are correctly classified, as shown in Table 10.4.

It is not surprising that the allocation by means of probability of group membership achieves a higher rate of correct classification than does the allocation using the joint-probability index. For, as stated earlier, the joint-probability system does not purport to reproduce the actual group-membership pattern, whereas discriminant analysis does, especially when used as a descriptive method of the sample for which the discriminant functions were computed.

Table 10.4 *Classification of Normative-Sample Members in Accordance with Probability of Group Membership*

Actual / Classified as	Passenger Agents	Mechanics	Operations Control Agents
Passenger Agents	72	11	2
Mechanics	16	67	10
Operations Control Agents	3	14	49

Finally, merely by way of illustration (for, as we have emphasized, it is based on logically untenable grounds), we present the outcome of allocation by predicted probability of success (regression analysis). Table 10.5 shows that 170 of the 244 employees (about 70%) are correctly classified by this scheme. The rate of "hits" is surprisingly high considering that prediction of success has nothing to do with *prediction* of group membership, and much to do with *assumption* of group membership in using the regression equations. The rate of correct classification achieved here must be attributed largely to an artifact in the way the success scores were generated.

Table 10.5 *Classification of Normative-Sample Members in Accordance with Predicted Probability of Success*

Actual \ Classified as	Passenger Agents	Mechanics	Operations Control Agents
Passenger Agents	62	22	1
Mechanics	17	68	8
Operations Control Agents	16	10	40

Classification of Applicant-Sample Members

As stated earlier, no figures can be obtained for percentages of correct classification by any topology in a cross-validation sample in our fictitious example. Nevertheless, an application of the joint-probability scheme to the as-yet-unclassified applicants' group is not entirely devoid of meaning. We may subdivide the applicants' group into passenger agents, mechanics, and operations control agents subgroups in accordance with the allocation dictated by the joint-probability index. Then each of these subgroups may be compared with the corresponding group in the normative sample to assess the degree of resemblance in some relevant aspect. In particular, it seems most pertinent to compare the matrix of intercorrelations among the three activity preference scales in each of the three putative job-specialty subgroups with that in the corresponding specialty group of the normative sample.

Classifying the 135 members of the applicants' group by the joint-probability method, it was found that 35 applicants were allocated as passenger agents, 73 as mechanics, and 27 as operations control agents. The correlation matrix for each of these three subgroups was as shown in Table 10.6, which also shows the correlation matrices for the corresponding job-specialty groups in the normative sample.

Examination of Table 10.6 shows that the resemblance between the corresponding pairs of correlation matrices is not great. Nevertheless, it should be noted that, among the nine distinct correlation coefficients in the three applicants' subgroups, only two are of substantial magnitude when the corresponding coefficients in the normative group are essentially zero (the r_{32} in the mechanics and operations control agents subgroups); two coefficients are substantially positive in both the applicants' and normative

Table 10.6 *Correlation Matrices for the Three Activity Preference Scales in Subgroups of the Applicants' Group as Classified by Joint-Probability Index, and in Corresponding Job-Specialty Groups of the Normative Sample*

	Applicants' Group			Normative Sample		
Passenger Agents	1.000	.536	.009	1.000	.237	−.170
	.536	1.000	−.059	.237	1.000	.184
	.009	−.059	1.000	−.170	.184	1.000
Mechanics	1.000	−.022	.264	1.000	−.097	.218
	−.022	1.000	.349	−.097	1.000	.006
	.264	.349	1.000	.218	.006	1.000
Operations Control	1.000	.001	−.075	1.000	.108	.045
Agents	.001	1.000	.350	.108	1.000	.010
	−.075	.350	1.000	.045	.010	1.000

samples (the r_{21} for passenger agents and the r_{31} for mechanics); the remaining five coefficients are essentially zero in both samples.

Tenuous as the foregoing indications of resemblance between the applicants' and normative-sample correlation matrices may be, they give some grounds for expecting that the regression equations constructed for the job-specialty groups in the normative sample will be at least approximately valid for predicting success for applicants allocated to the respective groups by the proposed method. We thus have partial evidence—as much as we can expect for our fictitious example—that the joint-probability method will lead to "reasonable" allocations. Further evidence, using real data, may be found in Tatsuoka (1956).

In conclusion, it must be reiterated that the method proposed in this chapter does not run counter to the principle that data on group membership should be of prime concern in the problem of personnel classification. The joint-probability index merely augments group-membership information with a possibility of incorporating the prediction of success. It thus offers a means for a personnel adviser to temper the *status quo* of employee choices with his desire for particular levels of accomplishment in the various job categories to which he has to allocate individuals from the applicant pool.

Chapter 11

Personnel Selection, Allocation, Classification, and Advising

America's entry into World War I occurred at a time when Karl Pearson had only recently developed the correlation coefficient and Truman Lee Kelley had introduced the idea of multiple regression into his work on educational guidance. Psychologists called into the service employed these techniques which allowed them to demonstrate that they could do a better-than-chance job of distributing drafted men into one of the many categories of jobs that had to be manned. The coincidence of these events represents the beginnings of personnel psychology in this country. The theory of multiple regression has dominated the course of personnel psychology ever since.

This technique flourished with the publication of Hull's book on aptitude testing (1928). Hull simply extended the concept of personnel classification by means of multiple regression to its logical limit. He suggested that for a given battery of tests, a multiple regression equation could be determined for each job in the United States; a client wishing to be advised could be given this battery of tests; his success in each of the jobs could be predicted by means of the multiple regression equations; and the client could choose his job in terms of this knowledge.

This logic dominated the personnel assignment procedures of the air force during World War II and is continued in its present career guidance and personnel allocation program. The air force and other armed services, however, have introduced one further modification, that of guiding and allocating predominantly in terms of the several highest predicted standardized criterion scores for an airman.

On employing this logical method, it is assumed that all individuals are of equal worth; all individuals should have equal opportunities; all individuals should know what they can do best and should make career decisions accordingly. The method is consistent with our belief that we

357

may allocate individuals to jobs in a way that maximizes the productive efficiency of the society, the armed services, or an industrial plant, provided that we are acting in the best interests of the individuals allocated. And we feel that we act in their best interests when we allocate them to that which we think they can do best.

However, Hull's suggestion and the use of it in industry and armed services ignores one basic fact of the validity of multiple regression—the person must first be a member of a particular occupational population to estimate his rank in the occupation he has chosen. We seldom bother to estimate an individual's similarity to those who are in the occupation before using the multiple regression relationship for the occupation. And yet members of various occupations are not randomly distributed throughout the test space from which the multiple regression relationship is developed.

Visual acuity does not correlate with pilot proficiency. And yet no officer with duty assignment as a pilot wears glasses. The air force has introduced perfect visual acuity as a criterion for admission to the occupational population, pilot. But not all of the criteria defining occupational membership are as obvious as this. The Dunn study (1955) of Brown University freshmen who became chemistry or history majors is illustrative (see page 323). Stewart (1947) has shown that occupations are differentiated by scores on the Army General Classification Test. Bennett, Seashore, and Wesman (1952) have shown both that college students differ from noncollege students in their scores on the Differential Aptitude Test and that later members of various occupations also score differently on this test. Other studies demonstrate other differences among occupational groups. However, studies of this kind are few in number for the problem has not-been investigated very thoroughly. The results can not be highly systematized from the present sparse data. This question should concern us more. It raises doubts about the use of multiple regression, even for selection for a single job.

There have been a few psychologists who have pursued the question of occupational differences at various times. Probably the greatest amount of systematic investigation of this kind was made by the Minnesota Employment Stabilization Research Project during the 1930's. These investigations, however, were hindered by the lack of an adequate statistical model.

For some reason this line of research lay dormant during World War II. Even now this type of research for personnel problems is not popular, seemingly because of the inability of psychologists to free themselves from the multiple regression orientation in their evaluation of personnel research. Such confusion is epitomized by Mosier (1951).

Beginning with the work of Du Mas on a coefficient of profile similarity (1949), a series of articles by Cattell (1949) and Cronbach and Gleser

(1952), among others, appeared dealing with the profile problem. However, the interest in profiles has been in the comparison of the profile for one individual with that for another rather than in personnel classification itself.

In this book we have developed a consistent logic for inferring the occupational population of which an individual of unknown occupation is likely to be a member. We started with a series of test scores on an experimental sample of men who were allowed to distribute themselves among jobs in World Airlines as they wished. Later we determined the job in which they were, their satisfaction with the job, and the airline's satisfaction with the men. Satisfaction with the job and satisfaction of the airline with the men were taken as criteria for group membership. We then returned to the previous test scores.

We found that the test scores of the n_g men in the gth job could be conceived of as a group of points in the test space. This conception of the test scores had considerable merit. First, the model showed that not all satisfactory and satisfied individuals in a job were at the same point in the test space. The model allowed us to examine the amount of overlap in the test space existing among satisfactory and satisfied apprentices in each of the G jobs. We are able to determine for a particular point in a particular job the relative frequency of points in the job that occurred with a lesser frequency. These fractions when multiplied by 100 were called centour scores.

A table of centour scores proved to be very handy for a personnel adviser for inferring typicalness of a particular set of test scores to those of known later job classification.

This test score model resolved a number of profile problems. These problems concern the type of scale that should be used, the group on which scores should be standardized, the representation of joint performance, the representation of dispersion of the specialty, the order in which profile stalks should be depicted, the problem of connecting profile points, the problem of incorporating job differences in personnel advising, and particularly the problem of inferring the job of which a particular profile is representative.

As the number of test variates increases beyond three, centour scores based upon the test space itself become impractical because of the large number of test score combinations ordinarily involved. Consequently, a logical procedure is necessary for some reduction of the number of variates.

Personnel advising is essentially a procedure of trying to infer the later job classification from a knowledge of the test scores. Consequently, personnel advising will be most accurate when based upon a system in which the number of correct classifications of personnel in the sample would be maximum if the job classification were lost. Rao (1952, pp. 308–309) has proven that in the multivariate normal model the number of correct classifications of the sample is maximal when the boundary regions are defined as we have indicated in Chapter 6. We found in Chapter 8 that when the dispersion matrices in each specialty were approximately the same, the topology in a multiple discriminant space placed almost all points in the same region in the discriminant space topology as they had been in the test space topology. Consequently, the multiple discriminant function is a very useful technique for this problem when this condition exists. Even when it does not exist, the multiple discriminant function probably provides a better method of reducing the number of variates than other available multivariate methods.

We found that the principal component method of factor analysis did not have this desirable property. In order to keep points in the same region as they were in the test space, it is necessary to use all of the principal components, and this is not likely to result in a very considerable reduction in the number of test variates.

Multiple regression methods of reducing the number of variates to one on a standardized predicted criterion scale led to a number of problems that were discussed in Chapter 9. The technique has little to recommend it as a procedure for inferring group membership.

The topology criterion discussed in Chapter 6 defined the boundary between two groups in the multivariate test space as the locus of points where the frequency in the two multivariate normal populations was the same. This boundary may be easily illustrated for the two-group univariate case, as in Fig. 11.1. If we define n_{gh} as the number in group g classified as group h members, for this isofrequency boundary, $n_{12} + n_{21}$ is a minimum. In other words, when the topology is used to classify persons whose group

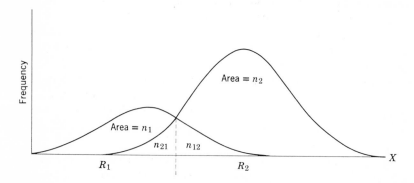

Fig. 11.1 *Boundary between two groups.*

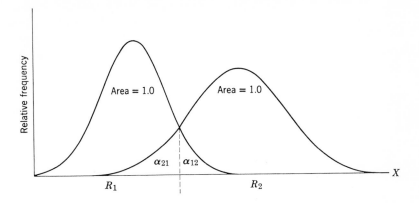

Fig. 11.2 *Boundary between two groups.*

is unknown from a knowledge of their score X, a minimum number of misclassifications results. This is true for the multivariate, as well as the univariate, case.

A second criterion for a topology could have been used had relative frequencies in each group been known instead of the actual frequencies. The boundary between any two groups would then be the locus of points of equal relative frequency in the two groups. For the two-group univariate case the boundary is represented in Fig. 11.2. If α_{gh} is defined as

$$\alpha_{gh} \equiv \frac{n_{gh}}{n_g}$$

where n_g is the number of observations in the gth group, the iso-relative-frequency boundary establishes regions where the sum of the *proportions* of misclassification is a minimum, that is $\alpha_{12} + \alpha_{21}$ is a minimum. We have seen in Chapter 6 that the boundaries of the topology may also be established in terms of equal centour scores. For the two-group univariate case, the boundary might be like that of Fig. 11.3. This isocentour score scheme of classification establishes regions where $\alpha_{12} = \alpha_{21}$. This is true in the bulk of multivariate normal cases, as well as in the univariate normal case. For multivariate normal populations with dispersion matrices whose *determinants* are equal (the matrices themselves do *not* have to be equal), the centour score concurs with the scheme of using the equal relative frequency boundaries.

When the proportion of apprentices who will be members of each group is more or less constant over recruitment intervals, the isofrequency scheme is the best to use for personnel classification provided the sample

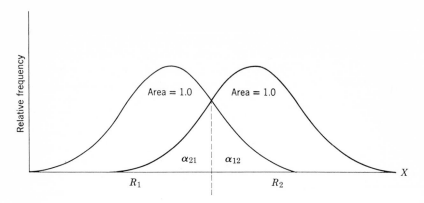

Fig. 11.3 *Boundary between two groups*

used for determining the decision rule is stratified. Advising according to this rule will result in a minimum number of men who would be mis-classified as to their actual choice.

If the proportion of individuals who become members of each job is believed to vary over the recruitment intervals in such a way that in the long run the average proportions in all jobs are more or less equal, the iso-relative-frequency scheme is the best. This scheme results in a minimum proportion of apprentices who would be misadvised.

When we do not know how the proportions in the several groups will vary over recruitment intervals, the centour score would seem best. In this instance, we have no good *a priori* estimate of the possibility for a random apprentice to be a member of group *g*; therefore, we cannot use the isofrequency scheme, which is the maximum likelihood rule when these *a priori* probabilities are known. Since the *a priori* probabilities are not known, this means that we cannot presume that they are equal, which would be necessary if we were to use the iso-relative-frequency scheme which is the maximum likelihood scheme under this condition of equal *a priori* probabilities. The centour score scheme provides only this kind of probability statement: *If this individual is indeed a member of this group*, then the probability is such and such that his score combination would be as deviant from the centroid as it was observed to be, or more deviant. Therefore the centour score makes no use of *a priori* probabilities. This is both an advantage and a disadvantage.

If there are marked differences in the *a priori* probabilities, an individual with a high centour score with reference to a group with a very small *a priori* probability might actually become a member of another job with reference to which his centour is somewhat lower but which has a much larger *a priori* probability. That is, the centour score scheme has a tendency to oversupply small groups. On the other hand, the centour score does identify the proximity of a point to the centroid of the group that has a very small *a priori* probability. That job may actually have a nonexistent region in either the isofrequency or the iso-relative-frequency topologies. This is possible because the density of a group may be completely over-shadowed by the density of another group throughout the entire region of the smaller group.

In the situations just discussed, no quotas regulate the number classified in each group. This assumption is always made in the logic of discrimi-natory topology. It will be noticed in the misclassification counts recorded in Chapter 6 that when individuals are *classified* according to the dis-criminatory topology, the number of points in the region R_g is not necessarily the number of apprentices actually in the group g. This is why the logic of topology is consistent with the logic of personnel advising. When advising an apprentice the logic that maximizes the probability of hitting upon the apprentice's choice is used. The classification topology has this property.

Personnel officers have the additional problem of *allocating* apprentices to jobs after personnel advising. Now it is necessary that the personnel officer get the number of apprentices needed in each job or, at least, the proportion of apprentices needed in each job. Rao (1952, pp. 322–324) presents a solution for the problem of assigning n_1 individuals to group 1 and n_2 individuals to group 2 out of a population of $n_1 + n_2$ candidates. In essence, Rao's results show that, when we have predetermined quotas, the best allocation rule is independent of the *a priori* probabilities for a random individual to be a member of any group, that is, independent of the relative sizes of the several groups in the population at large. Although Rao's conclusion appears to hold for any number of groups, Rao's *method* seems to be readily applicable only in the two-group instance where the rule of procedure amounts to computing the value of

$$\frac{f_1(X_1, X_2, \ldots, X_T)}{f_2(X_1, X_2, \ldots, X_T)} = \lambda$$

for each of the $n_1 + n_2 = N$ individuals, and assigning the n_1 individuals with the largest values of λ to group 1, the rest to group 2. The expression

$$f_g(X_1, X_2, \ldots, X_T)$$

stands for the relative frequency function for group g in the foregoing equation.

For the three-group instance, Rao proposes a geometric device (pp. 327–328). This is a trial and error method which appears rather tedious to apply in practice, and apparently cannot be used when $g > 3$ unless we go to the trouble of repeating the trial and error process

$$\frac{(G - 1)(G - 2)}{2}$$

times on as many charts.

Thus the *best* decision rule appears difficult to practice when the number of groups is large. If so, it would seem that the centour score scheme is the best alternative because it is independent of *a priori* probabilities. The most reasonable way to use the centour scheme in this instance appears to be to start with the group with the *smallest* quota n_1, taking the n_1 individuals with the largest centours with respect to this group; then allocating the n_2 individuals (among those not already assigned to group 1) with the largest centours for group 2 to group 2, the group with the second smallest quota n_2; and so on.

Thus it appears that the pure simplicity of the centour score places it in an advantageous position in all three types of personnel psychology problems: selection; placement (allocation); and advising (classification). The centour score says merely that a given set of test scores is typical or atypical (in a centile sense) of the scores of persons who later became members of a particular group. If satisfaction and success are used in the definition of the group, the centour score for the group becomes a particularly useful number.

If applicants are to be selected for only one job, n_1 applicants with the highest centour scores for that job would be selected. This would ensure maximum homogeneity of the type of person satisfied with, and successful in, the position. If a pool of N men is to be placed in several jobs, the position needing the smallest number of men would be filled first, and this would be filled with the n_1 men with the highest centour scores for that job. The position needing the next smallest number of men would then be filled, supplying it with the n_2 men among those remaining after job one had been filled, and so on.

Centour scores also provide a basis for job advising. Since the centour indicates the typicalness or atypicalness of a client to the satisfactory and satisfied person in each of the jobs under consideration, the client could be informed of his typicalness in relation to this person quite readily. If some indication of the relative number of people actually employed in each job were given at the same time, the client would be in a position to evaluate his chances of being employed in a particular job by combining the information concerning his centour score for the job with the information about the relative number of people employed in the job.

The centour scheme may not be attractive for two reasons: (1) it does not seem to offer any opportunity to allocate people so that the maximum efficiency of the organization is obtained; and (2) it maintains the status quo.

We have already commented about the use of predicted standardized criterion scores in schemes to maximize the over-all efficiency of the unit. First, the regression equations may rule out variables that are actually important for adequate performance in a job because the population of people entering this job already select themselves on certain variates. Second, the use of the standardized criterion scale makes numbers appear similar that may be not similar. And, third, use of any regression equation for a given set of scores assumes that the scores are a part of the population of scores on which the regression relationship was based. This is undoubtedly not the case. As a result, allocation procedures based upon standardized proficiency estimates result in some of the ambiguous maximized efficiency that we have represented.

Rao and Slater (1949) offer this comment on the problem:

"...In developing a selection procedure for an occupation, it is usual to apply psychological tests to a group of entrants; and after allowing them to remain in the occupation long enough to provide a reasonably reliable indication of the degree of success each has attained, to correlate their scores on the tests with the criterion of success and calculate a multiple regression equation. This defines a method of 'weighted information' to apply to individuals' scores; and it is generally assumed that the higher the sum score obtained by any individual, the greater his probability of succeeding in the occupation. This assumption (unless supplemented by others) overlooks the fact that people are often unsuccessful in occupations too far beneath their abilities. In considering an individual's suitability, it might be better to examine the multivariate dispersion of the test performances of the men who proved to be normally successful in the occupation. Their averages will indicate a point in the multidimensional space defined by the test scores, and a dispersion will indicate a region of permissible variation about that point. Then the likelihood that an individual will succeed in the occupation, i.e., form a homogeneous member of the group of people who are normally successful in it, can be determined by relating the point in the multidimensional space indicated by his test score to the region of permissible variation about the multivariate mean point of the normally successful group." (pp. 17–18)

Kelley (1940) also has offered this short comment on the problem in considering his index of slant distance:

"...The comparison of the individual with the average participant instead of, say, with the highly successful participant is appropriate in view of the fact that superior individuals should not spend their energies upon inferior tasks. If one's profile is well above that of the average participant in a job, it is presumptive evidence that he is fitted for a different and more advanced job." (p. 28)

The country has a pool of ability and personality available in every group of school graduates. Manpower research groups now have what appears to be a profitable new line of research. The purposes of this research would be to map out the regions of the country's available supply of human ability and personality. This task will be neither easy nor small. There are few guides in the literature because the problem has seldom been approached in this way. Regression studies will be of some assistance, but the data of the regression studies that will be of most importance are the previously neglected means and standard deviations.

If this research is done right, manpower research agencies will probably not worry about maintaining the status quo because the status quo will be what accomplishes the desired purpose. Of course, a prediction system such as this must be subject to continual review. The requirement for a particular specialty may change, which will mean that the manpower research agency will have to draw applicants for this job from a new region of its pool of human ability and personality. Some readjustment of the supply region for the job may be necessary. Adjustments of the status quo would be easier to make in the original test space than they are in the discriminant space because the discriminant space depends upon the location of the job centroid and the dispersion on the job centroid. But methods can be found for making adjustments in decision rules derived for centour scores in a discriminant space. One such method is given in Chapter 10. The index of joint probability of electing a group and of reaching a predetermined level of success in the elected group is promising for the study of this problem. Variation of the predetermined success levels of the several occupations under study can point to more effective ways of uniting individual preference for work and societal preference for efficiency at work.

Appendix A

Contour Ellipses for a Large Sample of Airmen

The normalized standard scores for 4696 airmen on the Armed Forces Qualification Test (AFQT) and the aural section of the Signal Corps Code Aptitude Test (SCCAT) are shown in the bivariate frequency distribution in Table A.1. The same data are graphically represented in Fig. A.1. Even

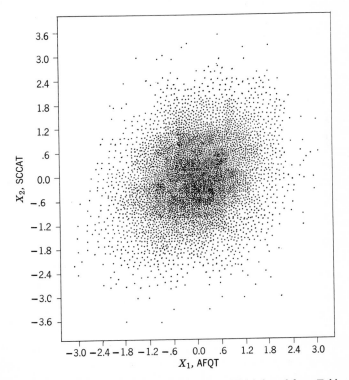

Fig. A.1 *Scatter diagram of a large sample; N = 4696 (plotted from Table A.1).*

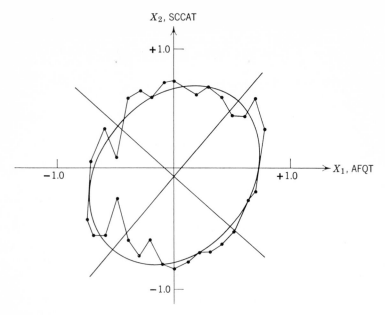

Fig. A.2 *Plot of an isofrequency contour and the equivalent ideal normal ellipse for the bivariate distribution of Table A.1* ($\chi = .74120$).

with as large a sample as this it is not possible to locate precisely the cells of equal frequency by empirical methods of counting. An estimate of the locations of isofrequency points can be obtained by fitting a normal distribution to each column of the table and computing the SCCAT score for a fixed abscissa. A plot of this kind is shown in Fig. A.2, together with the equivalent ideal contour ellipse.

The probability is that a point drawn at random from the bivariate normal distribution will be in the small rectangle $dX_1 . dX_2$ is

$$
\begin{aligned}
y = {} & \frac{1}{2\pi\sigma_1\sigma_2 \sqrt{1 - \rho^2}} \\
& \times \exp\left\{ -\frac{1}{2}\frac{1}{(1 - \rho^2)} \left[\left(\frac{X_1 - \mu_1}{\sigma_1}\right)^2 - 2\rho\left(\frac{X_1 - \mu_1}{\sigma_1}\right)\left(\frac{X_2 - \mu_2}{\sigma_2}\right) \right.\right. \\
& \left.\left. + \left(\frac{X_2 - \mu_2}{\sigma_2}\right)^2 \right] \right\} dX_1 \, dX_2 \quad \text{(A.1)}
\end{aligned}
$$

The population means μ_1 and μ_2, the population standard deviations σ_1 and σ_2, and the population correlation ρ are constants in the equation for a given population. The only variables are X_1, the score in variate 1,

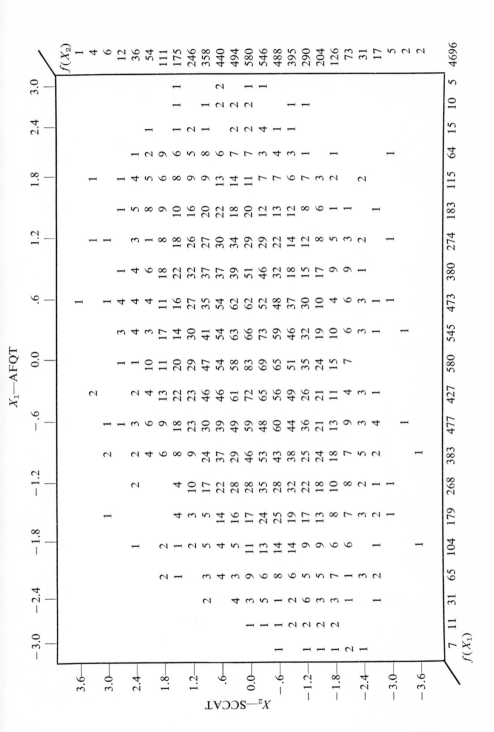

and X_2, the score in variate 2. The foregoing expression will be constant for all values X_1, X_2 for which

$$\frac{1}{1-\rho^2}\left[\left(\frac{X_1-\mu_1}{\sigma_1}\right)^2 - 2\rho\left(\frac{X_1-\mu_1}{\sigma_1}\right)\left(\frac{X_2-\mu_2}{\sigma_2}\right) + \left(\frac{X_2-\mu_2}{\sigma_2}\right)^2\right]$$
$$= \chi^2 \text{ (constant)}\quad\text{(A.2)}$$

This equation specifies an ellipse for each value assigned to χ^2. The center of each ellipse will be μ_1, μ_2; the axes will be oriented in the same way; the ellipses will differ only in the length of their major and minor axes. Such a set of ellipses is called *homothetic*.

The statistics describing the bivariate sample are given in Table A.2.

Table A.2   *Statistics of a Large Sample of Airmen—Two Variables*

	AFQT, X_1		SCCAT, X_2
N	4696		4696
Mean	$-.0029$		$-.0514$
Variance	.9424		1.1014
Standard deviation	.9708		1.0071
Correlation		.2507	

The data were first obtained in a roster in the form illustrated in Table A.3.

Table A.3   *Roster of Scores*

Airman Number	AFQT	SCCAT
1	1.8	1.7
2	$-.9$	.6
3	1.5	-1.2
$\vdots$	$\vdots$	$\vdots$
4696	-1.3	$-.7$

The roster is represented in the 4696×2 matrix X.

$$X = \begin{Vmatrix} 1.8 & 1.7 \\ -.9 & .6 \\ 1.5 & -1.2 \\ \vdots & \vdots \\ -1.3 & -.7 \end{Vmatrix} \quad \text{(4696 rows)}$$

The sum of squares and cross-products matrix in the original scores is

$$X'X = \begin{Vmatrix} 4425.78 & 1151.77 \\ 1151.77 & 4775.22 \end{Vmatrix}$$

The sum of squares and cross-products matrix in deviation scores is

$$S = X'X - \bar{X}'\bar{X} = \begin{Vmatrix} 4425.7406 & 1151.0715 \\ 1151.0715 & 4762.8313 \end{Vmatrix}$$

The dispersion matrix of the variances and covariances is

$$D = \frac{1}{n}S = \begin{Vmatrix} .9424490 & .2451174 \\ .2451174 & 1.0142315 \end{Vmatrix}$$

And the correlation matrix is

$$R = \begin{Vmatrix} 1.0000 & .2507 \\ .2507 & 1.0001 \end{Vmatrix}$$

Equation A.2 may be simplified by introducing deviation scores and multiplying both sides by $(1 - \rho^2)\sigma_1^2\sigma_2^2$ as follows.

Writing the substitution

$$x_1 = X_1 - \mu_1$$
$$x_2 = X_2 - \mu_2$$

and multiplying by $(1 - \rho^2)$ we obtain

$$\sigma_2^2 x_1^2 - 2\rho\sigma_1\sigma_2 x_1 x_2 + \sigma_1^2 x_2^2 = \chi^2(1 - \rho^2)\sigma_1^2\sigma_2^2 \qquad \text{(A.3)}$$

as the equation of the contour ellipses of a normal bivariate population.

The elements of the dispersion matrix D are the coefficients σ_1^2, σ_2^2, ρ.

$$D = \begin{Vmatrix} \sigma_1^2 & \rho\sigma_1\sigma_2 \\ \rho\sigma_1\sigma_2 & \sigma_2^2 \end{Vmatrix}$$

The determinant of the dispersion matrix is

$$|D| = \sigma_1^2\sigma_2^2(1 - \rho^2)$$

And the adjoint of the dispersion matrix is

$$\text{adj } D = \begin{Vmatrix} \sigma_2^2 & -\rho\sigma_1\sigma_2 \\ -\rho\sigma_1\sigma_2 & \sigma_1^2 \end{Vmatrix}$$

In matrix notation the equation of the ellipse may be written

$$x \cdot \text{adj } D \cdot x' = |D|\chi^2$$

where the row matrix x contains the two elements x_1, x_2 representing values measured from the centroid on the two test axes.

We assume that the sample data are reasonably described by the ideal bivariate normal distribution and take the sample statistics as estimates of μ, ρ, and σ^2. The numerical results are

$$\begin{aligned} |D| &= (.9424490)(1.0142315) - (.2451174)^2 \\ &= .8957790 \end{aligned}$$

$$x \cdot \text{adj } D \cdot x' = \left\| x_1 \quad x_2 \right\| \cdot \left\| \begin{array}{cc} 1.0142315 & -.2451174 \\ -.2451174 & .9424490 \end{array} \right\| \cdot \left\| \begin{array}{c} x_1 \\ x_2 \end{array} \right\|$$

$$= 1.0142315x_1{}^2 - 2(.2451174)x_1 x_2 + .9424490x_2{}^2$$

The locus of the ellipse defined by a fixed value of χ^2 is, from Eq. A.3,

$$1.0142315x_1{}^2 - .4902348x_1 x_2 + .9424490x_2{}^2 = .8957790\chi^2$$

We may now choose any value of χ^2 and find the coordinates of the points on the χ^2 ellipse. To determine the coordinates or to plot the ellipse on the scatter diagram for any particular centour value requires only a knowledge of the proper numerical value of χ^2 to substitute in the equation. We choose for numerical illustration the problem of finding the C_{50} or 50th centour ellipse. This ellipse is of such size that one-half the frequency in the total test space lies inside the ellipse and one-half lies outside the ellipse. We shall find first the numerical value of χ^2 to insert in Eq. A.3; second, the angle which the major axis of the ellipse makes with the test axes; and third, the length of the semiaxes of the C_{50} ellipse.

The value of χ^2 may be determined in two ways. Fisher and Yates' (1953) Table of χ^2 gives the values of χ^2 for selected values of P, the probability of a greater divergence than the tabled value. For $P = .50$ and two degrees of freedom the tabled value is $\chi^2 = 1.386$. Since the existing tables do not give χ^2 for all values of P in which we are interested, a more general method is illustrated.

Pearson's Table of the Incomplete Moment Function (Table IX, pp. 22–23 in *Tables for Statisticians and Biometricians*) may be used to compute the proportion of a bivariate normal distribution which lies outside an ellipse fixed by a given value of χ^2. The table gives values of $m_{T-1}(\chi)$ for the argument χ by increments of .1. The T in the subscript stands for the number of variates (tests). Since we are considering two tests we are interested in the value $m_1(\chi)$. When T is an even number, as in this example, the proportion of the distribution *inside* an ellipse with a fixed χ^2 is given by

$$q = \sqrt{2\pi} m_1(\chi)$$

The proportion outside the specified ellipse is the quantity

$$p = 1 - q$$

For the centour score 50 the numerical value of q is

$$q = 1 - .50 = .50$$

Substituting in the expression $q = \sqrt{2\pi} m_1(\chi)$ we obtain

$$.50 = \sqrt{2\pi} m_1(\chi)$$

$$m_1(\chi) = \frac{.50}{\sqrt{2\pi}}$$

$$= .1994711$$

In Pearson's Table IX we find the entries

χ	$m_1(\chi)$
1.1	.1810901
1.2	.2047562

The value of χ for $m_1(\chi) = .1994711$ obtained by linear interpolation is

$$\chi = 1.1 + \frac{1}{10}\left(\frac{.1994711 - .1810901}{.2047562 - .1810901}\right) = 1.1776681$$

Linear interpolation in this table does not give the value of χ to as many significant figures as are required in an example. The value of χ to seven decimal places, as obtained by quadratic interpolation, is

$$\chi = 1.1774062$$
$$\chi^2 = 1.3862854$$

When this value is substituted in Eq. A.3 the 50th centour ellipse for the AFQT and SCCAT data is

$$1.0142315x_1{}^2 - .4902348x_1x_2 + .9424490x_2{}^2 = (.8957790)(1.3862854)$$

In matrix form the same equation is written

$$x \cdot \text{adj } D \cdot x' = \chi^2 |D|$$

$$\|x_1 \quad x_2\| \cdot \begin{Vmatrix} 1.0142315 & -.2451174 \\ -.2451174 & .9424490 \end{Vmatrix} \cdot \begin{Vmatrix} x_1 \\ x_2 \end{Vmatrix} = 1.2418054$$

The angle θ between the test axis and the major axis of the ellipse is given by the equation

$$\tan 2\theta = \frac{2r_{12}\sigma_1\sigma_2}{\sigma_1{}^2 - \sigma_2{}^2}$$

Substituting numerical values taken from the dispersion matrix we obtain

$$\tan 2\theta = -\frac{.6796054}{.0995110}$$
$$= -6.8294500$$
$$2\theta = 98° \; 20'$$
$$\theta = 49° \; 10'$$

The family of contour ellipses is now known to be symmetrical about an axis inclined 49° 10′ to the axis in the test space and centered at $\bar{X}_1 = -.0029$, $\bar{X}_2 = -.0514$. If we now choose a new coordinate system y_1y_2 in which the origin is the centroid of the sample and the axes are rotated to form an angle of 49° 10′ with the X_1X_2 axes, the ellipses will be symmetrical around the new y_1y_2 coordinate axes. The major axes of the ellipses will be coincident with y_1 and the minor axes will be coincident with y_2.

When the equation for the ellipse is rewritten by the usual substitution for the rotation of axes

$$x_1 = y_1 \cos \theta - y_2 \sin \theta$$
$$x_2 = y_1 \sin \theta + y_2 \cos \theta$$

the cross-product term vanishes and the equation reduces to the standard form

$$\frac{y_1{}^2}{a^2} + \frac{y_2{}^2}{b^2} = 1$$

in which a is the length of the semimajor axis and b is the length of the semiminor axis. After substitution of the numerical values, the equation of the C_{50} ellipse expressed in the new coordinate system becomes

$$\frac{y_1{}^2}{(1.3037)^2} + \frac{y_2{}^2}{(1.0064)^2} = 1$$

The semiaxes are thus found to be 1.3037 and 1.0064. We are now able by geometric construction to draw the C_{50} ellipse on the scatter diagram of Fig. A.1. The result is shown in Fig. A.3.

If the scatter diagram is plotted accurately on a sufficiently large scale and the drafting of the ellipse is precise, the adequacy with which the ideal model describes the actual data can be estimated by inspection. In this example Fig. A.3 was plotted on a large scale and the number of score points lying outside the ellipse was counted. A total of 2359 dots were found outside the C_{50} ellipse. This number is 50.2% of the 4696 dots in the sample.

In matrix notation the equation of the χ^2 ellipse was found to be

$$x \cdot \text{adj } D \cdot x' = \chi^2 |D|$$

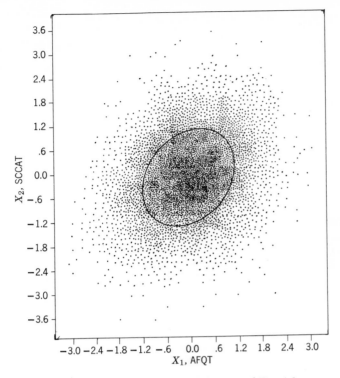

Fig. A.3 C_{50} *ellipse on scatter diagram of Fig. A.1.*

When the variate axes x_1, x_2 are transformed by a rotation to new axes y_1, y_2, the elements of the dispersion matrix D_x are transformed to form the matrix D_y. If the transformation is chosen so that the new coordinate system reduces the cross-product elements to zero, the dispersion matrix D_y representing the variance-covariance matrix in the y_1, y_2 axis system will be diagonal, and the diagonal elements will be the squares of the semiaxes of the particular contour ellipse for which $\chi^2 = 1.0$.

The dispersion matrix D may be reduced to diagonal form Δ in two ways. The elements of the diagonal matrix Δ will be the roots λ of the characteristic equation of D given by the expansion of the determinant of the characteristic matrix $D - \lambda I$.

$$
D - \lambda I = \begin{Vmatrix} \sigma_1{}^2 & r_{12}\sigma_1\sigma_2 \\ r_{12}\sigma_1\sigma_2 & \sigma_2{}^2 \end{Vmatrix} - \begin{Vmatrix} \lambda & 0 \\ 0 & \lambda \end{Vmatrix}
$$

$$
= \begin{Vmatrix} \sigma_1{}^2 - \lambda & r_{12}\sigma_1\sigma_2 \\ r_{12}\sigma_1\sigma_2 & \sigma_2{}^2 - \lambda \end{Vmatrix}
$$

The determinant of the characteristic matrix of D is

$$|D - \lambda I| \equiv \lambda^2 - \lambda(\sigma_1^2 + \sigma_2^2) + \sigma_1^2\sigma_2^2(1 - r_{12}^2) = 0$$

The two values of λ which satisfy the characteristic equation are the diagonal elements of Δ

$$\Delta = \begin{Vmatrix} \lambda_1 & 0 \\ 0 & \lambda_2 \end{Vmatrix}$$

$$= \begin{Vmatrix} 1.226 & 0 \\ 0 & .731 \end{Vmatrix}$$

When the required transformation is known, as it is in the example, the diagonal matrix Δ may be computed by the matrix multiplications indicated in the equation

$$\Delta = \Gamma'D\Gamma$$

where Γ is the transformation matrix containing as elements the direction cosines of the second, or y_1y_2, coordinate system referred to the first, or X_1X_2, coordinate system:

$$\Gamma = \begin{Vmatrix} \gamma_{11} & \gamma_{12} \\ \gamma_{21} & \gamma_{22} \end{Vmatrix}$$

The elements of Γ are cosines of the angles identified by subscripts. The subscript ij identifies the angle between the ith axis in the first system and jth axis in the second system. Thus γ_{11} is the cosine of the angle between the x_1 and y_1 axes of the two systems and γ_{21} is the cosine of the angle between x_2 and y_1. The relations are completely detailed in Fig. A.4 and Table A.4.

Table A.4   *Direction Cosines of the Transformation Matrix*

$$\theta = 49° \, 10'$$

$\gamma_{11} =$	$.65386$	$= \cos \theta$
$\gamma_{12} =$	$-.75661$	$= \cos (90° + \theta)$
$\gamma_{21} =$	$.75661$	$= \cos (90° - \theta)$
$\gamma_{22} =$	$.65386$	$= \cos \theta$

The transformation matrix is written numerically as

$$\Gamma = \begin{Vmatrix} .65386 & -.75661 \\ .75661 & .65386 \end{Vmatrix}$$

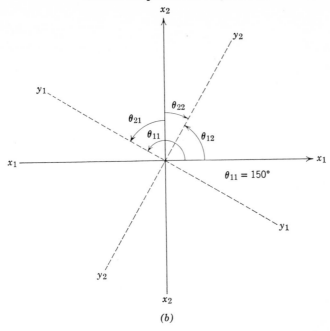

$$\theta_{11} = 150°$$

(b)

Fig. A.4a *Designation of the angles relating two axis systems—rotation through 60°.*

We note that the matrix Γ is orthogonal and that $\Gamma\Gamma' = I$ and $|\Gamma| = 1.0$. The fact that the determinant of the product of square matrices is equal to the product of their determinants leads to the useful result that the determinant of the dispersion matrix in the first axis system $|D|$ is equal to the determinant $|\Delta|$ of the dispersion matrix in the second axis system:

$$\Gamma'D\Gamma = \Delta$$
$$|\Gamma'D\Gamma| = |\Delta| = |\Gamma'| \cdot |D| \cdot |\Gamma|$$
$$|D| = |\Delta|$$

These facts, together with the theorem that the inverse of a matrix product is the product of the inverses taken in opposite order, lead to

$$\Gamma' \cdot \text{adj } D \cdot \Gamma = \text{adj } \Delta$$

The equation for the general contour ellipse may be written in either coordinate system. With reference to the original $x_1 x_2$ axes the equation is

$$\|x_1 \quad x_2\| \cdot \text{adj } D \cdot \left\|\begin{matrix} x_1 \\ x_2 \end{matrix}\right\| = \chi^2 |D|$$

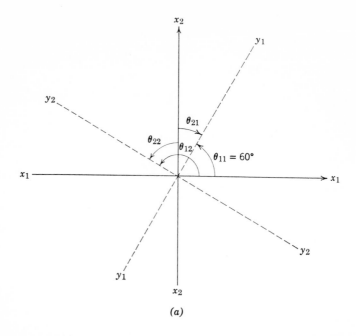

(a)

Fig. A.4b   *Designation of the angles relating two axis systems—rotation through* 150°.

In the new axis system $y_1 y_2$ the equation is

$$\| y_1 \ \ y_2 \| \cdot \operatorname{adj} \Delta \cdot \left\| \begin{matrix} y_1 \\ y_2 \end{matrix} \right\| = \chi^2 |\Delta|$$

The relation

$$\Gamma' \cdot \operatorname{adj} D \cdot \Gamma = \operatorname{adj} \Delta$$

may be used to write the equation of an ellipse in standard form. The equation is

$$y \cdot \operatorname{adj} \Delta \cdot y' = |\Delta|$$

In this special equation χ^2 has the value 1.0. We are seeking the ellipse which satisfies the equation

$$x \cdot \operatorname{adj} D \cdot x' = \chi^2 |D| = 1.2418054$$

where χ^2 takes the value 1.386+. Multiply both sides of this equation for the 50th centour of the AFQT and SCCAT data by $\chi^2 = 1.386+$

$$1.3862854 \left\{ x \left\| \begin{matrix} 1.0142315 & -.2451174 \\ -.2451174 & .9424490 \end{matrix} \right\| x' \right\} = (1.3862854)(1.2418054)$$

The numerical result is

$$x \cdot \begin{Vmatrix} 1.4060143 & -.3398027 \\ -.3398027 & 1.3065033 \end{Vmatrix} \cdot x' = 1.7214967$$

We now write the product of χ^2 and the dispersion matrix D as

$$\chi^2 D = \begin{Vmatrix} .9424490 & .2451174 \\ .2451174 & 1.0142315 \end{Vmatrix} \cdot 1.3862854$$

$$\chi^2 D = \begin{Vmatrix} 1.3065033 & .3398027 \\ .3398027 & 1.4060143 \end{Vmatrix}$$

and observe that the product of χ^2 and the adjoint of the matrix D is identical to the adjoint of the matrix product $\chi^2 D$. The determinant of the matrix $\chi^2 D$ is

$$|\chi^2 D| = 1.8369623 - .1154659$$
$$= 1.7214964$$

Thus it is apparent that multiplication of both sides of the equation

$$x \cdot \text{adj } D \cdot x' = \chi^2 |D|$$

by the scalar quantity χ^2 changes the equation to the form

$$x \cdot \text{adj } \chi^2 D \cdot x' = |\chi^2 D|$$

By applying the transformation Γ to the adjoint of the matrix $\chi^2 D$ we obtain the equation

$$y \cdot \text{adj } \chi^2 D \cdot y' = |\chi^2 \Delta| = |\chi^2 D|$$

The numerical values of the direction cosines are

$$\gamma_{11} = \cos \theta = .65386$$
$$\gamma_{12} = \cos (90° + \theta) = -\sin \theta = -.75661$$
$$\gamma_{21} = \cos (90° - \theta) = \sin \theta = .75661$$
$$\gamma_{22} = \cos \theta = .65386$$

The transformation matrix is

$$\Gamma = \begin{Vmatrix} .65386 & -.75661 \\ .75661 & .65386 \end{Vmatrix}$$

The transformed adjoint of the matrix $\chi^2 D$

$$\Gamma' \cdot \text{adj } \chi^2 D \cdot \Gamma$$

is easily computed in two steps as follows:

$$\Gamma' \cdot \mathrm{adj}\ \chi^2 D = \begin{Vmatrix} .65386 & .75661 \\ -.75661 & .65386 \end{Vmatrix} \cdot \begin{Vmatrix} 1.4060143 & -.3398027 \\ -.3398027 & 1.3065033 \end{Vmatrix}$$

$$\Gamma' \cdot \mathrm{adj}\ \chi^2 D \cdot \Gamma = \begin{Vmatrix} .6622384 & .7663301 \\ -1.2859879 & 1.1113684 \end{Vmatrix} \cdot \begin{Vmatrix} .65386 & -.75661 \\ .75661 & .65386 \end{Vmatrix}$$

The final result is

$$\Gamma' \cdot \mathrm{adj}\ \chi^2 D \cdot \Gamma = \begin{Vmatrix} 1.01282 & .000016 \\ .000016 & 1.69967 \end{Vmatrix} = \mathrm{adj}\ (\chi^2 \Delta)$$

This result is a diagonal matrix within the limits of accuracy imposed by the number of significant digits in the computation. When this result is substituted in the equation

$$y \cdot \mathrm{adj}\ \chi^2 \Delta \cdot y' = |\chi^2 \Delta|$$

we obtain

$$y \cdot \begin{Vmatrix} 1.01282 & 0 \\ 0 & 1.69967 \end{Vmatrix} \cdot y' = 1.7214967$$

The determinant of the matrix $\chi^2 \Delta$ is computed to provide a computational check with the algebraic equality $|\chi^2 D| = |\chi^2 \Delta|$

$$\begin{vmatrix} 1.01282 & 0 \\ 0 & 1.69967 \end{vmatrix} = 1.72146$$

which agrees with the determinant of the matrix $\chi^2 D$ to the extent of the significant figures in the transformation matrix Γ. The *square root* of the term in the lower right-hand corner of the adjoint of the $\chi^2 \Delta$ matrix is 1.3037. This is the semiaxis of the ellipse along the new reference axis y_1. The *square root* of the term in the upper left-hand corner of the adjoint of the $\chi^2 \Delta$ matrix is 1.0064. This is the semiaxis of the ellipse along the new reference axis y_2. Since the semiaxis of the ellipse along the reference axis y_1 is the larger value, the major axis of the ellipse lies on the reference axis y_1 and the minor axis lies on y_2.

The locus of points satisfying the equation

$$x \cdot \mathrm{adj}\ D \cdot x' = |D|$$

and its equivalent expression

$$y \cdot \mathrm{adj}\ \Delta \cdot y' = |\Delta|$$

in terms of the rotated axes is of special interest because each equation represents the ellipse for $\chi^2 = 1.0$. The equation in transformed axes

$$y \cdot \text{adj } \Delta \cdot y' = |\Delta|$$

may be calculated from the original equation

$$x \cdot \text{adj } D \cdot x' = |D|$$

by use of the transformation matrix Γ. The desired matrix is adj $\Delta = \Gamma' \cdot \text{adj } D \cdot \Gamma$. For the AFQT and SCCAT data the matrix products are

$$\Gamma' \cdot \text{adj } D = \begin{Vmatrix} .65386 & .75661 \\ -.75661 & .65386 \end{Vmatrix} \cdot \begin{Vmatrix} 1.0142315 & -.2451174 \\ -.2451174 & .9424490 \end{Vmatrix}$$

$$\Gamma' \cdot \text{adj } D \cdot \Gamma = \begin{Vmatrix} .4777071 & .5527939 \\ -.9276502 & .8016880 \end{Vmatrix} \cdot \begin{Vmatrix} .65386 & -.75661 \\ .75661 & .65386 \end{Vmatrix}$$

$$= \begin{Vmatrix} .73060 & .000012 \\ .000012 & 1.22606 \end{Vmatrix}$$

Thus the adjoint of the matrix Δ is

$$\text{adj } \Delta = \Gamma' \cdot \text{adj } D \cdot \Gamma = \begin{Vmatrix} .73060 & 0 \\ 0 & 1.22606 \end{Vmatrix}$$

and the matrix Δ is

$$= \begin{Vmatrix} 1.22606 & 0 \\ 0 & .73060 \end{Vmatrix}$$

The determinant of this matrix is

$$|\Delta| = .89576$$

which is equivalent to the determinant of the original matrix D

$$|D| = (.9424490)(1.0142315) - (.2451174)^2$$
$$= .8957790$$

Thus the ellipse specified by choosing $\chi^2 = 1.0$ is, in terms of the rotated axes,

$$y \cdot \begin{Vmatrix} .73060 & 0 \\ 0 & 1.22606 \end{Vmatrix} \cdot y' = .89578$$

which in expanded form is

$$.73060 y_1^2 + 1.22606 y_2^2 = .89578$$

By dividing both sides of the equation by .89578 the equation may be expressed in the standard form

$$\frac{y_1{}^2}{a_2} + \frac{y_2}{b_2} = 1$$

In this numerical example the result is

$$\frac{y_1{}^2}{\dfrac{.89578}{.73060}} + \frac{y_2{}^2}{\dfrac{.89578}{1.22606}} = \frac{y_1{}^2}{1.22606} + \frac{y_2{}^2}{.73060} = 1$$

In terms of the original axes x_1 and x_2, the same ellipse for the AFQT and SCCAT data has the equation

$$x \cdot \begin{Vmatrix} 1.0142315 & -.2451174 \\ -.2451174 & .9424490 \end{Vmatrix} \cdot x' = .8957790$$

which is a specific one of the general equation

$$x \cdot \text{adj } D \cdot x' = |D|\chi^2$$

It is apparent that these are equations in which χ^2 has the value 1.0. We use Pearson's Table IX to find the value $m_{1\chi} = .1569716$. The proportion of the total distribution inside the ellipse is given by

$$q = \sqrt{2\pi}(.1569716)$$
$$= 2.5066283(.1569716)$$
$$= .3934695$$

Therefore the proportion outside the ellipse is

$$p = 1 - .3934695$$
$$= .60653$$

so that this is the centour ellipse 60.653. In other words, the ellipse specified by the equation

$$x \cdot \text{adj } D \cdot x' = |D|$$

is one such that 60.653% of a normal bivariate distribution is outside of it. When the equation is divided by the determinant of D

$$x \cdot \begin{Vmatrix} \dfrac{\text{adj } D}{|D|} \end{Vmatrix} \cdot x' = 1$$

which may be written

$$x \cdot D^{-1} \cdot x' = 1$$

Similarly the equation of the ellipse in the rotated axis system may be written

$$y \cdot \Delta^{-1} \cdot y' = 1$$

Certain details of this ellipse are helpful in plotting it. It is tangent to the line $x_2 = \sigma_2$ at the point $(\sigma_1 r, \sigma_2)$; tangent to the line $x_2 = -\sigma_2$ at the point $(-\sigma_1 r, -\sigma_2)$; tangent to the line $x_1 = \sigma_1$ at the point $(\sigma_1, \sigma_2 r)$; tangent to the line $x_1 = -\sigma_1$ at the point $(-\sigma_1, \sigma_2 r)$. The ellipse intersects the line $x_1 = 0$ at the two points

$$(0, \sigma_2 \sqrt{1 - r^2})$$
$$(0, -\sigma_2 \sqrt{1 - r^2})$$

and intersects the line $x_2 = 0$ at the two points

$$(\sigma_1 \sqrt{1 - r^2}, 0)$$
$$(-\sigma_1 \sqrt{1 - r^2}, 0)$$

These points lead to a simple method of sketching the ellipse. Draw the $x_1 x_2$ axes through the centroid. Mark off on each axis the distance $\pm 1.0\sigma$. Draw the rectangle indicated by these four points with sides parallel to the axes. The desired ellipse is tangent to the rectangle at four points. In other words, the ellipse is contained in the 1σ rectangle. For this reason we call the ellipse defined by the equation

$$xD^{-1}x' = 1$$

the *one-standard deviation ellipse*. The four points at which the ellipse intercepts the axes are easily determined. They indicate the relative magnitude of the minor axis, and the orientation of the ellipse with reference to the coordinate system can be determined from the equation $\tan 2\theta = 2r\sigma_1 \sigma_2 / (\sigma_1^2 - \sigma_2^2)$. The rectangle is illustrated in Fig. A.5. The precise lengths of semimajor and semiminor axes of the ellipse are obtained from the elements of the diagonal matrix Δ formed from the product $\Gamma' D \Gamma$. These elements are the variances of the score points projected on the new axes to which the original axes have been rotated. The standard deviations of the scores along the y_1 and y_2 axes are the square roots of the elements of Δ.

The one-standard deviation ellipse in the y_1, y_2 coordinate system will be contained in and tangent at four points to the rectangle determined by the standard deviation of scores on the $y_1 y_2$ axes. The ellipse is tangent to the line $y_2 = \Sigma_2$ at the point $(0, \Sigma_2)$ (Σ denotes the standard deviation in the rotated coordinate system); tangent to the line $x_2 = -\Sigma_2$ at the

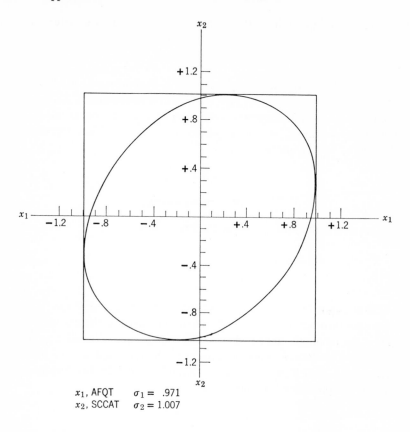

x_1, AFQT $\sigma_1 = .971$
x_2, SCCAT $\sigma_2 = 1.007$

Fig. A.5 *The one-sigma ellipse and circumscribed rectangle.*

point $(0, -\Sigma_2)$; tangent to the line $x_1 = \Sigma_1$ at the point $(\Sigma_1, 0)$; and tangent to the line $x_1 = -\Sigma_1$ at the point $(-\Sigma_1, 0)$.

Thus 12 points are readily available for sketching the one-standard deviation ellipse. The construction of this ellipse proceeds easily in either coordinate system, as in Fig. A.6.

For the AFQT and SCCAT data the matrix R is

$$R = \begin{Vmatrix} 1 & .2507 \\ .2507 & 1 \end{Vmatrix}$$

and the matrix D is

$$D = \begin{Vmatrix} .9424490 & .2451174 \\ .2451174 & 1.0142315 \end{Vmatrix}$$

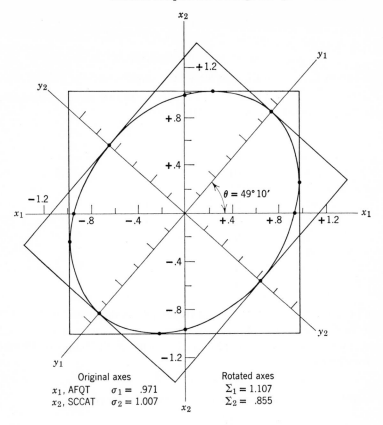

Original axes

x_1, AFQT $\sigma_1 =$ .971
x_2, SCCAT $\sigma_2 =$ 1.007

Rotated axes

$\Sigma_1 =$ 1.107
$\Sigma_2 =$ .855

Fig. A.6 *The one-sigma ellipse and circumscribed rectangles in two coordinate systems.*

The standard deviations of the scores along the x_1x_2 axes are

$$\sigma_2 = \sqrt{.9424490} = .9708$$

$$\sigma_2 = \sqrt{1.0142315} = 1.0071$$

The y_1y_2 axes are rotated to a position which is 49° 10′ counterclockwise to the x_1x_2 axis system. The dispersion matrix on the y_1y_2 axes is

$$\Delta = \begin{Vmatrix} 1.22606 & 0 \\ 0 & .73060 \end{Vmatrix}$$

The standard deviation of the scores along the y_1 axis is

$$\Sigma_1 = \sqrt{1.22606} = 1.1073$$

and the standard deviation of the projections of the scores on the y_2 axis is

$$\Sigma_2 = \sqrt{.73060} = .8548$$

These values Σ_1, Σ_2 are the lengths of the semiaxes of the ellipse. Since $r = .2507$, $\sqrt{1 - r^2} = .9681$. The 12 points of the one-standard deviation ellipse for the AFQT and SCCAT data are then

x_1	x_2	y_1	y_2
.24	1.01	0	.85
−.24	−1.01	0	−.85
.97	.25	1.11	0
−.97	−.25	−1.11	0
.94	0		
−.94	0		
0	.97		
0	−.97		

These points are sufficient to sketch the ellipse as illustrated in Fig. A.6.

One further property of the one-standard deviation ellipse is worth noting since it simplifies computation of any one of the family of ellipses. Suppose the equation

$$y \cdot \text{adj } \Delta \cdot y' = |\Delta|$$

has been evaluated and that we want to evaluate the equation

$$y \cdot \text{adj } \Delta \cdot y' = \chi^2 |\Delta|$$

By multiplying both sides of the equation by χ^2 we obtain

$$y \cdot \text{adj } \chi^2 \Delta \cdot y' = \chi^4 |\Delta| = |\chi^2 \Delta|$$

which indicates that when the adjoint of Δ has been computed for the standard ellipse

$$y \cdot \text{adj } \Delta \cdot y' = |\Delta|$$

the adjoint of the matrix $\chi^2 \Delta$ is simply

$$\chi^2 (\text{adj } \Delta)$$

Applying this relationship to the data to obtain the 50th centour ellipse of the AFQT and SCCAT data gives

$$\chi^2 \cdot \text{adj } \Delta = 1.3862854 \cdot \begin{Vmatrix} 0.73060 & 0 \\ 0 & 1.22606 \end{Vmatrix}$$

$$= \begin{Vmatrix} 1.01282 & 0 \\ 0 & 1.69967 \end{Vmatrix} = \Gamma' \cdot \text{adj } \chi^2 D \cdot \Gamma$$

which agrees to five decimal places with previous computation. Thus, to determine ellipses for several different values of χ^2, it is more convenient to determine the adjoint of the matrix Δ from

$$\Gamma' \cdot \text{adj } D \cdot \Gamma$$

and then to multiply the result successively by the selected values of χ^2. The series of products

$$\chi^2(\text{adj } \Delta)$$

will provide data for the computation of the major semiaxis and the minor semiaxis of each of the ellipses desired.

The locus of the 75th centour score is the ellipse for which χ^2 has a probability equivalent of $P = .75$. This value of P does not appear in the argument of most tables of χ^2. We therefore use Pearson's Table of the Incomplete Normal Moment Function. The value sought in Pearson's Table is $m_1(\chi)$ for $q = 1 - .75 = .25$. Substituting this value of q in the equation for $m_1(\chi)$ we obtain

$$.25 = \sqrt{2\pi} m_1(\chi)$$

$$m_1(\chi) = \frac{.25}{\sqrt{2\pi}} = \frac{.25}{2.50662827}$$

$$= .0997394$$

In Pearson's Table IX we find the entries

χ	$m_1(\chi)$
.7	.0866883
.8	.1092507

and by linear interpolation compute

$$\chi = .7 + \frac{1}{10}\left(\frac{.0997394 - .0866883}{.1092507 - .0866883}\right)$$

$$= .7 + \frac{1}{10}\left(\frac{.0130511}{.0225624}\right)$$

$$= .7 + .05784447 = .7578445$$

The value of χ is approximately .7578.

For comparison and illustration of methods of using Pearson's Table IX we compute χ to more significant figures by one of the methods of quadratic interpolation described by Pearson.

x	$m_1(x)$	First Difference	Second Difference
.7	.0866883		
		.0225624	
.8	.1092507		.0010439
		.0236063	
.9	.1328570		

$$x = .7 + \frac{1}{10}\left\{.5784447 + \frac{(.5784447)(.4215553)(.0010439)}{2(.0225624)}\right\}$$

$$= .7 + \frac{1}{10}\left\{.5784447 + \frac{.0002545513}{.0451248}\right\}$$

$$= .7 + \frac{1}{10}\{.5784447 + .0056411\}$$

$$= .7 + \frac{1}{10}\{.5840858\}$$

$$= .7584086$$

It is a convenient coincidence that the 75th centour in two-test space is approximately the three-quarter standard deviation ellipse.

χ^2 for the 75th centour ellipse is $\chi_{75}^2 = .5751836$. This value multiplied by the adjoint of Δ gives

$$\chi_{75}^2 \cdot \text{adj}\,\Delta = .5751836 \left\|\begin{array}{cc} .73060 & 0 \\ 0 & 1.22606 \end{array}\right\|$$

$$= \left\|\begin{array}{cc} .4202291 & 0 \\ 0 & .7052096 \end{array}\right\|$$

Consequently, the semiaxis of the 75th centour ellipse along the axis y_1 is

$$a = \sqrt{.7052096} = .8398$$

and the semiaxis along y_2 is

$$b = \sqrt{.4202291} = .6482$$

These values are the same as

$$\Sigma_1\chi_{75} = (1.1073).7584086 = .8398$$
$$\Sigma_2\chi_{75} = (.8548).7584086 = .6483$$

Thus we find a simple method of computing the length of the major and

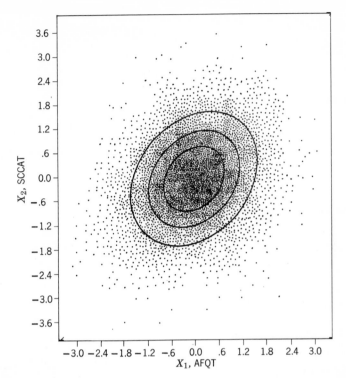

Fig. A.7 C_{75}, C_{50}, and C_{25} *ellipses on scatter diagram of Fig. A.1—C_{25} is outermost ellipse.*

minor semiaxis for any ellipse from the elements of the diagonalized dispersion matrix Δ.

The 75th centour ellipse is constructed on Fig. A.7. When constructed on a suitably large scale the number of score points lying outside the C_{75} ellipse can be accurately counted. In this example the count was 3547, which is 75.5% of the total sample of 4696 airmen. Thus we verify empirically that the AFQT and SCCAT data are consistent with the ideal model chosen to summarize the important characteristics of the sample.

The 25th centour ellipse C_{25} is similarly found. The value $q = 1 - .25 = .75$ is substituted in $q = \sqrt{2\pi} m_1(\chi)$

$$.75 = \sqrt{2\pi} m_1(\chi)$$

$$m_1(\chi) = \frac{.75}{\sqrt{2\pi}} = \frac{.75}{2.50662827} = .2992067$$

The tabled values of $m_1(\chi)$ most closely approximating this value are

χ	$m_1(\chi)$
1.6	.2880214
1.7	.3048932

Linear interpolation for χ gives

$$\chi_{25} = 1.6 + \frac{1}{10}\left(\frac{.2992067 - .2880214}{.3048932 - .2880214}\right)$$

$$= 1.6 + \frac{1}{10}\left(\frac{.0111853}{.0168718}\right)$$

$$= 1.6662958$$

and quadratic interpolation gives

χ	$m_1(\chi)$	First Difference	Second Difference
1.6	.2880214		
		.0168718	
1.7	.3048932		−.0017729
		.0150989	
1.8	.3199921		

$$\chi_{25} = 1.6 + \frac{1}{10}\left\{.6629583 + \frac{(.6629583)(.3370417)(-.0017729)}{.0337436}\right\}$$

$$= 1.6 + \frac{1}{10}\left\{.6629583 + \frac{-.000396145}{.0337436}\right\}$$

$$= 1.6 + \frac{1}{10}\{.6629583 - .0117399\}$$

$$= 1.6 + \frac{1}{10}\{.6512184\}$$

$$= 1.6651218$$

The values of χ_{25} obtained by linear and quadratic interpolation are equivalent for practical applications. For illustration we prefer the more precise value obtained by quadratic interpolation. The value of χ indicates immediately that the 25th centour ellipse is contained within the 1.67 standard deviation rectangle. The values of the semiaxes are

semiaxis on $y_1 = \Sigma_1\chi_{25} = (1.1073)(1.6651218) = 1.8438$
semiaxis on $y_2 = \Sigma_2\chi_{25} = (.8548)(1.6651218) = 1.4233$

The 25th centour ellipse is shown on Fig. A.7. The count of score points lying outside the ellipse was 1166 = 24.8% of the total group.

The three ellipses chosen for illustration are the bivariate analogues of the quartiles of a single-variate distribution. The relationship between the one-standard deviation ellipse and the value $\chi = 1.0$ and the notion of the rectangle with sides equal to $\chi\sigma$ which contains a tangent ellipse suggests a two-dimensional analogue of the probability table of the normal curve. In the two-variate case, we can tabulate the probability of a greater divergence from the centroid for loci given by the $\chi\sigma$ ellipse. An illuminating comparison of the entries in such a table with the single variate probabilities is presented in Table A.5.

Table A.5 *Comparison of Centour Equivalents in Univariate and Bivariate Normal Distributions*

Sigma Ellipse	Centour Score	
$\chi\sigma$	Two Variates	One Variate
.5	88.92	61.71
1.0	60.61	31.73
1.5	32.47	13.36
2.0	13.53	4.55
2.5	4.39	1.24
3.0	1.11	.27

Normality and Centour Ellipses

The actual number of airmen outside the quartile ellipses approximated the expected values fairly closely. The ideal bivariate normal distribution served as an adequate model. The AFQT and SCCAT scores had been separately standardized and approximately normalized before the analysis of the bivariate relations. In this section we examine the AFQT and SCCAT scores of the same 4696 men but in their original raw score form, neither standardized nor normalized.

The roster of AFQT and SCCAT obtained scores reads

Airman Number	Raw Score	
	AFQT	SCCAT
1	37	63
2	71	30
3	43	29
⋮	⋮	⋮
4696	97	68

These scores are represented in a matrix:

$$X = \begin{Vmatrix} 37 & 63 \\ 71 & 30 \\ 43 & 29 \\ \vdots & \vdots \\ 97 & 68 \end{Vmatrix}$$

The dispersion matrix is

$$D = \begin{Vmatrix} 654.91244841 & 43.44943891 \\ 43.44943891 & 48.24422462 \end{Vmatrix}$$

The element 654.91244841 in the upper left-hand corner of D is the variance of the AFQT scores and the lower right-hand element is the variance of the SCCAT scores. It is apparent that the AFQT scores are dispersed much more widely than the SCCAT scores. The term in the off-diagonal cell is the covariance of AFQT and SCCAT raw scores. The covariance is positive, indicating that the correlation is positive. The covariance is small relative to the product of the two variances. The correlation turns out to be .2444.

The adjoint of D is

$$\text{adj } D = \begin{Vmatrix} 48.24422462 & -43.44943891 \\ -43.44943891 & 654.91244841 \end{Vmatrix}$$

and the one-standard deviation ellipse is given by the equation

$$x \cdot \text{adj } D \cdot x' = |D|$$

In a bivariate normal distribution with dispersion matrix as in the sample, the equation of the one-standard deviation ellipse is

$$x \cdot \begin{Vmatrix} 48.24422462 & -43.44943891 \\ -43.44943891 & 654.91244841 \end{Vmatrix} \cdot x' = 29707.88951$$

The orientation of the principal axes of the contour ellipses is given by the angle θ which is found from the equation

$$\tan 2\theta = \frac{2\sigma_1\sigma_2 r}{\sigma_1{}^2 - \sigma_2{}^2} = \frac{86.8988778}{654.912448 - 48.244225}$$

$$= .14324$$

The angle θ is $4° 5'$. The transformation matrix Γ, containing as elements the direction cosines of a related axis system, is

$$\Gamma = \left\| \begin{matrix} \cos\theta & \cos(90° + \theta) \\ \cos(90° - \theta) & \cos\theta \end{matrix} \right\| = \left\| \begin{matrix} .99746 & -.07121 \\ .07121 & .99746 \end{matrix} \right\|$$

The computation of $\Gamma' \cdot \mathrm{adj}\ D \cdot \Gamma$ is

$$\Gamma' \cdot \mathrm{adj}\ D = \left\| \begin{matrix} .99746 & .07121 \\ -.07121 & .99746 \end{matrix} \right\| \cdot \left\| \begin{matrix} 48.2442246 & -43.4494389 \\ -43.4494389 & 654.9124484 \end{matrix} \right\|$$

$$\Gamma' \cdot \mathrm{adj}\ D \cdot \Gamma = \left\| \begin{matrix} 45.0276497 & 3.2972381 \\ -46.7745486 & 656.3430053 \end{matrix} \right\| \cdot \left\| \begin{matrix} .99746 & -.07121 \\ .07121 & .99746 \end{matrix} \right\|$$

$$= \left\| \begin{matrix} 45.1480758 & .0824442 \\ .0824442 & 658.0067097 \end{matrix} \right\|$$

Thus the adjoint of Δ is

$$\mathrm{adj}\ \Delta = \left\| \begin{matrix} 45.1480758 & .0824442 \\ .0824442 & 658.0067097 \end{matrix} \right\|$$

Since the off-diagonal term of the matrix is zero within the number of significant digits in the elements of the transformation matrix Γ, we shall regard its true value as zero. The matrix Δ is then

$$\Delta = \left\| \begin{matrix} 658.0067097 & 0 \\ 0 & 45.1480758 \end{matrix} \right\|$$

The upper left-hand corner of this matrix is the variance of the scores along the axis y_1. The standard deviation along this axis is

$$\Sigma_1 = \sqrt{658.0067097} = 25.6516$$

The lower left-hand term of Δ is the variance along the axis y_2, and the standard deviation along this axis is

$$\Sigma_2 = \sqrt{45.1480758} = 6.7192$$

The values of χ associated with the three quartile centours obtained in the preceding section from $q = \sqrt{2\pi m_1(\chi)}$ and Pearson's Table are

Centour	q	χ
25	.75	1.6651218
50	.50	1.1774062
75	.25	.7584086

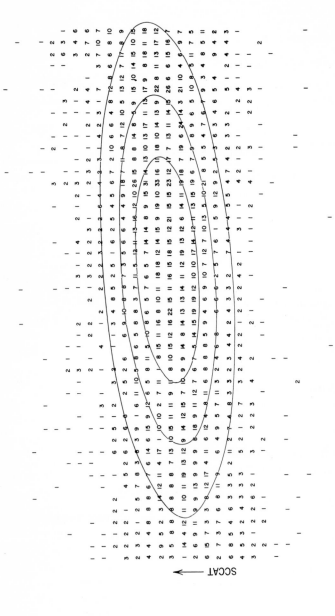

Fig. A.8 *Scatter diagram—AFQT and SCCAT raw scores.*

The semiaxes of these centour ellipses are given by the product $\chi\Sigma$

Centour	Semimajor Axis	Semiminor Axis
25	42.713	11.188
50	30.202	7.911
75	19.454	5.096

These three quartile centour ellipses are constructed in Fig. A.8. The number of airmen with pairs of AFQT and SCCAT raw scores outside the 75th, 50th, and 25th centours are 3620, 2566, and 1076. Thus 78.1%, 54.6%, and 22.9% are the observed results where 75%, 50%, and 25% are the values expected if the data are well described by normal distributions. The deviations from expectation (error) do not appear excessively large in an absolute sense, but we note three pertinent observations. First, centour scores estimated from the sample would be used for describing the location of a very large number of men—small percents may become large frequencies. Second, the relative size of the errors of small centours indicating very divergent points in the scatter diagram is large. For C_{75}, a quite typical point, the relative error is $3.1/75 = 4\%$. For C_{50} and C_{25} the values are 11% and 8%. The frequency counted outside C_{10} was 330 or 7%. The relative error in this case is 30%. Thus we see that deviations from normality may have serious effects at the extremes where divergence from the typical is likely to have most influence in advising decisions. Therefore, it is desirable to construct or scale the tests so that the marginal frequency distributions will be approximately normal if centour scores are to be adequate descriptions of divergence from the typical.

Appendix B

Rosters of Passenger Agents, Mechanics, Operations Control Agents

Table B.1 *Roster*—Passenger Agents

| Apprentice Number | Number of Activity Preferences* | | | Success Score |
	X_1	X_2	X_3	Y
1	10	22	5	.7
2	14	17	6	5.5
3	19	33	7	7.5
4	14	29	12	8.2
5	14	25	7	4.9
6	20	25	12	5.2
7	6	18	4	5.4
8	13	27	7	3.1
9	18	31	9	6.1
10	16	35	13	8.5
11	17	25	8	4.6
12	10	29	11	4.4
13	17	25	7	3.1
14	10	22	13	3.6
15	10	31	13	10.0
16	18	25	5	3.0
17	6	27	11	6.0
18	10	24	12	7.2
19	15	23	10	6.7
20	8	29	14	9.6

Table B.1 (*Continued*)

21	6	27	11	7.5
22	10	17	8	2.2
23	1	30	6	7.0
24	14	29	7	7.7
25	13	21	11	5.6
26	21	31	11	6.1
27	12	26	9	3.6
28	12	22	9	9.1
29	5	25	7	5.5
30	10	24	5	.7
31	3	20	14	7.6
32	6	25	12	5.7
33	11	27	10	7.4
34	13	21	14	5.2
35	11	23	5	3.4
36	8	18	8	6.1
37	5	17	9	4.7
38	11	22	11	3.6
39	14	22	11	5.1
40	22	22	6	4.7
41	16	28	6	5.5
42	12	25	8	4.3
43	12	25	7	2.8
44	15	21	4	5.4
45	11	28	8	5.9
46	11	20	9	4.3
47	15	19	9	3.4
48	15	24	7	3.2
49	15	21	10	4.5
50	17	26	7	4.5
51	12	28	13	4.9
52	7	28	12	7.0
53	14	12	6	3.9
54	22	24	6	3.5
55	22	27	12	2.2
56	18	30	9	7.0
57	16	18	5	5.4
58	12	23	4	6.1
59	16	22	2	5.5
60	15	26	9	6.2

Table B.1 (*Continued*)

Apprentice Number	Number of Activity Preferences*			Success Score
	X_1	X_2	X_3	Y
61	7	13	7	3.8
62	6	18	6	7.1
63	9	24	6	6.7
64	9	20	12	5.9
65	20	28	8	8.5
66	5	22	15	7.7
67	14	26	17	5.1
68	8	28	12	7.7
69	14	22	9	7.8
70	15	26	4	4.7
71	15	25	10	5.7
72	14	27	6	4.3
73	15	25	11	4.6
74	11	26	9	7.8
75	10	28	5	4.8
76	7	22	10	4.7
77	11	15	12	1.4
78	14	25	15	8.5
79	18	28	7	6.3
80	14	29	8	4.0
81	17	20	6	5.2
82	13	25	14	4.6
83	9	21	12	4.4
84	13	26	13	8.7
85	16	24	10	6.2

* X_1—Outdoor, X_2—Convivial, X_3—Conservative

Table B.2 *Roster*—Mechanics

Apprentice Number	Number of Activity Preferences*			Success Score
	X_1	X_2	X_3	Y
1	20	27	6	5.3
2	21	15	10	7.5
3	15	27	12	5.4
4	15	29	8	6.0
5	11	25	11	1.5
6	24	9	17	2.7
7	18	21	13	4.8
8	14	18	4	4.8
9	13	22	12	4.6
10	17	21	9	5.6
11	16	28	13	7.9
12	15	22	12	7.1
13	24	20	15	9.9
14	14	19	13	1.1
15	14	28	1	7.8
16	18	17	11	6.6
17	14	24	7	5.2
18	12	16	10	3.5
19	16	21	10	6.9
20	18	19	9	7.2
21	19	26	7	6.5
22	13	20	10	4.7
23	28	16	10	8.1
24	17	19	11	4.5
25	24	14	7	6.9
26	19	23	12	7.0
27	22	12	8	7.3
28	22	21	11	3.8
29	21	19	9	6.7
30	18	24	13	4.9
31	23	27	11	6.9
32	20	23	12	4.1
33	19	13	7	5.8
34	17	28	13	6.3
35	20	24	5	8.3

Table B.2 (*Continued*)

Apprentice Number	Number of Activity Preferences*			Success Score
	X_1	X_2	X_3	Y
36	21	23	11	6.1
37	17	21	15	4.7
38	11	25	12	6.2
39	14	19	14	3.0
40	18	24	5	4.2
41	13	14	7	5.0
42	22	18	16	4.4
43	25	17	13	6.0
44	19	25	13	4.5
45	20	20	9	6.5
46	21	25	11	5.2
47	17	24	11	5.3
48	18	26	10	8.2
49	21	29	11	6.7
50	17	21	12	5.6
51	17	19	12	3.7
52	17	16	6	5.4
53	16	22	5	6.3
54	22	19	10	6.8
55	19	23	12	6.6
56	16	23	9	4.6
57	18	27	11	7.3
58	21	24	12	6.4
59	15	22	13	4.3
60	19	26	12	4.9
61	14	17	11	2.1
62	15	23	7	2.9
63	23	20	16	7.3
64	22	26	15	8.1
65	13	16	11	4.2
66	25	29	11	7.1
67	23	24	7	8.3
68	17	29	9	7.7
69	21	19	7	6.5
70	15	13	6	5.3

Table B.2 (*Continued*)

71	19	27	14	7.0
72	22	24	14	6.8
73	17	18	8	6.6
74	21	19	8	1.2
75	24	18	13	6.9
76	21	12	9	7.3
77	15	17	8	3.1
78	24	22	14	4.9
79	19	19	7	3.9
80	23	16	10	3.9
81	21	29	12	8.7
82	20	19	11	5.1
83	18	28	0	5.4
84	23	21	16	7.4
85	17	17	8	7.0
86	17	24	5	3.8
87	17	18	15	5.1
88	17	23	10	7.3
89	19	15	10	5.5
90	17	20	8	7.5
91	25	20	8	6.9
92	16	19	8	3.7
93	19	16	6	4.6

* X_1—Outdoor, X_2—Convivial, X_3—Conservative

Table B.3   *Roster*—Operations Control Agents

Apprentice Number	Number of Activity Preferences*			Success Score
	X_1	X_2	X_3	Y
1	19	19	16	2.4
2	17	17	12	8.5
3	8	17	14	2.6
4	13	20	16	4.4
5	14	18	4	1.4
6	17	12	13	7.6
7	17	12	17	7.4
8	14	21	16	2.8
9	19	18	12	6.0
10	18	16	15	6.0
11	15	14	17	6.9
12	20	15	7	2.6
13	24	20	13	6.6
14	16	16	17	9.4
15	17	15	10	7.1
16	17	10	12	7.9
17	11	16	11	4.7
18	15	18	14	6.9
19	20	19	16	6.6
20	14	22	16	5.2
21	13	15	18	5.0
22	16	14	13	4.7
23	12	12	6	2.0
24	17	17	19	7.8
25	10	8	16	6.0
26	11	17	20	4.5
27	13	16	7	3.5
28	19	15	13	4.7
29	15	11	13	5.4
30	17	11	10	6.2
31	15	10	13	5.6
32	19	14	12	4.2
33	19	14	15	8.1
34	4	12	11	4.5
35	13	12	15	6.6

Table B.3 (*Continued*)

36	20	13	19	7.7
37	14	18	14	2.9
38	10	12	9	5.2
39	11	12	19	6.7
40	8	20	8	1.4
41	14	16	7	5.6
42	18	20	15	6.9
43	19	7	13	5.5
44	21	13	11	4.3
45	14	26	15	1.7
46	25	16	12	6.1
47	18	11	19	6.4
48	14	16	6	4.7
49	13	20	18	5.4
50	20	16	14	6.9
51	12	14	8	2.1
52	16	19	12	5.8
53	21	15	7	5.3
54	18	23	15	3.3
55	19	11	13	4.0
56	17	18	9	2.9
57	4	10	15	2.7
58	17	17	14	5.8
59	14	13	12	7.2
60	15	16	14	7.3
61	20	13	18	4.7
62	20	14	18	4.8
63	16	22	12	4.2
64	9	13	16	5.1
65	15	13	13	7.1
66	18	20	10	6.7

* X_1—Outdoor, X_2—Convivial, X_3—Conservative

References

Bennett, George K., Harold G. Seashore, and Alexander G. Wesman, "Aptitude Testing: Does It 'Prove Out' in Counseling Practice?" *Occupations*, **XXX**, 584–598 (1952).

Brodgen, Hubert E., "An Approach to the Problem of Differential Prediction," *Psychometrika*, **XI**, 139–154 (1946).

Bryan, Joseph G., *A Method for the Exact Determination of the Characteristic Equation of a Matrix with Applications to the Discriminant Function for More than Two Groups*. Harvard University Graduate School of Education, Cambridge, Massachusetts. (Unpublished doctoral dissertation), pp. xi and 292, 1950.

Cattell, Raymond B., "*rp* and Other Coefficients of Pattern Similarity," *Psychometrika*, **XIV**, 279–298 (1949).

Cronbach, Lee J. and Goldine C. Gleser, *Similarity between Persons and Related Problems of Profile Analysis*, Technical Report No. 2. Bureau of Research and Service, College of Education, University of Illinois, Urbana, Illinois, 1952.

Cronbach, Lee J. and Goldine C. Gleser, *Psychological Tests and Personnel Decisions*. University of Illinois Press, Urbana, Illinois, p. 164, 1957.

Du Mas, Frank M., "The Coefficient of Profile Similarity," *Journal of Clinical Psychology*, **V**, 123–131 (1949).

Du Mas, Frank M., "A Note on the Coefficient of Profile Similarity," *Journal of Clinical Psychology*, **VI**, 300–301 (1950).

Dunn, Frances E., *Guiding College Students in the Selection of a Field of Concentration*. Harvard Graduate School of Education, Cambridge, Massachusetts. (Unpublished doctoral dissertation), 1955.

Edwards, W., H. Lindman, and L. Savage, "Bayesian Statistical Inference in Psychological Research," *Psychological Review*, **70**, 193–242 (1963).

Fisher, R. A., "Inverse Probability," *Proceedings Cambridge Philosophical Society*, **26**, 528–535 (1930).

Fisher, R. A., "The Use of Multiple Measurements in Taxonomic Problems," *Annals of Eugenics*, **VII**, 179–188 (1936).

Fisher, R. A. and F. Yates, *Statistical Tables for Biological, Agricultural, and Medical Research*, 4th Edition. Oliver and Boyd, Edinburgh, 1953.

Gragg, D. B. and Mary Agnes Gordon, *Validity of the Airman Classification Battery AC-1*. Human Resources Research Center, Lackland Air Force Base, San Antonio, Texas, Research Bulletin 50-3, December 1950.

Hathaway, Starke R., "A Coding System for MMPI Profile Classification," *Journal of Consulting Psychology*, XI, 334–337 (1947).

Hotelling, Harold, "Analysis of a Complex of Statistical Variables into Principal Components," *Journal of Educational Psychology*, XXIV, 417–441, 498–520 (1933).

Hull, Clark L., *Aptitude Testing*. World Book Co., New York, 1928.

Kelley, Truman L., *Essential Traits of Mental Life*. Harvard University Press, Cambridge, Massachusetts, p. 145, 1935.

Kelley, Truman Lee, *The Kelley Statistical Tables*. The Macmillan Co., New York, p. 136, 1938.

Kelley, Truman Lee, *Talents and Tasks: Their Conjunction in a Democracy for Wholesome Living and National Defense*. Harvard Graduate School of Education, Cambridge, Massachusetts, Harvard Education Papers, No. 1, p. 48, 1940.

Kogan, Leonard S., "Statistical Methods," *Progress in Clinical Psychology*, Vol. I, Section 2, 519–535 (1953).

Lord, Frederic M., "Notes on a Problem of Multiple Classification," *Psychometrika*, XVII, 297–304 (1952).

Mahalanobis, P. C., "On the Generalized Distance in Statistics," *Proceedings of the National Institute of Science, India*, XII, 49–55 (1936).

Mosier, Charles I., "Batteries and Profiles," E. F. Lindquist (editor), *Educational Measurements*. American Council on Education, Washington, D.C., 794–807 (1951).

Pearson, Karl, *Tables for Statisticians and Biometricians, Volume I*. University College, London, The Biometric Laboratory, Second Edition, pp. 143 and xxxiii, 1924.

Rao, C. Radhakrishna, *Advanced Statistical Methods in Biometric Research*. John Wiley and Sons, New York, pp. xvii and 390, 1952.

Rao, C. Radhakrishna and Patrick Slater, "Multivariate Analysis Applied to Differences between Neurotic Groups," *The British Journal of Psychology* (*Statistical Section*), II, Part I, 17–29 (1949).

Schreier, A. and E. Sperner, *Introduction to Modern Algebra and Matrix Theory*. Chelsea Publishing Co., New York, p. 378, 1951.

Sokolnikoff, Ivan S. and Elizabeth S. Sokolnikoff, *Higher Mathematics for Engineers and Physicists*. McGraw-Hill Book Co., New York, p. 587, 1941.

Stewart, Naomi, "A.G.C.T. Scores of Army Personnel Grouped by Occupation," *Occupations*, XXVI, 5–41 (1947).

Tatsuoka, Maurice M., "The Relation between T-Space and D-Space Topology" (Unpublished paper), 1953. [Summarized in Tatsuoka, M. M., *Multivariate Analysis in Educational and Psychological Research*. John Wiley and Sons, Inc., New York (in press).]

Tatsuoka, Maurice. M., *Joint Probability of Membership in a Group and Success Therein: An Index which Combines the Information from Discriminant and Regression Analysis.* Harvard Graduate School of Education, Cambridge, Massachusetts. (Unpublished doctoral dissertation), 1956.

Thorndike, Robert L., "The Problem of Classification of Personnel," *Psychometrika*, **XV**, 215–235 (1950).

Tiedeman, David V. and Joseph G. Bryan, "Prediction of College Field of Concentration," *Harvard Educational Review*, 122–139 (1954).

Tiedeman, David V., Joseph G. Bryan, and Phillip J. Rulon, *The Utility of the Airman Classification Battery for Assignment of Airman to Eight Air Force Specialties.* Educational Research Corporation, Cambridge, Massachusetts, second printing, March 1953.

Tiedeman, David V. and Frank L. Field, "Measurement for Guidance," Dean K. Whitla (editor), *Handbook of Measurement and Assessment in Behavioral Sciences.* Addison Wesley Publishing Co., Reading, Massachusetts (in press).

Tiedeman, David V. and Jack J. Sternberg, "Information Appropriate for Curriculum Guidance," *Harvard Educational Review*, **XXII**, 257–274 (1952).

United States Department of Labor, *Guide to the Use of the General Aptitude Test Battery.* The Department, Bureau of Employment Security, Washington, D.C., 1962.

Uspensky, J. V., *Theory of Equations.* McGraw-Hill Book Co., New York, p. 353, 1948.

Votaw, D. F., Jr., "Methods of Solving some Personnel-Classification Problems," *Psychometrika*, **XVII**, 255–266 (1952).

Votaw, D. F., Jr., and J. T. Dailey, *Assignment of Personnel to Jobs.* Human Resources Research Center, Lackland Air Force Base, San Antonio, Texas, Research Bulletin 52-24, pp. 20 and v, 1952.

Welsh, George S., "Some Practical Uses of MMPI Profile Coding," *Journal of Consulting Psychology*, **XV**, 82–84 (1951).